D0758391

PHILOSOPHY AND THE CHRISTIAN FAITH

University of Notre Dame Studies

in the Philosophy of Religion

NUMBER 5

Philosophy and the Christian Faith

Thomas V. Morris, Editor

University of Notre Dame Press
Notre Dame, Indiana

Library of Congress Cataloging-in-Publication Data

Philosophy and the Christian faith.

(University of Notre Dame studies in the philosophy
of religion; no. 5)
1. Christianity—Philosophy.   I. Morris, Thomas V.
II. Series.
BR100.P53   1988   230'.01   87-40618
ISBN 0-268-01570-8

To

REV. THEODORE M. HESBURGH, C.S.C.

Contents

III. CHRISTIAN DOCTRINE AND THE POSSIBILITIES
FOR TRUTH

Preface

Early in 1984, I began reflecting on an interesting and, indeed, striking fact about contemporary philosophy. Little more than a decade ago, philosophy of religion was a backwater. Moreover, you could count the number of known or suspected Christian philosophers at the cutting edge of philosophical research on one hand. Then, in 1978, a professional group was formed, known as the Society of Christian Philosophers. From a handful of organizers, this group has grown in less than a decade to a membership of over eight hundred, a membership which includes a significant number of highly respected philosophers who are among the most creative and active members of the profession. Along with this development, there has been an explosion of activity in the philosophy of religion, reflected in a multiplication of both articles in the professional journals and books produced by the best publishers.

In all this whirlwind of activity, however, it struck me that there was one remarkable void — a near total lack of any contemporary philosophical attention to the claims and commitments special to the Christian faith. As ontological, cosmological, and other forms of theistic arguments were attended to as never before since the days of the schoolmen, the doctrines of the Incarnation and the Trinity seemed to pass by almost unnoticed by Christian philosophers, philosophers who were otherwise doing a great deal of important new work on religious belief. The ideas of sin, atonement, and sanctification were suffering the same apparent neglect.

In reflecting on this state of affairs, it seemed to me that there might after all be a fairly good sociological explanation, and even a bit of a logical justification, for this recent philosophical emphasis, with its attendant neglect of Christian doctrines. No one can deny that it would have seemed a bit unusual for philosophers to work hard on explicating what it might be for God to exist as three persons in one substance at a time when the existence of any sort of God at all, and the very cognitive meaningfulness of theistic discourse, had been called into serious question. Basic theism required a vigorous defense. And of course, a conception of God is logically, although not altogether epistemically, prior to an account of distinctively Christian doctrines. But, for a number of reasons, it also seemed to me some three years ago that the contemporary explication and defense of theism was well enough on its way to provide some elbow room for Christian philosophers who felt it important to examine their special religious commitments as well.

Such a development was bound to occur. It seemed to be "in the air," around the next corner of philosophical history. At the time, I was already engaged in a small bit of this new work myself, completing a project begun a few years earlier which focused on a defense of the central Christian doctrine of the Incarnation (subsequently published as *The Logic of God Incarnate* by Cornell University Press). In addition to this, I determined to approach a number of leading philosophers about writing a group of essays to initiate and further encourage the inevitable return of philosophical attention to Christian doctrines.

I was extremely gratified by the responsiveness of James Langford, Director of the University of Notre Dame Press, when I approached him about the publication of such a book. Our conversations led to the idea that a research conference should be held at Notre Dame, in connection with the project, for the presentation and discussion of initial drafts of the papers being commissioned. I was also pleasantly surprised and greatly encouraged in these plans by the enthusiastic responses and agreements to participate from those I contacted to provide papers for the book and conference.

Sponsorship of the conference was undertaken jointly by Notre Dame's Center for the Philosophy of Religion, through funding generously provided by the Pew Memorial Freedom Trust, and by the National Endowment for the Humanities, through their grant RX-20696-85. I would like to express my heart-felt thanks to these organizations for their generous support. I would also like to thank those philosophers who served as commentators for the conference papers. They were Jonathan Kvanvig, George Mavrodes, Richard McClelland, Robert McKim, Philip Quinn, Kenneth Sayre, Charles Taliaferro, Edward Wierenga, Keith Yandell, and Linda Zagzebski. Their role in the evolution of this project was vital. I also would like to express appreciation to all the other many participants in the conference whose presence and incisive discussions of these issues during those few days will continue to bear fruit for years to come.

Finally, I want to express my deep gratitude for the environment here at the University of Notre Dame, which made it the perfect place to hold such a conference and launch such a project. My thanks in this regard are directed especially to one man who for the past thirty five years labored to make Notre Dame the special and exciting place it is for such philosophical activity, the priest, president, and philosopher to whom this volume is respectfully dedicated, the Reverend Theodore Hesburgh, C.S.C.

Contributors

MARILYN MCCORD ADAMS is professor of philosophy and chair of the department at UCLA. Currently president of the Society of Christian Philosophers, she has authored numerous articles in the philosophy of religion and has recently published a major two volume study of Ockham.

ROBERT MERRIHEW ADAMS is professor of philosophy at UCLA, and a past president of the Society of Christian Philosophers. He is the author of a great many articles in moral philosophy, metaphysics, and the philosophy of religion, some of which have been collected into the book *The Virtue of Faith*.

WILLIAM P. ALSTON is professor of philosophy at Syracuse University and editor of *Faith and Philosophy*, the official journal of the Society of Christian Philosophers, as whose president he also has served. He is the author of *Philosophy of Language*, and an editor of both *Readings in Twentieth Century Philosophy* and *Religious Belief and Philosophical Thought*. He has published a great number of papers in the philosophy of language, epistemology, and the philosophy of religion.

NORMAN KRETZMANN is Susan Linn Sage Professor of Philosophy at Cornell University. He is the author of *Elements of Formal Logic*, the editor of *Infinity and Continuity in Ancient and Medieval Thought*, a general editor of the *Cambridge History of Later Medieval Philosophy*, and the author of numerous articles in medieval philosophy and the philosophy of religion.

JAMES F. ROSS is professor of philosophy at the University of Pennsylvania. He has written books in the philosophy of religion, including *Introduction to Philosophy of Religion*, and *Philosophical Theology*, and one in the philosophy of language entitled *Portraying Analogy*. He has edited *Inquiries into Medieval Philosophy* and introduced Suarez's *On Formal and Universal Unity*. In addition, he has published many journal articles.

ELEONORE STUMP is professor of philosophy at Virginia Polytechnic Institute and State University. She is assistant editor for the *Cambridge History of Later Medieval Philosophy* and has published Boethius' *De topicis differentiis* as well as numerous essays in medieval philosophy and the philosophy of religion.

RICHARD SWINBURNE is Nolloth Professor of the Philosophy of the Christian Religion at Oxford University. He is the author of many articles and of numerous books in the philosophy of science and the philosophy of religion, including *Space and Time, The Concept of Miracle, The Coherence of Theism, The Existence of God, Faith and Reason*, and *The Evolution of the Soul*.

PETER VAN INWAGEN is professor of philosophy at Syracuse University. He is the author of *An Essay on Free Will* and *Material Beings* and is editor of both *Time and Cause* and *Alvin Plantinga*. He has also published several professional articles.

WILLIAM J. WAINWRIGHT is professor of philosophy at the University of Wisconsin-Milwaukee. He is the author of many articles, the massive bibliographical study entitled *Philosophy of Religion*, and the book *Mysticism*. He is also co-editor of *Rationality, Religious Belief, and Moral Commitment*.

NICHOLAS WOLTERSTORFF is professor of philosophy at Calvin College and at the Free University of Amsterdam. He has published a great number of articles and books in metaphysics, aesthetics, moral philosophy, and the philosophy of religion, including *On Universals, Reason*

Within the Bounds of Religion, Worlds and Works of Art, and *Until Justice and Peace Embrace.*

Introduction

THOMAS V. MORRIS

This is a book of new essays by eminent philosophers on some of the most important themes in traditional Christian thought. I believe that, within the context of modern philosophy, these papers represent the beginnings of an exciting new direction of philosophical exploration—a careful and sustained conceptual investigation into the distinctive doctrines and concerns of the Christian faith, as expressed in its scriptures, creeds, conciliar decrees, and other seminal documents.

It has been a very long time indeed since numerous prominent philosophers have devoted themselves to serious reflection on such topics as sin, salvation, atonement, the triune nature of God, the indwelling of the Holy Spirit, the contours of Christian liberty, and the implications of eschatology. Since at least the time of Kant, philosophical attention to religious matters has been limited, for the most part, to very general considerations relevant to nearly any traditional form of theism, whether Judaic, Christian, Moslem, or even Hindu. During this period, philosophers have dealt with questions concerning the existence and basic nature of God, the problem of evil, the possibility of miracles, the import of religious experience, and the cognitive status of religious language, among other topics pertaining to the rudiments of theism. The examination of such issues with the tools of modern logic and the categories of modern metaphysics, epistemology and moral theory has yielded philosophical results of great interest, and certainly will continue to do so. But the authors represented in this collection are of the conviction that the commitments and perspectives distinctive to the Christian faith also have philosophically intriguing implications which will richly repay detailed scrutiny. I think that the following essays, which display the first fruits of this conviction, amply corroborate its truth. They should serve well to stimulate a great deal more philosophical reflection on these fascinating issues in future years.

There is no little irony in the fact that this comes at a time when a great number of respected academic theologians have, on *philosophical* grounds, largely abandoned the traditional claims distinctive of the Christian faith throughout most of its history. In the writings of many contemporary theologians, the doctrinal foundations of the church are labelled as myths, reinterpreted as symbols, or reassessed as grammatical rules merely intended to govern a particular religious "language-game." As straightforward claims about the way things are, they seem to be thought of as something of an embarrassment. This, to put it mildly, is a remarkable turn of affairs. Until fairly recently, the existential force of the Christian gospel was understood in the context of a Christian story about God, the world, and human beings which, as a conjunction of claims about the way things are, was believed to be *true*, metaphysically and morally correct. Of course, the apostles and the authors of the New Testament documents were not viewed as metaphysicians or moral philosophers. But it was generally recognized that their message has presuppositions and implications as well as central components which fall within the province of metaphysics and moral philosophy, and which can be very usefully elucidated in the technical terms appropriate to these important domains of human thought.

This view of the Christian message is now often termed 'propositionalism' or 'cognitivism' by prominent theologians and is thought to be a pre-modern mistake which arose only out of a philosophical innocence now long lost. In fact, anyone who thinks otherwise is nowadays quite often said to be naive, unsophisticated, a-historical (a charge shortly to be explained) and — nearly everyone's favorite term of disapprobation now that 'heretic' is unfashionable — a fundamentalist. How is this aversion to the tradition's self-understanding on the part of leading academic theologians to be explained? What motivates their large scale move away from what they call propositionalism? What, if anything, grounds their charges? In light of the wide divergence between such theologians and a great many contemporary philosophers on this issue, and especially in light of the fact that the authors of this collection take the straightforward cognitivism of the tradition seriously, as providing the framework for their own efforts, a few words in answer to these questions will not be out of place here.

A dominant trend in modern theology is to reinterpret the traditional Christian doctrines as symbols whose function is merely to express and evoke certain sorts of evaluative and religious *attitudes* and *experiences*. Representing one variant of this trend quite candidly and succinctly, John Hick once remarked concerning the central Christian claim that Jesus was, and is, God Incarnate, the claim captured in the classical doctrine of the incarnation, that

> the real point and value of the incarnational doctrine is not indicative but expressive, not to assert a metaphysical fact but to express a valuation and evoke an attitude.[1]

This systematic focus on human attitudes and experiences has become so firmly entrenched in modern theology since the work of Schleiermacher as to become a hoary tradition unto itself. In his recent and enormously influential book *The Nature of Doctrine*, George Lindbeck makes some very revealing comments about this "long and very notable experiential tradition" in theology. Expressing at one point a very common assessment, he says:

> The origins of this tradition in one sense go back to Kant, for he helped clear the ground for its emergence by demolishing the metaphysical and epistemological foundations of the earlier regnant cognitive-propositional views. That ground-clearing was later completed for most educated people by scientific developments that increased the difficulties of accepting literalistic propositional interpretations of such biblical doctrines as creation, and by historical studies that implied the time-conditioned relativity of all doctrines.[2]

These statements from Lindbeck are enlightening in a number of ways.

First of all, there is a conviction expressed here which is widespread among contemporary theologians, the belief that Kant, or Hume, or both together some two centuries ago dealt death blows to natural theology and to the sort of classical theistic metaphysics underlying traditional approaches to revelational theology. In a strange way, these philosophers have become the unlikely patron saints of current academic theology, as the popular appraisal of their work has shifted the whole theological enterprise into its now common non-metaphysical directions. What is particularly interesting about the references theologians make to Kant or Hume is that most often we find the philosopher merely mentioned, in a somewhat deferential and even slightly appreciative tone, but we rarely, if ever, see an account of precisely which arguments of his are supposed to have accomplished the alleged demolition of cognitivism, and exactly how they may be supposed to have had that effect. In fact, I must confess to never having seen in the writings of any contemporary theologian the exposition of a single argument from either Hume or Kant, or any other historical figure, for that matter, which comes

anywhere near to demolishing, or even irreparably damaging traditional
theistic metaphysics, historical Christian doctrine, or the epistemology
of what we might call 'theological realism', the construal of theology as
a discipline whose intent is to represent religious realities as they, in fact,
are. An editorial introduction such as this is clearly not the place to
survey and critique any such attempts as there may have been to accomplish this task. It must suffice here merely to point out that the essayists
whose work is being presented in this volume, who are numbered among
the foremost contemporary philosophers, and who are quite well
acquainted with the work of Hume and Kant, reject this conclusion
common among theologians about what their writings show concerning
traditional religious belief.

The developments of modern science that Lindbeck alludes to no
more clearly proscribe a traditionalist understanding of Christian doctrines than do the writings of Hume and Kant. His reference, of course,
is to scientific developments since the time of Kant, although he does not
specify the precise developments he finds to be troublesome. It is unlikely
that he has in mind recent strides in molecular biology, quantum mechanics, or cosmology, although the last of these fields has been thought by
some to pose challenges to religious belief. (Of course, just as many
have hailed its details as corroborating the ancient theistic claims of cosmic design.) But, in any case, Lindebeck's mention of the biblical doctrine of Creation indicates that what he probably means to invoke here
is modern evolutionary theory. If, however, one draws the simple distinction which must be drawn between the biblical *doctrine* of Creation
and the literary *representations* of creation to be found in, for example,
the book of Genesis, it is unclear how this development of scientific the-
orizing is supposed to increase the difficulty of construing a sentence like

(1) Everything in the universe is created by God and depends on
    him for its existence moment to moment

as the expression of a proposition which is true. How other scientific
developments could increase the difficulty of accepting the rest of Christian doctrine as cognitively available propositional truth is even more
difficult to see.

In addition to the spectres of Hume and Kant and the apparently
bullying image of modern science, historical studies are cited by Lindbeck
as contributing to the downfall of cognitive-propositional views of Christian doctrine. Now, there are many ways in which historical studies since
the time of Spinoza might be thought to have had a negative impact on
traditional Christian thought. First, in reference to biblical studies, it

might be argued that we have discovered the classical Christian doctrines not to be clearly present within the biblical corpus. Further, it is sometimes added, they are not even hinted at in "the earliest strata" of the core New Testament documents and their sources. And so, the conclusion is drawn, if we are historically sensitive to the earliest roots of the Christian faith, we will recognize the standard church doctrines to be later accretions inessential to, and even corrosive of, the most authentic Christian witness.

I must admit that during my own training in biblical studies before I came to philosophy, I often wondered whether it was the heavy hand of philosophical presuppositions which, usually unacknowledged, guided the work of biblical scholars, in everything from their exegetical and critical efforts to their application of procedures for dating documents. This is how I suspected it often went: No theologian or biblical scholar who identifies himself in any sense as a Christian wants to recognize in the earliest and foundational beliefs of his own faith community metaphysically implausible, cosmologically incongruous, or logically absurd claims about reality. If on the basis of some philosophical argument or, more commonly, rumors of such an argument, the biblical scholar comes to believe that one or another traditional doctrine is deeply flawed in any of these ways, he or she may well be less inclined to acknowledge intimations or anticipations of the problematic formulation in the *authentic* sayings of Jesus or in the earliest witness of the church. Since there is no purely mechanical procedure for textual archaeology on complex ancient documents, there is ample room within the parameters of accepted scholarly practice for such philosophically inspired subjective disinclinations to have their effect. If this, or anything like this, has been an operative dynamic in the development of biblical studies in the recent past, then we clearly have from this quarter no *independent* historical challenge to a classical conception of Christian faith and doctrine—we are merely directed back to purely philosophical arguments as potential sources of trouble.

Whatever the merit of this speculation about the possible psychological dynamics behind some recent work in biblical studies, the Christian faith has been traditionally understood to be rooted in the entirety of its canonical scriptures, as well as in the creeds, confessions, and conciliar decrees of the believing community. Any Marcionite picking and choosing of favorite sources is unacceptable. Whether the first Christian to commit faith to papyrus had a propositionally oriented, incipiently doctrinal mindset or not, this is a fundamental orientation of the Christian church throughout the centuries, and one which cannot be abandoned lightly.

We may suppose, however, that it is not primarily to the domain of historical biblical studies that Lindbeck alludes when he cites broadly "historical studies" as implying "the time-conditioned relativity of all doctrines." It is likely that he has in mind rather something like this: Quite simply, modern historical research has made us sensitive to the fact that thought forms vary from culture to culture, and from one historical period to another. Religious thought forms are no exception. They seem to be thoroughly conditioned by the times and places within which they arise. As Lindbeck himself says later on in his book:

> The first-order truth claims of a religion change insofar as these arise from the . . . shifting worlds that human beings inhabit. What is taken to be reality is in large part socially constructed and consequently alters in the course of time. The universe of the ancient Near East was very different from that of Greek philosophy, and both are dissimilar from the modern cosmos. Inevitably, the Christianized versions of these various world pictures are far from identical.[3]

The argument that Lindbeck, in effect, goes on to give is that since Christian claims about reality have been made in very different times and places, those claims themselves must be viewed as deeply different; thus, if doctrines are claims about God, the world, and human existence, first-order claims about reality, then they have been importantly changing and differing over space and time—there is no single doctrine of Creation, or Incarnation, or Salvation, but a set of very different time-conditioned cultural expressions of the faiths of different Christians. Surely we want a conception of doctrine such that there *is* continuity in Christian doctrine. Thus, we cannot view doctrines as first order truth claims about reality. They are instead, in Lindbeck's view, grammatical *rules*. Or so he argues.

But what of "the time-conditioned *relativity* of all doctrines" that historical studies are supposed to unveil for the cognitive-propositional view of doctrine? What is relative to what? Perhaps Lindbeck means to suggest that since religious claims are, on his conception, functions of socially constructed world-views, the truth of such claims can be understood only as intra-systemic truth, or truth-relative-to-the-operative-world-view. But the mere existence of different conceptual schemes does not alone entail the semantic relativity of claims made within those schemes, any more than the existence of differing theories in some domain of scientific inquiry alone entails scientific anti-realism. An argument is needed. And no argument is forthcoming whose contours are easily discernible and which might have any chance at all of contributing in a forceful way to dispatching the cognitive-propositional conception of Christian doctrine. What is at work here is one particular, philosophically loaded, sociology of knowledge, or perhaps better, of belief which seems strangely attractive to many contemporary theologians. But for such a view there is no compelling argument or independent purchase on truth, aside from a stipulative truth-within-its-own-conceptual-framework which we are free to ignore.

Of course, Platonistic and Aristotelian metaphysics and moral theory were presumably unavailable to the great majority, if not all, of the biblical authors. It does not follow at all from this that their own perspectives and claims cannot be captured and unfolded in such philosophically attuned thought forms. The development of doctrine which ensued from appropriating such thought forms is something quite different from, and much more deeply continuous than, a mere succession of distinct, time-conditioned linguistic artifacts. We can understand the medievals, the patristics, and the biblical authors about as well as we can understand each other. And we can disagree with them. We are not limited to just noting that what is true-in-our-framework sometimes differs from what is true-in-their-framework, and to admitting that the very existence of such a difference is itself a fact only in-our-framework. We can really engage the past. Nothing within the purview of modern historical studies has shown otherwise. Thus, again, from this direction there is not, after all, any decisive obstacle to working within the traditional understanding of Christian faith and doctrine.

The mere existence of ongoing doctrinal disputes through the history of the church, and the existence of metaphysical disputes related to these doctrinal controversies, seems to be deeply troubling to many modern theologians. Or, more specifically, the fact that there is no humanly available Archimidean point from which to resolve such disputes, no single, simple decision procedure for adjudicating rival doctrinal positions, seems to have been a cause for dismay among recent theologians contemplating the history of Christian thought. I believe that it is concern over such matters which has served as a powerful motivation in recent years for the move toward theological anti-realism, or at least toward the attempt to develop a practically metaphysics-free form of theological reflection. And yet all too often, the resulting reflection has not been free of metaphysics at all, but rather has been constrained by a naturalistic or materialist metaphysics alien to the gospel and the whole body of traditional Christian thought. If Christian thinkers do not, as part of their theological work, seek to develop and refine suitable philosophical tools for the expression of their faith, they inevitably just inherit their philosophical assumptions and dispositions from the culture around them. Here is a modicum of truth behind one of Lindbeck's convictions noted above. And, as I think Lindbeck on reflection would agree, not all such cultural legacies are equally suitable to the expression of Christian faith.

The lack of a simple algorithm for resolving doctrinal, or metaphysical, differences does not prevent rational adjudication of such differences. It just makes it much more difficult. Nor, as most epistemologists agree, does the unavailability of such a procedure in many departments of human thought prevent the attainment of genuine propositional knowledge in these spheres. It has often been said that a little philosophy is a dangerous thing. I suspect that one reason for the significant divergence of assumptions between most contemporary academic theologians and the professional philosophers now doing Christian philosophical theology is that the theologians have had a dangerous amount of philosophy in the course of their theological training. They have had enough to see problems in the tradition, but not enough to equip them to work carefully through those problems. This, the contributors to the present volume are amply equipped to do.

It is not the conviction of the philosophers brought together here that traditional theologizing is without any serious flaws. The contrary conviction on the part of many will become clear in reading their papers. The shared assumption is rather that the tradition has substantive commitments well worth exploring and refining, resources which merit detailed philosophical scrutiny, and contemporary re-appropriation. Whatever flaws there are should be brought to light as clearly and precisely as possible, so that we might seek to eliminate them and do our part to capture anew the deep truths heretofore imperfectly expressed.

The first four papers in this collection address problems in soteriology, or the Christian conception of salvation. In a broad ranging piece, Richard Swinburne launches our investigations by seeking to map out some of the general conceptual terrain within a broadly orthodox Christian account of human sin and salvation—hence, his title, "The Christian Scheme of Salvation." The next two papers explore the efforts of a couple of great philosophical theologians of the past to articulate lineaments of a cogent Christian soteriology. In "Original Sin," William J. Wainwright scrutinizes Jonathan Edwards' attempt to develop an Augustinian picture of inherited human guilt. Highly critical of many of its details, Wainwright succeeds in garnering from his examination numerous insights and constraints for a more adequate philosophical delineation of the common features of human sinfulness. In her essay "Atonement According to Aquinas," Eleonore Stump seeks to draw upon Thomas Aquinas's thought to correct a very common, unreflective account of the atonement which seeks to be orthodox but can easily be seen to be, according to Stump, "so full of philosophical and theological problems as to be irremediable." Reversing a popular image, Stump points out that "Aquinas sees the problem of alienation between God and man as consisting not in God's wrathfulness toward man but rather in man's withdrawal from God." The change of perspective thus effected is seen to have significant implications. Rounding out this section, Marilyn Adams leads us through some important biblical texts for theological reflection on salvation, with her paper "Separation and Reversal in Luke-Acts." The methods and procedures of this work bespeak the new-found commitment among many analytic philosophers to ground their philosophical theology firmly in the relevant biblical materials.

In "The Indwelling of the Holy Spirit," William P. Alston takes a look at Christian conceptions of the work of God, in particular God the Holy Spirit, in the created world. His focus is on the respective roles of God and the Christian believer in the process of sanctification, the spiritual growing to be more like God, which is intended to be a vital facet of the Christian life. Examining various possible models for conceiving of such divine activity, Alston begins to marshall considerations in favor of what he calls 'the sharing model', according to which the believer literally comes to share in the life of God.

In "Christian Liberty," Robert M. Adams tackles another problem for understanding, from a traditional point of view, the life of a committed Christian. The central issue that charts the direction of his reflections is the problem of how to provide a proper place in the ethical life for beliefs about what one *ought* to do without letting them drive out other springs of action such as the avowedly Christian one of *love* for other human beings. In the course of working through this problem, Adams suggests that the best model for a Christian ethics is not provided by anything like classical utilitarianism, but rather by what John Rawls calls 'intuitionism', with the distinctively Christian twist that, here, intuitions will be understood in categories traditionally used to elucidate the nature of divine inspiration. In this exciting and edifying paper, Adams draws interesting conclusions on such topics as supererogation, value maximization, and friendship.

Throughout the long history of Christian literature, one of the passages which has proved most fascinating and perplexing, comforting and troubling is Paul's famous confession in Romans 7, that "the good that I wish, I do not do; but I practice the very evil that I do not wish" (verse 19), along with its surrounding reflections. The passage which extends from verse 14 to verse 25 at the end of the chapter has been a source of illumination for many readers, a cause of irritation for others. Norman Kretzmann is convinced that medieval biblical commentaries contain a wealth of philosophical insight waiting to be mined by contemporary philosophers. To display such riches he draws upon the work of Thomas Aquinas to aid in understanding Paul here. The result, his paper "Warring Against the Law of my Mind," is an exemplary piece of philosophical appropriation and analysis which provides an absolutely excellent lesson as to how we can benefit immensely from an intimate acquaintance with the work of our philosophical forebears, especially within the rich vein of traditional Christian reflection on the deepest issues in moral philosophy.

With his essay "Suffering Love," Nicholas Wolterstorff seeks to rescue from the distortions of Stoic thought the proper biblical perspective on suffering and joy, and to reorient theological thinking on the relation of God to these extreme states of mind. Wolterstorff recounts how Augustine, a dominant influence in the classical Christian tradition, derived from the Stoics and peripatetics his view that a life free of disturbing emotions is a better form of life than one encompassing such states. Augustine rejected the Greek claim that *we* should be free of such emotions, arguing that we are sinners and thus, at least, should grieve over our sin. But he insisted on the view that God, who lives the best form of life, must be free of such states. Demonstrating how philosophical anthropology interacts with philosophical theology, Wolterstorff lays out what he presents as a needed corrective to this view.

Our last section consists of two papers which are in many ways the most technical and demanding in this collection. In his interesting paper "And Yet They Are Not Three Gods But One God," Peter van Inwagen explores the use of relative identity to defend the classical doctrine of the Trinity. He thus brings to bear on one of the most central and problematic doctrines of the Christian faith some of the most recent relevant developments in philosophical logic and metaphysics. The result is undeniably hard going for the philosophical novice, but presents possibilities for theological construction which well repay the careful attention they demand.

In "Eschatological Pragmatism," James F. Ross confronts questions about the nature of truth in general, religious truth in particular, and the development of doctrine. He denies that there is any single "being true" relation across all subject matters, offers arguments against a standard correspondence theory of truth, and adumbrates a conception of what it could be for the differing expectations of Christians in different ages all to come out "true" in the eschaton. Such truth, he suggests, will consist in large part in the fulfillment of earlier cognitive states by later cognitive states produced by God.

The authors of these papers, I suspect, do not agree with one another on all points. Nor will there be found many readers who find them all equally agreeable. One point on which they do agree, however, as I have emphasized earlier, is the importance of careful philosophical reflection on such topics as these. And this is a point on which, I hope, there will be found few readers who disagree.[4]

NOTES

1. John Hick, "Jesus and the World Religions," from John Hick, ed., *The Myth of God Incarnate* (London: SCM Press, 1977), p. 178.

2. George Lindbeck, *The Nature of Doctrine: Religion and Theology in a Post-liberal Age* (Philadelphia: The Westminister Press, 1984), pp. 20, 21.

3. Ibid., p. 84.

4. I would like to thank Alfred J. Freddoso for his comments on an earlier draft of this introductory essay.

PART I

Sin and Salvation

The Christian Scheme of Salvation[1]

RICHARD SWINBURNE

Christianity offers to us salvation, salvation from the guilt of our past sin, salvation from our proneness to present sin, salvation for the enjoyment of the Beatific Vision of God in the company of the blessed in Heaven. This salvation was made available to humans by the life, death, and resurrection of Jesus Christ. This paper is concerned to analyze how this life, death, and resurrection made available salvation from the guilt of past sin. In so doing I shall be spelling out a theory of Atonement which I believe to be in essence very similar to the theory expounded by St. Thomas Aquinas and also to the view of Christ's death as a sacrifice developed in the Epistle to the Hebrews. I shall, however, start from scratch and try to avoid using their technical terms without definition and to avoid using their implicit assumptions without bringing them out into the open.

I

Before anyone can understand how Christianity provides salvation from the past, he needs to understand three crucial concepts — guilt, atonement, and forgiveness. These concepts are crucial for understanding relations between one person and another, as well as relations between humans and God; and it is tragic that so much modern moral philosophy has neglected their study. I shall need to devote the larger part of this paper to analyzing these concepts before applying my analysis to the Christian message.

Among good acts, some are obligatory — duties owed to particular individuals, such as keeping promises or educating one's children. Good acts which go beyond obligation are supererogatory good acts. Giving one's life to save the life of a comrade is a plausible example of such an act. The scope for goodness is unending; however many good acts one has done, there is always another one waiting to be done. But it is a matter of dispute how wide is the range of obligation. Whether our obligations are a narrow set which can easily be fulfilled or a large set (including duties to help the poor in distant lands), which leaves little room for supererogatory goodness, is disputed.[2] Wherever the line is drawn, guilt belongs to a person only in respect of his failure to perform his obligations, or his doing what it is obligatory not to do, i.e., something wrong. (I shall often omit this second negative clause in future discussions of guilt, for the sake of simplicity of exposition. It will be obvious how it is to be inserted.)

The guilt is objective guilt if the agent has failed to fulfill a moral obligation (or done an act obligatory not to do) whether or not he realized that this was his moral obligation or that he was failing in respect of it. I am objectively guilty for failing to educate my children properly even if I believe that I have no duty to educate my children or if I believe that sending them to a certain school, which unknown to me is totally incompetent, is educating my children properly. The guilt is subjective if the agent has failed to fulfill what he believes to be his moral obligation (or done what he believed to be obligatory not to do), whether or not there was such an obligation—so long as the agent was free to do or refrain from doing the action, in whatever sense of "free" makes him morally responsible for that action.

But the assertion that someone is guilty is not just an assertion about the past; it makes two further claims about the present. The first is that the guilty one owes something to the one whom he has wronged, his victim. If I fail in an obligation, I do not just do a wrong, I do a wrong to someone. If I promise you that I will give a lecture and then do not turn up, or if I kick you in a fit of anger, I have done a wrong to you. By hurting you, I put myself in a moral situation somewhat like the legal situation of a debtor who has failed to repay money borrowed from a bank. But the kind of debt owed by failure to perform one's moral obligations is often no mere financial one. Insofar as the victim is a person, that person is known personally to the wrongdoer, the failure is a failure of personal trust, and above all if there is ill-will (deliberate malice or negligence) on the part of the wrong-doer, then there is a totally new kind of harm involved—the harm done to personal relations by a wrong attitude by the wrongdoer. Yet there is still more to moral guilt than past failure and present debt. Through his past failure the guilty one has acquired a negative status, somewhat like being unclean,[3] which needs to be removed. By making a promise a person puts himself under certain obligations, but his status is in no way bad or unclean in consequence. There is more in the present to being guilty than incurring new obligations.

There is something wrong with a person even if his guilt is purely objective. If I unintentionally break your best vase or light the fire with the manuscript of your book, I acquire the status of a wrongdoer even if my actions were done in total ignorance of their nature or consequence (and even if I had taken all reasonable precautions to ensure that they had no such nature or consequence). It is, I suggest, a virtually unanimous moral intuition that this is so, that in such circumstances I acquire a status which needs purging by reparation if possible, and certainly by apology. This is because in interacting with my fellows, I undertake responsibility for seeing that certain things are done and certain things are not done (e.g., in holding your vase, I take responsibility for its not getting broken); and bad luck (my actions having bad consequences, despite my taking reasonable precautions) no more removes the responsibility, than it excuses you from repaying a man a sum of money which you have borrowed from him, even if you have that same amount stolen.

But of course the guilt is of a different kind if I knowingly fail in my obligations toward you — if my guilt is subjective as well as objective. Here again I suggest that a virtually unanimous moral intuition suggests that far more is wrong, and far more needs doing to put it right. If I deliberately break your best vase, it is no good my saying "I really am very sorry." I have got to make several speeches distancing myself from the act and I have got to make reparation very quickly. I have wronged you so much the worse that my guilt is of a qualitatively different kind. The Book of Numbers differentiated between "sins committed unknowingly" and "sins committed with a high hand" (i.e., knowingly), declaring various kinds of ritual reparation suitable for the former and some very serious punishment for the latter.[4] The reason for the vast difference is that when I deliberately break your best vase, I have failed not merely in my outward obligations toward you, but also in that attitude of purpose toward you which I owe you, the attitude of seeking no harm for you.

What if there is no objective guilt, but I fail in what I believe to be my obligations toward you? I try to break your best vase, but by accident break my own instead. Have I wronged you? My argument suggests that the answer is yes; and we can see that the answer is correct from considering more serious cases. I try to kill you but the shot misfires. From the obvious need for reparation of rather more than a short apology, we can see that wrong has been done and guilt acquired. Both subjective and objective guilt are stains on a soul requiring expunging;

but subjective guilt is embedded in the soul while objective guilt lies on the surface.

Such, I have suggested by example, is the common understanding of moral guilt, the status acquired by one who fails in his obligations. When modern moral philosophers neglect this concept, they ignore the fact that letting someone down hurts, and matters. We cannot undo the past, but we can remove its consequences—How is the taint of guilt to be removed? For perfect removal, the guilty one must make atonement for his wrong act, and the wronged person must forgive him.

Atonement involves four components: reparation, repentance, apology, and what, for want of a better word, I shall call penance (though not all of these are always required). They are all contributions to removing as much of the consequences of the past act as logically can be removed. The consequences are, first, the harm caused by and distinguishable from the act of causing it and second, the purposive attitude of the guilty one toward the wronged one manifested in the causing of harm. By removing the former harm the guilty one makes reparation. Sometimes he can literally restore the status quo. If I steal your watch and have not sold it, I can return it to you. Sometimes I can only make things rather similar to the way they were, so that the victim is almost equally happy with the new state. I can compensate him adequately, that is. If I steal and sell your watch, I can buy you another one. If I smash up your car, I can pay for the repairs. Sometimes, alas, full compensation is not possible. If I run you over with my car, and paralyze you for life, nothing I can do can compensate you fully for that. Full reparation is not possible. But some things which I can do can compensate you in part. I can pay for wheelchairs and machines to lift you out of bed in the morning.

But the consequences of the act are not merely such harm, but the fact that by doing the act the guilty one has made himself the one who has harmed the wronged one. He cannot change that past fact, but he can distance himself from it by privately and publicly disowning the act. The wronged one has been hurt, and so it is to the wronged one that the disowning is owed and must be shown. But the disowning which is owed must be sincere and so must reflect the attitude that the guilty one now has and naturally expresses to himself. The natural expression to oneself is repentance, the public expression to the wronged one is apology. Repentance involves, first, acknowledgment by the guilty one that he did the act and that it was a wrong act to do. Thereby the guilty one distances the act from his present ideals. Repentance also involves a resolve to amend—you cannot repent of a past act if you intend to do a similar act at the next available opportunity. Preachers often draw our attention to the etymology of the Greek word translated "repent," Μετανοεῖν, which means literally to "change one's mind." By resolving to amend, the guilty one distances the past act from his present purposes. In acknowledging his initiation of the past act, but distancing it both from his present ideals and from his present purposes, the guilty one makes the sharp contrast between the attitude behind the past act and his present attitude. He disowns the past act publicly by expressing to the wronged one the repentance which he expresses to himself privately, assuring the wronged one that he recognizes its wrongness and that he purposes to amend. There are conventional ways of doing this; one may say "I'm very sorry" or "I really do apologize." An agent cannot alter the fact that he did the past act, but what he can do is make the present "he" in his attitude as different as possible from the past "he" who did the act; that is the most he can do toward undoing the act.

The above account of repentance and apology applies insofar as there is an element of subjectivity in the guilt, insofar as deliberately or through negligence the guilty one has some moral responsibility for doing the harm. If the guilt is purely objective, arising from the performance of an unintentional act in which there was not even the slightest negligence involved (e.g., dropping your best vase when startled by a loud noise), an apology of a sort is still owed, for the reason that in interacting with others we accept responsibility in advance for not causing them certain kinds of harm. If unintentionally we are the agents of harm, we must distance ourselves from that agency. But insofar as we never intended it in the first place (and had every intention of preventing it), what we must do is to emphasize that our present benevolent ideals and purposes were our past ones also. An apology (but one which brings out the unintentional character of the action) is needed; but it needs behind it no repentance in the form of change of mind, only sincerity in the reemphasis of ideals and purposes.

Apology can often be very difficult. It costs many of us a lot to say "I'm sorry." But sometimes, for some people, apology can be very easy. We all know the smooth, amiable people who say "I'm frightfully sorry" with such a charming smile that our reaction is "Yes, but do you really mean it?" And what else can show "meaning it," what else can show the sincerity of the apology? You lend your friend a considerably large sum of money. He forgets to return it until you remind him five times; in consequence of which you have to borrow money yourself and disappoint your own creditors. He then acknowledges his wrongdoing and resolves not to do it again (publicly, and, let us suppose, also privately). He pays you the money back and compensates you financially for extra financial costs, and says he is sorry. And yet that is not quite good enough, is it? We feel something else is required. The "something else" would be some token of his sorrow—a favor which we did not expect, interest on the money which was not part of the original bargain, perhaps a bunch of flowers—something more than mere compensation.[5] The giving of the extra gift does not have the function of making clear something which was true whether or not the agent made it clear; that he meant the apology. Rather it is a performative[6] act whereby he disowns the wrong act (in a way which mere words do not do when the wrong is a serious one). By doing his act of disowning, by doing something which costs him time, effort, and money, he constitutes that act as a meant and serious act. To give what we cannot too easily afford is always a serious act. The penitent constitutes his apology as serious by making it costly.

With reparation, repentance, apology, and penance, the guilty person has done what he can toward removing his guilt, toward atonement for the past, toward making him and the wronged one at one again. Not all such are needed in every case. For some wrongs reparation is inappropriate—there is no reparation for an insult; for the less serious wrongs, penance is not needed. But sincere apology is always needed. In the case of subjective guilt, apology involves repentance of the kind described.

The final act belongs to the wronged party—to forgive. In making apology, reparation, and penance, I am giving you something. All gifts have to be accepted (explicitly or implicitly) or else they remain with the giver. Gifts are accepted by the recipient completing the process which the giver is trying to effect by presenting them to the recipient. You accept my box of chocolates by taking it from me, the elephant I give you by accepting responsibility for its upkeep. What I give you in making reparation, penance, and apology is my contribution toward destroying the consequences (physical and not so physical) of my act of hurting you. You accept my reparation and penance by taking over the money, flowers, or whatever. My apology is my disowning of the past act. You accept my disowning by forwarding the purpose I had in showing you this disowning—to make it the case, as far as logically can be done, that I was not the originator of an act by which I wronged you. You do that by undertaking to treat me and think of me in future not as one who has hurt you, by agreeing not to hold my act against me. Your acceptance of my reparation, penance, and, above all, apology, is forgiving. Forgiving is a performative act—achieved perhaps by saying solemnly "I forgive you" or perhaps by saying "that's all right" or maybe just by a smile.

A person's guilt is removed when his repentance, reparation, apology, and penance find their response in the victim's forgiveness. Can the victim forgive him without any act of atonement on his part? The victim can indeed disown the act, in the sense that he explictly says something like "let us regard this as not having happened" and then acts as though it had not happened. Such disowning could be done at any time, even if the guilty one makes no atonement; but unless it was done in response to atonement it would not be acceptance of that. And it will not then suffice to remove guilt, for the guilty one has not distanced himself from that act. We can see this by example. I borrow your car and damage the bodywork. I do not even apologize, but all the same you say "That's quite all right." But I remain one who has wronged you and I need to purge myself of my guilt, as I may well realize in later life. A mere financial debt can easily be removed by the creditor, but the unclean status of guilt requires some work by the debtor.

Indeed, not merely is it ineffective but it is wrong, in the case of serious acts, for the wronged person to treat the acts as not having been done, in the absence of some atonement at least in the form of apology from the guilty person. In the case of acts done to hurt us which are not done with much deliberation and where the hurt is not great, this may indeed be the right course of action. (It would be wrong to treat very seriously acts which were not in their intentions or consequences very serious.) But this would be the wrong course in the case of a serious hurt, and, above all, one done deliberately. Suppose that I have murdered your dearly loved wife; you know this, but for some reason I am beyond the power of the law. Being a modern and charitable man, you decide to overlook my offence (insofar as it hurt you). "The past is the past," you say, "What is the point of nursing a grievance?" The party we are both going to attend will go with more of a swing if we forget about this little incident. But, of course, that attitude of yours trivializes human life, your love for your wife, and the importance of right action. And it involves your failing to treat me seriously, to take seriously my attitude toward you expressed in my action. Thereby it trivializes human relationships, for it supposes that good human relations can exist when we do not take each other seriously.[7]

It is both wrong and ineffective for a victim of a serious hurt to disown the hurt when no atonement at all has been made.[8] What, however, is within the victim's power is to determine, within limits, just how much atonement is necessary before he is prepared to give the forgiveness which will eliminate guilt. The guilty one must offer some atonement — certainly repentance and apology and some attempt at reparation insofar as it lies within his power. But the victim may, if he chooses, let the guilty one off from doing any more; his forgiveness, without insisting on more, would be efficacious. But if he chooses, the victim can insist on substantial reparation, and sometimes it is good that he should do so, that he should insist on the guilty one, for his own sake, making a serious atonement; for that allows him to take seriously the harm that he has done.

What now if the guilty one makes due amends, gives a serious apology with due reparation and penance, but the victim fails to forgive? Does the guilt remain? My answer is that it does remain initially; the victim has the power to sustain it for a while. But if the apology is pressed, the penance increased, and still the victim refuses to forgive, the guilt disappears. Ideally both those involved—the guilty one and victim—need to disown the act, but if the guilty one does all that he can both to disown the act and to get the victim to disown the act, he will have done all he can to remove his involvement in the act. All that is logically possible for the guilty one to do to remove his status has been done.

If by my past act I have wronged you, that gives you a certain right against me—a right to accept or ignore my plea for pardon. If we were to say that the guilty party had, as it were, a fixed fine to pay in the way of atonement, that guilt did not disappear before the fine was paid but that it disappeared automatically when the fine was paid, that would have the consequence that I can wrong you and then remove my guilt at will. That would not take seriously the fact that the act is an act by which you are wronged, and in the wiping out of which you ought therefore to have a say. One consequence of my harming you is that it is in part up to you whether my guilt is remitted. But although my act gives you a right against me, it does not give you an infinite right. The harm which I have done you and the guilt which in consequence I acquire is limited. Hence your power to keep me guilty is limited. The victim has the right, within limits, to judge when the guilty one's atonement suffices. He can take an apology which sounds sincere and so indicates repentance as sufficient, or refuse forgiveness until the apology is renewed with reparation and penance. He cannot forgive when the apology is totally casual and so shows no repentance, and if he refuses forgiveness after a serious, repeated genuine apology with reparation and penance, the guilt vanishes despite the lack of forgiveness. But, within those limits, the final remission of guilt depends on the victim.

There is, in general, no obligation on the victim to forgive. How can my hurting you and then trying to undo the harm, actions all of my choice and not yours, put you under an obligation to do something, which did not exist before? Barring an exception to be explained below, your positive obligations arise from your choices, including your acceptance of my favors, not from my choices. However, forgiving the serious penitent is clearly good—a work of supererogation. (There is, however, an obligation to forgive others, on anyone who has solemnly undertaken to do so. For this reason Christians, unlike others, have an obligation to forgive all who seek their forgiveness. For it is a central theme of the gospel, embedded in the Lord's Prayer, that God's forgiveness can only be had by those prepared to forgive others; Christians who accept God's forgiveness thereby undertake the obligation to forgive others.)

In this paper so far I have in general been assuming that a person acquires guilt and so the need for atonement and forgiveness only in respect of actions which he has done himself, that atonement is owed only to those hurt (in an obvious and direct sense) by his actions, and that he alone can make atonement for the actions which he has done. It is time to bring in third parties.

We live in a network of obligations, some of them undertaken voluntarily—as are our obligations to care for our spouses and children—and some of them incurred involuntarily, as are our obligations to care for our parents and other benefactors of our youth. Normally it is only the accepting of a benefit which creates any positive obligation, and that together with the accepting of the obligation is something which we do voluntarily. But the greatest benefits—of life, nurture, and initial education—are ones which a benefactor must convey without the recipient being able to choose whether to accept or refuse them—because only when he has them does he have the ability to accept or refuse benefits. A benefactor reasonably assumes that a recipient would, if he had the choice, accept such benefits; and the conferring of the benefit, given that reasonable assumption, creates, I suggest, an obligation on the recipient to do something in return—to care for parents, teachers, and other members of his nurturing community in their need.

The web of obligations to care stretches further than to parents and teachers, spouses and children. Voluntarily we have accepted friendship and cooperation with many, and that acceptance brings obligations to help our friends in their need. Involuntarily we have received benefits from a very wide community in space and time, stretching back to the first human who was sensitive to moral distinctions, and first chose intentionally to confer what was good on his children including some knowledge of what was good and bad. Many of our benefactors are dead. But the dead can still be benefited by bringing about what they would wish to have brought about, e.g., by conferring benefits on their descendents, our siblings and cousins and ultimately all members of the human race.

Among our obligations to our benefactors is the obligation to make some good use of benefits received. Of course if some one gives us a gift, we are not obliged to use it exactly as they wish. For it is the essence of a gift that, within limits, the recipient can do as he wishes with it. If I "give" you some money and tell you exactly what to buy for me with it, I have not given you a gift. But there are limits as to what a recipient can do with the gift. To accept an expensive present and then to throw it away is to wrong our benefactor. A recipient has *some* obligation to try to put what he has been given to some good use.

Given this web of obligations, what guilt have we for the actions of others? Those who are responsible for the moral education of children often have some guilt for the wrong acts of the children. Of course, a parent cannot make his children be good; there are other influences on the child, and also in the view of many, the child has some indeterministic freedom of choice. But the parent has a responsibility to influence, and if bad behavior results when he has failed to do so, the parent has some responsibility for this. Also, there is the responsibility of a member of a community to deter a fellow member from doing some particular grossly immoral act, on which he is intent. A husband has a duty to try to deter his wife from shop-lifting; a German a duty to protest against his country's extermination of Jews. Failure to protest involves a share in the resulting guilt.

Yet with these exceptions a person is surely not responsible for, not guilty in respect of, the acts of others; above all, he is not guilty for the acts of others which he could not have prevented. And yet, there is a sense in which a person is "involved" in the objective or subjective guilt of others of his community — although he bears no guilt for it himself. Our duty to help others of our community in their need includes a duty to help them with perhaps their greatest need, to get rid of their burden of past guilt. I cannot share my friend's guilt, but I can treat it as my burden and help him to cope with it in the ways in which he needs to cope with it — to acknowledge that it is his, and to help him by atonement to get rid of it.

Just as others are involved in our moral failures, so they can indeed help us get rid of our guilt. But the word is "help"; unless the guilty party participates in the process of "atonement," his guilt is not removed. If my child damages your property, and I tell you that he apologizes profusely, I pay the damage and give you a bottle of whisky at Christmas, my child's guilt remains. But I can help my child carry out the process of atonement — first, by encouraging him to set about it and second, by paying such of the reparation and proper penance as lies beyond his resources.[9] I can even help him say the words of apology — go along with him to knock at your door and provide him with cues. But beyond that I cannot go, if the atonement is to be his. Some offerings which others may give us to use as our reparation and penance are ones useful for other purposes. When my child damages your window and I give him money in the hope that he will pay for the repair, he could use the money for another purpose. But if I tell him that if he orders the glazier to mend the window, I will settle the bill, he does not give in reparation something which he could have used for another purpose. Nevertheless, in allowing me to do this for him, especially if it was something which I could ill afford and which required trouble to arrange, he is doing the only thing he can do and thereby he is showing humility (in recognizing the wrong he has done and his inability to right it by himself) when he transfers my generosity to you. And that is sometimes all that a wrong-doer without resources can do.

II

Such is the structure of guilt, atonement, and forgiveness. I now introduce a theological assumption—that there is a God, that is, a perfectly good, omnipotent, omniscient creator, who made the world and the natural laws which govern its operation and so (indirectly) made us and the framework within which we operate, that he became incarnate in Christ who was both God and man, lived a perfect human life, foreseeing correctly that such perfection would have the consequence that he would be crucified, intended that that life and death should be available to us to offer to God in full atonement for our sins, rose from the dead, founded a church to carry on his work and seeks our eternal well-being in friendship with himself. This very detailed assumption is of course provided by parts of the Christian credal package other than the doctrine of the Atonement. In calling it an assumption I do not, of course, in the least imply that it cannot be the subject of rational argument, only that I need to take it for granted in a short paper on another subject. My aim is to show that, given what I have shown about the nature of guilt, atonement, and forgiveness, my assumption has the consequence that Christ's life and death is indeed, as he intended, efficacious for anyone who pleads it as a perfect atonement for his actual sins and the sins of others with whom he is involved.

If there is a God, the moral worth of humans is far lower than it would otherwise be. As I have argued, we owe it to our parents and educators to obey them and to do what they wish to some limited extent, in view of all that they have done for us. *A fortiori*, if there is a God, we have a greater duty by far to obey his commands and fulfill his wishes. For our existence at each moment and all that we have depends on him; our dependence on our parents and educators is very limited in time and degree, and their ability to benefit us arises from God's gift to them. Our dependence on God is so total that we owe it to God not merely to obey any explicit commands — to worship and evangelize, say — but also generally to fulfill God's wish by making something good out of our lives, something better than what we owe to our parents and educators. When we fail in any objective or subjective duty to our fellows, we fail also in our duty to God our creator.

If, further, as I have assumed, God seeks our eternal well-being in friendship with himself, then there is a pattern of life and a goal of fulfillment open to us, which would not otherwise be available. The greatest human well-being is to be found in friendship with good and interesting people in the pursuit of worthy aims. God is a better friend with more interesting aspects of himself to reveal than human friends (given his necessity and perfect goodness an infinitely better friend with infinitely more aspects) and he has worthwhile tasks which humans can share with him in bringing themselves and others to reconciliation with each other and God, to growth in the contemplation of God and the universe which he made, and to beautifying that universe. If there is a God, such tasks will necessarily be vastly more worthwhile than secular tasks — for there will be a depth of contemplation of the richness of life of a person, God, open to us which would not be open if there is no omnipotent and omniscient being; and there will be the infinite time of an after-life which God, seeking our well-being, is able to make available to us to help in the beautifying of the world and the spiritual healing of our fellows. And God, unlike humans, is a necessary being, who is the ultimate source of being and therefore of a kind quite other than finite things; the entering into contact with him has a richness and mystery and meaning which Rudolf Otto so vividly described as the "numinous." The existence of God, which makes human moral worth far lower than it would otherwise be, makes our prospects for the future infinitely brighter.

If there is no God, humans have no obligations to give their lives to prayer or philosophical reflection or artistic creativity or helping to enrich the spiritual, intellectual, and physical lives of others, good though it is that these things be done. But if all talents depend totally on God, and if doing these things is the way to form our characters and those of others over a few years of earthly life to fit us for the life of heaven, then to use our lives in some such way passes into the realm of the obligatory.

Because of our total dependence on God, and because the possibilities for us are of a vastly different kind in quality and quantity, it follows that, if there is a God, acts which otherwise would be supererogatorily good or not good at all become obligations; and failure to perform them is a breach of obligation to God. Failure in a duty to

God is called sin. If a person does what is wrong (whether or not he realizes it), he sins objectively. If he does what he believes to be wrong, he sins subjectively.

Yet we have sinned, all humans have sinned, all humans have sinned considerably. So much is obvious, given the understanding which I have spelled out of what sin is. Hence all of us are guilty for our own sins, and also in part for the sins of those whom we ought to have influenced for good but failed to influence, and are involved in the way, which I have analyzed, in the sins of so many others of the human race. This responsibility for and involvement in the sins of others is a natural understanding of one part of original sin. (Original sin involves both some element of guilt for the sins of others, which I have analyzed, and also a proneness or tendency to sin.)[10] Each of us suffers from the burden of actual and original sin.

And so, each human owes atonement to God for the sins which he has committed and he owes it to God to help others make atonement for their sins, atonement in the form of repentance, reparation, apology, and penance. If you take seriously the theological background to human wrongdoing, you realize both the extent of atonement needed and the difficulty of making it — especially in respect of reparation and penance. For if God has given us so much, we have a duty to live a worthwhile life; and, if we have failed to do so, it's going to be very difficult to find a bit extra to offer to God in compensation for past misuse. We are too close to the situation of the criminal who has spent his ill-gotten gains and is unable to make reparation. We need help from outside.

But why in that situation would a good God not simply ignore our sins? I argued earlier that it is wrong for any victim to ignore serious harm done to him by another — for it involves not taking the other seriously in the attitudes expressed in his actions. But why would not God forgive us in return for repentance and apology without demanding reparation and penance? Aquinas claimed that he could have done so if he had so chosen.[11] But since our actions and their consequences matter, it matters that if we do wrong, *we* should take *proper* steps to cancel our actions, to pay our debts, as far as logically can be done. Just as a good parent may put in the way of a child an opportunity for making amends (an opportunity which he would not otherwise have had) rather than just accept an apology, so a good God also may do just that. God cannot literally atone for our sins, but he can help us to atone for our sins by making available to us an offering which we may offer as our reparation and penance, and by encouraging us to repent and apologize. He could give to us the opportunity to be serious enough about our sins to use his life and death as man to be our atoning offering.

And what is a suitable offering to God for our sins? Many offerings might suit, but a perfect human life would suit very well. For our sins make our human lives less worthwhile than the lives we owe to God; the best way of making it up to him would be for us to offer him a life which is perfect and so better than the life which is owed to God. The best reparation is that in which the reparation restores the damage done rather than gives something else in compensation; and the best penance is that which more than makes it up to the victim in the respect in which he was harmed rather than in some irrelevant respect. Having damaged the rusty bumper of your car, I can do penance better by giving you a new bumper, rather than restoring the old one and giving you a box of chocolates at the same time. This is because penance, to be good, must evince a concern that the particular harm which was done was done. The living of perfect human life by God himself forms a far more perfect offering for us to offer to God than a perfect life lived by an ordinary human. For the ordinary human has an obligation to God to live a worthwhile life, and so some of the perfection of his life would be owed anyway. An incarnate God does not owe it to any benefactor to live any particular kind of life, and so the whole of the perfection of that life would be available to others to use as their offering.

So if, as our theological assumption claims, God did indeed become incarnate in Christ and lived a human life so perfect that it ended in a foreseen death, and if he intended that that life should be available to be used by us to make our atonement, it is indeed the sort of thing which we could offer to God as our reparation and penance. Whether or not it would be a full reparation for the sins of all humans, it is good reparation such that a good God could indeed forgive us without demanding more. Given that Christ the man who made the offering intending it to avail fully for our atonement, is also the God to whom it was offered, he will forgive us without demanding more.

Christ offered the sacrifice on behalf of all. But it can only atone for me, if I use it—if I join my feeble repentance and halting words of apology to it, if I use it to pay my fine, to make my peace. There has to be a formal association with it in the process of my disassociating myself from my own sins and from involvement in those of others. A further part of my theological assumption was that Christ founded a body to carry on his work. The Christian Church provides a formal ceremony of association in the pledges made by the candidate for admission in its initiation ceremonies of baptism and confirmation, and before participation in the Eucharist in which, as Paul put it, we "proclaim the Lord's death until he comes."[12]

I plead the sacrifice of Christ in joining and rejoining myself to the new humanity, the new and voluntary association of those who accept Christ's offering on their behalf, the Church. And as it is difficult to repent and utter the words of apology, that too, the Church in its evangelistic and pastoral capacity helps me to do.[13]

NOTES

1. This paper has been read on many occasions. I am grateful to all who have provided those critical comments which helped me to give it its final form, and among them I am especially grateful to George Mavrodes and others who commented on the paper at the Notre Dame conference.

2. The importance of the notion of supererogation was first brought to the attention of modern moral philosophers by J. O. Urmson in his article, "Saints and Heroes," in *Essays in Moral Philosophy*, ed. A. T. Melden (Seattle: University of Washington Press, 1958), and reprinted in *Moral Concepts*, ed. J. Feinberg (London: Oxford University Press, 1969). For the history of this concept, and its elaboration and defence, see David Heyd, *Supererogation* (Cambridge: Cambridge University Press, 1982).

3. For this analogy, see St. Anselm, *Cur Deus Homo* 1.19.

4. Numbers 15:28–31.

5. "When anyone pays what he has unjustly taken away, he ought to give something which could not have been demanded of him, had he not stolen what belonged to another" (Anselm, *Cur Deus Homo* 1.11).

6. J. L. Austin introduced the terminology of "performative utterances" to describe such utterances as "I promise," "I solemnly swear," "I name this ship," which do not report already existing states of affairs but themselves bring about states of affairs. (See, e.g., his "Performative Utterances" in his *Philosophical Papers*, Oxford: Oxford University, 1961.) The man who promises does not report an interior mental act but creates an obligation upon himself to do something, an obligation which did not previously exist. Actions other than utterances may create or abolish states of people or relations between them, describable in such moral terms as responsibility and obligation. I convey money to you and thereby abolish my debt, and in the context of an auction a nod is enough to constitute a bid (i.e., a promise to pay).

7. To say that it would be wrong for me to treat an act done deliberately to hurt me as not having been done in the absence of some apology from the guilty person is not to say that one ought to seek revenge or continually harbor malevolent thoughts. It is only to say that I should not treat the wrongdoer with such disdain as to ignore his seriously intended actions.

8. Whether we call the disowning of a hurtful act by the victim "forgiveness," when no atonement at all has been made, seems to be a matter which requires a linguistic decision. In view of the fact that forgiving is normally

thought of as a good thing, I suggest that a victim's disowning of an act hurting him is to be called "forgiveness" only when it is in response to some minimal attempt at atonement, such as an apology. One of the very few recent philosophical discussions of the issues of this paper is William Neblett's "The Ethics of Guilt," *Journal of Philosophy* 71 (1974):652–663. As I do, he claims that men become guilty through performing wrong actions, and that this guilt needs atonement; but he claims that a man can be forgiven, even when he has not made atonement.

One recent article, which in my view fails to see what forgiveness is about, is Anne C. Minas, "God and Forgiveness," *Philosophical Quarterly* 25 (1975):138–150. She claims that God cannot forgive because forgiveness is either changing one's moral judgment, or remitting deserved punishment, or abandoning a feeling of resentment; and she has arguments to show that a good God will not do any of these. However, forgiveness does not involve changing any moral judgment, and feelings need not be involved (I can easily forgive that which I do not resent). It is true that if I forgive you for some act, I ought not subsequently punish you for that act. Yet forgiveness still has application in contexts where there is no question of punishment.

9. Aquinas urges that although confession has to be made and contrition shown by the sinner himself, "satisfaction has to do with the exterior act, and here one can make use of instruments" (*Summa Theologiae* III q. 48, a.2, ad 1), i.e., one can use reparation provided by others.

10. For the history of Christian views of original sin, see N. P. Williams, *The Ideas of the Fall and Original Sin* (London: Longmans, 1927). For analysis and assessment of the doctrine of the proneness or tendency to sin, see my "Original Sinfulness," *Neue Zeitschrift für Systematische Theologie*, 27 (1985): 235–250.

11. St. Thomas Aquinas, *ST* III q. 46, a. 1–4.

12. 1 Corinthians 11:26.

13. The account of atonement which I have given in this paper is that provided in the New Testament by the metaphor of sacrifice. We make a sacrifice to God by giving him something valuable, often as a gift to effect reconciliation. This is, of course, the way in which the doctrine of Atonement is worked out in the Epistle to the Hebrews, and is, I think, despite the emphasis on the Law Court metaphor in the Epistle to the Romans, the way of expressing the doctrine which has the widest base in the New Testament.

Original Sin

WILLIAM J. WAINWRIGHT

Western conceptions of sin and grace have been significantly shaped by a doctrine of Original Sin first clearly formulated by Augustine. Four claims are essential to it. First, human behavior is wicked. Second, the human heart is corrupt. Third, we are born guilty. Finally, Adam's sin is the source of our corruption and guilt.

Are these claims intellectually and morally acceptable? One of the most plausible defenses of the doctrine is Jonathan Edwards's.[1] I shall argue that it partly succeeds and partly fails.

We must be clear about what Edwards tries to do. One well-known commentator, Perry Miller, thought that Edwards was engaged in "a strictly empirical investigation, an induction in the manner of Boyle and Newton, of a law for phenomena," and that on this ground Edwards argued that "the Arminian position is refuted as an inadequate hypothesis to account, scientifically or historically, for the facts, either because it does not take cognizance of all of them, or because it does not explain those it recognizes."[2] This reading of Edwards is mistaken.

Edwards sometimes appeals to the facts of common human experience to support the claim that human behavior is wicked and its heart corrupt. (See, for example, OS 160, 161, and 167–168.) But empirical evidence is only adduced to confirm or illustrate a doctrine *established* by scripture.[3] Metaphysical and moral truths that support the doctrine are also typically backed by appeals to scripture rather than philosophical arguments.

Nevertheless, Edwards does not rest his case entirely upon scripture. While most of the empirical, moral, and metaphysical assertions which support the first and second claims are found in scripture, there are independent reasons for believing them to be true. For example, there is good empirical evidence that "all fail of keeping the law [of love] perfectly" (OS 120), and Edwards clearly believes he can *prove* that any deviation from this standard is infinitely heinous. He also believes that the conjunction of these propositions implies that human behavior is wicked, and that the wickedness of human behavior is a sufficient reason for concluding that our hearts are corrupt. If Edwards is correct, the first and second claims can thus be established by reason and experience as well as by scripture, but the third and fourth claims cannot. That we are guilty from birth and have inherited our corruption and guilt from Adam can only be established by the Bible. Edwards nevertheless believes that these components of the Augustinian doctrine can be shown to be *compatible* with reason and the facts of common human experience.

I.

A.

In its "primary" sense, "true virtue consists in love to being in general" (*TV* 4). Virtuous benevolence is directed toward being;[4] its aim is the general good. Those who love the general good, however, also love the disposition that promotes it. Because they love being, they love those who love being. Truly benevolent people thus love two things — being and benevolence.

A truly virtuous person, however, does not value benevolence simply because it promotes the general good. He also relishes it for its own sake. (Edwards calls this "truly virtuous complacence.") Hence, while virtue "most essentially consists in benevolence to being in general" (*TV* 3), there is a wider sense in which it includes not only benevolence but a delight in benevolence's intrinsic excellence or beauty.[5]

But "God is infinitely the greatest Being" and "infinitely the most beautiful and excellent," the "foundation and fountain of all being and all beauty . . . the sum and comprehension of all existence and excellence" (*TV* 14–15). True virtue thus primarily consists in "a supreme love to God, both of benevolence and complacence" (*TV* 15). One cannot consistently identify virtue with benevolence toward being in general, acknowledge God's reality and preeminence, and yet "insist on benevolence to the created system in such a manner as would naturally lead one to suppose" that it is "by far the most important and essential thing" (*TV* 16–17). Nor can one consistently acknowledge God's reality and preeminence and deny that a relish of his beauty and excellence must form the chief part of a truly virtuous complacence. Thus "a determination of mind to union and benevolence to a particular person, or private system which is but a small part of the universal system of being . . . is not of the nature of true virtue" unless it is dependent on or "subordinate to benevolence to being in general" (*TV* 18). Nor is a complacence in benevolence to particular persons or private systems truly virtuous unless it is subordinate to a complacence in God's benevolence. Since few lives are primarily governed by the love of God and a delight in his beauty, humanity in general is not truly virtuous.

B.

But even if human behavior is not truly virtuous, is it infinitely heinous?[6] Edwards thinks that an affirmative answer can be established "from the nature of things" (*OS* 130) as well as from scripture.[7]

As we have seen

(1) Sinful behavior proceeds from an attachment to private systems rather than being in general. But because God is "the sum and comprehension of all existence and excellence,"
(2) He is, "in effect," being in general.[8] It follows that
(3) All sin is against God. (From 1 and 2. To see the plausibility of this inference, consider a parallel case. Suppose that a person who is under the strongest obligations to his community and should govern his behavior by a regard for its interests is instead governed by an obsessive preoccupation with his own family and therefore neglects the common good. In these circumstances, he has committed an offense against his community.) But
(4) God is infinitely worthy of regard. Since
(5) The gravity of an offense against a being is principally determined by its worth or dignity,
(6) There is "infinite demerit in all sin against God" (*OS* 130).[9] (From 4 and 5.) Hence,
(7) All sin is infinitely heinous. (From 3 and 6.)

Edwards's argument hinges upon the truth of 5. Marilyn Adams has argued that the principle is false, and "that guilt and liability to punishment" are not "directly proportional . . . to the offended party's worthiness of honor." She asks us to consider Schweitzer and Gandhi who "are equally saintly," and Green and White who "are equally unsavory characters with long criminal records." "On separate occasions Green gratuitously slaps Schweitzer in the face, Schweitzer gratuitously slaps White in the face, and Gandhi gratuitously slaps Schweitzer in the face." If the principle in question was sound, Green and Gandhi would be guiltier than Schweitzer, but in fact "Schweitzer's action in slapping White is, if anything, more culpable than Green's action in slapping Schweitzer. In view of Schweitzer's long-standing habits of self-control and moral behavior, we should expect more from him than from Green. . . . Similarly, we should expect more from Gandhi. Nor would we say that Gandhi's act was more culpable than Schweitzer's. We might even have some inclination to be less outraged at Gandhi since he was at least 'picking on someone' of his own moral stature."[10]

I do not find this convincing. Even though there is a sense in which we expect more from Schweitzer, his offense may not be as grave as Green's. "Expect more" is ambiguous. It may mean that we demand more, i.e., that we apply higher standards to Schweitzer than to Green. Or it may mean that while Schweitzer and Green are subject to the same standards, Schweitzer's failure to conform to those standards would be more surprising or less excusable than Green's failure to do so. Adams's remark is *clearly* true only if "expect more" is taken in the second sense.[11] We should also distinguish the heinousness of an offense from the heinousness of the offender. The offense of striking Schweitzer may be more heinous than the offense of striking White, even though the commission of the first offense *by Green* is less heinous than the commission of the second offense *by Schweitzer*. (Green is morally ignorant and the prisoner of evil habits, and Schweitzer is not. Schweitzer's action is, therefore, less excusable.)

The most important point is that the principle in question is *not* clearly false if it is restricted to differences in ontological kinds and not applied to differences between more or less valuable members of the same ontological kind. For consider the following series of actions — destroying a flower, destroying a dog, destroying a human being, and destroying an archangel. Each action in this series appears to be intrinsically worse than its predecessor (presumably because, for example, human beings are a more valuable kind of thing than dogs). But a restricted principle is all we need since God is a unique kind of being, and the value of the relevant kind ("divinity") infinitely surpasses the value of other kinds. Marilyn Adams points out that the nature of an offense and the harm caused by it are as relevant to its assessment as the dignity or worth of the being against whom the offense has been committed. This is true but irrelevant. Edwards needs only assume that in cases in which the dignity of the person against whom an offense has been committed is very great, the offense is quite serious even though the act which constitutes it is comparatively insignificant when considered by itself, and causes little or no harm. I do not find this implausible. For example, it may be worse to treat a very good and holy person with mockery and contempt than to lie or commit a minor theft, and this may be true even if the offender fails to disturb the saint's serenity, and even if lying and theft are intrinsically more serious offenses. But if the assumption *is* plausible, it may *also* be plausible to suppose that when the offended party has infinite worth and dignity, one's offense has infinite disvalue even though it causes no harm and may be comparatively minor if considered by itself.[12]

It can also be argued that an offense of this sort is *not* intrinsically minor—that not only are its consequences extremely harmful, it is "infinitely heinous" in its nature. The content of the offense is not, except incidentally, a theft or a lie, negligence in worship, or a failure to commend the faith which is in us. It is, rather, placing creatures above God or, as Edwards puts it, loving private systems more than being in general. This offense perverts the order of creation (the direction of all creatures toward the Highest Good). Because it is the root or essence of all other offenses, there is a sense in which no offense could be more serious (even when considered in abstraction from the worth or dignity of the being against whom it is intentionally or unintentionally committed).

Edwards thus appears to have made a reasonable case for the claim that most men and women lack true virtue and that their behavior is, *when objectively considered*, infinitely heinous. In the next section, however, I shall argue that these claims do not imply that human behavior is usually wicked—that is, that it involves a settled malignancy which deserves infinite punishment.

C.

At one point, Edwards argues that humanity's depravity is confirmed by its "folly and stupidity in matters of religion" (*OS* 147). His discussion has an important bearing on our question.

Although spiritual things are infinitely more important, maxims of prudence that are normally observed in worldly affairs are neglected in religious affairs. Edwards invites us to consider "how careful and eagle-eyed" the merchant is "to observe and improve his opportunities and advantages to enrich himself," or how easily people are "alarmed at the appearance of danger to their worldly estate" and how "they bestir themselves in such a case . . . to avoid the threatened calamity" (*OS* 154). Yet in religious matters, we ignore familiar and obvious considerations like "the difference between long and short, the need of providing for futurity, the importance of improving proper opportunities, and of having good security, and a sure foundation, in affairs wherein our interest is greatly concerned, etc." (*OS* 156). We can only conclude that our hearts are so corrupt and our sinful inclinations so obsessive that when we deal with spiritual matters we willfully disregard the dictates of prudence. (Cf. "His love was so obsessive that he threw caution to the winds.")

Edwards's argument is not fully persuasive. Dictates of prudence are frequently disregarded in temporal affairs. More importantly, the reality of eternal goods may not be as obvious as the reality of temporal goods. If this is the case, we need not appeal to the corruption of the human heart to explain differences between our conduct with respect to our temporal and spiritual interests. Edwards believes that because "the things of this world" were "made to be wholly subordinate to" eternal things, and because we were given understanding "chiefly" in order to know these things, there is "sufficient evidence of their truth." He therefore concludes that "if men have not respect to 'em as real and certain things," it can only be from "a dreadful stupidity of mind, occasioning a sottish insensibility of their truth and importance" (*OS* 157).

I do not find this convincing. Our selfishness and attachment to private systems is wicked and argues an incredible sottishness, stupidity, and perversity *if* God is clearly apprehended, or our failure to acknowledge his reality and splendor is an expression of culpable negligence or self-deception. But the first is false and the second is plausible only if the evidence of God's being, greatness, and excellence is widely accessible and coercive.

Is the evidence coercive or widely accessible? Edwards himself thinks not. God's existence and nature are not manifest to unaided reason.[13] Revealed knowledge, i.e., the gospel, may be intrinsically clear (see, e.g., *OS* 156–157), but revealed knowledge is not available to everyone. (Until the age of discovery and "the gospelizing" of Australia and America, "and all those yet undiscovered tracts of land," "the devil had reigned quietly from the beginning" in the greatest part of the world.)[14] Furthermore, revealed knowledge is not clear *to* most of those who live under the gospel dispensation. Edwards believes that our failure to perceive the clarity and force of the gospel evidence is not the fault of the evidence but of ourselves—of our corruption and wickedness. But he cannot appeal to this consideration in the present context without begging the question.

Sin may be infinitely heinous in its own nature. Nevertheless, a person who commits an offense against God is not infinitely wicked if he is not aware of the real nature of his act. Behaving disrespectfully toward one's father may be a grave offense, but an offender is judged less harshly if he does not know he is in his father's presence (his father is disguised) or is ignorant of the proper deportment (he has been improperly brought up). To show that human behavior is wicked Edwards must show that humanity understands the nature of its offense. Perhaps this can be established by scripture. It cannot be established by the facts of common experience. Common experience shows that our loves are restricted, partial, and private, and thus fall infinitely short of love to being in general. It does not show that our neglect of God is normally deliberate.

There is another difficulty. True virtue consists in love toward being in general, and vice in love toward "private systems." Virtue and vice are dispositions of the heart, or affections. Since they are not directly subject to our control, our corrupt affections are largely involuntary.[15] It thus seems inappropriate to speak of infinite guilt or claim that we deserve infinite punishment. It seems unfair to blame someone for failing to will (love) the good when he cannot will (love) the good.

Edwards addresses a form of this difficulty in "The Justice of God in the Damnation of Sinners" (*Works* VI) where he argues that those whom God rejects are justly condemned because they are unwilling to accept Christ.[16]

But granting that those whom God rejects are unwilling to accept Christ, can they make themselves willing? And if they cannot, is it fair for God to reject them for being unwilling? Edwards responds to this objection as follows:

(1) The fact that A cannot do x excuses A only if A would do x if he could. Hence.

(2) The fact that A cannot will x excuses A only if A would will x if he could. (From 1.) Now,

(3) "A would do x if he could" is logically equivalent to "A is sincerely willing to do x but cannot do x." Therefore

(4) "A would will x if he could" is logically equivalent to "A is sincerely willing to will x but cannot will x." (From 3.) Hence

(5) The fact that A cannot will x excuses A only if A is sincerely willing to will x but cannot will x. (From 2 and 4.) It follows that

(6) The fact that A cannot will x excuses A only if A is sincerely willing to will x. (From 5.)

(7) "A sincerely wills to will x" entails "A wills x." ("To suppose the contrary . . . would be to suppose that a man's will is contrary to itself, or that he wills contrary to what he himself wills" [*Works* VI, 387]). Therefore,

(8) The fact that A cannot will x excuses A only if A wills x. (From 6 and 7.) But

(9) Those who *cannot* make themselves willing to adopt God's way of salvation are obviously *not* willing to adopt it. Consequently

(10) Their inability is no excuse. (From 8 and 9.)

Since the argument is valid, its conclusion can only be evaded by denying one or more of its premises. Premise 9 is true. What about the others?

Some apparent counterexamples to 7 are irrelevant. A person may sincerely *want* to will something which he cannot will and therefore does not will. The distressed addict is a case in point. But cases of this sort do not provide counterexamples. *Wanting* to will *x* is not the same thing as willing to will *x*. Even those who, like Edwards, assimilate inclination and will, identify willing with *preponderant* desire and not with desire as such. The addict's whole problem is that no matter how strong his desire not to preponderantly desire drugs may be, his desire for drugs is stronger, i.e., no matter how sincere, the addict's desire not to desire drugs is not a preponderant desire and is hence not a "willing."

Nevertheless, if Edwards's analysis of willing is correct, "*A* sincerely wills to will *x*" does not entail "*A* wills *x*." Consider the following propositions:

> (11) If *A* has a preponderant desire to preponderantly desire *x*, then *A* has a preponderant desire for *x*.
> (12) *A* has a preponderant desire for *x* and it is not the case that *A* has a preponderant desire for *x*.
> (13) *A* has a preponderant desire to preponderantly desire *x* and it is not the case that *A* has a preponderant desire for *x*.

Premise 12, of course, is formally incoherent. But the denial of 11 is not 12 but 13, and 13 is not self-contradictory, i.e., formally or syntactically incoherent. Nor does 13 appear to be logically impossible in the broad sense. There is nothing obviously absurd, for example, in saying that someone's strongest desire is to be mastered or consumed by passion for a member of the opposite sex, but that he loves no one. Since the antecedent of 11 can be true and its consequent false, it is not a logical truth. If Edwards' analysis of willing is correct, however, 11 is equivalent to

> (14) If *A* sincerely wills to will *x*, then *A* wills *x*.

It follows that 14 is not a logical truth, and that 7 is therefore false.

I think, though, that Edwards's analysis of willing is mistaken — that willing should be distinguished from (preponderant) desire and identified with choice or volition. If this is correct, 7 is plausible. While I can choose to do something at a future date and not do it, or choose to take steps which will reinforce a disposition to choose in certain ways and not choose in those ways, it is doubtful whether I can literally choose to choose to do *x* without choosing to do *x*. If there is no real distinction between choosing to choose to do x and choosing to do x, then "A wills to will x" entails "A wills x," and 7 is true.

Both 1 and 3, however, seem false. They *may* be true if the scope of "doing x" is restricted to physical behavior and to mental activities like attempting to solve a chess problem, framing an hypothesis, conjuring up a mental image of one's brother, etc. That is, 1 and 3 may be true if their scope is restricted to behavior which expresses our volitions.[17] They are not clearly true of volitions themselves.

Our argument up to this point suggests the following. Unless it can be shown that humanity's inversion of the true order of values is deliberate, and that it is within men and women's power to love God, then even though the situation of humanity without God may be wretched, its neglect of God does not imply some sort of settled malignancy and thus is not appropriately described as wicked.[18]

But is this conclusion superficial? Does the prevalence of sin, and the profound evil of so many of its expressions, point to some terrible perversity or corruption of the human heart? Edwards thinks that it does.

(1) "Where we see a stated prevalence of any kind of effect or event, there is a tendency to that effect in the nature and state of its causes. . . . 'tis the commonness or constancy of events, that gives us a notion of tendency in all cases" (*OS* 121). But

(2) "All fail of keeping the law perfectly" (*OS* 120) and thus act sinfully. Furthermore, this behavior occurs in "an immense diversity of persons and circumstances . . . never failing in any one instance, of coming to that issue, viz., that sinfulness which implies . . . eternal ruin" (*OS* 122). We must therefore suppose that

(3) There is a "prevailing tendency," or "propensity" or "stated preponderation" to sin. (From 1 and 2.) Since

(4) "An infallible tendency to [acts which deserve] eternal destruction [i.e., to sinful acts], is an infinitely dreadful and pernicious tendency" (*OS* 128), we can only conclude that

(5) Our "nature and frame of mind . . . must be an infinitely dreadful and pernicious frame of mind"; that "the soul of man, as it is by nature, is in a corrupt, fallen, and ruined state" (*OS* 128f). (From 3 and 4.)

But this too is unconvincing. Edwards is correct in thinking that the prevalence of sin and its occurrence in a wide variety of circumstances implies a "pernicious tendency" to sin. He is also correct in thinking that this disposition is best explained by the hypothesis that "the soul of man . . . is in a corrupt, fallen, and ruined state." The evidence does not, however, justify the ascription of malignancy since it can as easily be explained by our ignorance, the imperiousness of our passions and appetites, and the weakness of our wills.

D.

How much of Edwards's version of the Augustinian conception of sin is rationally defensible? At least this much can be defended. First, when objectively considered, our outward actions and the inner movements of our souls are "infinitely heinous." Second, since what is demanded is a change of heart, we cannot extricate ourselves from sin. Third, we strengthen the power which sin has over us when we turn our backs on the glimpses of the sovereign good which we sometimes have or deliberately choose a lesser good when we know we should choose a greater. To that extent our corruption is voluntary and can appropriately be blamed and punished. Fourth, it may also be appropriate to blame us for our involuntary blindness and hardness of heart. As Robert Adams has pointed out, we can sometimes appropriately be blamed for desires, states of mind, and beliefs which are morally defective but involuntary. Nazis' beliefs about and attitudes toward Jews were culpable regardless of how they were acquired.[19] Even if our behavior is not wicked, it may still be true that we should be blamed for failing to love God as we ought even though, given our ignorance and weakness, we cannot do so.

On the other hand, two components of the Augustinian conception seem indefensible. The first is the claim that human behavior in general can appropriately be described as wicked. Adams may be correct in saying that a member of the Hitler Jugend can appropriately be blamed for his attitudes toward non-Aryans. What is not clear is that a member of the Hitler Jugend who had no real control over his upbringing and no clear awareness of alternative values can appropriately be described as wicked. The latter implies a degree of control and self-consciousness which is lacking. To describe the young Nazi's attitudes and behavior as wicked blurs an important distinction between two qualitatively different sorts of failure. Objective wrongness should be distinguished from subjective wrongness or culpability. Even if our offense against God has infinite disvalue, our guilt may be finite.

Second, insofar as its behavior is involuntary, it is not clear that humanity should be *punished* for its failure to love God. While it may sometimes be appropriate to blame people for involuntary sins, it is not clearly appropriate to punish them.[20] Nevertheless, the implications of this for the Augustinian conception of sin may not be that drastic. Punishment involves inflicting pain or some other positive evil upon someone or depriving a person of a good which rightfully belongs to him (such as his life, liberty, or property). Failure to bestow a good (e.g., an academic position) on a person who is unqualified for it is not properly regarded as punishment even though lack of the good may make him more miserable than the deprivation of goods which rightfully belong to him or the infliction of a positive evil. Eternal punishment has traditionally been thought to include two things — exclusion from God's presence and the infliction of torment. My argument implies that the second and lesser of the two penalties is generally inappropriate. The first may be in order. The greater "penalty" is appropriate if exclusion from God's presence is not the deprivation of a good which rightfully belongs to us, and if our hardness of heart disqualifies us for this good. Both claims are defensible. It is plausible to suppose that the enjoyment of God is a supernatural good which exceeds the capacities of (even unfallen) human nature and can thus not properly be said to (rightfully) belong to us. It is also plausible to suppose that only those who love God are qualified to enjoy him.

If my argument is correct, the Augustinian conception of sin appropriated by Edwards must be modified at certain points. Its core, however, remains largely untouched. Whether it is possible to salvage anything like an Augustinian notion of hereditary taint is less clear.

II.

Augustine thought that Adam's corruption *and guilt* were transmitted to his posterity. The Western church has followed him. Is the doctrine of Inherited Guilt defensible?

Edwards fails to show that the doctrine is scriptural. He does show that (1) the state of redemption described in the New Testament presupposes a prior state of sin (*OS* 361–371) and that (2) the claim that Christ alone can save us presupposes that we are trapped in sin and cannot extricate ourselves (*OS* 353–359). But when he concludes that we can thus see that "what the Scripture teaches of the application of Christ's redemption, and the change of state and nature necessary to true and final happiness" affords "clear and abundant evidence to the truth of the doctrine of original sin" (*OS* 371), he overstates his case. Edwards's texts do not clearly show that Adam's guilt is ours.[21] Our concern, however, is not the doctrine's scriptural warrant but Edwards's defense of its rationality.

Edwards's defense weaves together two distinct strands of argumentation: First, that there is a legal or moral bond between Adam and his descendants in virtue of which his fault is ours; and second, that Adam and his posterity somehow form one thing, a natural unity, and that, in virtue of the union between the parts of this thing, Adam's fault is ours.

Edwards sometimes uses legal metaphors, speaking of Adam as a "public person, or common head" (*OS* 396). These suggest that, in virtue of certain "legal" or "moral" arrangements, Adam's acts are regarded as acts of the species and thus of each individual. This theme was important in Puritan theology. It was widely held that "Adam had stood as the agent, the 'federal' head of the race; when he, the spokesman for all men in the Covenant, broke it and incurred the penalty, the guilt was 'imputed' to his constituents as a legal responsibility."[22] John Preston, for example, said that there was "a compact and covenant between God and him, that if *Adam* stood, all his seed should stand with him; but if he fell, then that all that were borne of him should by virtue of that covenant, compact or agreement have his sinne imputed to them, and so should be corrupted, as he was, and die the death."[23]

The second strand of argumentation is more prominent in Edwards. Adam and his posterity are one thing as a tree and its branches are one thing. On this view, Adam's act is not an act of his posterity in virtue of a legal fiction. It is literally their act.[24]

Both approaches are intrinsically interesting, and both present a similar problem—how guilt can be transmitted from one person to another.

A.

In the "Book of Controversies," Edwards observes that "it seemed to be natural among the Jews to be conscious of the guilt" of their ancestors "and their being justly exposed to punishment for it and the same is observable among other nations, that have refined their notions by metaphysical principles."[25] In *Original Sin* he points out that it is not "a thing strange and unheard of, that men should be ashamed of things done by others, whom they are nearly concerned in" (*OS* 407).

These facts are undeniable, but are easily misinterpreted. I may be ashamed for my father, assume responsibility for the consequences of his behavior, and yet not accept blame for it. Again, as H. D. Lewis has pointed out, the prime minister who assumes responsibility for the actions of his chief of staff does not thereby become *morally* responsible for them if there has been no negligence on his part. He only incurs "certain consequences for what another person has done."[26] The question at issue is whether there are circumstances in which a person can be *guilty of*, or *blamed for*, another's conduct. The fact that people are sometimes ashamed for others, or assume responsibility for the results of their behavior, or incur legal and non-legal consequences because of it does not show that they believe themselves to be, or are, guilty of another's conduct.

Nevertheless, there *are* cases in which persons are held responsible for the behavior of other individuals or for the behavior of groups to which they belong. I will consider five of these. Although the first three fail to provide plausible models of the moral or legal relation between Adam and his descendents, it is instructive to see why they are inadequate.

1. Consider cases in which members of one's society commit morally bad actions " 'which are approved by the popular mores' . . . and which are not merely 'things done by sharply differentiated subgroups' " — for example, violence committed against blacks in postbellum Southern society.[27] There is a sense in which every member of the society who has not deliberately dissociated himself from it can be said to share the blame for these acts even though he did not perpetrate them and may have been unaware of them at the time they were committed.

This model is inadequate for two reasons. First, Adam's sin is not an *expression* of the "popular mores" of humanity but their cause. More importantly, it is not clear that members of the society in our example *were* to blame for the deeds in question. Those who did not perpetrate the crimes against blacks but shared the popular mores can be blamed for not taking issue with those mores, for in failing to do so they contributed to a climate in which deeds of that type were likely to occur. It does not follow that they were guilty *of those deeds*. The model is inadequate because it does not show how the guilt or fault of one person can (literally) be another's.

2. Virginia Held distinguishes between the responsibility of organized groups (i.e., groups with decision procedures such as corporations, countries, and political parties) and the responsibility of unorganized groups.[28] She argues that responsibility is not distributive in the first type of case but is distributive in the second. For example, consider a situation in which, by acting together, the passengers on a subway could easily prevent an unarmed person from strangling a weaker. Instead, they watch and do nothing. Or consider a situation in which there are several ways to rescue a person trapped in a burning building but each requires cooperative effort. A crowd gathers to watch the blaze. Its mem-

bers wish to help but waste their time arguing over which method should be adopted while the victim burns to death.

These cases might seem to provide a better model. Humanity does not appear to be an organized group, and it sometimes looks as if we are trying to explain how collective responsibility (the responsibility of a humanity which has rebelled against God) can be distributive (the responsibility of each man and woman). But this model, too, is defective. In the first place, Held's cases are cases in which a *group* refrains from taking action[29] when "the action called for . . . may be said to have been obvious to the reasonable person."[30] In the case of humanity, no group action is obviously called for or even possible. (How can a humanity which is scattered through time and space act as a group?) In the second place, if Adam is our "federal head," then (in spite of appearances) humanity is a community and not an unorganized group. That is, humanity has "a decision method for taking action that is distinguishable from such decision methods . . . as are possessed by all persons."[31] Since Adam acts for humanity his decisions are decisions of humanity as a whole. Most importantly, even though the members of Held's groups are (partly) responsible for the failure of the groups to which they belong, they are not responsible for the acts *of another person.*

3. Feinberg discusses cases "where every member of a group shares the same fault, but only one member's fault leads to any harm, and that not because it was more of a fault," but merely because he was more unfortunate. For example, consider a situation in which everyone drives home from a party drunk, but only one person kills a pedestrian. "Many outsiders will be inclined to ascribe collective liability to the whole group" (a liability which distributes to each of its members). Of course others may not, "but for a group member himself to take this public stand would be an unattractive piece of self-righteousness. It would be more appropriate for him to grieve, and voluntarily make what amends he can."[32] While criminal punishment would be unreasonable,[33] it may be reasonable for private individuals to censure or snub those whose fault fails to result in harm "to the same extent" as those whose fault causes harm.[34]

There are interesting similarities between Feinberg's case and ours. All of us (or at least all of us who have reached the age of moral reason) have sinned as Adam sinned. Although Adam's sin is more harmful (since it resulted in the ruin of humanity), ours is equally faulty or grievous.[35] Nevertheless this model is also inadequate. While everyone who drove home from the party is equally at fault, they are not at fault *for striking the pedestrian.* They are equally faulty because their behavior was relevantly similar to the behavior of the person who had the accident, and not because his action was somehow their own. The most this model would justify is that each of us is justly exposed to a punishment of the same kind as that to which Adam was exposed since each of us commits a similar fault upon reaching moral maturity. But this is a much weaker claim than Edwards's that Adam's fault is somehow *numerically* the same as our own first or original fault.

The last two models are more promising because, in each, an individual *is* liable or responsible for the fault of another.

4. Feinberg argues that a reasonable case can be made for vicarious liability where (1) a person has authorized another to act as his agent (for example, by giving him the power to sign contracts and checks and to buy and sell in his name), where (2) another is either under one's strict command as in the army, or acting in one's employ, or where (3) one has undertaken to stand surety for another (for example, by putting up bail).[36] While these liability arrangements differ, each is reasonable because the liability is voluntarily assumed and the arrangement is beneficial.

At first, these cases might not seem relevant. We did not authorize Adam to act for us, he is not under our command or in our employ, and we did not agree to stand surety for him. Nevertheless, there are important similarities between these cases and the one that interests us. It was more beneficial for Adam to be appointed to act "as the moral head of his posterity" than for each of us to act for ourselves. Adam was not only as likely to persevere as his posterity, "there was a *greater tendency* to a happy issue." Adam was "in a state of complete manhood," rather than "in a state of childhood and comparative imperfection." He also had a stronger motive to persevere since not only his own welfare but the welfare of his posterity was at stake. Furthermore, if "God had proceeded only on the foot of mere justice, and had gone no further than this required, he might have demanded of Adam and all his posterity, that they should perform *perfect perpetual* obedience," and that "without the promise of any positive reward," but God instead promised "an eternal happy life" to Adam and his descendents as a "consequence of his persevering fidelity" (*OS* 395–397). The arrangement was, therefore, highly beneficial. Our liability for Adam's behavior was not voluntarily assumed but this may not matter. Since we did not yet exist we could not have authorized Adam to act for us. Nevertheless, if we had been in a position to authorize Adam to act as our agent or representative, it would have been reasonable for us to have done so since the arrangement was beneficial to us. Our situation is analogous to one in which a guardian or trustee is authorized to act for a minor. The minor is not in a position to consent, but if he were able to consent, it would be reasonable for him to do so because the arrangement benefits him.

5. Feinberg argues that collective liability arrangements can be reasonable when groups possess a sufficient degree of "solidarity." Solidarity presupposes a "community of interest," i.e., that the interests of the group's members include one another. It "is ordinarily a function of the degree to which the parties share a common lot, the extent to which their goods and harms are necessarily collective and indivisible," and "is often associated with bonds of sentiment directed toward common objects, or of reciprocal affection between the parties."[37] In medieval Europe, for example, "everyone was . . . assigned to a neighborhood group every member of which was an insurer of his conduct. If an offender was not produced by his surety group . . . a fine was levied on each member of the group, and sometimes liability to make compensation as well."[38] This arrangement was reasonable because there was "a very high degree of antecedent group solidarity" and because it was advantageous ("efficient professional policing" and because it was not feasible).[39]

This model also appears promising. According to the doctrine of Original Sin, each man and woman is liable for the fault of a member of his or her group (viz., Adam), and the punishment which he deserved is distributed among its members. God's "constitution" thus appears to be a kind of collective liability arrangement. It also seems reasonable. The necessary community of interest exists. (The interests of Adam's posterity are included in his own interests as the interests of a child are included in the interests of its parents, and an indivisable good and evil are at stake, viz., eternal happiness and everlasting misery.)[40] The arrangement is also beneficial.

In spite of their attractiveness the last two models are inadequate. Both depict arrangements in which one person can reasonably be held liable for the faults of another. These arrangements are similar to the constitution by which God made Adam our "federal head." But both models break down at the crucial point. While I am liable for the faults which my agent or representative commits in my name, i.e., am exposed to the appropriate legal consequences, I am not *guilty* of the fault. If my agent overdraws my account, I am as exposed to the consequences as if I had signed the check myself. Nevertheless, I did not (literally) overdraw my account, nor am I *guilty* of an overdraft. (Although I may, of course, be guilty of other things such as failing to pay sufficient attention to the activities of my agent.) Similarly, the collective liability arrangements described by Feinberg are forms of *"liability without fault."*[41]

Although, the members of an individual's surety group are liable to penalties if they are unable to produce the offender, they are not guilty of his offense or of his failure to answer for his crime. These models do not, then, help us understand how "the guilt of the original apostacy" can be the same as that which each of us "has upon his soul at his first existence" (OS 390).[42]

Liability must be distinguished from guilt. Although it is sometimes reasonable to hold a person liable for the deeds of another, our legal and moral practice provides no situation in which a person can reasonably be judged guilty of another's offense. The reason is clear. One must have committed an act to be guilty of it, and one cannot commit another's act. Thus, even though liability can be transferred from one person to another, guilt cannot. Adam's posterity cannot be guilty of Adam's fault unless Adam's act is somehow *literally* their own. I suspect that an implicit recognition of this lies behind Edwards's attempt to show that Adam and his descendants constitute a "natural unity."

B.

Edwards maintains that Adam's posterity is in Adam as a tree's branches and fruit are in the tree (OS 385). Adam is the "head of the whole body, and the root of the whole tree" (OS 389). Just as head and body, or root and tree, are one thing, so Adam and his posterity are one thing. Humanity, of course, consists of a number of independent individuals existing at different times and places. But Edwards thinks this provides no more reason for denying that humanity is a single object than the (alleged) fact that particular minds and bodies are series of discrete and independent states provides reason for denying that particular minds or bodies are single objects.

1. God is the author of our criteria of identity. Since these criteria determine what counts as one thing, God ultimately determines what counts as one thing. He has decreed that Adam and his posterity are one. Therefore they are one.

The criteria of identity whose fulfillment constitutes our identity with Adam are presumably descent from Adam, and the covenant with Adam in virtue of which he was made our federal head. While these criteria differ from the criteria for personal identity, there is no reason to expect them not to. Criteria of identity vary from object to object. For example, there are different criteria of identity for trees, persons, industrial companies, musical compositions, and decks of cards. Thus, it is only to be expected that the criteria of identity for the object constituted by Adam and his posterity should differ from the criteria of identity for individual men and women. Nor is the object consisting of Adam and his posterity somehow less real than other objects. Since the natural order is whatever order God chooses to establish, Adam and his posterity are as much a natural unity as George Washington or the pen in my hand.

"Created identity or oneness with past existence, in general, depends on the sovereign constitution and law" of God. For example a tree which is "grown great, and an hundred years old, is one plant with the little sprout . . . from whence it grew . . . though it's now so exceeding diverse . . . and of a very different form, and perhaps not one atom the very same: yet God, according to an established law of nature, has in a constant succession communicated to it many of the same qualities . . . as if it were one. It has been his pleasure, to constitute an union in these respects, and for these purposes, naturally leading us to look upon all as one" (OS 397f). Similarly, "the communication or continuance of the same consciousness and memory . . . through successive parts of duration, depends wholly on a divine establishment. There would be no necessity, that the remembrance and ideas of what is past should continue to exist, but by an arbitrary constitution of the Creator" (OS 398f). Since Edwards believes that "identity of consciousness" is the same thing as "sameness of consciousness" or memory, he concludes "that personal identity, and so the derivation of the pollution and guilt of past sins in the same person, depends upon an arbitrary divine constitution" (OS 398–399). And, in general, because things are created new each moment, "what exists at this moment . . . is . . . simply and absolutely considered, not the same with any past existence, though it be like it, and follows it according to a certain established method. And there is no identity or oneness in the case, but what depends on the *arbitrary* constitution of the Creator" who "*treats them as one*, by communicating to them like properties, relations, and circumstances; and so leads us to regard and treat them as one" (OS 402f).

Edwards's remarks are ambiguous. He sometimes speaks as if God determines what the criteria of identity for various things will be; that he decides, for example, that such things as spatio-temporal continuity and qualitative similarity will be criteria of identity for physical objects, or that memory will be a criterion of identity for persons. At other times, Edwards seems only to be saying that God brings it about that things meet these criteria (for example, by successively producing oak-tree stages in such a way as to ensure that they exhibit spatio-temporal continuity, similarity between adjacent stages, etc.). I think, however, that Edwards wishes to say both.

The second claim is not especially controversial. By creating and preserving bodies and minds, God brings it about that things meet criteria of identity. But the first claim may not even seem intelligible.

The fact that spatio-temporal continuity and qualitative similarity are criteria of identity for physical objects or that memory is a criterion of personal identity appear to be logical facts. For example, it seems to be a conceptual truth that material objects exhibit spatio-temporal continuity and that persons can remember and anticipate. Edwards nowhere suggests that God constitutes logical facts. It might therefore seem that Edwards cannot coherently claim that God determines criteria of identity. Why, then, did he believe the claim to be not only coherent but true?

It is plausible to suppose that the criteria of identity for a thing (an oak tree, a mind, a hydrogen atom) are determined by its nature. Now in the seventh section of the notes he called "the Mind," Edwards argues that while "the various distributing and ranking of things, and tying of them together under one common abstract idea" is "arbitrary," "there is much more foundation for some distributions than others." This foundation is "the common circumstances and necessities of mankind, and the constant method of things proceeding." As a result of these factors, "most of the inhabitants of the earth" classify things in the same way ("The Mind," Section 41). "If the world had been created without any order or design or beauty, indeed, all species would be merely arbitrary" but God has in fact created a world in which things agree "either as to their outward appearance, manner of acting, the effects they produce or that others produce on them, the manner of their production, or God's disposal concerning them, or some peculiar perpetual circumstances that they are in" ("The Mind," Section 47; cf. "The Mind," Section 43.).

Edwards's position appears to be that kinds or natures (what he calls "species") are the ways in which we classify things. These classifications are arbitrary in the sense that we could have carved the world up in different ways. Nevertheless, they are not capricious since our classifications reflect our needs and interests and the character of the world we live in. But God has determined both what we are and the character of our world. He has therefore determined how things will be classified, i.e., what will count as a kind or nature or species. Since the criteria of identity for a thing are determined by its kind or species, God is the ultimate ground of these criteria. In short, laws determine kinds and kinds determine criteria of identity. In establishing the laws that govern creation, God thus establishes criteria of identity.

Up to a point, Edwards's position may be defensible. Compare the concept of a material object with the concept of a chair. If I remove the backs of my dining room chairs, shorten their legs, and use them as a place for setting drinks, magazines, and other objects, I will stop calling them "chairs." While there is a perfectly good sense in which the objects that were formerly picked out by "chair" continue to be the same *objects*, they are no longer *chairs*. This suggests that the properties which define "chair" are not essential to the *objects* to which the term is applied, but only to their being called "chairs." However, if the same objects were to lose the properties which lead us to speak of them as material objects, it is doubtful that we would be entitled to speak of the continued existence of the same entity. The properties which define "material object" thus seem essential to the things to which "material object" applies. They could not lose these properties without ceasing to be.

These considerations suggest that while the "essence" or "nature" expressed by a term like "chair" is conventional, the essence or nature expressed by "material object" is not. If this is correct, then Edwards's account of criteria of identity is only plausible in certain cases. Where species are conventional, it makes sense to speak of constituting or inventing the criteria for the application of a term. Where species are not conventional, Edwards's account is less convincing.[43]

But a limited conventionalism may be all Edwards needs, for he could argue that God has created a world in which it is reasonable to single out Adam and his posterity by an appropriate concept ("the body of Adam," for example), thus treating Adam and his posterity as one thing. That is, Edwards could argue that "the body of Adam" expresses a conventional essence, and that the criteria of identity for the body of Adam are thus ultimately constituted by God.

However, this would not be sufficient by itself. Edwards must not only show that Adam and his posterity are one thing, he must also show that Adam's fault is the fault of his posterity. Edwards appears to think that by establishing the first, he has established the second. But this is mistaken. A biological family constitutes a natural unity[44] but children are not guilty of their parent's faults. The collection of thoughts, volitions, and feelings which (according to Edwards) constitutes a human soul is also a natural unity but in this case the fault or guilt of earlier parts *is* "inherited" by later parts. Whether the fault of one part of a natural unity can be ascribed to another depends upon the *kind* of natural unity it is. Edwards must therefore show that the natural unity constituted by Adam and his descendants is the right sort. On the face of it, it is not. The "thing" in question (Adam and his posterity) resembles families and communities, i.e., natural unities in which fault does not transfer, more than it resembles particular minds, i.e., the only natural unity in which fault *clearly* transfers from one "part" to another. Edwards must therefore not only show that God constitutes the criteria of identity for the body of Adam, he must also show that these criteria permit the ascription of Adam's guilt to his descendents.

2. Edwards believes that personal identity depends upon sameness of consciousness or memory. Since the latter depends upon God's sovereign decrees, "the derivation of the pollution and guilt of past sins in the same person, [ultimately] depends on an arbitrary divine constitution" (i.e., on a set of decrees which are contingent expressions of God's wisdom and goodness) (*OS* 399). But if God can "arbitrarily" bring about the "derivation of pollution and guilt" in persons, he can arbitrarily bring about "the derivation of the pollution and guilt" of Adam's sin to his descendents. (cf. *OS* 405).

But there is a problem. That it is reasonable to impute guilt to a person for offenses committed by someone to whom he is linked by personal memory and bodily continuity does not imply that it is reasonable to impute guilt to a person for offenses committed by someone to whom he is connected in other ways. That x can inherit y's guilt is not itself a criterion of identity, but a logical *consequence* of the fulfillment of certain kinds of criteria of identity. For example, "x is at fault for sins committed by y" is entailed by "x is the same person as y" or "x is the same corporation (nation, etc.) as y." It presupposes that the criteria of personal or corporate identity are fulfilled. Even if God constitutes these criteria, he does not constitute the fact that *if* these criteria are fulfilled, and x is therefore the same person or corporation as y, y's sins can be imputed to x. This fact is a *logical* fact and Edwards nowhere suggests that God constitutes facts of this kind.[45]

God cannot, then, simply impute guilt as he pleases. Whether he can do so depends upon the *nature* of the natural unity, i.e., upon the nature of its criteria of identity. God cannot, for example, make it true that a person's gun is at fault for his robbery or that his tongue is at fault for his lie. A person and his possessions are a kind of unity, and a person's tongue is literally part of him, but it is logically false that fault transfers in these cases. The criteria of identity for persons differ from the criteria of identity for the natural unity constituted by Adam and his posterity. Edwards must therefore show that the sort of identity which God has established entails that Adam's descendents can inherit his guilt.

3. Let us suppose "that [1] all mankind had *coexisted*, . . . that [2] Adam's posterity had actually . . . grown out of him, and yet remained continuous and literally united to him, as the branches to a tree, or the members of the body to the head," and that God brought it about that

[3] "the heart of every branch should at the same moment participate with the heart of the root, be conformed to it and concurring with it in all its affections and acts" (*OS* 405f n). Adam and his posterity would then "constitute as it were *one* complex person, or *one* moral whole" (*OS* 391f n). If the root or head were to sin, the whole body would sin. Adam's posterity would "concur" in his act and share his guilt. But, says Edwards, if God "might by his sovereign constitution, have established such an union of the various branches of mankind, when existing in different places," he could "do the same, though they exist in different times" (*OS* 406 n).[46]

That the first condition is not met is irrelevant. True, "the difference of time shows, there is no absolute numerical identity of the things existing in those different times," but so does "the difference of the place of existence" (*OS* 406 n). Edwards does not comment on the fact that the second condition also is not met — perhaps because he regards physical descent as analogous to a "continuous" and "literal" union. In any case, the weight of the analogy rests on the third condition.

There is an obvious problem with the analogy. If a man's hand strikes someone, or his eyes look lustfully on another man's wife, then the man as a whole (body and soul) can be said to have committed the act and be guilty of it. It does not follow that each part of him can be said to have committed the act or be guilty of it. If someone commits a theft, we do not infer that his hand committed it. We do not blame the hand, and we do not punish the hand. (We may, of course, injure the hand, and in so doing punish the person, but that is a different matter.) Faults committed by a person do not distribute to that person's parts. If Adam and his posterity constitute one moral person, then Adam's fault may be the fault of the whole. It does not follow that it is the fault of his descendants.

Edwards's third condition may have been introduced to meet this objection. Indeed, the first two conditions are superfluous. If the third condition is met, his conclusion is established. The problem is that it does *not* appear to be met. If it were, each soul would be *literally* affected as Adam's soul was affected, and would literally consent to, or concur in, Adam's act. That God *could* have brought this about is beside the point since, as a matter of fact, he has not.

Our hearts may, of course, "concur" with Adam's in the sense that our inclinations agree with, or are similar to, his. But this no more involves concurring in, or consenting to, Adam's sin than having thievish inclinations involves concurring in, or consenting to, someone else's theft. It may even be true that our hearts are "disposed to *approve* of the sin of [the] first father, as fully as he himself approved it when he committed it, or so far as to imply a full and perfect consent of heart to it" (*OS* 391). But this, too, is insufficient. That someone would consent to an evil deed if he knew of it or had been present when it was committed does not make him guilty of it. We cannot blame him for it or punish him for it although we can, of course, deplore his faulty disposition. What is needed is an *actual* consent or concurrence which is given at the moment one comes into being. Nothing less than this will show that we are born guilty of Adam's fault. Yet to suppose that this consent has been given is absurd for it implies that as soon as we come into being as persons we function as moral agents and are conscious of Adam's fault.

I think Edwards failed to see this because his psychology makes it comparatively easy to confuse the inheritance of corruption and the inheritance of guilt. Once one assimilates inclination and choice, it is easy to assimilate sinful (corrupt) inclinations and sinful (guilty) choices. It is then easy to suppose that since the first can be inherited, so can the second.

Edwards's analogies may illuminate the inheritance of corruption, i.e., of morally disordered or unhealthy inclinations and desires. The corruption of a tree's roots can pass to the whole tree and so to each of its parts. Similarly, the sickness of one of its organs can infect the whole body and thus each of its members. Since Edwards believed that he had shown how Adam and his posterity can be legitimately regarded as one thing, i.e., as a natural unity such as a tree or a human body, it was natural for him to think that he had shown that corruption can be transmitted from Adam to his descendents. His assimilation of corrupt inclinations and guilty choices would make it difficult for him to see that the transmission of guilt involves a different issue, and that this issue has not been satisfactorily resolved.

C.

If I am correct, Edwards has not shown that God can reasonably impute Adam's guilt to his descendents. He has, at best, shown that (1) we can reasonably be held liable for Adam's failure, i.e., that the arrangement in virtue of which we are exposed to certain "legal" consequences because of Adam's failure, is reasonable and, perhaps, that (2) Adam's fault can in some sense be regarded as the fault of the "species," i.e., of humanity as a whole. He has not shown how Adam's fault can be the fault of each of his descendents and has, therefore, not shown how his descendents can share Adam's guilt. But I do not think that the doctrine should simply be dismissed.

Guilt is usually thought to entail three things — one's offense was within one's control, one should be blamed for it (if only by oneself), and one is an appropriate candidate for (legal, social, or divine) punishment. The standard objects of guilt are actions. Robert Adams thinks that we can also be guilty of, and blamed for, beliefs and attitudes which are not within our control although he concedes that punishment may be inappropriate. This seems correct. It may therefore be useful to distinguish two senses of "guilt." In its primary sense, guilt presupposes control and entails that one is an appropriate candidate for punishment as well as blame. In a secondary sense, guilt does not imply control and only entails that blame is appropriate.

Pelagius was correct in thinking that a person cannot be guilty of something in the primary sense unless it springs from his own will or affections. He was mistaken in thinking that sin is no more than "the performance of a deed wrongly done."[47] As Augustine realized, sin is ultimately a state or condition which sinful deeds express. Whether the human sickness is diagnosed as sinful self-reliance or a disorder of love, it is ultimately a sickness of the heart. In the primary sense, we are guilty of sinful dispositions and attitudes only insofar as they are shaped and reinforced by our choices. But we may be wholly guilty of them in the secondary sense.

Furthermore, there are at least two senses in which these guilty dispositions and attitudes are inherited. Our egocentricity and our pre-occupation with temporal goods are partly a biological inheritance. These dispositions have survival value and seem to be traits of the species. We are also implicated from birth in sinful social structures. Each of us initially receives his ideas and values from the sinful social groups to which he belongs. Our understanding of ourselves and our relation to the world, and the attitudes and feelings with which this self-understanding is inextricably intertwined, are thus tainted at their source. Guilt is there-fore inherited in the sense that we inherit sinful dispositions and atti-tudes of which we are guilty in the secondary sense. Can we also inherit guilt in its primary sense?

Immanuel Kant and Paul Ricoeur call our attention to an impor-tant aspect of our *experience* of evil — that whenever we reflect on our freedom, we find that we have already *chosen* evil, that our *will* has already deflected. We experience our own evil as at one and the same time springing from our freedom and as "already there for freedom." That is, as soon as we begin to choose reflectively, we recognize that the situation in which we must choose, and our nature as choosers, has been shaped by guilty choices we have already made. Guilt (in its primary sense) precedes reflective choice.[48]

A further observation may also be relevant. There is a significant sense in which our identity is socially constituted. Our metaphysical identity is not a social product. Nevertheless, there is a sense in which who or what I am is partly defined by my most fundamental convictions, my deepest loyalties, and my most heartfelt allegiances. To deny these, as we say, is to deny myself. But most (if not all) of these convictions, loyalties, and allegiances are reflections of purposes, goals, beliefs, and practices which are not only common to the members of a community but are *shared* by them in the sense that they recognize, affirm, and endorse one another as persons who, at least partly, are what they are in virtue of these common bonds.[49] Because of this, there is a significant sense in which the history of my community is part of my own history. But orthodox Christians believe that all social groups and structures — families, nations, classes, and so on — are more or less fallen, alienated from God and distorted by sin. Furthermore, to the extent to which these institutions and groups are capable of acting corporatively, they are guilty in the primary sense. There is thus a significant sense in which the sin *and guilt* (in its primary sense) of my community is mine.

I do not wish to press these observations too far. That guilt precedes *reflective* choice does not entail that guilt precedes choice. And though there is a sense in which the guilt of the communities to which I belong is mine, it is mine only in the *same* sense in which the histories of those communities are part of my history. Neither observation implies that I can literally be guilty of another's offense and, hence, neither implies that I can literally be guilty of the offenses of my ancestors.

Should orthodox Christians be troubled by this conclusion? Augustine, Luther, and Calvin insisted that sin can only be understood in the light of grace. The doctrine of Original Sin, like the doctrine of Predestination, is at best a corollary of the story of God's redemption of a humanity which is unable to extricate itself from its own egoism and blindness. I submit that nothing is essential to an adequate account of the nature and origin of sin that is not implied by the offer of grace. I also submit that the components of the Augustinian conception of sin which I have criticized are not implied by that offer.

NOTES

1. Edwards's defense is presented in *Original Sin (OS)*, ed. Clyde Holbrook (New Haven, 1970). Relevant material is also found in *The Nature of True Virtue (TV)* (Ann Arbor, 1970); *The Works of President Edwards (Works)* (10 vols., 1968 reprint of the Leeds edition reissued with a two volume supplement

in Edinburgh, 1847); the "Miscellanies" (a number of which can be found in *The Philosophy of Jonathan Edwards from his Private Notebooks*, ed. by Harvey G. Townsend [Eugene, Oregon, 1955]), and "The Mind" (in *Scientific and Philosophical Writings*, ed. by Wallace E. Anderson [New Haven, 1980]).

2. Perry Miller, *Jonathan Edwards* (New York, 1959), p. 267. "Arminianism" refers to the system of theology named after Jacobus Arminius (1560–1609), and condemned by the Synod of Dort in 1618. Arminius was primarily concerned with the harsh consequences of the Calvinist theory of predestination. Edwards and other eighteenth-century Calvinists used the term more broadly "to stand for a complex of notions involving an elevated confidence in freedom of choice, a sharply upward revised estimate of human nature, and a form of commonsense moralism, all of which were related to an acute dissatisfaction with Calvinism" (Clyde Holbrook, *Original Sin*, introd., p. 4.)

3. The doctrine of Original Sin is "plainly and fully taught in his [God's] Holy Word," and *"confirmed* by what is found in the experience of all mankind in all ages." (*OS* 409, emphasis added.)

4. Like Berkeley, Edwards thinks that being is essentially *conscious* being.

5. The relation between benevolence and virtuous complacence is not entirely clear. In *Religious Affections* (*RA*) (New Haven, 1959), Edwards argues that "affections that are truly holy, are primarily founded on the loveliness of the moral excellency of divine things. Or (to express it otherwise), a love to divine things for the beauty and sweetness of their moral excellency" (*RA* 253f). Similarly, in the *Treatise on Grace* (*TG*) (Cambridge, 1971), Edwards argues that "the first thing in Divine Love [true virtue], and that from which everything that appertains to it arises, is a relish of the excellency of the Divine nature" (*TG* 49). A love of complacence, i.e., a relish of God's beauty, or a delight in his moral excellence, is thus said to be the ground or foundation of all virtuous love. Edwards appears to have abandoned this view by the time he wrote *True Virtue*. He continues to believe that benevolence toward being in general and a delight in spiritual beauty are inseparable but no longer thinks the latter is the foundation of the former. Edwards appears to have come to the conclusion that his earlier view was incoherent. Since one prizes the love of *x* only if one prizes *x*, one would not delight in the consent to, or love of, being unless one already loved being. The love of true beauty presupposes a love toward being and thus cannot be its ground. The manuscript of the *Treatise on Grace* has been lost but A. V. G. Allen believed that it was written after 1752. If this is correct, then Edwards's rejection of his earlier view occurred quite late, perhaps at the time he was writing the essay on true virtue.

6. What does Edwards mean by saying that an offense is infinitely heinous? He certainly means that there is a point of view from which no offense could be worse, and I shall also use the expression in that sense. Edwards may also wish to imply that no matter how severely the offense is blamed or punished, still more blame or punishment would be appropriate.

7. Edwards believes that the infinite heinousness of sin follows from what scripture tells us of "God's own constitutions and dispensations towards mankind."

Since (1) scripture informs us that all who sin are "exposed to be wholly cast out of favor with God" and "made the subject of perfect and eternal destruction," since (2) this punishment would be unjust if sin was not infinitely heinous, and since (3) we know from scripture that God judges and acts according "to the exact truth and real demerit of things," (4) all sin must be infinitely heinous (*OS* 130–131).

8. What does Edwards mean by this? (1) God is the head of the system of beings, its "chief part." (2) God's being, power, and perfection are so great that "particular beings" are nothing in comparison. (3) God is the only real substance and the only true cause. (The third point reflects Edwards's idealism, mental phenomenalism, and occasionalism.)

9. By contrast, the merit of our respect or regard for another is "diminished in proportion to the obligations we are under in strict justice to pay him that respect. There is no great merit in paying a debt we owe . . . but there is great demerit in refusing to pay it" (*OS* 130). Since our obligations to God are infinite (we owe him all that we are and all that we have), there is no merit in our love and obedience.

10. Marilyn Adams, "Hell and the God of Justice," *Religious Studies* 11 (1975); p. 443.

11. Professor Marilyn Adams has informed me that she wishes "expect more" to be taken in its first sense.

12. This does not entail that no sin is worse than any other. In the corollary to Miscellany 713, Edwards argues that just as two infinitely long cylanders may be unequal in width, so infinitely heinous sins may be unequal in other respects (*OS* 41f n). Sins can be considered from several points of view. Regarded as offenses against God, murder and deceit are both infinitely heinous. Regarded as offenses against our neighbor, murder is (normally) more heinous than deceit.

13. Edwards insists upon the difficulty of discovering spiritual truths and also upon the difficulty of discerning their truth once they have been discovered. See, e.g., "Miscellanies" 986, 1297, 1298, and 1340.

14. *Apocalytic Writings*, ed. by Stephen J. Stein (New Haven, 1977).

15. As Augustinians have pointed out, *expressions* of our evil dispositions are not normally involuntary. But this should not be confused with the voluntariness of sin itself.

16. Their unwillingness is evinced by (1) the fact that they are not sensible of deserving infinite punishment, by (2) the fact that they have no sincere conviction, i.e., no sense or relish, of the excellency of Christ, and by (3) their reluctance to set their own goodness at naught. No one can sincerely accept Christ's offer to discharge his debt unless he acknowledges his debt. He might, of course, be glad if Christ were to offer him the means of escape from eternal torment. Nevertheless, he cannot sincerely accept this offer *under the description "discharging our debt"* if he does not believe that he owes one. Nor can one sincerely accept an offer of help unless he believes that the person who offers help is able to help. Since Christ's holiness and splendor are the foundation of his death's efficacy, one cannot sincerely believe that Christ is able to help if he is

blind to his beauty and excellency. Finally, God's way of salvation sets human goodness at naught. Salvation is an unmerited favor, not a response to human deserving. No one can sincerely embrace God's way of salvation while rejecting God's estimate of his own real worth.

17. One might argue that 1 is not even *clearly* true of overt behavior. Consider a case in which a private is ordered to stand guard. He fails to stand guard, and excuses himself by pointing out that he had been struck by a car and was therefore unable to do so. Is he excused from punishment even if it is false that he would have stood guard if he could have done so, and even if we *know* that he would not have done so? Perhaps. But while he might be excused from punishment, he would not be excused from blame.

18. At one point, Edwards asserts that "sin . . . wishes ill, and aims at ill, to God and man; but to God especially. It strikes at God; it would, if it could, procure his misery and non-existence" (*Works* VIII, 460). If this were true, sin would be wicked and eternal punishment appropriate, but human sin is not typically like this. The most that could be maintained is that the nature of sin is such that if the sinner were to become fully conscious of God's greatness, splendor, and infinite opposition to sin, then if he were to persist in sin, he would hate God, would "strike at" him, etc. There may, then, be a sense in which sin is *potentially* malignant. Potential malignancy, however, is not malignancy.

19. Robert Adams, "Involuntary Sins, "*The Philosophical Review* 94 (1985); 3–31.

20. As Robert Adams admits.

21. It is important to distinguish the following claims: (1) Because of Adam's sin, we are subject to death. (2) Because of Adam's sin, our nature has been vitiated, i.e., our mind has been darkened, our concupiscence awakened, our will weakened, etc. (3) Because of Adam's sin, we are guilty. The first is clearly taught by scripture; 2, and possibly 3, might be inferred from (e.g.) Romans 5. Nevertheless, it is worth remembering that 3 was not widely held before Augustine. (It is significant that the belief in the guilt of infants was not generally accepted before Augustine. See J. N. D. Kelley, *Early Christian Doctrines*, 5th rev. ed. [London, 1977], ch. 13.)

22. Perry Miller, *The New England Mind: The Seventeenth Century* (New York, 1939), p. 400f. As Miller points out, these legal metaphors should be distinguished from Augustine's quasi-biological metaphors. According to Augustine, sin, like an hereditary disease or a genetic defect, is passed on from parent to child in the act of physical procreation.

23. Quoted, ibid., p. 401.

24. Edwards's preference for the second approach may reflect an uneasiness about the first, but he does not clearly distinguish them. The two are connected by the assertion that Adam is not only the organic root of his posterity but also its head and representative, the "hegemon" of the "single thing" constituted by Adam and his descendants. (There may be an inadvertent (?) play on two senses of "head," viz., the part of a human body containing the brain, ears,

eyes, nose and mouth, thought of as its "executive" organ, and chief, representative, ruler, or "federal head.")

25. P. 251. Quoted in *OS*, p. 398 fn.

26. "Collective Responsibility," *Philosophy* 23 (1948): p. 12.

27. Joel Feinberg, "Collective Responsibility," in *Doing and Deserving: Essays in the Theory of Responsibility*, by Joel Feinberg (Princeton, New Jersey, 1970), p. 247. The internal quotation is from Dwight MacDonald.

28. Virginia Held, "Can a Random Collection of Individuals be Morally Responsible?" *Journal of Philosophy* 67 (1970); 471–481.

29. Either a direct action by the group such as restraining an assailant or the action of organizing into a temporary community in order to decide how best to deal with an emergency.

30. Ibid., p. 477.

31. Ibid., p. 471.

32. Feinberg, "Collective Responsibility," p. 241.

33. Feinberg thinks that criminal punishment would be unreasonable because (1) where the group is fairly large or diverse, "the less likely it is that they all share—or share to anything like the same degree—the fault in question," and (2) where "the fault is properly ascribed distributively to a group of great size, the probability increases that the fault is common also to judge, jury, and prosecutor" (ibid., 242–243). This does not seem to capture our intuitions about cases of this kind. The guests who drove home may have been equally drunk, and the judge, jury, and prosecutor may never drive when drunk. Should the lucky drivers therefore receive the same penalty as the person who struck the pedestrian?

34. Ibid., pp. 242–243.

35. Though one might argue that we do not exhibit the same fault to "the same degree," since our sin is an expression of a corrupted constitution and ruined environment, and Adam's is not.

36. Ibid., pp. 226–229.

37. Ibid., p. 234. Feinberg suggests that "there is perhaps no better index to solidarity than vicarious pride or shame." He concedes that Lewis in "Collective Responsibility" may be right in saying that parental pride is often "a consequence of the belief" that the achievements of one's children "reflect the influence of the parent," and that pride in the achievements of one's ancestors or countrymen frequently rests upon the belief that one shares the qualities for which they are noted, but thinks there is a type of vicarious pride or shame which is "unrelated to any doings or qualities" of the person who feels pride or shame (236–237).

38. Ibid., p. 239.

39. Ibid., p. 241.

40. Adam's fall involves the fall of his posterity whereas his adherence to the good would have guaranteed the eternal happiness of his descendants. God has constituted things in such a way that our well-being and ill-being are necessarily intertwined with Adam's well-being and ill-being.

41. Ibid., p. 241.

42. There is another problem with the fifth model. As Feinberg observes, "justice requires that . . . those held vicariously liable have some reasonable degree of *control* over those for whom they are made sureties" (ibid., p. 241). We have no control over Adam.

43. The argument of the last two paragraphs is heavily indebted to chapter 13 of Richard Swinburne's *Coherence of Theism* (Oxford, 1977). Even so limited a conventionalism as this is probably indefensible. If no one had invented chairs, it is unlikely that our language would have contained a term for them. It is nevertheless true that in all possible worlds, something is a chair only if it meets our criteria for a chair. This is a necessary fact, and necessary facts are not invented (by God or anyone else). The concepts which are explicitly enshrined in a language will be partly determined by the interests of its speakers, their environment, and other contingent circumstances. (Classical Latin contains no term for quarks.) It does not follow that the natures (i.e., properties) which are the contents of these concepts are somehow invented. (Indeed what would it *mean* to say this?) It must be conceded, however, that this point depends upon the truth or adequacy of certain currently fashionable views about possible worlds, essences, etc. James Ross and others have called these into question.

44. We can meaningfully speak of *one* biological family, distinguish biological families from one another, etc. The criteria employed in picking out these objects and making these distinctions are no more arbitrary than the criteria employed in picking out and distinguishing between mountains or baseball teams.

45. There is another problem with Edwards's argument. He wants us to conclude that just as it is reasonable to impute guilt to individuals for past offenses even though persons are series of discrete thoughts, choices, and feelings which God treats a single thing, so it is reasonable to impute Adam's sin to his posterity even though Adam and his descendants are discrete individuals whom God treats as one. But aren't we likely to develop doubts and scruples about ascribing blame to individuals for "their" past actions if we become convinced of the truth of Edwards's occasionalism, phenomenalism, and views on personal identity? Edwards's case depends upon the reasonableness of the practice of ascribing guilt to people for past actions *together with* his philosophy of mind. It is not clear that the two are compatible.

46. Edwards owes some of these ideas to Johann Friedrich Stapfer (1708-1775). See the long quotations on p. 392f (n).

47. Robert F. Evans, *Pelagius, Inquiries and Reappraisals* (New York, 1968), p. 97.

48. See, e.g., Paul Ricoeur, "The Hermeneutics of Symbols and Philosophical Reflection: I," in *The Conflict of Interpretations* (Evanston, 1974), pp. 287-314.

49. See, e.g., Michael J. Sandel, *Liberalism and the Limits of Justice* (Cambridge, 1982).

Atonement According to Aquinas

ELEONORE STUMP

I

The doctrine of the Atonement, the doctrine that God has resolved the problem of moral evil in the world by means of the suffering and death of Christ, is the central doctrine of Christianity; and yet very little attention has been paid to it by contemporary philosophers of religion. There are no doubt many reasons for the neglect; but among them is embarrassment, for many of us know this doctrine only in the version which tends to be promulgated by unreflective believers who are more to be admired for devotion than for philosophical expertise. This unreflective account of the Atonement is often assumed to be just the theory of the Atonement held by Anselm (or Luther, or some other notable philosophical theologian), but careful study of the work of such theologians will show that their theories differ significantly from the unreflective account with which most of us are familiar. That account tends to consist in the following set of claims (or something approximately like it).

(A) Human beings by their evil actions have offended God. This offense against God generates a kind of debt, a debt so enormous that human beings by themselves can never repay it. God could, of course, cancel this debt, but God is perfectly just, and it would be a violation of perfect justice simply to cancel a debt without extracting the payment owed. Therefore, God cannot just forgive a person's sin; as a just judge he must sentence all people to everlasting torment as the punishment for their sin. God is also infinitely merciful, however; and so he brings it about that he himself pays their debt in full, by assuming human nature as the incarnate Christ and in that nature enduring the penalty which would otherwise have been imposed on human beings. In consequence, the sins of ordinary human beings are forgiven, and by God's mercy exercised through Christ's passion, they are saved from sin and hell and brought to heaven.

There are many problems with this version of the doctrine of the Atonement. To begin with, contrary to what it intends, it does not, in fact, present God as forgiving human sin. To forgive a debtor is to fail to exact all that is in justice due. But, according to (A), God does exact every bit of the debt owed him by humans; he allows none of it to go unpaid. As (A) tells the story, God himself fully pays the debt owed him. This part of the story is perplexing; but what it shows is that God himself has arranged that the debt be paid in full, not that he has agreed to overlook any part of the debt.

The proponent of (A) might claim that God's forgiveness consists precisely in his not requiring that *we* pay the debt for sin but rather he himself paying it for us in the person of Christ. But it is hard to see what constitutes forgiveness on this claim. Suppose that Daniel owes Susan $1000 and cannot pay it, but Susan's daughter Maggie, who is Daniel's good friend, does pay Susan the whole $1000 on Daniel's behalf. Is there any sense in which Susan can be said to forgive the debt? On the contrary, Susan has been repaid in full and has foregone none of what was owed her.

The proponent of (A) will say that God's justice precludes his overlooking the debt and that therefore he has shown mercy and forgiveness in the only way he can, by he himself paying the debt owed him. And, the proponent of (A) might say, surely our intuitions about Susan's forgiveness would be different if it turned out that although her justice did not allow her to cancel Daniel's debt, Susan had instructed her daughter to pay the debt. The case for (A) is also strengthened by remembering that, on the doctrine of the Trinity, Christ is one in being with God the Father, so that the one paying the debt is the same as the one to whom the debt is paid.

Apart from the other perplexities raised by this rejoinder, however, it seems not to emphasize God's justice but to rest on a denial of it. For all the talk of debt is really a metaphor. What (A) is really telling us is that any human being's sins are so great that it is a violation of justice not to punish that person with damnation. What God does in response, however, is to punish not the sinner but a perfectly innocent person instead (a person who, even on the doctrine of the Trinity, is not identical with God the Father, who does the punishing). But how is this just? Suppose that a mother with two sons, one innocent and one very disobedient, inflicted all her disobedient son's justly deserved punishment on her innocent son, on the grounds that the disobedient one was too little to bear all his punishment and her justice required her to punish someone. We would not praise her justice, but rather condemn her as cruel and barbaric, even if the innocent son had assented to this procedure. If the mother could after all forego punishing the disobedient son, why did she not just do so without inflicting suffering on the other child? And how is justice served by punishing a completely innocent person?

Furthermore, the account given in (A) is inconsistent both with itself and with another fundamental Christian doctrine. In the first place, (A) claims that in his suffering and death on the cross Christ paid the full penalty for all human sin so that humans would not have to pay it. And yet it also claims that the penalty for sin is everlasting damnation; but no matter what sort of agony Christ experienced in his crucifixion, it certainly was not (and was not equivalent to) everlasting punishment, if for no other reason than that Christ's suffering came to an end. Second, (A) maintains that Christ pays the penalty for all sin in full so that humans do not have to do so. But it is a fundamental Christian doctrine that God justly condemns some people to everlasting punishment in hell. If Christ has paid the penalty for sin completely, how is God just in demanding that some people pay the penalty again?

The proponent of (A) may try to answer both these objections by altering his account to say that the penalty Christ pays for humans is his death and suffering. But this answer is no help. On Christian doctrine, the punishment for sin is not just death but hell, so that this alteration of (A) has the infelicitous result that what Christ undergoes in his sub-stitutionary suffering is not the assigned penalty for sin. But even if it were, his suffering would not remove the penalty from humans since they all suffer death anyway.

Finally, it is not clear what the Atonement accomplishes, on the account given in (A). According to Christian doctrine, the main problem with sin is that it leaves humans alienated from God. Human beings tend to will what they ought not to will, and so their wills are not in conformity with God's will. Consequently, they do not live in peace with God now, and in that state they cannot be united to God in heaven. According to (A), the Atonement consists in Christ's paying the penalty for sin. But nothing in (A) suggests in any way that the Atonement alters the human nature and proclivities which were responsible for sin. In (A)'s version of it, the Atonement is efficacious to remove not sin, but only the penalty for sin. In that case, however, the Atonement is not really an At-one-ment; for, as (A) tells it, the Atonement leaves humans with just the same tendencies to will what is contrary to God's will, so that their wills are no more conformable to God's will, they are no more tending toward unity with God, than they were before the Atonement.

It seems to me, then, that the version of the Atonement in (A) is really hopeless, so full of philosophical and theological problems as to be irremediable. But often enough when we find a piece of Christian doctrine which looks hopeless in popular theology, it turns out to be a garbled version of an idea which was once presented with philosophical sophistication in the work of Christian theologians. In the rest of this paper I want to present a carefully worked out theory of the Atonement, one that can be found in the work of Aquinas. Aquinas's theory is by no means the only alternative to (A) worth taking seriously. Other alternatives can be found in the work of John Calvin, for example, or John of the Cross. But I have picked Aquinas's theory to focus on largely because his is the most philosophically rigorous and complete of the accounts I know. At the end of the paper I will say something more about Aquinas's theory in the history of Christian theology.

II

Aquinas assigns a number of roles to Christ's passion and death;[1] but they can all be subsumed under two general functions, namely, making satisfaction and meriting grace. These functions correspond, roughly, to two different problems posed by moral evil.

Consider two friends, Susan and David. They have been best friends for years; but recently David has become an alcoholic, and he is given to driving while drunk. On one such occasion he has a bad accident while driving with Susan's little daughter Maggie in his car, and, because in his drunken state he had neglected to buckle the child in, Maggie is killed. If Susan and David are not to be alienated despite this dreadful event, there will be two obstacles to their friendship: first, the problem of dealing with the moral wrong David has done (I will call this the problem of past sin) and, second, the problem of dealing with the moral wrong David is likely to do, given that he is still an alcoholic (I will call this the problem of future sin).

Aquinas believes that the Atonement is God's solution to both those sorts of problems.[2] Christ's passion and death, understood as making satisfaction, is the solution to the problem of past sin and, understood as meriting grace, is the solution to the problem of future sin. So, he says, Christ's suffering has two principal effects: satisfaction for our past sins and salvation from our sinful nature.[3] I will begin with his understanding of the Atonement as making satisfaction for sin.

At first glance, the Thomistic account of the Atonement as making satisfaction to God for sins sounds perilously like (A):

> [Christ] willed to suffer that he might make satisfaction for our sins.
> And he suffered for us those things which we deserved to suffer because of

the sin of our first parent. The chief of these is death, to which all other human sufferings are ordered as to their end. . . . Accordingly Christ also willed to suffer death for our sins so that, by himself without any fault of His own bearing the penalty we owed, he might free us from the sentence of death, in the way that anyone would be freed from a penalty he owed if another person undertook the penalty for him.[4]

To understand Aquinas's account of this function of the Atonement, it is important to be clear about what he means by satisfaction and what importance he attaches to it. Satisfaction, he says, removes the debt of punishment for sin.[5] Now if God had willed to free humans from sin without any satisfaction, he would not have acted against justice; for if he forgives sin without satisfaction — without removal (that is) of the debt of punishment — he wrongs no one, just as anyone who overlooks a trespass against himself acts mercifully and not unjustly.[6] Nonetheless, there was no more suitable way of healing our nature than by making satisfaction.[7]

These remarks show that for Aquinas the problem of past sin is understood very differently from the way it is understood in (A). On (A) the problem with the sins a person such as David has committed is that they have resulted in God's alienation from David and in God's consequent inability to refrain from punishing him. But on Aquinas's account, the problem is rather that David is alienated from God, who is free to punish him or not. That this is so can be seen most clearly from Aquinas's general account of satisfaction as one of the three integral parts of penance (the other two being contrition and confession).[8] Aquinas sees penance as a kind of medicine for sin:[9] It consists in detesting one's sin and purposing to change one's life for the better,[10] and it aims primarily at the restoration of friendship between the wrongdoer and the one wronged.[11] The function of satisfaction for Aquinas, then, is not to placate a wrathful God but instead to restore a sinner to a state of harmony with God. So, Aquinas says, sins are remitted when the soul of the *offender* is at peace with the one offended.[12]

We can understand the gist of his idea by considering a homely example of minor evil. Suppose Anna is the mother of a feisty little boy, Nathan, who loves soccer. Anna, on the other hand, loves flowers and has asked him repeatedly not to practice soccer on the side of the house where her flower beds are. But Nathan does play with his soccer ball near the flower beds, and the inevitable occurs: some of the flowers are trampled. Nathan, however, is so interested in his ball playing that he stops just long enough to run into the house and say, "Sorry, Mom, I trampled your flowers" before he returns to his game. What he has done presents his mother with two problems, one regarding the flowers and one regarding her son. She has lost some of her flowers, and it will take her some time and energy and money to replace them. But her real problem is with her son, because from this episode she sees two things about him. In the first place, he does not love what she loves; if he had had any care for the flowers, he would have played with his soccer ball in a different place. And second, he does not love her as she would like him to, because although he knows *she* loves her flowers, he does not have a care for the flowers for her sake. So what Nathan has done has created some distance between himself and his mother. His will and hers are not in harmony and he does not love her as he might; and her recognition of both these facts makes her sad.

Nothing in Nathan's response to his own action will lessen her sadness. In recognition of his misdeed he has offered a hasty and casual apology and nothing more. If he had any real care for his mother or her flowers, if he had really been sorry for what he had done, he would also have done what he could to fix the damage. And his mother would have been very glad of his efforts, even if they were clumsy and ultimately unsuccessful, because they would have manifested a change of heart: after the fact, at any rate, Nathan would have had a care for his mother and for her flowers. And so by his efforts at undoing the damage caused by his action, he would have restored a harmony of will and love between himself and his mother which his wrong action had disrupted. In Aquinas's terms, Nathan would then have made satisfaction for his sin. The chief value of this satisfaction is not so much that it restores Anna's flowers — if Nathan's efforts are clumsy enough, the flowers may even be worse off than if he had not tried to improve their condition — rather, the value of the satisfaction is that it restores the harmonious and loving relationship between Anna and her son.

Considerations of this sort, I think, underlie Aquinas's claim that in assigning the penalty or satisfaction for sin one considers the sinner, rather than the one sinned against.[13] On Aquinas's view, the will moves away from sin by moving in a direction opposed to those movements which inclined it to sin. Doing so requires being sorry for past sin in such a way that the past sin comes to be against one's present will.[14] When Nathan attempts to rectify the damage he has done, he shows that he is truly sorry for his action, that if he had it to do over again, he would be more careful — in short, that he now wills the opposite of what he willed when he hurt his mother's flowers and feelings.

But now suppose that Nathan is too little to make any satisfaction for his misdeed. Perhaps to rectify the damage he would need to buy and plant new flowers, but he has no money and is too small either to go to the store or to use a shovel. If he is truly sorry, what can he do? Suppose that he has an older brother Aaron, who can do what Nathan cannot. And suppose that Nathan explains his predicament to his brother and asks his brother to buy flowers and plant them for him. If Aaron loves his brother enough, he may then use his own time and money to undo his brother's mischief. Now when Anna learns of this situation, she may have a special love for Aaron because of his kindness to his brother. But if Nathan's will really is set on some restitution for his misdeed, he will have returned to harmony with his mother even if all the actual work of restitution was done solely by Aaron. In this context, just in virtue of allying himself with Aaron's restitution, Nathan shows he cares for his mother and for the things she values; and so he restores the close relationship with his mother although Aaron is the one who restores the garden.

In this way, then, it is possible for one person to make satisfaction for another's sins. Because the point of making satisfaction is to return the wrongdoer's will to conformity with the will of the person wronged, rather than to inflict retributive punishment on the wrongdoer or to placate the person wronged, it is possible for the satisfaction to be made by a substitute, provided that the wrongdoer allies himself with the substitute in willing to undo as far as possible the damage he has done. Thus Aquinas says that one person can make satisfaction for another only to the extent to which they are united,[15] or that one person can atone for another insofar as they are one in charity.[16]

Now the story in which Aaron makes satisfaction for Nathan's wrong action has obvious parallels to Aquinas's theory of Christ's Atonement, but it is also disanalogous in many ways which might be thought to make a difference to the plausibility of Aquinas's account. We can, however, alter the story till many of the disanalogies vanish. Suppose, for example, that instead of Nathan's asking Aaron for help, he just continues playing soccer but that *Aaron* comes to *him* and asks if he would like to have Aaron fix the damage for him. That the initiation of restitution lies with Aaron increases his merit but is no hindrance to the subsequent reconciliation between Nathan and his mother. Provided that Nathan does now have a care for his mother and her concerns, it does not matter to their reconciliation whether the credit for his change of heart is due to Nathan himself or to his brother. The salient fact is that Nathan's will is now in harmony with his mother's.

Or, finally, suppose that Nathan has no brother or anyone else who could fulfill the same function for him. And suppose, further, that he shows no signs of any interest in restitution or reconciliation with his mother. If Anna were, like the mother of Aeneas, endowed with the power of transforming herself, and if she really loved her son, she might appear to him in disguise and in that disguise try to talk him into letting *her* make his restitution for him. If we think of the problem between Nathan and Anna as consisting in her loss of flowers or her distress over the damage to the flowers, then, of course, this story is just farcical, for in this story Anna is in effect giving flowers to herself. But if we understand, as Aquinas would, that the real problem lies in Nathan's will, which is turned away from his mother, and if we suppose not that Anna is wrathful and vengeful towards her little sinner but rather deeply loving, then the story makes very good sense. For by this complicated and somewhat demeaning method Anna may succeed in turning her son's will and love back to her, so that the harmony of their relationship is restored. As long as Nathan wills heartily to undo the wrong he did, it does not matter whether he himself or someone else, including even Anna, actually does the work of making restitution. And this version of the story of Anna and Nathan is analogous in all relevant respects to Aquinas's account of the Atonement as making satisfaction.

So although both (A) and Aquinas's account are couched in terms of a debt of punishment for sin, they reflect two different ways of understanding the notion of incurring a debt of punishment. That in (A) rests on a conception of God that makes him seem something like an accountant keeping double column books on the universe. When a person commits a sin, a debt of guilt is registered in one column which must be balanced on the same line in the other column by the payment of a punishment which compensates for the guilt. This view raises a problem about how the books could ever balance if the debt is to be paid by someone other than the sinner, because the debt is one of guilt, and guilt is not a transferable commodity.

Aquinas, on the other hand, has a different understanding of the notion of incurring a debt of punishment, which in turn rests on a different conception of God. This is a conception of God not as accountant but as parent. A good parent believes that a misbehaved child incurs a debt of punishment for his misbehavior, not because the parent is trying to keep the spiritual books of the household balanced, but rather because the parent loves the child, and everything from old wives' tales to contemporary psychology suggests that negative reinforcement extinguishes undesirable behavior. The parent's concern is with the child, that the child develop into the best person she can be and that there be a loving relationship between the child and her parent. Any punishing, then, is strictly a means to an end, the end of making the child a good person in harmony with the parent. If punishment is the only hope for achieving that end, then a good parent will not omit punishment — but for the parent, unlike the celestial accountant, the punishment by itself does not accomplish the end desired.

When a person sins, both on (A) and on Aquinas's theory, he incurs a debt of punishment. On (A), the sin results in a debt of guilt in that person's celestial accounts, which must be paid back somehow. And if the sinner could pay back the debt, as on (A) he cannot, then God would be satisfied (in more than one sense of the term). But on Aquinas's account, God is not concerned to balance the accounts. He is concerned with the sinner, with his child. What he wants is for that person to love what God loves and to be in harmony with God. His aim, then, is to turn that person around; and what will satisfy him is not punishment and repayment, but the goodness and love of his creature.

Punishment is one means to that end; but it is a desperate, last ditch effort, because while punishment is known for its efficacy in extinguishing certain behavior, it is not famous for its effectiveness at winning hearts. So while Anna in my story may well hold some punishment in reserve for her little sinner, if she is a wise as well as a loving mother, she will try some other means first. If she forces Nathan to fix the flower bed as punishment for his sin, he may repent, or alternatively he may hate flowers all his life. On the other hand, if she provides vicarious satisfaction for her son, in the way I think Aquinas understands vicarious satisfaction, she eases his return to her. She invites rather than forces his compliance. She counts as sufficient for reconciliation his willingness to undo his mischief and does not require his actually restoring the garden. And finally, in the person of the substitute making vicarious satisfaction, she sets before him a living model of what he should be if he were up for it, so that he does not need to initiate the desired state of mind in himself, but needs just to watch and copy someone else's. So if Anna sends Aaron to offer in a spirit of love to fix the damage on his brother's behalf, she stands a better chance of getting what she wants: not compensation, but the heart and mind of her disobedient son.

For Aquinas, then, the *aim* of any satisfaction (including vicarious satisfaction) is not to cancel a debt incurred by sin but to restore a sinner to harmony with God. And the person making the vicarious satisfaction is not paying a debt so much as acting the part of a template representing the desired compensatory character or action, in accordance with which the sinner can align his own will and inclinations to achieve a state of mind which it is at least unlikely he would have achieved on his own.

Focusing on this aim of satisfaction helps to answer an important question.[17] If the aim is just a sinner's repentance, why bother restoring the garden? Why not just forget about the garden and the whole notion of vicarious satisfaction and aim solely at producing repentance? Aquinas says that it *was* open to God to deal with sin in just that way, that nothing required God to deal with sin by means of vicarious satisfaction, but that there is nonetheless something appropriate about God's doing so.[18] The appropriateness seems to me of two sorts. In the first place, if a person is truly sorry for a sin, he will *want* to do whatever he can to undo what he did; and there is something loving about gratifying his desire to undo or compensate for the wrong he has done. In the second place, having eased a sinner into repentance by vicarious satisfaction, one wants to be sure he is not readily eased out of it again. True repentance, being sorry for a sin and resolving not to repeat it, is very difficult; and people are apt to deceive themselves into thinking that they have repented when they have, in fact, just had some short-lived remorse. Participation in making compensation for the wrong done—even the indirect compensation involved in making satisfaction vicariously—helps cement the remorse into repentance; the willing of compensation, voluntarily undertaken in contrition, helps strengthen the will in its resolution of repentance.

These considerations show that there is some value in making satisfaction for a wrong action, and they also explain how one person can make satisfaction for the sins of another, even when the one making satisfaction is the same as the one wronged. But it is not yet clear *how* Christ is supposed to make satisfaction, on Aquinas's account. It is not clear, that is, what the theological equivalent of restoring the flowers is.

According to Aquinas, Christ makes satisfaction for all the sins of the human race in his passion, that is, in the suffering which leads up to and includes his dying in physical and psychological pain.[19] Something in what Christ endured in dying, in other words, rectifies for God what was disordered or destroyed by human beings in sinning. But what is it that human sin ruins? In general, a person sins by preferring his own immediate power or pleasure over greater goods. Human sin has pride and selfishness at its root, then, and it constitutes disobedience to God, whose will it contravenes. So what is most directly ruined by sin is human character; a proud, selfish, disobedient mind is the theological analogue of the trampled garden. In Aquinas's terms the immediate effect of sin is to leave something like a stain on the soul;[20] and the cumulative stains of sin lessen or destroy the soul's comeliness,[21] so that by sinning a person directly mars part of God's creation, namely, himself.

To make satisfaction for human sinning, then, is to present God with an instance of human nature which is marked by perfect obedience, humility, and charity and which is at least as precious in God's eyes as the marring of humanity by sin is offensive. But this is just what the second person of the Trinity does by taking on human nature and voluntarily suffering a painful and shameful death. By being willing to move from the exaltation of deity to the humiliation of crucifixion, he showed boundless humility; and by consenting to suffer the agony of his torture because God willed it when something in his own nature shrank powerfully from it, he manifested absolute obedience.[22] Finally, because he undertook all the suffering and humiliation out of love for sinful humans, he exhibits the most intense charity. So in his passion and death Christ makes restitution to God for the marring of human nature caused by sin because he gives God a particularly precious instance of human nature with the greatest possible humility, obedience, and charity. And one answer to the question why Christ had to suffer is that humility, obedience, and charity are present in suffering that is voluntarily and obediently endured for someone else's sake in a way in which they could not be, for example, in Christ's preaching to the Jews or healing the sick.[23] (I will say more about the suffering of Christ later in this paper.)

In this way, then, because of his divine nature and because of the extent of his humility, obedience, and charity,[24] Christ has made satisfaction for all the sins of the human race,[25] both those committed before his death and those committed after it. On Aquinas's view, Christ's passion is like a medicine for sin[26] available to cure sin in all ages of human history.[27] But it is clear on Aquinas's account — as it is not clear on (A) — why Christ's having made satisfaction for all human sins does not entail that there be no humans in hell. Given the understanding of satisfaction on which Aquinas's theory of the Atonement is based, satisfaction for sin made by a substitute for the sinner effects reconciliation only in case the sinner allies himself with the substitute by willing the restitution the substitute makes. The medicine of Christ's satisfaction is unavailing unless a person applies it to himself by accepting Christ's suffering and death as making satisfaction for his own sins.

To ally oneself with Christ's making satisfaction involves, first of all, having faith in his passion. That is, it involves believing that the incarnate Christ suffered for the sake of humans and in their stead. But this belief by itself is not enough, as we can see by remembering the example of satisfaction considered earlier; for Nathan might believe that Aaron was restoring the flowers for his sake and in his stead and yet, in a fit of perversity, hate what Aaron is doing. In that case Aaron's action is not successful in producing reconciliation between Nathan and his mother. So, Aquinas says, for Christ's passion to be applied to a person, that person must have both faith and charity. He must not only believe that Christ has made satisfaction for his sin; he must also have the love of God and goodness which makes him glad of the fact. In such a case, then, the mind and heart of the sinner cleave to Christ, and he applies the medicine of Christ's passion to himself for the remission of his sin[28] and for reconciling himself with God.

Thus, we can see that although Aquinas's account superficially resembles (A), it is in fact very different. For Aquinas sees the problem of the alienation between God and humans as consisting not in God's wrathfulness toward humans but rather in human withdrawal from God. And he understands Christ's passion as atoning, as producing reconciliation between God and humans, not because God in his justice must inflict the punishment for sin on someone and the innocent Christ substitutes for guilty humans, but rather because humans by allying their hearts and minds with Christ in his passion as he makes satisfaction for their sins are converted to a state of mind in harmony with God's will.

There is real mercy and forgiveness on this account, because according to this view God does not require the penalties for sins either from humans or from Christ; God does not inflict Christ's suffering on him as a punishment for human sins, but rather accepts it as an act of making satisfaction. In accepting Aaron's restoration of her flowers Anna does not inflict restoration of the flowers on Aaron as punishment even if she was the instigator of his action. The purpose of Aaron's action (and Anna's participation in it) is not to punish Nathan's misdeed but to change his mind so that he is again in harmony with his mother. Furthermore, it is clear on this account as it is not on (A) why not all people experience the benefit of the Atonement, because on Aquinas's account it is not possible for Christ's atoning action to be efficacious for anyone unless that person freely wills to accept Christ's action on his behalf.

And, finally, this account, unlike (A), provides some comprehensible connection between Christ's atoning action and salvation from sin, because according to Aquinas's theory when a person accepts Christ's making satisfaction for him, he wills the contrary of the pride, selfishness, and disobedience he wills when he sins, and in so willing he moves away from sin.[29]

III

If we return now to the earlier example of Susan and David, her alcoholic friend, we can see that Aquinas's account of the Atonement as satisfaction for sins is only part of the solution to the problem of moral evil. According to the story in that example, David drove while drunk and in doing so killed Susan's child Maggie. No matter how forgiving Susan may be, David's action disrupts their friendship. Among other reasons, David will not be able to share with Susan the most important current event in her life, the death of her daughter, because his sense of guilt and regret will be too painfully exacerbated by witnessing her grief and pain; and what David may say to himself by way of diminishing his guilt will ring in his own ears as hollow excuses if said to Susan.

One way of restoring these people to friendship with each other, on Aquinas's view, is for David (or someone else acting for David) to make satisfaction for the wrong done by offering Susan something which she would not have had otherwise and which she values as much as what she lost, thereby evincing the real care for Susan and for what she loves which he lacked in those actions that resulted in Maggie's death. Suppose, for example, that Susan has a second daughter who is dying from kidney disease and for whom a donor has not been found; and suppose David's tissues are compatible with the daughter's. If David in a spirit of contrition donates one of his kidneys and thereby saves Susan's other daughter from death, he goes a long way toward restoring his friendship with Susan. But even in such rare felicitous circumstances, their friendship will not be completely restored. For David remains an alcoholic. In that state he does not share many of Susan's most important concerns and desires; and, as he and Susan both know, he may at any time again do something as terrible as killing a child.

Analogously, although Aquinas's account of the Atonement as satisfaction explains how Christ's passion remits past sin, this account by itself is not enough to show that Christ's passion reconciles humans and God, because human nature remains in its post-Fall sinful condition. Christ's passion considered as making satisfaction does not alter the disordered relationship among human reason, will, and emotions which, on Aquinas's view, is responsible for the tendency of human beings to do what they ought not to do.[30] This disordered condition of human nature and the consequent failure to develop positive virtuous dispositions constitutes the problem of future sin. According to Aquinas, when his account of Christ's passion as making satisfaction is supplemented by an explanation of the passion as Christ's meriting grace and thereby healing human nature and enabling it to become virtuous, it also provides a solution to the problem of future sin. And so, Aquinas says, Christ's passion and death are both a remedy of satisfaction and a sacrament of salvation;[31] Christ's suffering has *two* principal beneficial effects: satisfaction for one's past sins and salvation from one's sinful nature.[32]

This second part of Aquinas's theory of the Atonement is much more complicated and difficult than his account of the Atonement as satisfaction. It is couched in the technical terminology of medieval theology; it is set in the context of Aquinas's elaborate treatment of the nature and varieties of God's grace; and on first hearing it is likely to strike a contemporary audience as obscure and implausible at best. In what follows I will give a very brief summary of the salient points of Aquinas's account, presenting just as much of his work on grace as I need to make this part of his theory of the Atonement intelligible and without pausing to comment on the many questions Aquinas's views raise. After this uncritical presentation I will try to recast Aquinas's theory in more familiar terms in order to consider whether it is successful in arguing that the Atonement is a solution to the problem of future sin.

According to Aquinas, Christ is the head of the Church; and since all human beings are potentially members of the Church, Christ is (at least potentially) the head of the whole human race.[33] By saying that Christ is the head of the whole human race, Aquinas means that he is first among humans in order, perfection, and power;[34] but, more importantly, he also means that together Christ and human beings form one mystical body, analogous to the physical body formed by the head and other members of a human body.[35] All humans are potentially and believers are actually part of this mystical body. In his passion Christ merits grace sufficient to cure all human sin;[36] and as head of the body of the church, he infuses the grace he has merited into those persons actually united with him in this mystical body.[37]

The source of Christ's merit that provides grace for humans is his will.[38] For someone to merit something is for him to bring it about that some good thing should in justice be given him. In the last analysis, however, good things for humans are those which contribute to obtaining eternal life. Now an action meriting eternal life must be an action done out of charity.[39] And in fact charity is the root of all merit[40] because it is the love of God,[41] who is goodness personified,[42] and the love of other persons and things for the sake of goodness. Without charity, then, no true virtue is possible,[43] and charity is, as it were, the form of all virtuous acts.[44] But Christ in his passion suffered out of the deepest charity, for he voluntarily accepted great suffering and death out of love for all humans.[45] His suffering was intense, both physically and psychically, partly because during his passion he grieved for all the sins of the human race at once,[46] and partly because there is more charity involved when a greater person submits to suffering for the sake of others.[47] So because of the intensity of his love for human beings Christ merits grace leading to eternal life; and as the head of all humans (at least potentially), he merits this grace for all people.

To understand this part of Aquinas's account, we have to be clear about his complicated views of grace. In what follows I will generally mean by 'grace' only what Aquinas calls cooperating grace. He recognizes several other species of grace as well; but understanding his view of cooperating grace is sufficient for our purposes here. For Aquinas, then, grace is a habit or disposition bestowed in virtue of Christ's passion by the Holy Spirit on a person, inclining that person toward freely complying with God's precepts and prohibitions.[48] This disposition is bestowed when a person's mind is illuminated to know things which exceed reason and when his affections in consequence cleave to God in love, being inclined to do all the things such love requires.[49] The end or purpose of this grace is the union of a human person with God.[50] It accomplishes this end by inclining the natural powers of the mind to love of God and by making that love come easily and pleasantly.[51]

Nonetheless, this inclining of a person's mind to charity is always accomplished by the Holy Spirit by means of a free act of that person's will.[52] While grace is being infused into a person, that person assents to the process in an act of free will,[53] so that the infusion of grace is simultaneous with the movement of the will.[54] Thus, no one comes to God by grace without freely willing to do so. It is God who moves a person toward charity, from which the virtues flow; but God moves everything in accordance with the nature of the thing moved, and since it is part of human nature to have free will, God's movement of a person in the process of infusing grace does not take place without a movement of free will.[55] Furthermore, what grace confers is a habitual disposition. But one can always act against a disposition or habit, and so a person in grace is always capable of sinning.[56] And, finally, grace is available to all human beings; the only humans who are deprived of grace are those who offer an obstacle to grace within themselves.[57]

Grace itself is not a virtue;[58] but it prepares the will for virtue by giving it a disposition, by preparing it to love God and to act rightly.[59] So grace gives rise to all the virtues,[60] and especially the theological virtues.[61] The process of the infusion of grace and the consequent effects of grace on the mind of the person receiving it is the process of sanctification, in which a person's sinful nature is slowly converted into a righteous character. Thus, Aquinas says, there are five effects of grace in humans: (1) healing of the soul, (2) desire of the good, (3) carrying out the good desired, (4) perseverance in good, and (5) attainment of eternal life.[62]

Even if this account of grace were entirely clear and wholly plausible as a solution to the problem of future sin, it would not yet suffice as part of a theory of the Atonement, because so far we have no connection between the bestowal of grace and Christ's passion. That connection is provided by Aquinas's theory of the means by which God has chosen to bestow grace, namely, the sacraments. Grace is involved in all the sacraments, but the one most important for Aquinas's theory of the Atonement is the Eucharist. Christ's passion works its effect of saving humans from sin through faith, charity, and the sacraments, [63] he says, in particular the Eucharist. The sacraments are for the spiritual life what certain physical things are for bodily life;[64] the Eucharist is nourishment for the psyche, and it provides growth in virtue[65] by conferring grace.[66]

The sacrament of the Eucharist is also intimately related to Christ's passion. On Aquinas's view, in accordance with Christ's institution at the last supper Christians maintain that Christ's body and blood are actually, literally, present in the sacrament. Christ's body, however, is not in the sacrament as a physical body is in a place, that is, contained by the place and filling it. Rather it is in the sacrament only substantially, as being the substance of what was bread. Thus Christ's body is in the (apparent) bread in such a way that the whole body of Christ is comprised in every part of the bread.[67] Finally, the nature of the Eucharist is such that when a believer partakes of it, he does not turn the sacrament into his substance, as happens when he eats other food, but instead he becomes part of the body of Christ and is incorporated into him.[68]

The effect of the sacrament, then, for those who receive it properly (with the right sort of will) is that they are united with Christ and become part of the body of Christ.[69] But if a person is part of Christ, then the grace Christ merited on the cross by his passion flows into him; and so the grace won by Christ's passion is bestowed by the Eucharist on those who partake of it appropriately.[70] So union with Christ is the effect of this sacrament, since in the sacrament a believer receives Christ within himself in such a way as to become incorporated into Christ;[71] and the result of this union is the protection of the soul against future sin, because by the grace bestowed through the sacrament a believer's love of God and love of goodness is stimulated and strengthened.[72] In the sacrament, Aquinas says (in one of the few lyrical passages in his scholastic prose), a believer's soul is inebriated by the sweetness of the divine goodness.[73]

Although the grace Christ merited by his passion is sufficient for undoing bad habits acquired in the past and preventing further sin in the future, it is efficacious to cure the sin only of those joined to him. The joining is effected by faith and love.[74] And although love of God can be stimulated by other examples of God's love for his creatures, it is stirred especially by reflection on Christ's passion[75] and by the bond of charity brought about by participation in the Eucharist. When a person cleaves to Christ in faith and love, an act of free will is elicited in him simultaneous with the infusing of Christ's grace. This act of free will is directed in different ways both toward past sins and toward future righteousness.

In it a person hates his past sin and desires God's righteousness, so that by this act of will the mind withdraws from sin and draws nearer to righteousness.[76] Simultaneously with this willing God infuses grace into the believer's soul; that is, God adds to the soul a disposition inclining it toward the good and away from sin. The repetition of this cooperative action is the process of sanctification, conforming the believer's mind and character to Christ's and culminating in eternal life with him.

So the Atonement solves the problem of future sin because by means of the sacrament of the Eucharist a union of sorts is effected between the believer and Christ such that Grace merited by Christ in his passion is transferred to the believer in one cooperative divine and human action in which the believer desires goodness and hates sin and God adds to him a disposition for that state, with the result that in the course of time the believer comes to be more righteous and more like Christ.

IV

Because Aquinas's account of grace is complex and problematic, this part of his theory of the Atonement may leave us cold and uncompehending. It is, for example, not clear how a disposition toward a certain sort of willing could be infused simultaneously with a free act of such willing. And why should it take an intricate ceremony like the Eucharist for God to bestow this grace? Furthermore, the connection of Christ's passion to the Eucharist and the bestowal of grace is perplexing. The talk of the mystical body of Christ is more mysterious than helpful, and it is difficult to see why it was necessary for Christ to suffer in order to effect this mystical body. The transfer of grace merited by Christ in his passion to believers united to him raises moral and metaphysical problems. The nature of grace includes a disposition to love and goodness, and it is hard to understand how this disposition of Christ's could be directly transferred from him to another person, no matter how they are joined together. And finally, it is not clear why God could not simply bestow grace directly without the suffering of Christ's passion or the ritual of the Eucharist.

Part of the trouble we have in understanding Aquinas's account, I think, stems from the fact that he explains in medieval metaphysical terms what we would be more inclined to explain in psychological terms. I want to try, then, to present Aquinas's account in non-medieval terms more familiar to us. My attempt will not help elucidate the metaphysical perplexities of Aquinas's account; but I believe it will help to show his general idea of the way in which the Atonement solves the problem of future sin, and it will provide answers to some but not all of the questions I just raised about this part of Aquinas's account.

Consider again David, the alcoholic who has killed a child because he was driving while drunk. Suppose also that David is a lapsed Christian (of a Thomistic sort) and that shortly after his dreadful accident, full of sorrow and remorse, he returns to church and communion. What will this experience be like for David? Consider first what he believes. He believes that he has done something morally reprehensible and that he did it because of his continuing enslavement to alcohol; and he sees himself in consequence as a hateful person. But since he is a Christian, he also believes that God does not hate him but rather *loves* him intensely. God himself is perfectly good, holy in righteousness, and he also sees completely all the evil in David's heart and actions. And yet Christ's love for David, for the hateful, alcoholic David, was so great that he voluntarily undertook the shame and agony of crucifixion for him. And for what purpose? To heal David of his sin. To offer for David what David himself could not offer to God, so that he might be reconciled to God, no matter what awful evil he had done, and so that he might be transformed from something hateful into something holy, into someone like Christ.

Furthermore, Christ's great love for him is not just part of some old historical narrative or abstruse theological argument. For the person who loves David so intensely as to die for him in order to keep David from dying in his sin is right there then, present to David's spirit even if hidden from his eyes. In fact, not only is he present, but (David will believe) in the sacrament of the Eucharist the Christ who loves him comes closer to him and is more intimately united to him than it is possible for two created persons to be in this life; for in receiving the sacrament David will receive the body and blood of Christ in such a way that he himself becomes a part of the body of Christ, bound together with him into one spiritual entity.

If David believes all this, what is the effect on him likely to be?[77] In the first place, his guilt is assuaged; Christ has made satisfaction to God for David's sin and restored the relationship between David and God which David's past sin had disrupted. Second, David's hostility to himself is alleviated; the judge most in a position to despise and condemn him instead loves him and means to rescue him from his evil. Then, too, David's hope for himself will be strengthened. God, who sees David as he is and who can do anything, is himself on David's side. It is God's intention that David be turned into a righteous person, at peace with God and with himself. And if God be for him, what can be against him? Furthermore, David will feel a great debt of gratitude to Christ,

who suffered so to free him, and with that gratitude will come a determination that Christ's suffering should not be for nothing. Finally, David
will feel a surge of love for this person who first so loved him, and also
a sense of joy, for the person who loves him is present to him and united
with him.

As long as David is in this frame of mind, what chance has his
addiction got of retaining its mastery over him? To use Aquinas's terminology for a moment, what David has done in this state is to cleave to
Christ in charity and thus to will freely to draw near to righteousness
and withdraw from sin.

If at some other time out of love for David God were simply to
alter David's will to hate his addiction to alcohol, he would be destroying David's free will, because he would be making David will contrary to
what David himself would have willed. But if God acts on David's will
while he is in this frame of mind, if he strengthens David's will in its
resolution to stop drinking, he is not violating David's will, for in this
state David is in effect willing to have his will be set against drinking. In
other words, the beliefs and desires stimulated in David by the Eucharist
and reflection on Christ's passion evoke in David a powerful second-
order willing, namely, the will that his first-order willing be against drinking. In giving David grace on such an occasion, God is infusing him
with a disposition (of one degree of strength or another) to first-order
willing against drinking; but that God does so in no way detracts from
the freedom of David's will because it is David's own (second-order) will
that he have a (first-order) will against drinking. In strengthening David's
will in its resolution, then, God does not undermine the freedom of his
will but rather cooperates with it to produce the state of will which
David himself wills to have. And this is, I think, the sort of thing Aquinas
has in mind when he says that the grace bestowed by means of the
Eucharist *cooperates* with free will. He does say that this grace is infused
simultaneously with an action of free will; but since Aquinas also believes
that God is outside time, nothing prevents him from supposing that the
grace infused simultaneously with an act of free will is in fact infused
because of and as a response to that act of free will. (The worry that this
interpretation is on the road to Pelagianism will be discussed in the next
section.)

It is clear that if David's response during the sacrament is of the
ordinary human variety of emotion, if it is not the unusually powerful
and life-transforming emotion of a Paul on the road to Damascus, his
exalted state of mind will fade and his resolution will weaken. Even so,
however, he will have made some progress, because God will have acted
on David's second-order will to have his will altered. But not even omnip-

otence can make David's will stronger in its willing of righteousness than David wills it to be, on pain of violating David's will. Without the sudden wholesale conversion of will of the sort experienced by Paul, David will also have a strong disposition toward first-order willings to drink, which undermines his second-order willing to have a will not to drink and which thus resists God's grace.[78] So David's road away from his sin and toward righteousness will take time, during which some willing will bring with it some grace and consequently some fixing of his will, and these in turn will stimulate further willing and further fixing.

In telling this story of David, of course, I have picked an example of a person whose sense of himself makes him naturally likely to receive communion emotionally, and it might occur to someone to wonder whether the same story could be told about someone who came to communion with a relatively untroubled conscience. I know of no way to prove that communion would have similar effects on such a believer, short of some poll of communicants. But I offer as some evidence for the view that it could Aquinas's poem, *Adoro te devote*,[79] which shows the depth of emotion the Eucharist could stir even in a man whose life was apparently morally blameless.

On the basis of this psychological presentation of Aquinas's scholastic explanation of the Atonement, as regards the problem of future sin, we can provide some answers to the questions with which I began this section of the paper.

We can understand the bestowal of grace as God's response to the believer's willing to have his will altered, and such grace is tied to the Eucharist because it is the Eucharist which inspires and calls forth the willing. Both the bestowal of grace and the willing of a righteous will associated with the Eucharist are connected to Christ's passion, because it is Christ's love as manifested in his passion which elicits the believer's love and consequent willingness to will righteousness. It is also clear why God could not bestow grace directly without Christ's passion, because God's bestowal of grace is efficacious only in connection with an act of free will, which is called forth by the commemoration of Christ's passion in the Eucharist. On this interpretation, the mystical body of Christ is (or at least essentially includes) a union of minds, when the believer values and desires what Christ does, in the love engendered by the intimacy and poignancy of the Eucharist. It would be a mistake for someone, hearing the expression 'the mystical body of Christ' for the first time in this context, to ask what sort of thing this body is or where it is located, not because the expression is a figurative one which does not refer to anything, but rather because what it does refer to is a very complex set of shared experiences constituting the loving interweaving of human wills and minds with Christ's.

In this sort of way it is also possible to give a more understandable interpretation of Aquinas's claim that Christ's grace is transferred to a believer in the Eucharist. When David acquires grace on partaking of the Eucharist, it is not because some moral disposition of Christ is magically plucked from his soul and transplanted into David's. Instead in loving Christ because he believes Christ loves him and wants David's love in return, with all that that love implies in the context, David allies himself with Christ and takes on a frame of mind like that which he believes characterized Christ in his passion, namely, charity accompanied by a hatred of sin (in David's case, his own sin) and a love of goodness. In this frame of mind David forms a second-order willing to have first-order willings of the sort he believes he ought to have, so that God can infuse in David (to the degree warranted by David's second-order will) a disposition to will not to drink without thereby violating the freedom of David's will. In this way, then, Christ's grace is transferred from him to David, not in the way that tulip bulbs are transferred from one plot to another but rather in the way that understanding is sometimes transferred from one mind to another, by the two minds being joined together in certain aims and beliefs and one mind's being kindled and illuminated by the other.

V

If we combine these two parts of Aquinas's account, Christ's passion as satisfaction and Christ's passion as meriting grace, we can see that he has a theory of the Atonement which can handle both the problem of past sin and that of future sin. Return again to the story of Susan and David, close friends who are alienated because David in his ongoing alcoholism has killed Susan's daughter. This story is in many (but certainly not all) respects analogous to the Christian view of the relationship between God and human beings. They are alienated because humans in their on-going post-Fall nature tend to will the contrary of what God wills, generally their own pleasure or power in preference to greater goods. To reconcile Susan and David requires first David's doing what he can to make satisfaction for the evil he has done. On Aquinas's theory of the Atonement, God out of love for humans initiates this process by sending his Son to make satisfaction for a person's past sins, by offering in his passion what that person in his current state cannot offer to God, namely, an instance of human nature with perfect humility, obedience, and love of God. But making satisfaction for past sins is not enough to effect reconciliation. For David and Susan to be reconciled also requires David's abandoning his addiction, and similarly for human beings and God to be at one again requires a person's converting from his post-Fall disordered nature with its inclination to evil to a new Christ-like character inclined to righteousness. On Aquinas's theory, Christ also provides the means for effecting this conversion by his passion and its commemoration in the Eucharist. The love manifested by Christ's passion and the loving union experienced in the Eucharist call forth the believer's love of Christ, which generates a willingness to will goodness and withdraw from evil. Once the believer has been stimulated by God to this act of will, then God can give the believer's will supernatural aid, assisting and strengthening the will to will the good, without thereby violating the believer's free will.

It might occur to someone at this point to protest that in explaining Aquinas's account I have in effect changed it from an orthodox view of the Atonement into something perilously close to Abelard's theory of the Atonement, a theory repudiated by the medieval church. For Abelard, Christ's role in human salvation from sin amounts to little more than that of a moral example, guiding and stimulating right conduct on the part of believers. But according to Aquinas, as I have explained his position, the work of saving a person from his sin is done not by the struggling sinner himself but by God's grace won by Christ in his passion. Christ participates in this human reformation as its cause rather than just as a moral influence prompting it.

It is true that the causal efficacy of Christ's passion is dependent on human free will, however; and so someone might object that my interpretation of Aquinas is Pelagian even if it is not Abelardian. Here, I think, it is worth pausing to clarify the role of free will in my interpretation of Aquinas's account. Consider again Anna and her son Nathan: Suppose that Nathan loathes vegetables but that Anna means Nathan to eat them anyway. Anna lectures her son on the benefits of eating vegetables, offers rewards for eating them, threatens punishments for not doing so, and finally as a last resort spoons the vegetables into his mouth herself. Now, on the one hand, if Nathan does eat his vegetables, the credit goes to Anna, whose labor, ingenuity, persistence, and determination brought about the desired result. And yet, considered from the standpoint of Nathan and his attitude toward vegetables, the bare failure to keep his mouth closed, which is all he can claim as his share in the cooperative enterprise of Anna's getting him to eat his vegetables, may cost him a severe struggle with himself. And so although the credit for success is Anna's, there is nonetheless room in this story not just for exhortation but even for praise of Nathan. On the other hand, if Nathan does not eat his vegetables, the fault is all his, because no efforts to get him to eat his vegetables, no matter how clever or forceful, *can* succeed if he refuses to open his mouth.

This story is analogous to Aquinas's account of cooperative grace. What God infuses as grace is a disposition to righteous first-order willing; but God can do so only if a person is willing to have him do so, only if a person wills to will what he ought to will. It is open to a person to do what is in effect refusing to receive grace. So in a way analogous to that in my homely example, the credit for bringing about the desired result is God's, although exhortation of and praise for human actions is compatible with this fact; but any failure is entirely attributable to the sinner, whose persistence in sin stems from his refusal of divine aid. This view is hardly what we usually consider Pelagianism.

Whether it is Pelagian or not, it is considered a theological monster by the noted Thomist Garrigou-Lagrange. According to him, the doctrine according to which "man by his consent causes the grace of God to be efficacious" is "a monster, a chimera, or at least a puerile invention."[80] Garrigou-Lagrange takes this view because he holds that "God is either *determining* or *determined*, there is *no* other alternative;"[81] and, he goes on, "only anthropomorphism can admit the second term of the dilemma and therefore, from sheer necessity, we must keep to the first."[82] But if God must always be determining and can never be determined, then a person's use of his free will can make no difference to what God is or does.

A full examination of Garrigou-Lagrange's claim is beyond the scope of this paper, but two things should be said in answer to his charge. In the first place, Garrigou-Lagrange's general thesis seems based on a mistaken notion of God's greatness. A God who can create things like himself in their ability to act of their own accord, without determination by something else, is surely greater than a God who can create only things whose activities are entirely determined by himself. But if God creates entities which can act on their own apart from his determination of them, then he also brings it about that some of what he does is a response to what his creatures do; he brings it about, in other words, that he is sometimes determined rather than determining. In the second place, if Garrigou-Lagrange's thesis is correct, it seems to me that the monstrosity is all on its side, because then God is the determiner of all the evils around us, and the human sense of freedom is an illusion. Both David's alcoholic bouts and his trusting prayers to God for redemption from his addiction are equally and wholly determined by God. So

Garrigou-Lagrange's thesis seems to me to render the problem of evil (among others) insoluble and to make a mockery of some cherished religious practices. Consequently, I think a principle of charity can plausibly be invoked here. Aquinas need not be read as Garrigou-Lagrange reads him; as my preceding exposition shows, it is possible to interpret him consistently in a way which violates Garrigou-Lagrange's thesis. And since it is possible to read Aquinas in a way which frees him from the (to my mind) monstrous consequences of Garrigou-Lagrange's thesis, it is charitable and reasonable to do so.

Those familiar with other theories of the Atonement, such as Calvin's, for example, may also wonder at the fact that there is here hardly any mention of the work of the Holy Spirit, which features significantly in Calvin's account, as in others. In fact, Aquinas's theory does assign a prominent place to the Holy Spirit, because on Aquinas's view grace is the grace of the Holy Spirit,[83] so that the infusion of grace is the Holy Spirit working in the heart. But covering all the complexities and elaborations of Aquinas's account of the Atonement is more than could be managed in one paper, and so I have left to one side any issues which can be omitted without distorting the heart of his idea. The work of the Holy Spirit is one such issue; the relation of Christ's passion to original sin and the role of Christ's resurrection in the process of atonement are others.

There is, however, one idea found in other, more familiar theories of the Atonement which is not mentioned in this paper because it is not in Aquinas; the fact that it is not seems to me a serious flaw in his account. Luther, for example, in his theory of the Atonement, emphasizes the idea that Christ somehow actually bears all human sin; that is, in some way all the sins ever committed in human history are transferred to Christ's soul in his suffering on the cross. (I will refer to this claim as 'Luther's idea,' for the sake of convenience only.) There is no similar or analogous claim in Aquinas's account. The problem for Aquinas, then, is to square his account with the New Testament story of the passion. The cry of dereliction from the cross is certainly easier to explain on Luther's idea than on Aquinas's account. So is Christ's agony in the garden of Gethsemane. For Aquinas it is difficult to explain why the incarnate deity should have been in such torment over his death when so many of the merely human martyrs went gladly, even cheerfully, to death by tortures worse than crucifixion. Aquinas's interpretation of the relevant New Testament passages seems to me to eviscerate the text. Given that he is trying to provide a theory of the Atonement, his failure to do justice to these passages is a major fault.

We might be tempted to suppose that Aquinas does not include an idea such as Luther's because it makes no sense; sins cannot be transferred like money in bank accounts. But, in fact, Luther's idea is less counterintuitive than it seems at first, and Aquinas has the doctrines and distinctions necessary for supporting it. For example, Aquinas distinguishes between a sinful action and what he calls 'the stain on the soul' left by that sinful action.[84] By 'the stain on the soul' he understands, roughly, something which includes the distressing knowledge of what it feels like to have committed a particular sin and the tormenting awareness of what it is to desire such an evil action. On this understanding, it is, arguably, possible to have a stain on the soul without having the sin which usually precedes it. For example, a powerful scene in a movie portraying a brutal murder may succeed in evoking in receptive members of the audience a mild version of the stain on the soul ordinarily produced only by the evil action itself. Luther's idea could thus be explained in Aquinas's own terms by claiming that in his passion Christ acquires all the stains on the soul produced by all the sins of the human beings with whom he is united. The horror and pain of such a burden would explain the agony in Gethsemane and the cry of dereliction. And that Christ had to suffer in such a way could perhaps be explained as a necessary concomitant of Christ's uniting himself with human beings in the process of saving them from sin. If David is united with Christ, then Christ is also united with David. David experiences the uniting as allying himself with an overwhelmingly holy, loving person. But perhaps Christ experiences this uniting as allying himself with a selfish, alcoholic killer of a child. So it is possible for Aquinas's account of the Atonement to accommodate Luther's idea. That Aquinas has no equivalent idea stems, I think, from his tendency to emphasize the divine nature of Christ at the expense of his human nature, rather than from any philosophical absurdity (in Aquinas's terms or ours) in Luther's idea. But Aquinas's theory of the Atonement would have been theologically more powerful, and also perhaps more humanly compelling, if it had included something equivalent to Luther's idea.

Finally, it is, of course, clear that Aquinas's account is not the only theory of the Atonement that is an alternative to the unreflective (A) with which this discussion began. Anselm, Abelard, Luther, Calvin, and John of the Cross, to name just a few, also worked out sophisticated theories of the Atonement. What my examination of Aquinas's account shows is not the preferability of his version to any of these others but rather just the nature of one defensible theory of the Atonement and the general constraints on any acceptable account. Aquinas's theory of the

Atonement is a reflective version of (A). As Aquinas explains it, Christ in virtue of his passion really does solve the problem of human sinfulness and really does make people at one with God. Whatever the details of other theories of the Atonement, they must explain how the Atonement solves the problem both of past and of future sin; and they must do so, like Aquinas's account, in a way which does not undermine God's justice and mercy or human nature.[85]

NOTES

1. In *Summa theologiae* (*ST*) III, q. 48, Aquinas says Christ's passion operated as a source of merit, as a sacrifice, as a mode of redemption, and as satisfaction making atonement for human sins.

2. See, e.g., *Compendium theologiae* (*CT*), chapters 226–230. Robert Adams has suggested to me that alcoholism may be a bad example to illustrate the problem of future sin because we tend to think of alcoholism as a disease involving physical addiction, and perhaps his suggestion is right, although it seems to me that the cure of alcoholism typically includes a painful and difficult moral struggle which is illustrative of the problem of future sin. We could, however, readily replace the example involving alcoholism with other examples of habitual evil such as chronic marital infidelity.

3. See, e.g., *CT*, chapter 227.

4. *CT*, chapter 227. Cf. also *ST* III, q. 46, a. 1 and *Summa contra gentiles* (*SCG*) IV, chapter 55, n. 3952. This section in the Latin corresponds to section 22 in the translation of *SCG* IV by Charles J. O'Neil (Notre Dame, Ind.: University of Notre Dame Press, 1975); I will add section numbers to this translation in parentheses after the Latin section number.

. . . ut pro peccatis nostris satisfaceret, voluit pati. Passus est autem pro nobis ea quae ut nos pateremur ex peccato primi parentis meruimus, quorum praecipuum est mors, ad quam omnes aliae passiones humanae ordinantur sicut ad ultimum. . . . Unde et Christus pro peccatis nostris voluit mortem pati, ut dum poenam nobis debitam ipse sine culpa susciperet, nos a reatu mortis liberaret, sicut aliquis debito poenae liberaretur, alio pro eo poenam sustinente.

5. *ST* III, q. 22, a. 3.

6. *ST* III, q. 46, a. 2.

7. *ST* III, q. 46, a. 3. In conversation with me, Thomas Tracy raised a problem for this part of Aquinas's account and also helpfully suggested a solution. According to Tracy, it might occur to someone to wonder whether God would be justified in allowing the innocent Christ to suffer if his suffering was not necessary for salvation, as Aquinas claims it is not. In terms of my analogy (yet to come in the text), we might wonder whether Anna was morally justified in allowing Aaron to suffer in the process of restoring the garden if his suffering

was not necessary to bring about a change of heart in Nathan. Tracy's solution is to suggest that Aquinas's account requires a traditional Christology. In the case of Anna, we might very well be inclined to deny that she is justified in allowing the unnecessary suffering. But if we add traditional Christology to Aquinas's account of the Atonement, then the one who suffers unnecessarily is both truly man and truly God. Thus God does not allow the unnecessary suffering of some third party but rather himself endures it as a means of redemption. And just as we would have no moral qualms about the case if Anna herself chose to endure some unnecessary suffering to rescue her son, so there seems no basis for objecting to *God's* undergoing unnecessary suffering as a means to human redemption. So although Aquinas does not hold that the passion and death of Christ are necessary for salvation, once God has chosen to save people in that way it is necessary that God be the one suffering.

8. *ST* III, q. 90, a. 2.

9. *ST* III, q. 84, a. 5.

10. *ST* III, q. 85, a. 1.

11. *ST* III, q. 85, a. 3 and q. 86, a. 2.

12. *ST* I-II, q. 113, a. 2.

13. *SCG* IV, chapter 55, n. 3953 (23).

14. *SCG* III, chapter 158, n. 3305 (1).

15. *ST* I-II, q. 87, a. 7 and a. 8.

16. *ST* III, q. 48, a. 2.

17. I am grateful to Philip Quinn for raising this question in his comments on an earlier draft.

18. *ST* III, q. 46, a. 2 and a. 3.

19. *ST* III, q. 48, a. 2.

20. *ST* I-II, q. 86, a. 2.

21. *ST* I-II, q. 89, a. 1.

22. See, e.g., *Scriptum super libros Sententiarium Magistri Petri Lombardi episcopi Parisiensis (Sent.)*, Bk. III, d. 19, q. 1, a. 4, q. 2.

23. *ST* III, q. 48, a. 2; cf. *SCG* IV, chapter 55, n. 3947-48 (17-18).

24. *ST* III, q. 46, a. 3.

25. *ST* III, q. 49, a. 4.

26. *ST* III, q. 49, a. 1.

27. As for those who lived before Christ, Aquinas holds that all persons in hell were visited by Christ in the period between his crucifixion and resurrection; see, e.g., *ST* III, q. 52. Aquinas interprets this traditional doctrine of Christ's harrowing hell in a stern fashion; those whom Christ takes out of hell with him are only those who had some foreknowledge of him and were united to him in faith and love, namely, the righteous among the Jews who were awaiting him as Messiah.

28. *ST* III, q. 49, a. 1 and a. 3; cf. also *ST* III, q. 62, a. 5 and *SCG* IV, chapter 72.

29. Cf., e.g., *SCG* III, chap. 158.

30. See, e.g., *ST* I-II, q. 82, a. 3.

31. *CT*, chap. 227.
32. *ST* III, q. 49, a. 1 and a. 3.
33. *ST* III, q. 8, a. 3.
34. *ST* III, q. 8, a. 1.
35. Ibid.
36. See, e.g., *ST* III, q. 8, a. 5.
37. *ST* III, q. 8, a. 6 and q. 48, a. 1.
38. See, e.g., Sent., Bk. III, d. 18, divisio textus.
39. Sent., Bk. III, d. 18, q. 1, a. 2.
40. *ST* I–II, q. 114, a. 4.
41. *ST* II–II, q. 23, a. 1.
42. For an exposition and defense of the Thomistic doctrine of simplicity, on which this claim is based, see Eleonore Stump and Norman Kretzmann, "Absolute Simplicity," *Faith and Philosophy* 2 (1985):353–382.
43. *ST* II–II, q. 23, a. 7.
44. *ST* II–II, q. 23, a. 8.
45. Sent. Bk. III, d. 18, q. 1, a. 5.
46. *ST* III, q. 46, a. 6.
47. *SCG* IV, chapter 55, n. 3957 (27).
48. See, e.g., *ST* I–II, q. 108, a. 1 and q. 109, a. 4.
49. *CT*, chap. 143.
50. *ST* III, q. 7, a. 12.
51. *ST* II–II, q. 23, a. 2.
52. Ibid.
53. *ST* I–II, q. 111, a. 2.
54. *ST* I–II, q. 113, a. 7.
55. *ST* I–II, q. 113, a. 3.
56. *SCG* IV, chapter 70.
57. See, e.g., *CT*, chapter 144; *ST* I–II, q. 112, a. 4 and q. 113, a. 2.
58. *ST* I–II, q. 110, a. 3.
59. *ST* I–II, q. 109, a. 3–4.
60. Sent., Bk. II, d. 26, a. 4.
61. *ST* I–II, q. 110, a. 3.
62. *ST* I–II, q. 111, a. 3.
63. *ST* III, q. 49, a. 3.
64. *SCG* IV, chapter 58.
65. *SCG* IV, chapter 61.
66. *ST* III, q. 79, a. 1.
67. *ST* III, q. 75, a. 1 and q. 76, a. 4–5.
68. *ST* III, q. 73, a. 3.
69. *ST* III, q. 73, a. 3 and q. 80, a. 2.
70. *ST* III, q. 79, a. 1.
71. Ibid.
72. *ST* III, q. 79, a. 4 and 6.
73. *ST* III, q. 79, a. 1.

74. In fact, Aquinas goes so far as to say that faith and love are efficacious without the Eucharist if a person has an implicit desire for the Eucharist but is somehow prevented from acting on that desire; see, e.g., *ST* III, q. 73, a. 3.

75. Sent., Bk. III, d. 19, q. 1, a. 1, q. 2.

76. *ST* I–II, q. 13, a. 6.

77. 'Likely' is a necessary qualifier here, because grace is not efficacious without an act of free will. It is possible for David to react to the Eucharist with perversity or hardness of heart.

78. Compare, for example, Augustine's struggle for continence and his agonized prayer that God give him chastity—"but not yet;" *Confessions*, tr. Edward Pusey (New York: Macmillan Publishing Co., 1961), Bk VIII, p. 125.

79. Adoro devote, latens veritas,
   te qui sub his formis vere latitas:
   tibi se cor meum totum subicit,
   quia te contemplans totum deficit.

   Visus, gustus, tactus in te fallitur;
   sed solus auditus tute creditur.
   credo quicquid dixit Dei filius:
   nihil veritatis verbo verius.

   In cruce latebat sola deitas;
   sed hic latet simul et humanitas.
   ambo tamen credens atque confitens
   peto quod petivit latro poenitens.

   Plagas, sicut Thomas, non intueor;
   meum tamen Deum te confiteor.
   fac me tibi semper magis credere,
   in te spem habere, te diligere.

   O memoriale mortis Domini,
   panis veram vitam praestans homini,
   praesta meae menti de te vivere,
   et te illi semper dulce sapere.

   Pie pelicane, Iesu Domine,
   me immundum munda tuo sanguine,
   cuius una stilla alvum facere
   totum mundum posset omni scelere.

   Iesu, quem velatum nunc aspicio,
   quando fiet illud quod tam cupio,
   ut te revelata cernens facie
   visu sim beatus tuae gloriae?

80. R. Garrigou-Lagrange, *God, His Existence and Nature*, 5th ed., tr. Dom Bede Rose (St. Louis, Mo.: Herder, 1955), p. 540.

81. Ibid., p. 546.

82. Ibid., p. 547.
83. *ST* I–II, q. 112, a. 1; cf. *ST* I, q. 38, a. 2.
84. *ST* I–II, q. 86.
85. I am indebted to Robert Adams, William Mann, George Mavrodes, Alvin Plantinga, Philip Quinn, Richard Swinburne, Charles Taliaferro, and Thomas Tracy for comments or suggestions. I am especially grateful to Norman Kretzmann for his many helpful comments on an earlier draft of this paper.

BIBILIOGRAPHY

Many of the articles and books I consulted before writing this paper I did not have occasion to cite in the paper itself. This is a short list of the works I found most interesting or helpful on the topics covered in this paper.

Bracken, W. Jerome. *Why Suffering in Redemption? A New Interpretation of the Theology of the Passion in the Summa Theologica, 3, 46–49, by Thomas Aquinas*. Ph. D. Dissertation, Fordham University, 1978.

Crotty, Nicholas. "The Redemptive Role of Christ's Resurrection." *The Thomist* 25 (1962):54–106.

Daly, Mary. *The Notion of Justification in the Commentary of St. Thomas Aquinas on the Epistle to the Romans*. Ph. D. dissertation, Marquette University, 1971.

De la Trinité, Philippe. *What is Redemption?* Tr. Anthony Armstrong. New York: Hawthorn Books, 1961.

Dittoe, John T. "Sacramental Incorporation into the Mystical Body." *The Thomist* 9 (1946):469–514.

Lawler, Michael. "Grace and Free Will in Justification: A Textual Study in Aquinas." *The Thomist* 35 (1971):601–630.

Lonergan, Bernard. *Grace and Freedom: Operative Grace in the Thought of St. Thomas Aquinas*. Ed. J. Patout Burns. New York: Herder and Herder, 1970.

Lynn, William D. *Christ's Redemptive Merit: The Nature of its Causality According to St. Thomas. Analecta Gregoriana* 115, Series Facultatis Theologicae: sectio B, n. 37. Rome: Gregorian University, 1962.

Marinelli, Francesco. *Segno e Realita. Studi di sacramentaria tomista*. Rome: Lateranum, 1977.

McCormack, Stephen. "The Configuration of the Sacramental Character." *The Thomist* 7 (1944):458–491.

Moore, Sebastian. *The Crucified is No Stranger*. London: Darton, Longman and Todd Ltd., 1977.

O'Leary, Joseph M. *The Development of the Doctrine of St. Thomas Aquinas on the Passion and Death of Our Lord*. Chicago: J. S. Paluch Co., Inc., 1952.

Parente, Pietro. *De verbo incarnato*. 3rd ed. Rome: Marietti, 1949.

Rivière, Jean. *The Doctrine of the Atonement: A Historical Essay*. Tr. Luigi Cappadelta. St. Louis, Mo.: Herder, 1909.

Schleck, Charles A. "St. Thomas on the Nature of Sacramental Grace." *The Thomist* 18 (1955):1–30 and 242–278.

Separation and Reversal in Luke-Acts

MARILYN McCORD ADAMS

We Christians are dedicated to the proposition that while God and evil can coexist in the same world, evil is no match for the creator. God has evil "under control": From eternity he envisioned and even now he is implementing a plan which will guarantee him and his beneficiaries the ultimate and consummate victory. We also believe that God, in his mercy, has given us more than a hint of his strategy. For this revelation, the Bible is our principal source, with two others being the tradition of Christian experience and reflection throughout the ages, and the testimony of the Holy Spirit in our hearts. These presuppositions issue in a methodological moral for Christian philosophers: If we want to understand how God is solving the problem of suffering, we do well to mine the ore of scripture and tradition for insights into his saving work.

Some of us have accepted this "historical" assignment willingly enough, but with an emphasis on tradition, which from almost the beginning was formed by fellow-philosophers whose language we more or less readily speak. For my part, I think it is time to break disciplinary ranks and trespass into the field of New Testament studies. While scripture underdetermines doctrine, and doctrine underdetermines philosophical theology and Christian philosophy, such an excursus may offer philosophers a fresh perspective from which to correct or reinforce our own strategies.[1]

Luke-Acts is a good place to start because of its scope and probable time of composition. This two-volume work traces the redemptive hand of God not only in the ministry of Jesus but also during the first generation of the church. Moreover, most recent scholarship dates Luke-Acts between 80–90 A.D.,[2] in the midst of the crisis created for Israel by the second destruction of Jerusalem. The Romans destroyed the symbols of national identity (the city and its temple) and banished Jews from the place. The long seige dehumanized the inhabitants, even to the point of cannibalism. Such horrors urgently raised for Israel then the questions that Nazi Germany poses for us: What is/was God doing? Why did he let it happen? How can God's faithfulness, his will and power to save his people, be discerned in current events?[3]

Luke-Acts offers its audience the reassurance that everything has happened according to "the definite plan and foreknowledge of God" (Acts 2:23) and that his redemptive purpose will triumph through it. In what follows. I try to bring the soteriological plot of Luke-Acts into clear focus and explore points of contrast between it and its contemporary competitors. The result will expose the Luke-Acts picture of God's goodness, of how and to what extent he intends to rescue his people from the power of darkness.

APOCALYTICISM AND THE TWO-AGE THEORY

Jewish apocalyptic theology offered one interpretation of how God was being faithful to his people, despite their experience of abuse and oppression by the ungodly. Briefly, apocalypticism posits (1) a double distinction—between groups of people, the righteous and the wicked, and the two ages, the one old and present and the other new and yet to come. It explains that (2) in the present age, injustice prevails: the righteous suffer and the wicked prosper. It warns that (3) things will get worse before they get better; for while the old age is "wearing out" and coming to an end, it will not do so until it bears the full fruits of its unrighteousness. Typically, these involve undoing the very works of God in creation: cosmic upheavals with falling stars and planets, and geological reversals with mountains leveled and valleys raised. To the righteous suffering in the present, apocalypticism (4) counsels patient endurance and (5) offers the hope that when God comes to inaugurate the new age, the scales of retributive justice will be set right. There will be a separation of the righteous from the wicked and a reversal of destinies: the wicked will be confined to torture chambers to suffer, either eternally (as in the book of Revelation) or until they wither away to nothingness (as in 1 Enoch); while the righteous will be ushered into heavenly palaces to enjoy the light of God's company. Such consolation is available to the righteous, because (the two-age theory assumes) "they know who they are." Further, whereas now the wicked mock God and his people with flagrant abuse, in the age to come the righteous will be able to take satisfaction in the sufferings of the wicked, and enjoy the revenge God has taken on their behalf.

As a solution to the problem of evil, apocalyptic theology shares the defects of a grade B Western: the plot is too simplistic, assuming as it does a clear-cut separation of people into the "good guys" and the "bad guys." At one level, this is overly optimistic: the righteous are presented as mere victims, who are encouraged to locate the source of their problems entirely outside themselves. Once they are in a new environment, separated from external evil forces, everything will be pure bliss. At bottom, however, apocalyptic theology is highly pessimistic. God's victory over evil and the meaning of the experience of the present age is understood solely in terms of retributive justice: in the next age he will make sure that people will get the rewards and punishments they deserve for their performance in this one. But at a deeper level, this seems to mean a kind of defeat for God: there are some people, some states of affairs that he cannot turn to good. The forces of evil so dominate the present age as to make it irredeemable. God's only recourse is to revert to his strategy in the days of Noah: to destroy the whole thing (except for a righteous remnant) and start over (his promise in the rainbow notwithstanding)! Although God can separate the wicked and cut off their power to afflict the righteous, suffering and hatred last as long as the reprobate do. And if joy is banned from hell, rejoicing in evil continues (at least for a time) in heaven where the righteous are allowed the pleasures of revenge. This conceded, one wonders how long heavenly peace and bliss will last! Like revolution in politics, apocalypticism looks forward to a simple reversal in which different groups control power and prosperity. It looks for a change in caste, but not an end to separation. Such a game-plan seems neither subtle enough nor successful (much less loving) enough for God!

APOCALYPTIC ELEMENTS IN LUKE-ACTS

Or is it? For better or worse, apocalypticism is not entirely absent from the New Testament. Not only does the book of Revelation fall squarely within this genre; scholars[4] have argued that apocalyptic thinking pervades the synoptic gospels themselves. Focusing on our topic, Luke-Acts, we find (1) *a division of ages* in Jesus' remark, "The law and the prophets were until John; since then the good news of the kingdom of God is preached" (Luke 16:16). John the Baptist is the more-than-prophetic herald of the new age (Luke 7:2–27; cf. 1:76; 3:4–6, 15–16), but is not himself a member of the new age (Luke 7:28). On the other hand, Jesus is *the promised Davidic Messiah* in whom the everlasting reign of God will be established (Luke 1:32, 68–69; 2:4, 11, 26, 29–32; 3:31; 4:41; 9:20; 18:38; 20:41–44; Acts 2:25–36; 13:22–25, 33–37); He is *the chosen Son of God* (Luke 1:32, 35; 3:38; 4:3, 9, 41; 9:35; 22:70; cf.

Acts 9:20); He is *the apocalyptic Son of Man*, who exercises his "authority on earth to forgive sins" (Luke 5:24; 8:48-50; cf. Acts 7:60) and his lordship over the Sabbath (Luke 6:5), "who shall be seated at the right hand of the power of God" (Luke 22:69; cf. Acts 7:56), whose "coming at an unexpected hour" (Luke 12:40) "in a cloud with power and great glory" (Luke 21:27; Acts 1:11) will be as obvious as lightning (Luke 17:22-24, 37), will be accompanied by cosmic upheavals (Luke 21:33), and will bring judgment (Luke 21:36). Loyalty to him before men will bring acknowledgment by him before the angels of God, but denial of him will merit denial (Luke 12:8-9) and destruction (Luke 17:26-30; cf. John the Baptist's sermon, Luke 3:17).

(2) According to Luke-Acts, the Kingdom of God will be marked by a *reversal of fates*. Mary's Magnificat celebrates God's preference for the humble, the powerless, and the poor over the proud, the mighty, and the rich (Luke 1:46-55). Jesus' inaugural sermon proclaims that the good news is for the outcasts — the poor, the captive, and oppressed, the blind, etc. (Luke 4:17-19). And Jesus pronounces eschatological blessings on the poor, the hungry, the mournful, and those persecuted for loyalty to him, eschatological woes on the rich, the laughing, and those now enjoying human favor (Luke 6:20-26). Overall, in the judgment, "some are last who will be first, and some are first who will be last" (Luke 13:30).

(3) Likewise, *the apocalyptic theme of fruit-bearing* runs through the gospel of Luke (3:7-8, 17; 8:9-15; 13:6-9). And Jesus announces the eschatological harvest (Luke 10:2).

Again, (4) there are passages which suggest *a final separation* of the righteous and the wicked, with blessings for the former and destruction for the latter. John the Baptist forecasts that the Lord will come with geological upheavals (Luke 3:5), warns his audience to flee from "the wrath to come" (Luke 3:7), and proclaims of the Christ,

> His winnowing fork is in his hand to clear his threshing floor, and to gather the wheat into his granary, but the chaff he will burn with unquenchable fire. (Luke 3:17)

In the judgment, the Son of Man will acknowledge those who acknowledged him and deny those who denied him before the angels of God (Luke 12:10). At the end of the Sermon on the Plain, Jesus admonishes that those who do not build their lives on obedience to his words will be like ruined houses (Luke 3:46-49), and prophesies that it will be worse for unresponsive cities "in the judgment" than it was for Tyre and Sidon; that Capernaum will even be brought down to Hades (Luke 10:13-15). After the Beelzebul controversy, Jesus pronounces an anticipatory sentence on "this evil generation," saying that the Queen of the South and the men of Ninevah will condemn it "in the judgment" (Luke 11:32). There are first eschatological woes for the Pharisees (Luke 11:37-44; cf. 12:1-3) and lawyers (Luke 11:46-52) and later a prediction that in the judgment the scribes "will receive the greater condemnation" (Luke 20:45-47). Jesus renders the verdict over Jerusalem that its "house is forsaken" (Luke 13:34-35), and predicts the consequent destruction of the Temple (Luke 21:5-9) and the city (Luke 21:20-24; 23:28-31). The parable of the returning householder speaks of the heavy and light beatings due to wittingly and unwittingly disobedient servants (Luke 12:41-48); the parable of the fig tree echoes John the Baptist's sermon (Luke 3:9) with its warning that the unfruitful will be cut down (Luke 13:6-9); the parable of the householder who shuts the door against late comers warns that some may find themselves "thrust out" to "weep and gnash their teeth" (Luke 13:25-28); the parable of the banquet threatens that none of the originally invited guests shall taste the meal (Luke 14:16-24); the story of the rich man and Lazarus tells of "a great chasm" which "has been fixed" to prevent travel between the torture chambers of Hades and the bosom of Abraham (Luke 16:17-31); the Lucan version of the parable of the pounds has the king slay those who refused his reign (Luke 19:11-26); the parable of the wicked tenants predicts that "the owner" "will come and destroy those tenants and give the vineyard to others" (Luke 20:16); the simile of the cornerstone warns of destruction for those who reject the gospel (Luke 20:18). Again, Jesus prophesies that the day of the Son of Man will bring division within households (Luke 18:33-35) and destruction for the unsuspecting wicked (Luke 18:27, 29). Likewise, Peter's first sermon exhorts hearers to save themselves from "this crooked generation" (Acts 2:40), and his second threatens that those who do not listen to Jesus, the "prophet like unto Moses," "shall be destroyed from the people" (Acts 3:23; cf. Acts 13:40-41). On the other side, those who hear the word of God and keep it receive blessing (Luke 11:28; cf. Acts 3:19, 25-26), and the disciples who have continued with Jesus through many trials will "sit on thrones judging the twelve tribes of Israel" (Luke 22:28-30).

(5) Likewise, the gospel is dotted with *questions about the eschatological scenario* so typical of apocalyptic literature. Jesus, cast as the principal apocalyptic revealer, is asked, "Lord, will those who are saved be few?" (Luke 13:23). Likewise, the Pharisees inquire about time-table (Luke 17:20), and Jesus offers a number of enigmatic remarks about "when?" (Luke 12:40; 17:20-21; 19:11; 21:32; 22:69; 23:43; Acts 1:6-7), as well as warnings to his audiences to read the signs of the times (Luke 12:54-56). Again, the disciples ask, "where?" and are assured that when the time comes, it will be obvious (Luke 17:37; cf. 17:22-24).

Do we face the prospect that Luke-Acts simply offers us a repackaging of the two-age theory and inherits all of its limitations? Despite the above evidence, there are important features of the text which do not fit this hypothesis. If the ministry of Jesus inaugurates a new age, final division and reversal of fates, with bliss for the righteous poor and torment for the arrogant wicked, is not immediately put into place according to apocalyptic specifications. Moreover, not all of the Son-of-Man sayings in Luke-Acts depict him in full regalia: Not everybody recognizes him — the present generation find the Son of Man, who comes eating and drinking, to be "a glutton and a drunkard" (Luke 7:34–35; cf. Dt. 21:18–21); and Jerusalem does not know the hour of its visitation (Luke 19:44). Three times, (Luke 9:22, 30, 44; 18:31–33; cf. 24:6–7), Jesus predicts:

> The Son of man must suffer many things and be rejected by the elders and chief priests and scribes, and be killed, and on the third day be raised.

One of his own disciples will betray him into the hands of these enemies with a kiss (Luke 22:22, 48). In the meantime, "the Son of Man has nowhere to lay his head" (Luke 9:58), in his relentless pursuit of "the lost" (Luke 19:10). Such features have no place in the plot-line of conventional apocalyptic. Is another discernible in the text of Luke-Acts?

THE PLOT OF LUKE-ACTS: A PRELIMINARY LOOK

According to Luke-Acts, Jesus did come proclaiming the Kingdom of God, the inauguration of a new age. But in his view, it is a divine revolution aimed at reconciliation, an end of separation. This is God's game-plan, ironical in reversing the expectations not only of the two-age theory, but of the complacent conventional religion of his opponents as well.

Reversal of the Criteria for Citizenship

Internal versus External: In various official and unofficial ways, conventional religion made inclusion in God's people contingent upon externals. Traditional embellishments of Levitical codes (regarding priesthood) made physical defects — e.g., crushed hands or feet (Lev. 22:19), damaged sexual organs (Lev. 22:20), skin blemishes or bodily discharges (Lev. 12–15), being hunch-backed, lame, blind (Lev. 22:18–20), etc. — *sufficient conditions of exclusion*. Again, women are at best second class citizens, often numbered with the cattle among a man's possessions.[5] Further, tradition elaborated scriptural prescriptions for tithing, fasting, cleanliness of vessels, and Sabbath rest, while practice turned such observances into *necessary and sufficient* marks of election. And practice turned the natural advantages of wealth into a sign of *religious privilege*. As these conditions or their absence is clearly certifiable, it was possible for individuals to be self-confident of their religious position. And, given the Levitical assumption that ritual impurity is "catching" by contact (Lev. 7:19; 11:24, 39; 14:46; 15:8, 11, 22–24, 27), the pious felt justified in separating themselves from those who failed to "measure up" to these standards. These latter attitudes were natural breeding grounds for religious pride and contempt for others.

Throughout his ministry, Jesus reverses the primary religious focus from the outside to the inside, back to the Deuteronomic and prophetic injunction to whole-hearted love of God and correlative love of neighbor (Luke 10:25–28; 11:42). God looks on the heart and its fruits (external works rooted in heart-attitudes) (Luke 6:43–45; 8:9–15; cf. John the Baptist's sermon, 3:8–9). And he contradicts his opponents' externalization of religion by precept and example.

Poverty, gender, and physical deformity, so far from exclusionary, make people nodal points of intimate contact with the reign of God. Jesus' inaugural sermon announces that the good news of the reign of God is to be directed primarily at religious outcasts—the poor, the captives, the blind, and oppressed (Luke 4:18–19). Likewise, in the Sermon on the Plain, he pronounces blessings on the poor, the hungry, the weeping, the hated and excluded, and woes on the rich, the filled, the laughing (Luke 6:20–26; cf. the Magnificat Luke 1:46–55). And he exhorts the Pharisees to imitate God by inviting "the poor, the maimed, the lame, the blind" to their feasts (Luke 14:13). The Lucan Jesus consistently maintains that so far from being an asset, wealth poses special temptations and requires cautious stewardship (cf. Luke 16; 18:18–30).

Moreover, Jesus demonstrates *God's willingness to reverse the putative disqualifying conditions* by his miracles: He exorcizes demons (Luke 4:33–37, 41; 8:26–39); heals lepers (Luke 5:12–15; 17:11–19), the woman with the issue of blood (Luke 8:42–48), and the man with dropsy (a disease associated with immorality, Luke 14:1–6); releases the paralytic (Luke 5:17–26) and the woman who had suffered with spinal curvature for eighteen years (Luke 13:10–17); restores sight to the blind (Luke 18:43) and functioning to the man with the withered hand (Luke 6:6–11). The disciples are sent off to exorcize and to heal (Luke 9:1–2, 6; 10:9, 17–20), and Peter and John begin their post-Pentecost ministries by healing a lame man (Acts 3:1–16; cf. 5:12–16; 8:6–7, 12–13).

With elaborate sense of humor, women are woven into the inner circle of the plot—as the first prophets (Elizabeth and Mary, Luke 1:41–55;

Acts 2:18), as among those who travelled with and supported Jesus' itinerant ministry (Luke 8:1-3), as witnesses to the crucifixion (Luke 23:49) and the first to testify to the resurrection (Luke 24:1-12); they are numbered among the beneficiaries of his healing ministry (Luke 8:42-48; 13:10-17) and among the gathering crowds (Luke 11:27-28; 23:28-31), and commended as illustrations (Luke 7:36-50; 15:8-10).

To proclaim the truth that *holiness is both more contagious and less fragile than pollution*, Jesus touches or is touched by the leper (Luke 5:13), the bier of the widow of Nain's son (Luke 7:14), Jairus' dead daughter (Luke 8:54; cf. His treatment of the priest and the Levite in the parable of the Good Samaritan, Luke 10:31-32), the sinful woman at Simon's dinner party (Luke 7:39), the woman with an issue of blood (Luke 8:43-48), and the man with dropsy (Luke 14:2-6). He calls Levi the tax collector as a disciple (Luke 4:27-28), and regularly eats and drinks with tax collectors and sinners (Luke 4:29-32; 7:34; 15:1-2ff.; 19:1-9). Peter's vision at Joppa suspends kosher food laws (Acts 10:9-16). Cleansing by the Holy Spirit cancels the ban against social intercourse between Jews and Gentiles (Acts 11:18; 15:1-29, esp. 8).

By contrast, Jesus pronounces eschatological woes against those Pharisees, whose reliance on external rituals only masks decay within (Luke 11:44); those who clean the outside of the cup and dish, while failing to care for the poor from the heart (Luke 11:37-41); who tithe everything in sight, but neglect justice and the love of God (Luke 11:42); who look to human approval of the facade rather than God's judgment on the heart (Luke 11:43). Likewise, those lawyers are denounced who embroider the fine points of the law, while harboring murderous intentions toward God's prophets (Luke 11:45-52).

Pre-established Righteousness versus Repentance and the Forgiveness of Sins: Having externalized religion, Jesus' opponents regard salvation as something to which they (at least non-defective, economically solvent males) can gain *entitlement* by scrupulous observance (cf. the elder brother of the prodigal son in Luke 15:25-32, and the "unprofitable servants" of Luke 17:7-10). At least for the conscientious, external law-keeping, if strenuous, still lies within one's voluntary control. Conventional religion slides into regarding salvation as only the just payment for such efforts.

If God's attention is on the heart, however, pre-established righteousness is impossible, because emotions and attitudes, such as anger, jealousy, hatred, vindictiveness, contempt, and arrogance, lie no more within an agent's voluntary control than do lameness or blindness. Hence, Jesus joins his first reversal of criteria, from external to internal, with a second, from pre-established righteousness to *repentance and the for-*

giveness of sins. This is the content of John the Baptist's sermon (Luke 3:3; 3:8-9; cf. Zechariah's prophecy thereof in the Benedictus in 1:77). Likewise, when criticized for eating and drinking with "tax collectors and sinners," Jesus replies, "I have not come to call the righteous but sinners to repentance" (Luke 5:32); similarly, Jesus explains his approach to Zacchaeus with the comment, "The Son of Man came to seek and to save the lost" (Luke 19:10). Approach to God does not require that one become righteous first, but only recognition of oneself as a sinner and desire for reconciliation with God. Being thus loved by God begins the work of changing the sinner's heart—the weeping woman at Simon's feast loves much because she has been forgiven much; those who have not had such an interchange with God, having been "forgiven little, love little" (Luke 7:47)—and opens the way for fruits befitting repentance (cf. Luke 3:8-14; 19:8-9). And the post-Pentecost sermons extend the same offer of salvation by repentance and the forgiveness of sins (Acts 2:38-42; 3:19; 5:31)

Natural versus Supernatural Ties: Judaism was in many ways a family religion: its promises were to Abraham, Isaac, and Jacob and their descendants, to David and his dynasty. Since the days of Ezra and through the Greek and Maccabean periods, there were those who believed that faithfulness to God required *separation* from the Gentiles.[6] And religious complacency drifted into the assumption that heredity might be enough.

Such nationalism is consistently contradicted in Luke-Acts, for the real criterion is the acceptance of God's purpose for oneself (Luke 7:30; 8:19-21; 11:27-28). Simeon prophesies that Jesus will be "a sign for the fall and rising of many *in Israel*" (Luke 2:34), John the Baptist warns that "God is able from these stones to raise up children to Abraham" (Luke 3:8). The turn-about reception of Jesus in Nazareth precipitates his observation, "no prophet is acceptable in his own country" (Luke 4:24), and the response of neighboring Capernaum eventually prompts his judgment that the city will be dragged down to Hades (Luke 10:15). By contrast, already in the gospel, the (presumably Gentile) centurion is praised for a faith that exceeds Israel's (Luke 7:1-10), and the healed Gerasene becomes the first foreign missionary to spread work of the mighty works of Jesus (Luke 8:39). And Acts presents the rapid spread of the gospel among the Gentiles and their reception of the Holy Spirit as part of the definite plan and foreknowledge of God (Acts 10:1-11:21).

So far as immediate natural family is concerned, Simeon declares to Mary that "a sword will pierce through your own soul also" (Luke 2:35). Jesus recognizes God as his true father at age twelve (Luke 2:48-49), repeatedly identifies the family of God on whom the eschatological blessings will fall as composed of *those who hear the word of God and keep it* (Luke 8:19-21; 11:27-28). The message of Jesus will divide households (Luke 10:51-53). The disciple, too, faces similar alienation of natural ties: hating of "father and mother and wife and children and brothers and sisters" (Luke 14:26-27) and the renunciation of "all that he has" (Luke 14:33) for the sake of the gospel.

The Reversal of Order of Entry

Reversal of criteria for admission results in a reversal of populations who enter easily. Whereas external criteria were designed by and for the scrupulous and exclusive, the offer of salvation by the forgiveness of sins is open to all. This surprising news finds its most enthusiastic reception, not among the self-righteous whose capital was thereby devalued, but among outcasts—in Jesus' litany, "the poor, the maimed, the blind, the lame" (Luke 14:21), as well as to tax collectors and others with sins so obvious as to make self-deception impossible.

Thus, God's saving work finds its beginning among the righteous poor—an aged childless couple (Luke 1:5-25, 57-80) "righteous before God" and "blameless" (Luke 1:6), and an unmarried girl (Luke 1:26-56) and her betrothed who conform to the post-partem rites of purification and circumcision (Luke 2:22-35). It is hailed by the aged prophet Simeon, who was "righteous and devout, looking for the consolation of Israel" (Luke 2:25) and an eighty-four year old widow who spread the news to "all who were looking for the redemption of Jerusalem" (Luke 2:36-38). Likewise, such unsavory characters as shepherds rejoiced to be included by the angelic birth announcement (Luke 2:8-18). The multitudes (Luke 3:10), the tax collectors (Luke 3:12, 7:29), and soldiers (Luke 3:14) readily acknowledged their sinfulness and their need of God, and accepted God's purpose for themselves by submitting to the baptism of John (cf. Luke 7:29). Crowds flock to Jesus for teaching and healing (Luke 4:32, 36, 42; 5:15; 6:19). A leper (Luke 5:12-14), a paralytic's friends (Luke 4:18-20, 24), a Gentile centurion (Luke 7:1-10) are among the first to respond in faith. Fishermen (Luke 5:1-11) and Levi the tax-collector (Luke 4:27-28) accept his call to discipleship. Moreover, outcasts surprised by God's love are more easily thankful. Thus, the sinful woman loves and serves Jesus (Luke 7:37-38, 44-47), while Simon the Pharisee is rude and judgmental (Luke 7:36, 39, 44). And the Samaritan leper is the only one who returns to give thanks (Luke 17:11-19). The humble widow renders to God "her whole living" (Luke 21:4).

By contrast, those heavily invested in proving their own righteousness through external observance, will find it very difficult to admit they are sinners in need of divine forgiveness. The prodigal son is more readily reconciled with his father than the elder brother is (Luke 15:11-32). In the parable of the banquet, Jesus warns that by refusing to respond to God's invitation, the religious establishment may forfeit its place to the poor, the maimed, the blind, and lame (Luke 14:21) and even to Gentiles (Luke 14:23) who will accept it. The whole thrust of the book of Acts is that although the gospel is repeatedly taken to the Jews first, it repeatedly takes root more readily among the Gentiles. Jesus tells the parable of the Pharisee and the publican against the establishment, because they "trusted in themselves that they were righteous and despised others" (Luke 18:9; cf. 9-14), and declares the publican the one who "went down to his house justified" (Luke 18:14).

Role-reversal for the Elect

More surprises await us when we examine Luke-Acts' answer to the question, "elect for what?"

To be sure, Luke-Acts shares with the apocalyptic literature the idea that the elect will suffer in the present at the hands of those who reject God's purpose for their lives. Jesus himself, the righteous one par excellence (cf. the centurion's confession, Luke 23:47; Acts 3:14; 7:52; 22:14), forecasts that his proclamation of the Kingdom of God will lead to persecution and death at the hands of the religious establishment (cf. esp. Luke 9:22, 30-31, 44; 18:24-25). His disciples, who act in his name (Luke 10:16; cf. Acts 5:40-42) can expect the same:

> If any man would come after me, let him deny himself and take up his cross daily and follow me. For whoever would save his life will lose it; and whoever loses his life for my sake, he will save it. For what does it profit a man if he gains the whole world and loses or forfeits himself? (Luke 9:23-25)

Jesus commissions the twelve and then the seventy to go out and preach the Kingdom of God, giving them authority over demons to cure all diseases (Luke 9:1-2, 6; 10:17-20), but they are warned that their message will meet with a divided response: some will accept, and others reject (Luke 9:4-5; 10:5-11), and the latter will persecute them (Luke 21:12-19). This prediction is verified in Acts, where the disciples' testimony to Jesus wins them both converts and hostilities from the beginning to the end of the book.

Moreover, Luke-Acts agrees with conventional apocalyptic that the consummate vindication of the righteous will not happen before the hearts of the wicked bear their full fruit. The ministries of John the

Baptist, of Jesus, and later of the disciples accelerate this process, as people judge themselves by their response to these divine agents. John confronts his audience with:

> You brood of vipers! Who warned you to flee from the wrath to come? Bear fruits that befit repentance. . . . (Luke 3:7-8; cf. 3:17)

Later Luke offers a summary evaluation:

> All the people and tax collectors justified God, having been baptized with the baptism of John; but the Pharisees and the lawyers rejected the purpose of God for themselves, not having been baptized by him. (Luke 7:29-30)

Jesus sees the same pattern of response to his ministry as well: "wisdom is justified by all her children" (Luke 7:35) but "the men of this generation" will neither dance to his piping nor mourn with John the Baptist (Luke 7:31-34). Shifting the contrast from that between good fruits and bad to fruitfulness versus barrenness, the allegorical rendering of the Sower charts the range of this division (Luke 8:9-15), and the parable of the fig tree warns that the season remaining before the harvest is short (Luke 13:6-9; cf. Luke 10:2). And audiences throughout the book of Acts divide themselves in reaction to the disciples' testimony to Jesus.

Nevertheless, from here on, the plots diverge significantly: for where apocalyptic theology assumes the competence of the righteous to judge and discriminate the wicked from the holy and reinforces their tendency to include themselves among the elect, Jesus warns his disciples, "Judge not, and you will not be judged" (Luke 6:37). His rationale for this advice is two-fold and simple: The disciples, admitted into the Kingdom by repentance and the forgiveness of sins and not on the basis of pre-established righteousness, are themselves sinners whose faults obstruct their vision for the present (Luke 22:29-30) and thereby disqualify them from judging others (Luke 6:39-42). Second, the attempt to judge others drives a person deeper into sin. Those Pharisees "who trusted in themselves that they were righteous" were blind to their own "extortion and wickedness" (Luke 11:39), their "neglect" of "justice and the love of God" (Luke 11:42; cf. 18:11) and compounded the felonies of arrogance and complacency with the sin of contempt (Luke 18:9). Hence self-righteousness is the most disqualifying sin of all, insofar as it hinders a person from acknowledging (and hence from repenting of) his sins and so entering the Kingdom!

Further, where apocalyptic theology finds in the prospect of divine revenge a legitimation of hatred and vindictiveness toward the wicked, Jesus' disciples are to follow him in imitating the Father, who is "merciful"

(Luke 6:35) and "kind to the ungrateful and the selfish" (Luke 6:36).
Jesus commands his disciples to

> Love your enemies, do good to those who hate you, bless those who curse
> you, pray for those who abuse you. . . . (Luke 6:28; 29–36)

In this, they only pass on to others the favor God has already done for
them by including them in his Kingdom; thus, they are to pray, "forgive
us our sins, for we ourselves forgive everyone who is indebted to us"
(Luke 11:4). Jesus himself sets the example, as he prays for his killers,
"Father, forgive them; for they know not what they do" (Luke 23:34)
and is imitated by Stephen at his martyrdom (Acts 7:60). Likewise, repentance and the forgiveness of sins is to be the continuing rule within the
community:

> Take heed to yourselves; if your brother sins, rebuke him, and if he repents,
> forgive him; and if he sins against you seven times and says, "I repent,"
> you must forgive him. (Luke 17:3–4)

Finally, in the apocalyptic scenario, the fruit-bearing of the wicked
has no *redemptive* significance: their hearts are exposed for *condemnation*, not rehabilitation. In Luke-Acts, this situation is reversed. For the
disciples, persecution is a testing ground; fidelity to Jesus in the face of
hostilities constitutes the losing of one's life to find it (Luke 9:24–25;
6:22–23) and will win them acknowledgment by Jesus before the angels
of God (Luke 12:10). As the trials of discipleship so transform their
hearts that they are willing to lose their lives for the redemption of the
wicked, they are thereby fitted to sit in judgment over the twelve tribes
of Israel (Luke 22:28–29). For the wicked, "acting out" their inner attitudes on Jesus and the disciples who love and forgive them provides an
occasion for them to see who they really are, to recognize their sin and
their need of God, and to repent. The works themselves bear witness
against pretensions of righteousness. And to these, the disciples, like
Jesus, are to add the testimony of their words. When rejected, they are
not to call down fire from heaven onto the rejecting towns and villages
(Luke 9:54–55), but to shake the dust off their feet (Luke 9:5; 10:11; cf.
Acts 13:51) and to declare that "the kingdom of God has come near"
(Luke 10:11). Finally, the rejection of the gospel by presumed insiders
occasions its extension to outsiders: within the ministry of Jesus to reli-
gious outcasts—to the maimed, the ritually impure, and to public sinners (e.g. Luke 14:15–24, 19:1–10); in the early church, to Samaritans
(Acts 8:4–8) and then to Gentiles (Acts 10ff.)

The aftermath of the crucifixion plays out this scenario. The religious leaders win the temporary collaboration of the people in demand-

ing of Pilate the death of Jesus (Luke 23:13–25). But at Golgotha, the people stand by watching, while the rulers continue to blaspheme (Luke 23:35). They see Jesus pray for their forgiveness (Luke 23:34), exercise his kingly authority to admit the repentant criminal into paradise (Luke 23:39–43), and in an act of trust commit his spirit to the Father (Luke 23:46). They hear the centurion's verdict, "Certainly this man was righteous" (Luke 23:47). Although neither the religious leaders nor the people appreciated the full import of what they were doing (Luke 23:34; Acts 3:17), "all the multitudes who assembled to see the sight" begin to "catch on" by the end of the scene; "when they saw what had taken place, [they] returned home beating their breasts" (Luke 23:48). In his Pentecost sermon, Peter confronts the crowd with a blunt characterization of their deed:

> Men of Israel, hear these words: Jesus of Nazareth, a man attested to you by God with mighty works and wonders and signs which God did through him in your midst, as you yourselves know—this Jesus, delivered up according to the definite plan and foreknowledge of God, you crucified and killed by the hands of lawless men. But God raised him up, having loosed the pangs of death, because it was not possible for him to be held by it. . . . Let all the house of Israel know assuredly that God has made him both Lord and Christ, this Jesus whom you crucified. (Acts 2:22–24, 36)

The "devout" Jews "from every nation under heaven" (Acts 2:5),

> when they heard this . . . were cut to the heart, and said, "Brethren, what shall we do?" And Peter said to them, "Repent, and be baptized every one of you in the name of Jesus Christ for the forgiveness of your sins; and you shall receive the gift of the Holy Spirit. For the promise is to you and to your children and to all that are far off, every one whom the Lord God calls to him." (Acts 2:37–39)

Acts reports that three thousand responded to Peter's message (Acts 2:41) and two thousand more to his sermon occasioned by the healing of the man lame from birth (Acts 4:4). By contrast, the religious rulers in Jerusalem are first annoyed (Acts 4:2) and then filled with jealousy (Acts 5:17), first warn the apostles not to teach in the name of Jesus (Acts 4:18) and then imprison them (Acts 5:18). When their rage leads to the stoning of Stephen (Acts 7:54–60) and "a great persecution against the church in Jerusalem" (Acts 8:1), the resultant emigration spreads the gospel first to Samaria (Acts 8:4–8) and then to the Gentiles (cf. Acts 10ff.). Paul's ministry meets with a similarly divided response (Acts 13:45ff.). By contrast with apocalyptic theology, the plot of Luke-Acts thus celebrates the resourceful irony of divine goodness which turns every hostile response into a wider opportunity for reconciliation and redemption!

GOD'S LAST WORD: MERCY AND/OR WRATH?

Or does it? Does the script of Luke-Acts make God's last word univocally one of mercy? We are not entitled to this conclusion, unless we can give some coherent account of the passages (mentioned in the second section above) which speak of judgment, wrath, and destruction for the impenitent.

A Prophetic Interpretation of History

Such an explanation seems partially possible when we reconsider the historical context within which Luke-Acts was written: between 80-90 A.D., in the aftermath of the second destruction of, and exile of Jews from, Jerusalem. Apocalypticism encourages the oppressed to look for the source of such evil without, in the enemy (in this case, the Roman Empire). Without denying the wickedness of the conquering powers, the prophets always urged self-examination. According to them, political reversals occur, most fundamentally, because God allows them as punishment for national apostasy. The scriptures most quoted by Luke-Acts — Moses, the prophets, and the psalms (Luke 24:44) — chart the development of God's relations with his people — see the chart on page 107. Psalms 78 and 106 chart the repetition of this pattern. It is one in which disobedience has harsh consequences — the most staggering having been the forty year wilderness period and the first destruction of Jerusalem, along with the Babylonian exile — but in which God's last word is mercy and reconciliation. Some later prophecy looked forward to such an overflowing of divine mercy as would not stop with a definitive restoration of Jews to Jerusalem, but would move on to incorporate even the Gentiles into the gracious reign of God (cf. Jeremiah 12:15-16; 16:19; 43:39; Isaiah 40-55, 60:1-19).[7]

With all this in mind, David L. Tiede speculates that the attempt to locate the root of the trouble within Israel led to mutual accusations among the various factions of Judaism.[8] The Pharisees and Sadducees might have laid the charge of covenant-infidelity at the door of the Messianists (the Christians), who followed a false prophet (Jesus) into lax observance and contaminated the people by fraternizing with Gentiles. Luke-Acts is in part a piece of Christian apologetics, which reverses the charges: This catastrophe has fallen on Israel because the religious establishment

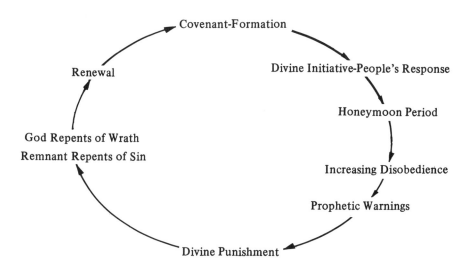

consistently rejected God's purpose for them (Luke 7:29) by refusing the baptism of John, and by failing to "recognize the time of [their] visitation" (Luke 19:44). By carrying their hostility toward Jesus to the point of arranging his execution and perverting the people into collaboration, they committed blasphemy (cf. Luke 23:35; Acts 7:37, 51–52) and were "even found opposing God" (cf. Acts 5:39). Furthermore, according to Luke-Acts, this most recent covenant infidelity has occasioned a reversal in Isaiah's scenario: God will come to establish his reign in a clear and definitive way; but Gentiles will enter first (hence the irony of Jesus' use of the quote in Luke 21:24; cf. Acts 13:44–49; 28:26–29) and those first-invited last. This was Luke-Acts' explanation of the ready reception of the gospel among Gentiles and its widespread rejection by Jews.

Wrath-Passages with Reference to the Destruction of Jerusalem

Tiede's interpretation has plausibility. Luke-Acts repeatedly characterizes the ministries of John the Baptist and Jesus as *the period of prophetic warning*. John is "a prophet and more than a prophet" (Luke 7:26): the herald of the Messianic age (Luke 1:76; 3:4, 15–17; 7:27–28). Likewise, Jesus styles himself a prophet. The Holy Spirit anoints him for ministry (Luke 3:22; 4:18–21). He sums up his home-town reception under the addage "no prophet is acceptable in his own country" (Luke 4:24) and compares himself with Elijah and Elisha (Luke 4:25–27). Further, what Jesus sows is the word of God (Luke 8:11), which in the apostolic period grows mightily despite obstacles (Acts 12:24, 19:20).

The crowds identify him as "a great prophet" (Luke 7:16), perhaps one of the old prophets *redivivus* (Luke 9:8, 19). In the great confession, Peter penetrates that Jesus is more than a prophet, "the Christ of God" (Luke 9:20), an insight confirmed by the heavenly Father's singling Jesus out above Moses and Elijah (Luke 9:33-35). Jesus truly prophesies the true prophet's fate of persecution for himself and his disciples (Luke 9:22, 30-34, 23-25; 11:47-51; 13:34; 22:64). The Emmaus-road disciples describe him as "a prophet mighty in deed and word before God and all the people" (Luke 24:19). And post-resurrection sermons identify Jesus as that "prophet like unto Moses," response to whom is criterial for inclusion or being "destroyed from among the people" (Acts 3:22-23; 7:37, 52-53).

Yet, throughout Luke-Acts, Jesus and the disciples are repeatedly styled as *law-breakers* by their enemies. Jesus is accused of *blasphemy*, when he takes authority to forgive the sins of the paralytic (Luke 5:21). His eating habits win the verdict that he is "a glutton and a drunkard" (Luke 7:34): he and his disciples broke tradition by not fasting (Luke 5:33) and they dine with tax collectors and sinners (Luke 5:30; 7:34; 15:2; 19:7). Later, Peter has to meet objections to his eating with the *uncircumcized* Gentiles (Acts 11:3). Again, Jesus ignores the traditions about ritual washing before meals (Luke 11:37). His views about Sabbath keeping are at odds with those of Pharisaic observance (Luke 6:1-5; 14:1-6). Likewise, Stephen is accused of blaspheming against Moses and God (Acts 6:12) and the Temple (Acts 6:14; 7:48) and of teaching that "this Jesus of Nazareth will destroy this place, and *will change customs which Moses delivered to us*" (Acts 6:14). Similarly, Paul is accused of telling the Jews "to foresake the laws of Moses" and "not to circumcize their children or observe the customs" (Acts 21:20-21), and of defiling the Temple by bringing Gentiles into it (Acts 21:28).

Luke-Acts counters these charges with the claim that John the Baptist and Jesus found their origins among pious observant Jews (cf. Luke 1-2, esp. the accounts of the circumcision, Luke 2:21; purification, Luke 2:22-24; Passover/bar mitzvah, Luke 2:41-51); that the true meaning of the law has been distorted by traditional elaborations, some of which are actually contrary to God's wishes (see the third section above); that Jewish Christians continue to observe it on its correct interpretation (e.g. Acts 21:28), but Gentiles are bound only by the Noachic covenant (Acts 15:6-29).

If Luke-Acts is working with a variation of the prophetic scenario, then many of the wrath-passages are plausibly construed with reference to *the intermediate punishment-stage*. From the mid-point of the gospel, Jesus begins to make *explicit* the connection between establishment-response to his ministry and the destruction of Jerusalem. First, there is his verdict that the house of that prophet-killing city is forsaken (Luke 13:34–35). Drawing near to Jerusalem at the end of the journey-narrative, Jesus weeps to predict that

> the days shall come upon you, when your enemies will cast up a bank and surround you, and hem you in on every side, and dash your children within you, and they will not leave one stone upon another in you; because you did not know the time of your visitation. (Luke 19:41–44)

This is followed with a prophecy of the destruction of the Temple (Luke 21:5–7) and the Gentile take-over of the city "until the times of the Gentiles are fulfilled" (Luke 21:20–24). Jesus again links these events with his own execution (arranged by the religious rulers) in the interchange with the "daughters of Jerusalem" on the road to The Skull (Luke 23:27–31).

The same message is thinly veiled in the parable of the fig tree that is given one last year to bear fruit (Luke 13:6–9); the parable of the banquet whose Lucan version has not only the outcasts within the city but people outside on the highways and in the hedges enter while "none of those men who were invited" "taste my banquet" (Luke 14:16–24); the Lucan version of the parable of the pounds in which those who refuse the king's rule are slain before him (Luke 19:11–27; which immediately precedes Jesus' drawing near to Jerusalem); and the parable of the wicked tenants whose verdict is that the owner "will come and destroy those tenants, and give the vineyard to others" (Luke 20:9–16).

A Lucan Modification of the Apocalyptic Scenario

Jesus marks the division of the ages with his comment,

> The law and the prophets were until John; since then the good news of the kingdom of God is preached. (Luke 16:16)

And we have seen how in Luke-Acts, contrary to conventional apocalyptic theology, the Kingdom comes in two stages: During the earthly ministry of the Son of Man, it is like mustard seed and leaven (Luke 13:18–21), small and unnoticed by some, but steady and swelling in its effect. During this period, people judge themselves by their response to Jesus, and later his disciples (see the third section above). The decisive battle with "the power of darkness" (Luke 22:53; cf. 4:13; 22:3) is won by Jesus on the cross; God's decisive vindication of the righteous, in his resurrection and exaltation of Jesus (Acts 2:22–36; 3:13–14; 13:30–39). Likewise, there are interim blessings (e.g., the gift of the Holy Spirit, cf. Acts

2:1-4; seeing and recognizing the mighty acts of God, e.g. Luke 2:25-32; 10:23-24), and curses (the destruction of Jerusalem, along with the Temple, the dispersal of the people). Yet, neither the latter division nor its consequences is final: Those who kill Jesus are invited to repent and enter the Kingdom (e.g., Acts 2:38-40; 3:19, 27), while the disciples are urged to vigilant loyalty (Luke 12:35; 21:34-36, 38-39). Second, the final, decisive consummation will come, if not immediately (Luke 19:11), not in the indefinite, distant future either (Luke 21:32).[9] The Son of Man will return "in a cloud with power and great glory" (Luke 21:27) and be manifest to all (Luke 17:22-24, 37). The resultant schema is shown on page 111. Luke-Acts thus seems to correct the apocalyptic scenario against the prophetic one, allowing the latter to dominate.[10]

Wrath Left-Over?

Or does it? For the outline of salvation history in late prophecy seems to promise a happy ending for everyone: not only will Israel be restored to Zion, but all the Gentiles will be enrolled as citizens as well (Psalms 87)![11] By contrast, the lines of Luke-Acts seem to threaten wrath at the end. After all, Jesus himself promises to judge the earth, greeting with shame and denial before the angels of God those who were ashamed of and denied him before men (Luke 9:26; 12:8-9), but acknowledging those who were not ashamed to confess him (ibid.) and who persevered through the trials of discipleship (Luke 12:32). Again, when all is said and done, Luke-Acts does appear to envision final (external) separation as the consequence of unrelenting opposition to God's purposes. John the Baptist speaks of the chaff which will be burned with *unquenchable fire*. Rejecting cities will be condemned *in the judgment* (Luke 10:13-15, 32) as will "the present generation" that scorns Jesus (Luke 11:31-32). Jesus answers the apocalyptic question, "Lord, will those who are saved be few?" with a warning to "strive to enter by the narrow door" before it is too late:

> When once the householder has risen up and shut the door, you will begin to stand outside and to knock at the door, saying, "Lord, open to us." He will answer you, "I do not know where you come from." Then you will begin to say, "We ate and drank in your presence, and you taught in our streets." But he will say, "I tell you, I do not know where you come from; depart from me, all you workers of iniquity!" There you will weep and gnash your teeth, when you see Abraham and Isaac and Jacob and all the prophets in the kingdom of God and you yourselves thrust out. (Luke 13:23-29)

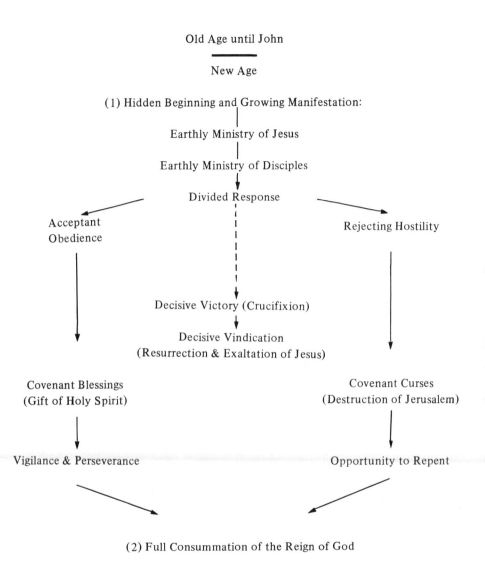

Similarly, the tale of the rich man and Lazarus presupposes that opportunities for efficacious repentance are restricted at least to one's life-time (Luke 16:19–31). Likewise, the obvious manifestation of the Son of Man will be accompanied by surprising destruction of the unrepentant (Luke 17:27, 29, 33–35).

Does this not mean that wrath is half of God's last word on history after all? Is the conclusion not unavoidable that either the Prodigal Son's father changes character after death and/or on judgment day, or his redemptive purpose is partially defeated? For all of its apparent subtlety, does not the scenario of Luke-Acts finally share the most serious defects of the two-age theory?

The Nature of Divine Defeat

Far from it! Within its own parameters, the two-age theory presents God as a success, because he effectively establishes an order of retributive justice in the new age. The principal defects of such apocalyptic lie in its premises—its naive view of human motivation on the one hand and its limited conception of divine goodness as retributive justice on the other—according to which God dismisses failed relationships with the coolness of a corporation executive writing off business losses. By contrast, the God of Luke-Acts is not interested in giving people what they deserve, but rather in reconciled relationships. Nor does he underestimate human perversity, but figures it into his redemptive calculations. And because intimate relationships are by nature collaborative, he thereby opens himself up to the possibility of divine defeat.

Graduated Judgment: The two-age theory and Luke-Acts agree that the advent of the new age brings judgment. Since for apocalyptic theology judgment serves merely to determine and announce just deserts, it can be scheduled right away. Luke-Acts, however, puts judgment in service of reconciliation. Right relationships between God and creatures must be based on truth, and judgment is a matter of exposing sin for what it is and God for who he is. Because the God of Luke-Acts aims to redeem the hard-hearted as well as the readily repentant, the process of divine judgment in the new age must be drawn out.

For Luke-Acts, *its first stage* comes in the ministries of John the Baptist and Jesus. In word and deed, Jesus is direct and explicit about divine opposition to external separation. He proclaims how divine ingenuity reverses the effects of sin, making the old source of alienation a potential occasion—through acknowledgment and repentance—of reconciliation and reunion with God, a source of heavenly rejoicing (Luke 15:7, 10).

In the gospel story, the ministry of Jesus reveals the thoughts of many hearts (cf. Luke 2:35; 8:17; 11:34–36; 12:1–3). Since table-fellowship is transitive, Jesus' association with outcasts and public sinners made the dogma of holiness-by-external-separation a source of alienation from Jesus. Because such "separatism" was a defense against facing the "darkness" within, hostility to Jesus was powered by so much emotional steam that his death is no surprise to the reader. Part of this darkness is an unconscious picture of God as a harsh, demanding tyrant, who has to be appeased, but from whom goods can be extorted by slavish external scrupulosity. Jesus characterizes this attitude in the parables. The elder brother sees his father as a stingy slave-driver, who gives him nothing "for free" but from whom earned wages can be extracted (Luke 15:29–30). The one talent man, who believes his master to be "a severe man" who exploits the labor of others for his own profit, adopts a policy of passive aggression and angrily goes "on strike" by burying rather than investing the money entrusted to him, only to be punished by the master, who "condemn[s] him out of his own mouth" (Luke 19:21–24). Their self-reinforcing pessimism[12] about life mirrors that of Jesus' opponents about God. This unconscious caricature drives the surface behavior, and leaves no room for thankfulness (Luke 17:11–19) or generosity toward those who have worked less hard at appeasement. Thus, their self-separation from Jesus "acts out" an unconscious sense of alienation from God.

The second stage of divine judgment comes in the apostolic ministry. At the time of their crimes, Jesus' opponents do not see their role in his crucifixion as opposition to God's purpose for their lives. They continue to mock him from the foot of the cross (Luke 23:35). But the preaching of Peter, Paul, and others makes this connection explicit, invites repentance, and offers forgiveness for this offense against the Son of Man. It is the thesis of Luke-Acts that the destruction of Jerusalem is louder testimony to this fact — that rejection of Jesus means self-separation from God — directed at those within Israel who would not listen to mere sermons.

The third stage will come with the glorious return of the Son of Man. To those who refuse to hear the lessons of history, Luke-Acts sounds a severe warning: In the last judgment, this alienating quality of their attitudes and actions will be made fully explicit in external separation. Any still "sot in the ways" of (external) separatism will find themselves definitively thrust out.

Unlike the apocalyptic version of the last judgment, however, Luke-Acts makes their threatened condemnation ironical for judge and accused alike. The separatists themselves are separated — not because of particu-

lar felonies such as extortion, adultery, or even the murder of Jesus—
but because they refuse to be inclusive. Their strategy, like that of the
elder brother and the one-talent man, is self-defeating.

But persistent separatism also stands in the way of God's aims. On
the one hand, it obstructs divine judgment; for, to the extent of their
entrenchment, separatists will be incapable of seeing the truth about
God's inclusive purposes. Like the elder brother and the one-talent man,
they will see this severe separation as unmerited, further evidence of a
tyrannical management. Where the separatists are concerned, there is no
way God can be sure to get the truth about his inclusive policy across.
External separation, by its very nature, cannot communicate divine inclusiveness to the separated. His external inclusion of outcasts, which is
part and parcel of the policy, strikes separatists as unfair and outrageous and provokes them to exclude themselves. And God cannot demonstrate his inclusiveness toward separatists if they refuse to be included.
God's efforts to *communicate* the truth in judgment, about himself and
about sinners, are thus partially frustrated. More than that, the persistent separatist thereby forces God to compromise his policy of inclusiveness itself: either he includes the separatist and excludes those with whom
the separatist refuses to associate; or he includes the latter and the former
separate themselves. In thus accepting the possibility of external separation "in the judgment," God opens himself up to a double defeat.

Aloofness Reversed: Yet, with this very possibility Luke-Acts reverses
apocalyptic scenario once more. The God of conventional two-age theology is aloof. He lives in a different world, above the fray, and commu-
nicates with the righteous who are mired in the present age only through
angelic intermediaries. Frail though they are, the righteous are enjoined
to "hang in there" through years of suffering, while God awaits the ripe
time in the undisturbed tranquillity of the realms of light. (Recall that
Job could not easily swallow such advice.) And God will be equally
remote from the sufferings of the wicked in the age to come.

By contrast, the God of Luke-Acts is the God of the prophets,
who not only directs but gets emotionally involved in human history. In
the gospel story, *he identifies himself with the righteous* in a radical way:
He sends his chosen Son, the apocalyptic Son of Man, to occupy a piv-
otal position in the long line of suffering righteous prophets. He has not
asked them and will not require the disciples to play a role in which he
was unwilling to cast himself. In Jesus, the decisive battle with Satan
and the power of darkness is waged on the cross (Luke 4:13; 22:53); in
him, God's decisive vindication of the righteous is accomplished (Luke
24:4–6, 26, 45; Acts 2:24–36; 3:13–16; 13:26–37), giving the disciples a
down-payment on the vindication to come.

Nor does God distance himself from the lost. According to the plot of Luke-Acts, the Son of Man comes to seek and to save them (Luke 19:10; cf. 5:32). It is the separatists, the ones who are the most lost of all, who try to remain aloof from him. Yet, in his mercy, God still finds some way to identify with them. The darkness in their hearts costs them something (the elder brother is not a happy person; in the longer run of eternity, his attitudes will drive him to the madness of teeth-gnashing); so God arranges for it to cost God something. The Son of Man allows them to "act out" the secrets of their hearts on himself, and calls the disciples to present themselves as such targets as well. The purpose of this is to judge them in such a way as to give them opportunity and psychological space to see their sins and repent. At the time Luke-Acts was written, some of God's lost chosen people had not repented; it was an open question whether this situation would be reversed. The book is written as a warning; the author may hope that the threats of final separation are conditional. Should they remain impenitent to the end, God's purpose will be partially defeated in those people. But for a God who identifies with his people, this is as it should be. To revert to that best loved of Lucan parables, the elder brother, so long as he remains locked into his patterns, loses something—loving family relationships. The gracious father by loving but failing to win the love of his son, shares the latter's loss.

NOTES

1. In fairness to the reader, I should say a word about my view of scripture. I believe that the Bible is the inspired Word of God to us and our principal source of divine revelation. I am not, for all that, a biblical literalist. I do not think that the inspiration of scripture, any more than our inspired reading of it, was a process in which the personality of the writer was shoved aside. Rather, in my opinion, the deliverances of scripture seem to me to have been filtered through the receptors of the writer(s) and shaped by his or her world view, historical context, etc. Because we receive these treasures in earthen vessels of different shapes, I would anticipate finding in various New Testament authors as well as later layers of tradition somewhat different angles on God's redemptive work. I want to learn from them all, and so project similar studies of other gospels, the Pauline epistles, etc. Nevertheless, much of what I say here does not depend on a rejection of biblical literalism.

2. Joseph A. Fitzmeyer, *The Gospel According to Luke I-IX, The Anchor Bible, vol. 28 (Garden City, New York: Doubleday & Co., Inc., 1981), pp. 53-57. Also, Donald Juel, Luke-Acts: The Promise of History* (Atlanta, Ga.: John Knox Press, 1983), pp. 5-8; and David L. Tiede, *Prophecy and History in Luke-*

Acts Philadelphia: Fortress Press, 1980), ch. 1, pp. 7–16. Dates at least this late are presupposed by Hans Conzelmann's argument in *The Theology of St. Luke* (New York: Harper and Row, 1957). Johannes Munck speaks for a minority in advocating an early date of composition, at the beginning of the sixties, on the hypothesis that Acts was intended as an apology for Paul at the time of his trial in Rome (*The Acts of the Apostles*, The Anchor Bible, vol. 31, [1967], pp, xlvi–liv).

3. Tiede's book, *Prophecy and History*, starts from this observation.

4. For example, Albert Schweitzer and Johannes Weiss. See summary by Richard J. Cassidy, *Jesus, Politics and Society: A Study of Luke's Gospel* (Maryknoll, N.Y: Orbis Books, 1980), pp. 139–140. Also, Earl Ellis, *Eschatology in Luke* (Facet Books), Biblical Series 30, ch. 2, pp. 5–6.

5. This tendency is epitomized in the benedictions of the Morning Prayer service recited daily by the Jewish male: "Blessed art thou, O Lord our God, King of the universe, who hast not made me a heathen . . . a bondsman . . . a woman" (*The Authorized Daily Prayer Book*, Revised Edition [New York: Bloch Publishing Company, 1948], pp. 19–22). Contrast Luke 15:4–10, where God and the angels are likened first to shepherds and then to a woman.

6. In the Bible, Ezra is a "separatist" tract, while Jonah and Ruth are arguably anti-separatist. Cf. Tiede, *Prophecy and History*, ch. 2, pp. 59–61.

7. Joseph Klausner, in his classic work *The Messianic Idea in Israel* trans. W. F. Stinespring (New York: Macmillan Company, 1955), traces the development of the so-called "Messianic chain" (which is really the plot-line of God's interactions with his people) in detail through biblical and post-biblical Jewish literature. He finds prophetic developments particularly important. According to Klausner, the prophet Amos depicts sin as the cause of punishment (understood retributively), and repentance as the necessary pre-condition for salvation (pp. 38–44). Hosea refines this idea by assigning punishment a purifying and not merely retributive purpose (p. 45). First Isaiah continues the scenario: Sin causes punishment; punishment causes repentance; and repentance occasions redemption (p. 57ff.). Some parts of Jeremiah extend salvation to those Gentiles from all over the world who will worship and obey God (pp. 106–107). Deutero-Isaiah sustains this universalistic theme, with the notion that after the exiles have returned to Jerusalem, Gentiles, too, will come to worship and glorify God. But Israel remains at the center and Gentiles at the circumference, her superiority based on her knowledge and love of the Lord which she will teach to the nations (pp. 159–161). Klausner holds that the prophets understood punishment and salvation in historical, political, and material terms, and not merely spiritually, and he tries to locate their different emphases in their varying historical situations.

8. *Prophecy and History in Luke-Acts*, especially ch. 1, pp. 1–16; ch. 2, pp. 58–62; ch. 3, pp. 66–68, 79–84, 94–95; ch. 4, pp. 99–103.

9. Cf. Richard H. Hiers, "The Problem of the Delay of the Parousia in Luke-Acts," *New Testament Studies* 20: pp. 145–155.

10. Cf. Earl Ellis, *Eschatology in Luke* (Philadelphia: Fortress Press, 1972), pp. 16–20. Ellis argues for the two-stage advent of the Kingdom, but claims that

the present stage brings covenant blessings, while covenant curses are deferred until the final judgment. But Tiede's argument for the destruction of Jerusalem as a down-payment on covenant curses seems to force a modification of Ellis' schema.

11. It may be argued that given the collective context of late prophecy, the promise is only of salvation to everyone who is left: to the remnant of faithful Israel and to the remaining Gentiles. Those who have died in the course of punitive national set-backs have simply lost out. Even so, the remaining wrath-passages in Luke-Acts seem to offer a different picture: that the impenitent may remain but be excluded, to burn in unquenchable fire and to weep and gnash their teeth.

12. Dan Otto Via suggests this "existentialist" diagnosis of the one-talent man in Matthew's version of the parable (see *The Parables*, [Philadelphia: Fortress Press, 1967], ch. 4, pp. 113–122).

PART II

God, the Good, and Christian Life

The Indwelling of the Holy Spirit

WILLIAM P. ALSTON

I

This paper deals with certain aspects of the work of the Holy Spirit in the world. Christian theology assigns the Holy Spirit a wide variety of functions: The Holy Spirit inspires, guides, and enlightens a person, and, according to some versions, even takes over the normal psychological functions in prophecy, in the composition of the books of the Bible, in preaching the word of God, in speaking with tongues, and other "charismatic" manifestations. Over and above these more dramatic manifestations, the Spirit acts as an internal witness to the faith, producing a sense of conviction in the mind of the believer. The Spirit is active in the church, the Christian community, knitting its members together in fellowship, guiding its decisions and activities, preserving its integrity. In this paper we will be concerned with another crucial function of the Holy Spirit, or family of functions; the transformation of the believer into a "saint," into the sort of person God designed him or her to be. In other terms, it is the function of initiating, sustaining, fostering, and developing the Christian life of the believer, or, as we might well say, the "spiritual" life, thinking of that term as encompassing all the ways in which the work of the Holy Spirit is manifested in the life of the believer.[1] My topic thus falls within the territory labeled "regeneration" and "sanctification" by much Protestant theology, and within certain parts of the territory labeled "grace" in Catholic theology, particularly "sanctifying grace."

In focusing on the work of the Spirit in the individual I do not mean to denigrate the importance of the corporate in the Christian life. Quite the contrary. I am aware, sufficiently aware I hope, of the point that the New Testament and the ensuing Christian tradition represents the Christian life as a full participation in the community of believers and makes no provision for the salvation of the solitary individual, isolated from her fellow Christians.[2] Indeed, the transformation of the individual with which I am concerned is a transformation into one who has both the capacity and the will to participate fully in the life of the church. One cannot advance in love, patience, kindness, faithfulness, and other "fruits of the Spirit," without exhibiting these characteristics in one's interactions with others in the community. These are not aspects of "the feelings, acts, and experiences of individual men in their solitude, so far as they apprehend themselves to stand in relation to whatever they may consider the divine," to quote William James' profoundly misguided characterization of religion.[3] They are inclinations to social behavior. But having said all this, it must also be recognized that at least an essential part of the work of the Holy Spirit in building up the Christian community is the regeneration and sanctification of its members.

Neither the New Testament nor Christian experience through the ages represents the Spirit as working on what we might call a purely corporate level, in such a way as to bypass the inner psychological development of each individual. The sanctification of the individual is as fundamental for the building up of the church as is the latter for the former. It is crucial to recognize both directions of dependence. On the one hand, the transformation of the individual is intimately dependent on the community, for without the Christian community we would not have the tradition that informs our Christian life, nor would we have the role models that play so central a role in spiritual growth. But, on the other hand, unless some members had made significant advances in the development of Christian character, there would be no communal spiritual life into which new members could be drawn and in the context of which each individual can receive resources to be used in further development.[4]

It will also be noted that I have chosen to concentrate on what might be called the "moral" aspects of the work of the Holy Spirit within the individual, the ways in which the Spirit modifies the character of the person, her values, tendencies, attitudes, priorities, and so on, rather than, for example, the work of the Holy Spirit in "inspiring" the person to various sorts of exceptional activities, such as prophecy and speaking in tongues. Again I do not mean to imply that the latter are without value or that they are not genuine manifestations of the presence of the Spirit. I only wish to suggest that these phenomena are not the heart of the matter; they are not what the divine plan of salvation is all about. We were not created in order to speak with tongues or exhibit various forms of "enthusiasm." If they do have a place in the divine scheme, and I am prepared to recognize that they do, it is by way of assuring the individual and those around him of the presence of the Spirit and/or by way of communicating certain messages to concerned parties. But it still remains that, by well nigh common consent, God's basic intention for us is that we should become like unto him, insofar as in us lies, and should thereby be in a position to enter into a community of love with him and with our fellow creatures. And the work of regeneration and sanctification is directly addressed to the carrying out of this intention.

Although I am discussing these matters in terms of the work of the Holy Spirit, I am not concerned here with problems concerning the Trinity or concerning the nature and status of the Third Person in particular. I am concerned with God's work in regeneration and sanctification, work that is traditionally assigned to the Third Person of the Trinity, and I am following that language. Moreover, as we shall see, the term 'spirit' is quite appropriate for certain aspects of the phenomenology of these proceedings. Nevertheless I want to avoid getting into controversies over which Person of the Trinity is doing a particular job at a particular time. I will adhere to the widely accepted theological view that all Persons of the Trinity are involved in the external operations (external to the Godhead) of any Person. From this perspective the work of regeneration and sanctification is primarily attributed to the Holy Spirit because these operations are centered around the development of love in the individual, and within the Godhead the role of the Holy Spirit is to be the love borne each other by the Persons of the Trinity.

By adhering to this principle we can handle the fact that in the Pauline epistles and the Johannine writings there is quite a bit of oscillation between speaking of the Spirit and speaking of Christ as working within one. A famous passage from the Epistle to the Romans clearly illustrates this:

> But that is not how you live. You are on the spiritual level, if only God's Spirit dwells within you; and if a man does not possess the Spirit of Christ, he is no Christian. But if Christ is dwelling within you, then although the body is a dead thing because you sinned, yet the spirit is life itself because you have been justified. Moreover, if the Spirit of him who raised Jesus from the dead dwells within you, then the God who raised Christ Jesus from the dead will also give new life to your mortal bodies through his indwelling Spirit. (8:9–11)[5]

Here the indwelling divine presence that gives the new life is indifferently referred to as "God's Spirit," "the Spirit of Christ," and "Christ." I can see no way of reading the passage as specifying three distinct divine agents. If Paul does not find it necessary to distinguish between the Holy Spirit at work in one and Christ at work in one, I do not see why it should be incumbent on me to do so, even though he and I are separated by the Council of Nicea. In pursuance of this policy I shall feel free to use biblical and other material put in terms of the indwelling of Christ, as well as material phrased in terms of the indwelling of the Spirit.

II

If this suffices for a demaracation of my subject matter, I can proceed to formulate my problem. Simply stated, it is this: How are we to think of this stretch of the activity of the Holy Spirit? Just what role does the Spirit play in bringing about these changes within the person? Just how is it brought off? These questions, to be sure, need further specification. They are not to be construed as a request for a delineation of the divine mechanisms employed or the divine flow chart employed. Even if there are such things we could not expect to grasp them. Moreover we should be aware of the possibility that God works differently with different people in different situations. It may be unreasonable to expect a simple account that applies univocally to every case. What I am specifically interested in exploring are two issues: First, to what extent is the transformation wholly God's work and to what extent is a human response, human effort, human voluntary choice, assent, or cooperation involved? And second, how intimately is God involved with the individual in this process? How internal is he to these proceedings?

The first question is one that inevitably forces itself on us as soon as we reflect on the matter, for it is of the highest practical as well as theoretical importance. It obviously makes a great deal of difference to how I should proceed, whether the course of sanctification is to any extent dependent on my actions, choices, or efforts; whether it is in any way "up to me" in what direction it goes, how fast it goes, or whether it goes at all. If, on the other hand, God is simply transforming me by his own immutable decrees according to some schedule of his own, that is quite a different ball game. And one or another position on this issue will have various theological and philosophical consequences that will tell for or against it and that will have an important bearing on one's conception of the divine-human relationship.

I will not say much about the second question now. It will become clear, I hope, at a later stage of the discussion just what external-internal contrasts are relevant here and what is involved in choosing between them.

Certain extreme views concerning regeneration and sanctification will be dismissed virtually without a hearing. First, I shall rule out of court any view according to which God is not active at all in the process, except for the sustenance that he is always exercising with respect to the entire creation. On such a more-Pelagian-than-Pelagius position we are left on our own with just such natural capacities as we were initially endowed with by our creator. God is not active in any special way. I take it that any such view goes radically against the mind of the church, as embodied in scripture, tradition, and normal Christian experience. The idea that God *acts* in order to redeem sinful humanity and bring those that respond to his redemptive action into a loving relationship with himself is so central to Christianity that its excision would leave nothing worthy of the name. Our problem is not *whether* God is active in personal transformation but *how* we should think of this activity.

At the other extreme we have the view that God alone is active in this matter, that God simply "takes over," replaces the human agent. God (the Spirit) lives one's life for one; the human person is simply the "location" or "receptacle" in which this particular bit of divine life takes place. There are famous scriptural passages that suggest this construal, most notably Paul's famous cry: "I have been crucified with Christ: the life I now live is not my life, but the life which Christ lives in me" (Galatians 2:20). (In the better known Revised Standard Version, " . . . it is no longer I who live, but Christ who lives in me.") However there are abundant reasons for taking this as a bit of hyperbole. Paul certainly does not lose his sense of continuing personal identity; he gives every indication of awareness that it is he, the same human being who once persecuted Christians, who is writing to the Galatians and pursuing his missionary journeys. Furthermore, if it really were Christ, or the Spirit, who is the agent from now on, why should it be, as it is according to universal Christian witness, including Paul's, that even after God has begun to work within them there is still a long job of combatting and rooting out sinful tendencies? If it is God, not I, who is the agent from now on, whence these sinful tendencies? Finally, it is our faith that God has created us for loving communion with him and with each other. If each of us were replaced by God as soon as he were firmly set on this path, the goal could not be reached; there would be no human agents left to enter into the desired communion. Thus any viable answer to our question must recognize both a divine and a human agent, both divine activity and human response.

Let me also point out that our problem does not pose the crucial issues for human free will that are notoriously posed by the Pelagian controversy. The latter, or at least an important segment thereof, has to do with putatively free, human voluntary acts. For example, it has to do with the decisive act of repentance, of turning one's back on sin, asking for divine forgiveness and divine assistance, and resolving to do one's best to amend one's life and to follow the commandments of God. The question was as to whether it is ever up to a human agent to make such a move, or whether any such move will be made only as the outcome of the irresistible grace of God. (On the latter alternative, God may be working through the will of the human person, though this will can no longer be considered free, in that instance, in a libertarian sense. It was not, in the strongest sense, "up to the human person" whether that move was made.) The latter, Augustinian, position on this issue really does deny that such acts of repentance are free in a libertarian sense. Likewise the Augustinian position that fallen human beings cannot do anything good except when moved by divine grace implies that none of us has any real choice between good and evil. But the problem of this paper, at least the central problem of this paper, does not concern putatively free voluntary acts; it has to do with personality or character changes, with changes in what we might call "motivational structure." That is, it has to do with changes in one's tendencies, desires, values, attitudes, emotional proclivities, and the like. It has to do with such changes as the weakening of a desire for illicit sexual intercourse, the strengthening of a desire for the awareness of God, the weakening of a tendency to be preoccupied with one's status or reputation, and the strengthening of one's interest in the condition of others. The issue is as to just what role the activity of the Holy Spirit has in such changes as these.

To see that the integrity of human free will is not at issue here, consider the most extreme attribution of divine responsibility for these changes, short of the "takeover" position we have already ruled out. Say that all such changes result from God's simply effecting them directly by an exercise of his omnipotence, without in any way going through natural psychological or social processes, and without in any way evoking a response from the creature in order to carry this out. God just decides that one of my tendencies shall be weakened and another strengthened, and Presto! It is done. Even on this view I could still have as much free choice, of a morally significant sort between good and evil, as the most dedicated libertarian would affirm. That is, this would still be a possibility unless it is further stipulated, as many Christian thinkers would wish to do,[6] that these new tendencies (or new strengths of tendencies) to holiness are irresistible, that they strictly determine my volitions. But that would be an additional thesis, one that does not follow from the attribution of changes in motivational structure to direct divine volition. If we allow that my altered desires, tendencies, and attitudes influence my volitions without strictly determining them, just as with my previous tendencies, then no negative consequences with respect to human free will ensue. After all, even the most convinced libertarian recognizes that human motivational structure results, for the most part, from factors other than the individual's own free voluntary acts and, indeed, from factors that were, to a large extent, not under any sort of voluntary control. When we first arrive at the point at which there is some possibility of taking oneself in hand and trying to do something about one's own habits, likes, interests, and desires, one already has a character that arose without one's deliberate intervention or encouragement. And even after deliberate intervention becomes a possibility, this is only one factor in personality changes, and by no means the most important. If there is any hope for libertarianism, it will have to be compatible with the fact that one's desires and tendencies are largely determined by factors over which one exercises no effective control. This being the case, why should we suppose that the effecting of personality changes by direct divine volition should be subversive of human free will?

After introducing our topic as having to do with both regeneration and sanctification, I have been discussing them together without differentiation, sometimes using sanctification as a catch-all label. But the two phenomena are typically treated in quite different terms, both in systematic theology and in reports of Christian experience. Regeneration, being born again, is often represented as an instantaneous transition that is vividly conscious and that involves acts of repentance and faith. While sanctification is a long, gradual process, much of which takes place below the level of consciousness. Regeneration is the decisive turning away from sin and toward God that initiates the process of which sanctification is the continuation. If these phenomena occupy such different positions in the scheme of salvation, it might well be that our central question would be answered differently for the two.

However, in the interests of concision, I am going to continue to discuss them together. I am encouraged in this policy by the fact that by no means all sectors of Christendom carve up our general territory in the same fashion. The picture I have just presented is typical of Protestantism, more specifically of evangelical Protestantism. In traditional Roman Catholic theology there is much less emphasis on a conscious deliberate act of repentance and faith as a prerequisite for God's work of sanctification. "Divine grace" is portrayed as working largely through the sacraments of the church. Insofar as there is a particular moment of initiation of the process it comes in baptism, often infant baptism when the individual is incapable of a conscious, deliberate repentance and acceptance of Christ as savior. And apart from theological differences, Christian experience indicates that the classic evangelical scenario is not always followed. As William James insisted, there are both "once born" and "twice born" believers. In many cases, even in evangelical circles, a person would be hard pressed to specify some particular moment at which the decisive conversion and rebirth took place.

In any event, I shall be focusing on common ground within mainstream Christianity. It is recognized on all hands that God is at work within the believer to transform her into the kind of person God wants her to be, the kind of person capable of entering into an eternal loving communion with God. I shall henceforth use the term 'sanctification' for this process of transformation as a whole, including any conscious, deliberate initiation there may be. Although I shall not assume that a rebirth of the classic evangelical sort is required in every case, I shall feel free to draw on descriptions of regeneration in seeking to understand the work of the Holy Spirit: For where these dramatic turnings do occur, the divine activity is more out in the open than in the lengthy gradual process of transformation that ensues.

In this connection I should make a general statement about the place of conscious manifestations in sanctification. We are often warned both by theologians and by spiritual writers not to identify grace or the work of the Spirit with feelings, emotional reactions, or "consolations." One should not expect the process of sanctification to be a perpetual "high," an uninterrupted train of ecstasies and exaltations. Most of it is a matter of digging out some deeply entrenched roots, and planting and nurturing new shoots; and that is certainly not all fun. God may well be hard at work within us when we are not feeling "spiritual," and feelings can, notoriously, be deceptive when they are present. But these sage counsels need to be balanced by the equally important point that spiritual transformation does manifest itself from time to time in a, perhaps obscure, awareness of what is going on; and this awareness is often affectively toned with feelings of joy, love, exaltation, etc. I shall also assume that by attention to these conscious manifestations we can get some clue to what is going on, though I would warn against expecting too much from this source.

III

Let us turn to the first of our two main questions, the one concerning the respective roles of God and the believer in sanctification. The simplest answer to this question is that the psychological changes are wrought directly by the will of God. God simply wills that at a certain moment my concern for the condition of others will increase and my concern for my own comfort, repose, and recognition will decrease; and it thereby happens, just as whatever God wills to happen thereby happens without any need for a further intermediary. Such a view can marshall considerable support. Many biblical passages are naturally read in these terms. The Psalmist sings: "Create a pure heart in me, O God, and give me a new steadfast spirit" (51:10). Ezekiel represents God as saying: "I will give them a different heart and put a new spirit into them; I will take the heart of stone out of their bodies and give them a heart of flesh. Then they will conform to my statutes and keep my laws" (11:19–20; see also 36:26–27). In the Epistle to the Philippians, Paul writes: "You must work out your own salvation in fear and trembling; for it is God who works in you, inspiring both the will and the deed, for his own chosen purpose" (2:13; see also 1:6). The Pauline love of paradox is such that this passage can be used to illustrate everything from the ultra-Pelagian view that it is all our doing to the ultra-Augustinian view that God has simply taken over and displaced the human agent. But, among other things, it expresses the conviction that God is at work in us altering our action tendencies. Some of the prayers in the Pauline epistles seem to be informed with this conception of the matter. "May God himself, the God of peace, make you holy in every part, and keep you sound in spirit, soul, and body, without fault when our Lord Jesus Christ comes" (1 Thess. 5:23). ". . . may the Lord make your love mount and overflow towards one another and towards all, as our love does towards you" (1 Thess. 3:12).

Though these utterances can be construed in other ways, we can see how they would encourage theologians to make statements like the following: "The power which regenerates is the power of God. . . . There is a direct operation of this power upon the sinner's heart which changes its moral character."[7] "In the primary change of disposition, which is the most essential feature of regeneration, the Spirit of God acts directly upon the spirit of man."[8] "But man cannot himself extricate himself from this revolt. For everything that he undertakes is infected with it. Only the Creator can overcome the revolt. He does it in the fact of reconciliation in Christ, when he cancels the revolt through His assurance which is accepted in faith. The self is restored to soundness through justification by faith."[9] "To say that God gives us grace is to say that the author of our existence realizes in us a quality or property grafted upon our natural being."[10] ". . . sanctifying grace: that is, of a divine sanctity which only God can give us and which cannot come from our works, but by which we are renewed and therefore capable of performing works that are really holy."[11]

The same picture of God directly producing new dispositions and tendencies in us is embodied in the traditional Catholic view that by grace we are "infused" with the theological virtues of faith, hope, and love, and endowed with such "gifts of the Spirit" as wisdom, fortitude and piety.[12] Let us dub this model of the work of the Holy Spirit in sanctification the "fiat" model.

On the fiat model the inner workings of the Holy Spirit constitute the same sort of divine activity as creation. It is just as if God had originally created me with these tendencies, the difference lying only in the context within which the divine activity takes place. Thus the present view ties in well with all those New Testament passages that represent the initiation of the moral changes in question as a· "new creation" or a "new birth." The former phraseology is more typical of Paul (See, e.g., 2 Cor. 5:17; Eph. 2:10, 4:24; Col. 3:10), whereas the latter is more typical of John (e.g., John 3:3–8). Since neither in being born nor in being created can I play any active part, the bearing on our question is the same.

Furthermore this construal is richly illustrated in the reports of dramatic conversions and regenerations which abound in Christian literature. A common scenario has the individual in the grip of sinful tendencies, apparently helpless to do anything about it, until at a crisis point he turns to God, throws himself on the divine mercy, and receives as a gift from God the transformation he was unable to effect himself. To the person it seems a bolt from the blue; it seems that God alone by his almighty power has effected a fundamental change in his personality.

Now there is no doubt that God could do things this way, and perhaps he does, at least sometimes. But there are reasons for doubting that this is his normal *modus operandi*. First there are general considerations concerning God's conception of human beings, his relations thereto, and his intentions for us. It is a major theme of the Christian tradition that God created us for loving communion with himself, for the richest and fullest possible personal interaction with him. God envisages us and created us as *persons*, beings that are capable of such distinctively personal activities as the formation of purposes and attempts to realize them, the acquisition and use of knowledge, the entering into social relationships, and the creation of beauty. Moreover he has created us as persons who have a share in the determination of their own destiny by the exercise of free choice between alternatives. Now if we enjoy this status in creation, we could expect God to relate himself to us in a distinctively interpersonal fashion. To be sure, our creation is not, and cannot be, an interpersonal relationship, for prior to being created there is no person on the human side to stand in relation. Again there is presumably nothing distinctively interpersonal about God's sustaining our existence at each moment. But against the background of creation and preservation, the Bible and the Christian tradition generally represent God as entering into distinctively interpersonal relations with human beings: making covenants, laying down requirements and prohibitions, making promises, providing guidance and support, punishing and rewarding, exhorting, condemning, communicating messages, consoling, encouraging, and so on. And there are abundant indications that the game has not changed in this regard in the New Covenant. Paul tells us that "The Spirit you have received is not a spirit of slavery leading you back into a life of fear, but a Spirit that makes us sons, enabling us to cry 'Abba! Father!' In that cry the Spirit of God joins with our spirit in testifying that we are God's children; and if children, then heirs" (Rom. 8:15–16).

The immediate point of all this is that on the fiat model the inner working of the Holy Spirit is not distinctively interpersonal in character. We have already noted that the present view represents the divine activity in sanctification as being of the same sort as in creation, and hence as lacking any distinctively interpersonal character. But if God is primarily concerned to enter into interpersonal relations with us, why should he relate himself to us here in such an impersonal manner, treating us as sticks and stones, or at least acting in a way that is indistinguishable from one that is equally appropriate to sticks and stones. If one human being succeeds in altering the desires or attitudes of another without the other's consent, perhaps by some form of conditioning, wouldn't that constitute a violation of the other's personal integrity? Why, then, should we suppose that God acts in a way in which it would be fundamentally wrong for us to act? Would it not be more appropriate to our God-given nature and to God's intentions for us for God to go about our transformation in a way that is distinctively appropriate to persons, a way that would involve calling us to repentance, chastising us for our failures, encouraging us and assisting us to get started and to persevere in the way, making new resources available to us, enlivening and energizing us, assuring us of his love, his providence, and his constant presence with us, leaving it up to us whether the desired response is forthcoming.

Indeed, the New Testament often speaks of the work of the Holy Spirit in these terms. One thinks particularly of the characterization of the Holy Spirit in the farewell discourses of the fourth gospel, in which the Spirit is characterized as an "Advocate," who will "bear witness" to Christ (15:27), will "teach you everything, and will call to mind all that I have told you" (14:26). Moreover, remembering that we are not restricting ourselves to what is specifically assigned to the Holy Spirit, we can note other references in these discourses to a distinctively personal activity of God within the believer. " . . . because I live, you too will live; then you will know that I am in my Father, and you in me and I in you.

The man who has received my commands and obeys them — he it is who loves me; and he who loves me will be loved by my Father; and I will love him and disclose myself to him." (14:19-21). "Anyone who loves me will heed what I say; then my Father will love him, and we will come to him and make our dwelling with him" (14:23). Thus in these discourses the Holy Spirit is represented as one who will engage in such distinctively interpersonal activities as teaching, witnessing, loving, and uniting others into fellowship.

Let us be more explicit as to how God's role in regeneration and sanctification could be depicted on an interpersonal transaction model (hereafter termed the "interpersonal model"). There are many possibilities. First and most obviously, God can *call* the individual to repentance, to obedience, to a life of love lived "in the Spirit." These are calls for deliberate, voluntary responses from the individual. And apart from voluntary responses, these communications can, suddenly or gradually, have effects on the individual's likes, desires, and attitudes through various conditioning mechanisms and other psychological processes that do not involve consciously directed effort. But the communication of divine messages, recognized by the individual as such, is only the most obvious possibility. God could affect the ideational processes of the individual in more subtle fashion. He could bring it about that facets of the person's present life appear to him in an unfavorable light and that the life of *agape* appears to him as highly attractive, without this being consciously taken by the individual as a communication from God. Again, God could present himself to the individual as a role model, giving the person more of a sense of things divine, thereby increasing the desire for holiness and communion with God. God could make his love and providence for the individual more obvious, more salient in the person's mind, thereby evoking responses of gratitude and yearning for closer communion. Finally, God could make new resources available to the individual, new resources of strength of will, of energy for perseverance in the face of discouragement, of inner strength that enable one to avoid dependence on the approval of one's associates. In these and other ways God would be seeking to *influence* the individual in the direction of holiness without stepping in and directly producing such a character structure by fiat. By proceeding in this more indirect fashion God would be relating himself to the human person as a person, influence the human being as one person influences another (albeit making use of some of his extraordinary powers in doing so), seeking to evoke responses, voluntary and otherwise from the other person, somewhat as each of us seeks to evoke responses from each other. The only item on the above list that may seem not to fit this description is the "secret" manipulation of the subject's ideational processes. This is indeed something that human influencers are incapable of. But we do seek to alter the ideation of others by such means as are available to us when we try to influence their motivations. Thus carrying out such alterations does not violate the distinctively interpersonal character of the transaction; it is just that the divine person has infinitely greater resources for the task.

For a live example of this way of approaching the matter, consider the excellent study by G. W. H. Lampe, *God as Spirit*.[13] One strand in this very rich book is an attack on "impersonal" ways of thinking of the action of the Holy Spirit. In opposition, Lampe suggests that in speaking of the Holy Spirit "we are speaking of God disclosed and experienced as Spirit, that is, in his personal outreach" (p. 11). In accordance with this orientation Lampe repeatedly emphasizes that the Holy Spirit works within us by entering into distinctively interpersonal interactions with us. That work is "a developing interaction, according to man's capacity, of the Spirit of God with the spirit of man" (p. 20). " . . . transcendent God creates man from within, as the immanent personal indwelling Spirit who inspires and guides and evokes that response of faith and love which is the human side of the relationship of sonship."[14] God's "creativity involves the personal interaction of divine Spirit with human spirits, by which persons who have the capacity to accept or to reject divine love are formed into the divine likeness" (p. 21). The Holy Spirit should be thought of as "forming the human personality from within by communion with it" (p. 22). The concept of Spirit provides material "for the construction of a theological framework in which to interpret our experience of God acting upon, and interacting with, thinking, feeling, and willing human persons" (p. 35).[15] "The concept of Spirit" is "more suitable as a way of thinking about personal God drawing created persons into communion with Himself" (pp. 41–42).

But can this interpersonal model of sanctification accommodate the facts? I do not think it runs into insuperable difficulties with biblical texts. The ones I quoted above as encouraging the idea of direct divine alteration of character are typical in that they affirm that God does this but are less than wholly explicit as to how God does it. As for experiential reports, first note that the phenomenology of sanctification, properly so called, tends rather to support the interpersonal model. The gradual process of mastering sinful tendencies and strengthening holy desires is typically punctuated by frequent prayers to God and the reception of messages therefrom—guidance, encouragement, exhortation, assurance, and so on. But what about regeneration? A very common picture here is that of a new character structure just appearing out of the blue, without the usual psychosocial prerequisites. Can we suppose that this process has been carried on by a distinctively interpersonal divine-human trans-action?

Although these accounts certainly do not suggest an interpersonal model they can be squared with it, provided we recognize that much of the action is carried on below the level of consciousness. After all, in these typical accounts of rebirth a great deal of conscious divine-human communication goes on before the crucial moment. It is clear from these accounts that God is exercising, or seeking to exercise, personal influ-ence on the sinner for some considerable period of time prior to the decisive shift. It is just that the individual is not aware of a series of individually small effects of this influence, effects that are accumulating during the process. But it should be obvious that motivational shifts, even large motivational shifts, can occur below the conscious level. Hence, if there were sufficient reason to adopt the interpersonal model, the phe-nomenology of regeneration could be made to fit it.

Having discussed the interpersonal model, it is time for a counter-attack from the fiat model, which might be developed as follows. All this talk of respecting the integrity of the human person is quite inappropri-ate in the light of the actual divine-human relationship. My opponent is thinking of a relationship between *adult* human beings. True enough, if I were capable of directly modifying my wife's attitudes, whether by hypnotism, brain-washing, or whatever, and I were to use this power to bring those attitudes more into line with my wishes, I would be violating her personal integrity in doing so. I would be exercising control over her that one human being has no right exercising over another. But our sta-tus vis-à-vis God is quite different from the status of one adult human being vis-à-vis another. We should take more seriously the idea that even after having been "born again" we are only "babes in Christ"; we have only begun the new life. Therefore the rules governing the interactions of adult human beings are quite unsuitable for divine-human interac-tion. Let us think for a moment of the parent-infant relationship. The conscientious parent does everything she can, within limits set by other constraints, to mold the motivational structure of the child in what she deems a desirable direction, *without obtaining the infant's consent for these proceedings.* Of course, the human parent is not capable of insti-tuting and extinguishing desires, scruples, and attitudes in the infant by fiat. But what if she were? Would she use this power to instill a good character in her child? I think she would. Would she be condemned for doing so? On what grounds? She certainly is not condemned for using every mode of influence at her command to see to it that the child devel-ops as good a character as possible. On the grounds that these changes have been brought about without the child's consent? But an infant is in no position to give consent; the infant has not developed to the point of being able to make a judgment on the matter. If the parent could accomplish her purposes by fiat she would merely have a more effective way of bringing about what she is already seeking to accomplish by the means at her command. Then why suppose that God would refrain from directly altering the character of the believer? Of course, the adult believer is not incapable of making a judgment about such things, as the child is. Nevertheless, it could be argued that the "babe in Christ" is in no position to make sound judgments as to what is best for him, what kind of person it would be best for him to be, or what kind of life he should be leading. And even if he is in a position to make sound general pronouncements on these matters he is incapable of working out the details. It is only *after* the right sort of character has developed that he is in a position to judge. The opposing view is one more manifestation of the basic sin of pride, the tendency to deny our proper relationship of subservience to God and to demand our rights before God.[16]

I will rule that this controversy between the fiat and interpersonal models is a standoff. However there are what I take to be weightier objections to the fiat model. The basic point is this. If God is to transform me into a saint by a fiat why should he do such an incomplete job of it, at least one that is far from complete at any given moment (up to now!), and why should the transformation be strung out over such an extended period? If the process depends on the creature's responses to divine influences we can understand both of these features; but on the fiat theory they seem to be inexplicable. Of course, God *could* have reasons we cannot understand for issuing his fiats in this kind of pattern; after all, we often fail to understand why God does things as he does. But insofar as we are in a position to form a judgment on the matter, the present consideration does provide a strong reason against the fiat theory and in support of some view according to which human responses play a significant role in the process.

IV

Now I want to call attention to an inadequacy in both the fiat and the communication models. Noting this will bring us to the second main issue of the paper, the externality or internality of the work of the Holy Spirit in sanctification.

The inadequacy is simply that both models represent God as relatively external to the believer. To be sure there is a way in which God is always internal to everything in his creation. God is omnipresent. In whatever sense he can be said to be located at all he is, at every moment, located everywhere. Whatever this comes to, and there are different views on that, God's activity of sustaining a tree, for example, in existence, and everything else he does vis-à-vis that tree, is done *within* the tree. God is always where he works. Our two models do not, of course, deny that God is internal to the person in this way in his sanctifying activity.

Nevertheless, the New Testament and much other Christian litera-ture represent God as internal to the believer in a special way in his work of regeneration and sanctification. This internality is represented as requir-ing the satisfaction of certain special conditions, whereas God's omni-presence obtains whatever conditions the believer does or does not sat-isfy. Thus in the farewell discourses of the fourth gospel Jesus says: "If you love me you will obey my commands; and I will ask the Father, and he will give you another to be your Advocate, who will be with you for ever—the Spirit of truth . . . he dwells with you and is in you" (14:15–17). "Anyone who loves me will heed what I say; then my Father will love him, and we will come to him and make our dwelling with him." Again, in the great figure of the vine and the branches, the integral connection of the branch to the vine is presented as optional. "No branch can bear fruit by itself, but only if it remains united with the vine; no more can you bear fruit, unless you remain united with me. I am the vine, and you the branches. He who dwells in me, as I dwell in him, bears much fruit; for apart from me you can do nothing. He who does not dwell in me is thrown away like a withered branch" (15:4–6). Finally, Christ, and the church, *prays* for mutual indwelling, and one does not request some-thing that will necessarily be the case. "But it is not for these alone that I pray, but for those also who through their words put their faith in me; may they all be one: as thou, Father, are in me, and I in thee, so also may they be in us, that the world may believe that thou didst send me" (John 17:20–21). And from the Anglican Eucharistic prayer," . . . hum-bly beseeching thee that we, and all others who shall be partakers of this Holy Communion, may worthily receive the most precious Body and Blood of thy Son Jesus Christ, be filled with thy grace and heavenly benediction, and made one body with him, that he may dwell in us, and we in him." But no extensive documentation is needed to make the point. It is fundamental to the whole Christian scheme of salvation that in order for the Holy Spirit to be within me in the way that is distinctive of the Christian life I must satisfy conditions over and above being a crea-ture of God; I must "repent and believe the Gospel," or I must be baptised, or I must do whatever is necessary to be drawn into the Chris-tian community. This indwelling is only a new birthright, not a creature right.

And now the point is that the fiat and interpersonal models do not embody this special mode of internality. Of course I cannot demonstrate this without making explicit just what sort of internality this is; and that is a goal of the ensuing discussion (or of the larger discussion of what this paper is a fragment). Nevertheless, prior to such specification, I can at least indicate why it seems to me that the models are deficient in this respect.

First, the fiat model, as we have already shown, represents God as acting on the believer in the same fashion God acts on all the rest of his creation. The particular effects he brings about in sanctification differ from any that he could bring about in a stone or a tree, but the manner of going about it is the same. God simply wills that a certain change shall be brought about, and thereby it is. The model does not deny that God is present to the believer in some more intimate fashion, but no such fashion is built into the account.

As for the interpersonal model, it does not represent God as more internal to the believer than one human person is internal to another when they are related as intimately as possible. At least it does not represent God as any more internal to the believer than that in its distinctive account of the work of sanctification.[17] The distinctive thrust of the interpersonal model lies in its construal of the sanctifying work of the Holy Spirit on the analogy of the moral influence one human being can exert on another, by speech, by provision of a role model, and by emotional bonds. But all this leaves the parties involved external to each other in a fundamental way; they are separate, distinct persons, each with his or her own autonomy and integrity. Of course, human relationships can be more or less intimate; and at their most intimate they are even spoken of, figuratively, in the language of mutual indwelling—"I just feel that you are a part of me," "I carry some of you around with me wherever I go." *Unless* the talk of the indwelling of the Holy Spirit can be interpreted in just such a figurative manner the interpersonal model does not embody the appropriate sort of internality. Let us now turn to the crucial question of whether the indwelling of the Holy Spirit is thought of in the New Testament, in the church, and in the articulation of Christian experience generally, as something different from any purely human intimacy that is only figuratively a case of indwelling.

I will not aspire to coercive proof in this matter; I will merely consider what sort of language has been deemed most appropriate by those who have most to report of these matters. Here I am struck by the way in which the work of the Spirit is so often spoken of in terms of the believer being *filled, permeated, pervaded*, with the Spirit, with love, joy, peace, power, confidence, serenity, energy, and other gifts of the Spirit, and of the Spirit being *poured out* into us.[18] The experience of the Spirit seems to lend itself to an articulation in terms of something like a *force*, a *gaseous substance*, or, to go back to the etymology of *pneuma* and *spiritus*, a *breath*, a movement of the air. One is impelled to report the proceedings in terms of one's being *pervaded* by something that provides one with new resources, new directions, new tendencies, a "new spirit." This language is, of course, eminently suited to the articulation of "charismatic phenomena"—prophecy, speaking with tongues, and the like—where one seems to have been seized by a power, indeed by an agent, from without, so that what one is speaking and doing is not really being done by oneself; one is simply a means used by the agent that has taken possession of one to do *its* work. Now whatever is to be said about these phenomena, we have already rejected this "takeover" model as adequate for the process of sanctification. But, and this is the important point, it is not only in cases of "possession" that one speaks of being filled or permeated by the Holy Spirit. This is richly illustrated by such biblical passages as those just cited.

These ways of talking about the work of the Spirit seem to present it as quite another matter than intercourse with another person that is separate from the believer in the way in which two human beings are separate from each other, however intimate their relationship. The root metaphor is much more materialistic than that. Being filled with the Spirit is like being plugged into a source of electricity, or being permeated by fog, or, closer to the etymology, being inflated by air pressure, or being filled with a liquid. Of course these material analogies are grossly inadequate. The Holy Spirit *is* personal; the believer is in a personal relationship with the Spirit, and the goal of sanctification is a distinctively personal goal, both as being a goal that involves a state of a person and as being the kind of goal a person would have. Nevertheless, the wide consensus on the appropriateness of this language of filling and permeating indicates that the indwelling of the Holy Spirit is of a fundamentally different character from the relationship of two human persons, however intimate, different by reason of being much more an internal matter. Or so I shall suppose. I shall endeavor to cast some light on just what different and more internal sort of interpersonal relationship it is.[19]

The answer is to be found, I believe, in the idea that by the indwelling of the Holy Spirit we "come to share in the very being of God" (2 Peter 1:4; see also 1 Corinthians 1:9), we partake of, or participate in, the divine nature. This concept has been made central in the Roman Catholic doctrine of "sanctifying grace." Thus Aquinas speaks of "the light of grace" as "a participation in the divine nature" (*Summa Theologica* I–II, 100, a. 4.).[20]

As an initial fix on this idea let us think of our being "drawn into" the divine life and living it, to the extent our limited nature permits. We realize in our life and, to some extent, in our consciousness, the very life of God himself. Once we have made this idea central, much of the biblical and other material with which we have been dealing falls into a new sort of pattern. The "new birth" can be understood as the initiation *in us* of the divine life, this life being *grafted* onto us, so that *we* are living this life; a rebirth indeed! All the talk in John (gospel and epistles) about our becoming "sons of God" is given a new depth. We become sons of God not just quasi-legally, by proclamation or decree, but also in a more intrinsic sense; just as a biological son shares a nature with the parents, so we, to some extent, come to share a nature with God. In the "high priestly prayer," when Jesus says, "as thou, Father, art in me, and I in thee, so also may they be in us. . . . The glory which thou gavest me I have given to them, that they may be one, as we are one; I in them and thou in me, may they be perfectly one" (John 17:21–23), he can be understood fairly literally as asking God to bring it about that believers may share, in the measure of which they are capable, in the same divine life that is his by nature. "God became man in order that man might become God" (St. Augustine); "Adoptive sonship is really a shared likeness of the eternal sonship of the Word" (St. Thomas Aquinas: *ST* III, q. 3, a. 8.) The Eucharistic reception of the consecrated bread and wine can be seen, according to one's sacramental theology, as an actual reinforcement of, or addition to, the divine life in which one is partaking, or as a symbol of that participation. An understanding of sanctification in these terms we shall dub the "sharing model."

But perhaps this is just to explain the partially unknown by the totally unknown. What sense can we make of a creature's *sharing* in the divine life? The rest of this paper will be devoted to this issue (and much more would be required to deal with it properly), together with the attempt to understand sanctification in these terms. Here are a couple of preliminary points, to smooth the way somewhat. First, let us set aside any mystical idea of a wholesale *identification* of the human person with God. The terms 'share in,' 'partake in,' and 'participate in' are to be distinguished from 'is' or 'is identical with.' Otherwise all the objections to the "takeover model" return in strength. If I were God I would not have the sinful tendencies I do, I would not have to struggle for an increase of sanctity, and so on. A human being shares in the divine life in a way that is possible for a finite being of that sort, one that is moreover disfigured by sin. Just what way that is we must consider. Second, the sharing must be compatible with a protracted process of growth in holiness. So the divine life one receives at the outset is not, in every respect, all that the individual is capable of. There may be some sense in which the participation is complete from the first, but that sense will have to be such as to allow for subsequent growth in the individual's moral character.

Now I would like to consider a certain Roman Catholic interpretation of our participation in the divine nature. For this purpose I shall use the excellent presentation in *The Theology of Grace* by Jean Daujat.[21] Quotations in this paragraph will be from this work. Since the life of God consists in a perfect knowledge of himself and a perfect love of himself for his own sake, our participation in the divine life will consist of our attaining a knowledge of God as he is in himself and a love of God for his own sake (rather than for what he can do for us). Needless to say, neither the knowledge nor the love, especially the former, can be exactly like the divine exemplars thereof; but, so far as our finitude will allow, we are enabled by sanctifying grace to enjoy the kind of knowledge and love of God enjoyed by God himself. Grace enables us to do in these regards what we are incapable of by our own nature. " . . . grace gives to our human intellect as an object of knowledge what is the proper object of the divine intelligence, that is, God himself in all his reality and all his divine perfection; and grace gives to our human wills as an object of love what is the proper object of the divine will, that is, God himself, loved for his own sake in his infinite divine goodness. Thus it is that grace deifies us, makes us share in what constitutes the very nature of God, and thereby establishes us, through the complete intimacy of knowledge and love, in a fellowship of love with God, whom we know and love in himself and for himself, as children know and love their father" (p. 73). Since "It is impossible for man to be God substantially, . . . it is not by our substance but by knowledge and love that the divine nature is imparted to us. Our union with God by grace is not substantial unity, but only in the order of knowledge and love" (p. 74). It is only as an *object* of knowledge and love that God is present within us by sanctifying grace. " . . . knowledge and love mean the presence of the object known and loved in the subject knowing and loving, which possesses within itself the known and loved object by knowing and loving it. Thus, then, does grace give us what does not belong to our nature, and what our nature cannot procure by itself—the possession of God present within us as the object of knowledge and love" (p. 73).[22]

My objection to this account is that it leaves God too external and so fails to account for the distinctive sort of internality we are seeking to understand. God is present within us *only* as something known and loved. It is stipulated that the knowledge and love is of a sort of which we are not naturally capable; but the way in which the object of this higher knowledge and love is present in the subject is the familiar Aristotelian-Thomist way in which *any* object of an intentional attitude is present within the subject. On this account, God is not present to me in any different, any more intimate way than that in which my wife is present to me as an object of knowledge and love. My "sharing" and "participation" in the divine life amounts to no more than my having, in infinitely lesser measure, a knowledge and love of God *of the same sort* as that possessed by God himself. What is shared are attributes, features, aspects. On this account I do no share in the divine life in any way other than that in which I share in your life when you and I know and love something (perhaps you) in the same way. And because the "sharing in the divine life" is of this relatively innocuous sort, the account provides us no new resources for understanding the divine role in sanctification. How does "sanctifying grace" as so understood *sanctify*? It will be by some combination of our first two models. First God, by fiat, will bestow on the individual the capacity and, presumably, the tendency, to know and love him in this higher way. Then, by virtue of this knowledge and love, the individual is in a closer interpersonal relation with God and so in a better position to receive influences from him by way of messages, example, loving encouragement, and so on. No new illumination of the work of sanctification is forthcoming.

By contrast, I should like to suggest a stronger, more literal, construal of the sharing notion. To my mind, all the talk of being filled, permeated, pervaded by the Spirit, of the Spirit's being poured out into our hearts strongly suggests that there is a literal merging or mutual interpenetration of the life of the individual and the divine life, a breaking down of the barriers that normally separate one life from another. You and I might be in close personal communion, we might have mutual liking, respect, regard, affection for each other, we might share many interests, attitudes, and reactions. But still our two lives are effectively insulated from each other, with perhaps minor exceptions to be noted below, by physical and psychological barriers. Mine is lived within my skin and yours within yours. When we have similar attitudes, still I have my attitude and you have yours; when we react alike to something, still each of us must react to it on his or her own. If we can now imagine some breakdown of those barriers, perhaps by a neural wiring hookup, so that your reactions, feelings, thoughts, and attitudes, or some of them, are as immediately available to me as my own, and so that they influence my further thinking and feeling and behavior in just the same way that my own do, there would have occurred a partial merging of our hitherto insulated lives. Some of your life would have become as intimately involved with my life as one part of my life is with another. When you are moved by a scene I will *thereby* be moved with your feelings; when you find a remark distasteful I will *thereby* find it distasteful. This is not to say that you will have taken over and eliminated me. Some of your life has been caught up in mine and vice versa, but caught up alongside what would have been there anyway. The details of this could be spelled out in various ways. The merging might be wholly egalitarian, with alien attitudes, thoughts, and reactions on exactly the same footing as the natives. This might lead to considerable incompatibility and tension. Another version would preserve a privileged status for the old settlers, relegating the new immigrants to a servile position. More soberly, your thoughts and reactions might influence the further course of events in me by virtue of being immediately accessible to me, but without being strictly speaking mine until I have taken them up in a certain way. And many other arrangements would be conceivable. However my aim at present is not to make an exhaustive catalogue of modes of life-sharing, but only to suggest that the concept of life-sharing between two persons is one that can be spelled out to some extent.

Another illustration of life-sharing is found in the breakdown of barriers between one psychological subsystem and another within a single human being. It is a truism of psychotherapy that people often wall off a certain sphere of thought, affect, or conation from the rest of the psyche. Perhaps I "never think of" my father and do not consciously feel anything about him and my childhood interactions with him. But it may be that I do have strong attitudes and emotional reactions toward all this that continue to exert influence on my thought and behavior in various ways, but not via the normal conscious route. I have shut it out from conscious thought and feeling, and so my attitudes to it are forced to express themselves in devious ways. If, through psychotherapy or otherwise, these retaining walls are breached, there may be a sudden rush of thought and feeling into consciousness. The conscious part of me has regained touch with a part of my own life; my reactions to my father can now be integrated with the rest of me, and I can enjoy a greater degree of wholeness. There is now a sharing of life, a mutual participation between that memories-of-and-attitudes-toward-the-father complex and the rest of the psyche.

Finally, a more tenuous source of the concept. Earlier I alluded to the possibility of an exception to the insulation of the lives of different human beings, actual exceptions not just conceivable ones. I was thinking of what happens when two people share a moving experience, like listening to a performance of a great piece of music. Why is it so much more satisfying to "share" something like this than to enjoy it alone? I find it hard to understand this without supposing that each listener actually experiences, to some extent, the reactions of the other; so that I am not just reacting to the music on my own but am also, to some extent, reacting with your reactions as well. This would account for the fact that a shared experience is so much richer. If this is a correct reading of the phenomenon, it is another example of the breakdown of the normal barriers between lives. Perhaps we have an analogous phenomenon in the "identification" of the individual with the group that occurs at political rallies, religious worship, and sports events. Here too, perhaps, there is an interpenetration of reactions, flowing through what are normally impermeable walls, so that each individual shares, to some extent, in the life of the others.

We could also turn to mystical experience as a help in getting a purchase on the notion of life-sharing. Such experience is typically reported as involving a drastic breakdown of barriers, a merging of the self with the One, God, Nature, or whatever. However, this might be an unwelcome ally, since mystics often report a complete identification of self and God, and I am seeking to build up a concept of a *partial* sharing in the life of God. A study of orthodox Christian mystics, who are careful to avoid any suggestion of human-divine identification, might be quite pertinent to our problem. However, we shall have to forego that in this paper.

Here are a couple of additional points about life-sharing. First, an advantage of the term 'life' for what is shared is that it does not restrict us to a sharing of consciousness or of conscious psychological states and processes. This is not to say that there will not be conscious reverberations for the individual, but it will not necessarily be limited to what the individual is conscious of. I may be in contact with the divine life, and the latter may be actively involved in the work of sanctification, in ways I am not aware of. Second, it may well be that the sharing is fuller, or different in some other way, for different aspects of life. I will just mention a few possibilities. The constant admonitions of spiritual directors not to put much stock in feelings which are evanescent and unstable, and which may or may not be present when the spirit is at work, suggests that feelings are an epiphenomenon of the basic part of the sharing, rather than constituting its essence. On the other hand, the abundant testimony to feeling "filled with the Spirit," feeling overwhelmed by love, joy, peace, etc., suggests that feelings and other experiences may be what is most readily and completely shared.[23] The sharing of attitudes, tendencies, and values, may require much more time for consummation.

Finally certain cognitive elements—beliefs, ways of looking at things, putting the divine scheme of salvation at the center of one's construal of the world, etc.—may be readily taken on by the individual from the Spirit, even while little progress has been made in the transformation of character.

Thus far I have, at most, lent some color to the idea of a literal sharing of divine life with the believer, and much work remains to be done to fill out the details. But the task remaining for this paper is to indicate how the work of sanctification might be accomplished through God's sharing his life with us. The first point to make is that this model is by no means exclusive of the other two. If the Holy Spirit is within me by virtue of a breakdown of barriers between my life and the divine life, God may still choose to carry out some alterations in my character by fiat; and he may seek to influence me by exhortation and loving encouragement. These moves will be made from a more "internal position" by virtue of the sharing, but they would still exemplify what is made central in the other models.[24] But even if sharing is compatible with the other means of sanctification, my present concern is to explore the distinctive implications of sharing for the work of sanctification; I want to show how, by virtue of sharing his life with us, God *thereby* provides us with resources for growth in the Christian life.

Let us recall that our specific interest in sharing is with its bearing on character development, rather than, for example, the experience and knowledge of God. We want to consider how a participation in the divine life might alter the nature and/or strength of tendencies, attitudes, desires, habits, emotional proclivities, and the like. Now just what possibilities there are for this depends on how we tie up some of the threads hitherto left dangling. Consider those aspects of the divine life that are shared. More specifically, think of an attitude of love toward all of creation, or, more modestly, toward certain people with whom I come into contact. Are we to think of my sharing that divine attitude as sufficient for my *having* that attitude in the same fully incorporated fashion in which I have all my other attitudes? Or are we to think of the sharing in itself as consisting in some relation in which I stand to that attitude that falls short of full blooded possession, albeit a relation that comes closer to full possession than a mere awareness of the attitude. On the former alternative the sharing model turns into a particular version of the fiat model. For presumably divine volitions play a crucial role in all these models. On the sharing model, in particular, it will be by divine fiat that I share whatever I share of the divine life. It is not as if participation in the divine life is at my beck and call; I participate when, and to the extent that, God permits me to. But then if the (partial) sharing of God's love itself constitutes my having that attitude of love, this is just a particular way in which God alters my motivational structure by fiat. This version of the fiat model will escape the curse of externality that haunts other versions; if God produces in me by fiat a loving attitude, by way of willing that, to some extent, the barriers should be broken down between his life and mine, this could hardly be deemed an *external* operation on his part. However, there will still be no room left for a human response to divine grace in the engendering of my attitude. That is not to say that no room is left for human activity, including free voluntary activity, at any stage of the work of salvation. It can still be up to me whether, or to what extent, I do what the infused habits and attitudes tend to lead me to do; it can be up to me whether these tendencies are to be encouraged, strengthened, and extended by my further thoughts and actions. Nevertheless, so far as the crucial changes in tendencies are concerned it will still be a matter of divine fiat alone.

Thus in order to explore the possibility of a place for human cooperation in this matter we will have to consider the idea that my sharing of divine love, in itself, amounts to something less than my fully taking on this attitude, while at the same time amounting to something that can be a push or a tendency in that direction. How might that be? I suppose that the weakest internalization of divine love that could lay claim to being a *sharing* in that love, in a way that goes beyond the mere exemplification of a common feature, would be an immediate awareness of that love, the kind of awareness that one has of one's own feelings, attitudes, and tendencies. This would, indeed, be a sort of breakdown of the walls that separate different lives, a breakdown of barriers to experiential accessibility. Normally I cannot be aware of your thoughts, feelings, and sentiments in the same direct and unmediated way in which I am aware of my own. If I could, then the walls that separate our lives would have been breached in a very significant respect, and I could be said, in an important sense, to share in your (conscious) life. This breach would be of a cognitive nature, in the first instance, but it could have conative implications.

If God has permitted me to be aware (to some extent) of his loving tendencies in the same direct way that I am aware of my own, that means that they are "available" to me as models in a maximally direct and vivid fashion. I now have a sense of what it is, what it feels like, to love others in this fashion. I can model my attitudes, not just on external manifestations of love, but on the inner springs of those manifestations. And by psychological processes the exact nature of which I will not try to delineate, processes that I very well might be able to facilitate or hinder by my own choices and my own effort, this may lead to similar loving tendencies in me, where these latter tendencies would be mine in the fullest sense. On this picture of the matter, the divine contribution is largely cognitive, the presentation in a specially vivid and intimate way of a role model; the actual changes in the individual's own motivational structure come from responses, voluntary and involuntary, to these models.

I believe that the preceding constitutes a possible model of (at least some of) the work of sanctification, a model that deserves further exploration. But having come this far, a further step beckons. Immediate cognitive accessibility is not the last stage on the road to conative assimilation that falls short of installation by divine fiat. If I can be directly aware of divine love without thereby taking it on as my own, why can't I have *some* tendency toward loving in that way without my being fully disposed to love in that way whenever the opportunity arises. Tendencies can enjoy all degrees of integration into the dominant motivational structure. I can have passing fancies or yens that, without active encouragement on my part, will never blossom into effective action tendencies. I can have idle wishes to take a voyage around the world, or to chuck it all and live on a yacht, or to take up the cello. These are genuine conative tendencies, not just purely cognitive awareness of possibilities. I do have some tendency to do these things (or to take steps in the direction of doing them). But those tendencies are so weak, or so effectively opposed by stronger interests or systems of interests, that unless I take active steps to encourage them and to dismantle the opposition there is no significant chance that they will influence my behavior.

Why shouldn't we think of participation in the divine life as consisting, in part, in the introduction into my conative system of initially weak, isolated, and fragile tendencies like those just mentioned, as well as consisting, in part, of my immediate awareness of God's tendencies of the same sorts? This would be a foot in the conative as well as in the cognitive door; it would be a foothold, a beachhead from which the progressive conquest of the individual's motivational system could get a start. This would be a decisive act on the part of God without which, let us say, the individual has no chance of sanctification. Without the infusion of these initially weak and isolated tendencies there would be nothing to effectively oppose the status quo, the domination of the person by sinful self-centeredness and self-aggrandizement. But there is plenty left for the individual to do, by way of building up the motivational system from the rudimentary beginning supplied by God. At this point the mechanical metaphor might well give way to the organic metaphors used so effectively in the New Testament. We have been talking about a particular way in which God might sow a seed the further fate of which depends on what the recipients do with it. One is put in mind not only of the parable of the sower, but of the striking images in the fourth gospel of "water springing up into eternal life" and of the "true bread come down from heaven." It may well be that in its concern to give glory to God and to put a check to sinful pride and presumption, the Christian theological tradition has been too ready to attribute all the work of salvation to divine activity and to neglect the roles we all, in practice, realize that we ourselves have. The model I have just been suggesting holds out the promise of according both partners their due share, while yet recognizing the necessity and the crucial initiatory role of divine grace.

In conclusion, I will summarize the advantages of the sharing model. First, as just intimated, it makes an important place in sanctification for human response and human effort, while at the same time recognizing the divine initiative as absolutely crucial.[25] Second, unlike the other two models it recognizes a distinctive and fundamental sort of internality in the process of sanctification, a mode of internality that goes beyond any *interpersonal* intimacy, however close, and that goes beyond the internality God necessarily enjoys with respect to all of creation. Furthermore it indicates how this mode of internality is (or can be) essentially involved in the divine work of sanctification. And because it makes this mode of internality central to the process of sanctification it reveals the goal of sanctification to be not just moral improvement, of whatever a pitch, but rather a full communion with God, the fullest possible sharing in the divine nature, with respect to which moral development is both a necessary prerequisite and an essential component. Finally, the sharing model permits a satisfactory interpretation of regeneration. To be born again is to come to share in the divine nature. Given our development of this latter notion, regeneration is thereby represented both as a decisive divine initiative that fundamentally transforms the human condition, and as something that in itself leaves the individual with a lot of work to do before she is ready for full communion with God.

NOTES

1. At one time I thought that in order to understand the concept of the Holy Spirit one would first have to understand what it is for a human being to engage in spiritual activities, to be spiritual, or to lead a spiritual life. This is, indeed, in accordance with the general rule for theological language: Concepts of divine attributes or aspects are formed by derivation from concepts of human matters. However, I am now convinced that in this case the derivation is in the

opposite direction. I cannot see anything that marks off what in Christianity is called the "spiritual life" or "spirituality" (for human beings) except for their explanation by the influence of the Holy Spirit. A human being is a *spiritual* person, manifests true *spirituality*, provides *spiritual leadership*, etc., to the extent that she exhibits such characteristics as love, peace, serenity, joy, and absence of self-centeredness, self-seeking, and dependence on recognition from others. I cannot see what differentiates this list of attributes from other commonly prized features of which we are capable, such as intelligence, resourcefulness, and prudence, except that the former are deemed to be especially prized by God, given special divine priority in his rescue operation for sinful human beings, and so are thought to be what the Holy Spirit is specially concerned to foster in us. Apart from this theological dimension, spirituality simply becomes a catalogue of those attainments of which human beings are capable by virtue of their mental capacities. (For a couple of examples of what spirituality becomes when shorn of its theological dimension, see George Santayana, *The Realm of Spirit* and Julian Huxley, *Religion Without Revelation.*)

2. This is not to say what constitutes isolation or participation. I do not intend these remarks to constitute a condemnation of monasticism. There are many ways in which the religious, even the cloistered religious, can be in vital contact with the community of believers.

3. *The Varieties of Religious Experience* (New York: The Modern Library, 1902), pp. 31–32.

4. I also believe, though this is not directly relevant to this paper, that the individual's awareness of the regenerating and sanctifying work of the Holy Spirit constitutes a crucial part of his basis or ground for Christian belief. See my "Christian Experience and Christian Belief," in *Faith and Rationality*, ed. Alvin Plantinga and Nicholas Wolterstorff (Notre Dame, Ind.: University of Notre Dame Press, 1983), even though the discussion there is not explicitly in terms of the work of the Holy Spirit.

5. This quotation and all other biblical quotations are from *The New English Bible* (New York: Oxford University Press, 1976).

6. "We must know that the only thing we possess of ourselves is evil. Good, on the contrary, comes from us but also from Almighty God who, by interior inspirations so forestalls us as to make us will, and then comes to our assistance so that we may not will in vain, but may be able to carry out what we will" (St. Gregory). "All good thoughts and all good works, all the efforts and all the virtues whereby since the dawn of faith we have made our way to God, have truly God as their author" (Pope Zosimus).

7. A. H., Strong, *Systematic Theology* (Philadelphia: Griffith & Rowland Press, 1909), pp. 818–819.

8. Ibid., p. 820.

9. Emil Brunner, *The Christian Doctrine of the Church, Faith, and The Consummation*, tr. D. Cairns & T. H. L. Parker (Philadelphia: Westminster Press, 1962), p. 272.

10. Jean Daujat, *The Theology of Grace*, vol. 23 of the *Twentieth Century Encyclopedia of Catholicism*, ed. Henri Daniel-Rops (New York: Hawthorn Books, 1959), p. 63.

11. Ibid., p. 68.

12. Consider also such traditional prayers as the following: "Almighty and everlasting God, who hatest nothing that thou hast made and dost forgive the sins of all those who are penitent: Create and make in us new and contrite hearts, that we, worthily lamenting our sins and acknowledging our wretchedness, may obtain of thee, the God of all mercy, perfect remission and forgiveness" (Collect for Ash Wednesday). "Lord of all power and might, who art the author and giver of all good things: Graft in our hearts the love of thy Name, increase in us true religion, nourish us with all goodness, and bring forth in us the fruit of good works" (Collect for the 17th Sunday after Pentecost). "Almighty and everlasting God, . . . make us to love that which thou dost command" (Collect for the 25th Sunday after Pentecost). "O God, from whom all holy desires, all good counsels, and all just works do proceed: Give unto thy servants that peace which the world cannot give, that our hearts may be set to obey thy commandments" (Evening Prayer). These prayers and all others quoted in this paper are taken from *The Book of Common Prayer, According to the use of the Episcopal Church* (New York: The Church Hymnal Corporation, 1977).

13. G. W. H. Lampe, *God as Spirit* (Oxford: Clarendon Press, 1977).

14. To understand some of these passages one must realize that Lampe considers creation and sanctification to be different stages of a single process, both involving an activity of God as a person. We are not concerned here with that aspect of his view.

15. The reference in this last quotation to God's "acting upon" as well as "interacting with" us is only one of many indications that Lampe has not broken completely with the fiat model. Nevertheless the main thrust of his thought is clearly in the direction of the interpersonal model.

16. A more complete treatment would give consideration to a mediating position according to which the divine fiat would be confined to removing our inability to respond in the right way to divine initiative. On this view God does not produce or install particular motivational tendencies in us by fiat. Those will develop, if they do, by response to divine influence, as on the interpersonal model. But it is not all interpersonal interaction. God does produce a crucial change in us by an act of will, viz., the removal of blocks that had hitherto made it impossible for us to make the appropriate responses. This does not determine those responses, but it makes them possible.

17. This last qualification is needed because the model will recognize divine omnipresence, and that constitutes a mode of internality that is not exemplified in human intercourse. But we have seen that this internality is not what is distinctive of the indwelling of the Holy Spirit.

18. For biblical references, see, e.g., Rom. 5:5, 1 Cor. 12:13, Eph. 5:18, 3:19, Luke 1:67, 4:1; Acts 2:1-21, 10:45. See also such prayers as "O God, who has prepared for those who love thee such good things as pass man's under-

standing: Pour into our hearts such love toward thee, that we, loving thee in all things and above all things, may obtain thy promises, which exceed all that we can desire" (Collect for the 6th Sunday of Easter).

19. To be sure, the permeation language might be taken to support the fiat model. One feels oneself permeated by a power not oneself, bringing with it a new joy, love, etc., just because God is producing this joy and love in the person directly by fiat. But the people who use this language mean to be reporting an activity of God that is not common to all of creation all of the time. They may just be mistaken as to the character of what is going on, but at least we can say that if they are not radically mistaken then what they are reporting is something other than God simply exercising his omnipotence to directly bring about an effect.

20. See also such a traditional prayer as "O God, who didst wonderfully create, and yet more wonderfully restore, the dignity of human nature: Grant that we may share the divine life of him who humbled himself to share our humanity, thy Son Jesus Christ" (Collect for the Second Sunday after Christmas).

21. Jean Daujat, *The Theology of Grace* (New York: Hawthorn, 1959).

22. See also St. Thomas Aquinas, *ST*, I q. 43, a. 3.

23. On the other hand, one might suppose that such feelings are our reactions to, rather than part of what is shared. That would certainly follow from the thesis that feelings are not involved in the divine life.

24. In this connection I would like to disavow any intention to try to place limits on God's action in our lives. I am suspicious of attempts to arrive at unrestrictedly universal conclusions as to how God achieves a certain effect, and still more suspicious of claims as to how God *must* carry out sanctification or any other divine operation. I do not feel that we are capable of that degree of insight into the possibilities for, or actualities of, God's activity. I am only seeking to lay out certain modes of operation that, so far as we can see, are real possibilities and, in addition, to suggest that some of these modes are more strongly suggested than others by the data at our disposal.

25. This is in contrast to the fiat model, which attributes the whole proceeding to God; the advantage over the interpersonal model will be brought out next.

Christian Liberty

ROBERT MERRIHEW ADAMS

The idea of freedom from the Law of God is one of the most important, and also one of the most deeply perplexing, themes in Christian ethics. It is widely agreed that Christian ethics ought not to be "legalistic." All too often, however, confusion sets in at this point, and the alternative to legalism that is offered us turns out to be irrationalism or act utilitarianism. From time to time, throughout the history of Christianity, the idea of Christian liberty has been carried to clearly unacceptable extremes of antinomianism. Even more disturbing, because more prevalent, are difficulties that have arisen in rejecting antinomianism; Christian liberty has been so interpreted as to be compatible with moralities that are very oppressive and ways of life that seem anything but free.

It is my hope to work out a conception of Christian liberty that avoids these dangers. There are two sides to the conception. Christian liberty is in the first place a feature of an ethical system, of the system of divine commands. But it is also a motivational ideal, a conception of the subjective freedom with which a person ought to respond to life's occasions. These two sides are inseparable; we are concerned with the kind of freedom that has to be built into the moral principles under which we see ourselves as living, in order to make it possible for us to be, or to become increasingly, the kind of people we ought to be, with the kinds of motives and projects we ought to have. My interest in this subject is part of a more general interest in the relation between the ethics of actions and the ethics of motives. In its most abstract form the central problem that will concern us in the present essay is how to provide a proper place in the ethical life for *beliefs* about what one *ought* to *do*, without letting them drive out other springs of action, such as *love* for human individuals.

In our study of relations between love and obligation, we will have occasion to discuss four main aspects of Christian liberty: I call them

freedom from fear (section 1), theonomy (section 2), friendship with
God (section 3), and the possibility of supererogation (section 4). There
are certainly other aspects of liberty that are important in Christianity—
political aspects of liberty, for example, and freedom from the bondage
of sin, which is the freedom most emphasized in the New Testament.
But I think the four aspects that will be examined here are the most
important for the idea of freedom from the Law of God.

1. FREEDOM FROM FEAR

One thing that is certainly meant when Christians say that Christ
has set us free from the Law is that we need not earn our salvation by
obedience and good works. Indeed we *cannot* earn salvation that way,
first of all because we are not good enough and more profoundly because
salvation is the enjoyment of God's love, which is in its very nature grace
and not the kind of thing that can be earned. Salvation is God's free
gift.

It remains, however, that Christians must (in some important ethical sense of 'must') fulfill many duties. For instance, they must not murder, steal, cheat, or do other immoral actions. Paul is quite emphatic
about this, despite his proclamation of freedom from the Law. Thus far
there is no inconsistency. To say that we do not have to do good works
in order to be saved, or to avoid damnation, is not to say that we are not
morally obliged to do them or that God does not command them. The
commands of a trusted authority are still commands and may strin-
gently bind our conscience, even if they are not enforced by threats of
punishment or promises of reward. There are things that we morally
have to do, even if we would not be punished for not doing them.

Suppose that as I braked my car when approaching a crosswalk
full of pedestrians, I believed I would incur no punishment, divine or
human, if I ran right over them. I hope I would still *want* to stop, just as
much as if I feared punishment. But I also hope I would still think I *had*
to stop. Failing to stop would be a truly horrible action in relation to the
pedestrians; ethically and religiously it would be wrong, a violation of
something sacred, a sin. We may try to articulate this by saying it is
forbidden by God. It would be a distraction in this context to add that it
will be punished by God. To say that an act is a sin is to say something
about the act itself, in relation to God, rather than about its consequences for the agent.

It is worth dwelling on this point about obligation, for theologians
have often not grasped it. Penitential practices, and the concept of mor-

tal sin, have led in some Catholic moral theology to a tendency to measure the stringency of some ethical obligation by the severity of punishment connected with it. In Protestant theological ethics, on the other hand, an emphasis on salvation by grace has sometimes led to an attempt to eliminate obligation from Christian ethics entirely, rather than to a rejection of the definition of obligation in terms of punishment.

Connected with this in Protestant thought is a dangerous temptation to flatten out ethical distinctions, due to an emphasis on the sinfulness of *all* our actions. The emphasis, I think, is correct; even our best actions are deeply infected with sin. It remains, however, that certain actions *have* to be done, and others do not. Conversely, an act may be sinful, in the sense of proceeding from motives that are sins, even if it is not itself *a sin* in the sense that concerns us here. This point about the relation between acts we ought to perform and motives we ought to have is important. Even if I know that I will have sinful motives for whatever I do now, I have also to recognize that ethically there are certain things I *must* do, and other things I *must not* do. For example, I *have to* stop my car to avoid hitting a pedestrian, whether or not my motives in stopping will be free of sin.

I have been arguing against suggestions that the fact that we need not, and cannot, earn our salvation frees us from all obligation to perform actions commanded by God. In what sense, then, does faith in salvation by God's grace free Christians from the Law? The answer commonly given is the correct answer. Faith in God's grace frees us from fear — more precisely, from the fear that he will hate us, or treat us as if he hated us, if we do wrong. We are still to do good works, but we are to do them out of gratitude and devotion to God and love for our neighbors, not out of fear of punishment.

Two sorts of questions arise about this claim of freedom from fear. (1) The replacement of fear by love as a motive is an important part of the Christian ethical ideal. But is there no place at all for fear in the Christian life? "Perfect love casts out fear" (1 John 4:18). But who is already perfect in love? Not being perfect in love, we ought perhaps to fear the sins themselves that we might commit, even if we ought not to fear that God will hate us for them. And surely Christians ought to be free from the fear of earthly potentates (Matt. 10:28, but cf. Rom. 13:4); but ought they in no sense to fear the Lord? How should the doctrine of salvation be understood, if it offers us freedom from fear of God's hatred and eternal punishment? But these questions will have to wait for another occasion. They would lead us away from the main lines of our argument.

(2) Love and gratitude are surely better motives than fear of punishment, but why should the replacement of the latter by the former be regarded as conferring *liberty*? The first thought that occurs to us in this connection is that to the extent that an action is done from fear of punishment it is not done gladly but under constraint. Actions done from gratitude to God are supposed to be done gladly—the more so the more one trusts in God for the assurance of one's own welfare in the long run. Indeed one may be glad to receive commands from God, so that one may have a way of serving him. This difference in motivation certainly has to do with freedom, for it is a sort of bondage or unfreedom to be constrained to do what one cannot gladly do.

On the other hand, making us like what we have to do is not enough to make us free. That is almost a commonplace in political thought where we have learned to be sensitive to the danger of talk about a "true freedom" which on accurate examination turns out not to be freedom at all. In theology as in politics such talk tempts us to give up the quest for freedom too easily. The replacement of fear by gratitude does not exhaust the meaning of 'Christian liberty'. For being bound in gratitude is still being bound, even if one likes it. And it would be sentimental to suppose that what is done out of love and gratitude is always done gladly.

Suppose one were bound in gratitude to the fulfillment of an arbitrary set of rules governing every detail of one's life. It would be odd to call that liberty, even if one liked it. Christian moralists would generally repudiate such an ethical system as "legalistic," and would do so in the name of Christian liberty. We must therefore look for other aspects of Christian freedom from the Law, besides freedom from fear.

2. THEONOMY

"Everything is permitted," wrote St. Paul, "but not everything is helpful" (1 Cor. 10:23). Both the context and the content of this statement make it clear that he is talking about Christian liberty. It is also very natural (at least for a philosopher) to take 'but not everything is helpful' as proposing a consequentialist morality. On this reading the message would be that the Christian is freed from deontology for a teleological ethics. This interpretation of freedom from the Law has been very influential in Christian ethics. It can even lead to equating the ethics of love with a form of act utilitarianism, as in Joseph Fletcher's *Situation Ethics*.[1]

Such a Christian utilitarianism does offer the most obvious way of constructing a complete moral guide to action on the basis of the single commandment, 'Thou shalt love thy neighbor as thyself.' It construes the commandment as directing us to promote the good of all people, weighing the interests of each person exactly as much as our own. Each person is to count for one, as the classical utilitarians insisted. Utilitarianism can thus be seen as a secular rendition of the commandment of neighbor-love. At worst it carries to an indefensible extreme one of the genuine central themes of Christian ethics. It is no accident that Christian philosophers such as Berkeley and Paley were among the first utilitarians.

Nonetheless the utilitarian version of Christian love is disastrously lopsided. I will not rehearse here all the standard criticisms of utilitarianism. But I will observe, in the first place, that Christianity has usually recognized a more than merely instrumental value in apparently deontological principles regarding, for example, truth-telling, fidelity, and sexual relations. This is so clearly true of Paul's own concrete ethical teaching that it is hard to believe that he really meant to propound a rigorously teleological ethics.

In the second place, it is not obvious what utilitarianism has to do with Christian liberty. It can be seen itself as a harsh slavery. There will virtually always be something it tells us we are obliged to be doing, for there is no limit to the demands of good to be maximized and harm to be prevented. As receptacles of happiness we may or may not have the good fortune to exemplify conveniently the end to be promoted; but as agents, where action has only instrumental value, we satisfy Aristotle's description of a slave, as a "living tool."[2] There is nothing so degrading, dishonorable, or evil, nothing so inimical to our loves or so opposed to our ideals, than we may not be obliged by utilitarianism to do it, if the results will be good enough.[3] Utilitarianism is not Christian liberty.

"Everything is permitted, but not everything is helpful" (1 Cor. 10:23; cf. 6:12). Many scholars think that Paul would not have chosen the words 'Everything is permitted' of his own accord, but that they were a slogan of Corinthian libertines against whom he was arguing, which Paul tried to turn to his own purposes with the qualification, 'but not everything is helpful'. Be that as it may, the sentence has to be stretched to fit much of Paul's ethical teaching. There are certainly kinds of behavior of which he has much worse to say than that they are not "helpful." This is true in particular about fornication, which is one of the topics to which he seems to apply the saying that everything is permitted but not everything is helpful (1 Cor. 6:12-20).

The saying agrees much more easily with what Paul has to say about the other topic to which he applies it — the eating of food that has been offered in pagan sacrifices (1 Cor. 10:14-11:1). Paul seems to be

saying that in this area at least, Christians ought to be governed by teleological considerations. He is fiercely insistent on certain non-teleological
principles — for instance, that idols must not be worshipped. With regard
to food, however, "everything is permitted." There are no kinds of food
intrinsically forbidden, no dietary rules deontologically binding on Christians. What concerns us here is not the difference between Christianity
and Judaism on this point, but the fact that the placing of dietary matters under teleological rather than deontological constraints seems to
Paul to be an instance of Christian liberty. Is there really a positive connection between teleology and liberty?

Yes. A person who is taking the means she judges most effective
toward an end she thinks she ought to pursue is freer, more independent, in an important way, than one who merely follows a rule. She has
made a certain project her own, and relies on her own judgment in carrying it out. But this sort of liberty does not require utilitarianism or a
rigorously teleological ethics. What it requires is that we be given *discretion*. If we are given discretion we need a sense of what is morally important; for we have the responsibility of weighing morally relevant considerations against each other and finding the best course of action, without
having a rule that can be applied mechanically to determine what we
ought to do. This responsibility may be found as well in weighing
deontological considerations against each other, or against teleological
considerations, as in weighing teleological considerations against each
other. A person is not necessarily less free or less responsible in choosing
to be truthful or to respect the rights of her neighbor, *rather than* to
bring about the best possible state of affairs.

Utilitarianism, therefore, does not provide the only model, nor in
my opinion the best, for understanding the sense in which an ethics
exemplifying Christian liberty must be "contextual." A better model is
provided by what John Rawls has called "intuitionism," which is "the
doctrine that there is an irreducible family of first principles which have
to be weighed against one another by asking ourselves which balance, in
our considered judgment, is the most just."[4] This is only a model, a
philosophical first approximation to an understanding of the structure
of this aspect of Christian ethics. We shall shortly question some features of it, but for the time being let us work with Rawls' conception.
He notes that the first principles in an intuitionistic theory could all be
teleological, endorsing competing *goods* whose claims are not to be adju-
dicated by any universally applicable formula.[5] But the intuitionism I
have in mind includes some first principles that are not teleological, not
concerned with the value of the resulting states of affairs. Such a doctrine allows for no less discretion, or reliance on one's own judgment,

than utilitarianism. Indeed it engages a wider range of faculties. It calls on one not only to calculate what action is most likely to have the best consequences, but also to judge, on occasion, whether something else is more imperative than obtaining the best result.

"I no longer call you slaves," says Jesus in John 15:15, "for the slave does not know what his master is doing; but I have called you friends, for I have made known to you everything I have heard from my Father." Slavery is found here in being obliged to do what one does not see the point of. If the slave is a "living tool," it is not necessary for him to see beyond his immediate task. Christians are said not to be God's slaves, but his friends, because he has not merely given them instructions, but has shown them what he is doing. God's friend is not a tool; he or she is invited to be a participant in God's projects, seeing the point of them. The point need not be understood teleologically, or in terms of goods to be maximized; it may sometimes be found more in what is expressed or symbolized by one's actions than in what results from them; it may also be found in a reckless, imprudent loyalty to principles or ideals. Insofar as God's friends see the point of the teachings and the lives that are given to them, they have the responsibility of deciding accordingly what they ought to do.

Shall we conclude, then, that Christians are never to accept any rules or obligations that they do not see the point of? Hardly. The moral development of a child involves much acceptance of rules and directives on authority, simply because they are commanded. In the process of learning to live the Christian life, as a child or as an adult, one will doubtless be wise to accept the authority of some Christian ethical teaching even when one does not see the value of the recommended course of action. But I think it is New Testament teaching that the blindness of such obedience, on any given point, is not to be acquiesced in as a permanent condition. Rather, there is to be a development — a development in Tillich's terms, not from heteronomy to autonomy, but from heteronomy to theonomy. "Autonomy asserts that man . . . is his own law. Heteronomy asserts that man . . . must be subjected to a law, strange and superior to him. Theonomy asserts that the superior law is at the same time, the innermost law of man himself, rooted in the divine ground which is man's own ground."[6] The Christian ideal is not one of heteronomous subjection to a law whose motives are alien to the human agent; it is an ideal of theonomous permeation of the human faculties by the Spirit of God, so that the human agent comes to love what God loves and to see ethical priorities as God sees them.

Paul describes just such a development, on a communal rather than an individual scale, as part of the history of the people of God. The

Law was our *paidagogos* to prepare us for Christ. We were kept under guardianship until Christ came, and until God sent his Spirit into our hearts; since then we are no longer slaves, but sons (Gal. 3:23-26, 4:17). Theonomous, internal guidance by the Spirit has replaced heteronomous, external control by the Law.[7] This development is to be recapitulated in the history of the individual Christian, as it was in Paul's own life.

Perhaps no Christian has completed this development. Perhaps all still have some occasion for obedience that is in some degree blind. Sin blinds us to the point and importance of many moral considerations, and we all have reason to want the advice of others when we face difficult decisions. Nonetheless the Christian is called to vision, not blindness. If intuitionism in Rawls' sense is a good model for the structure of Christian ethics, the Christian is not given a procedure that can be applied mechanically to determine the right course of action. Without such a mechanical procedure, Christian decision making calls for a just sense of the comparative importance of various ethical considerations; and it is not likely that one will have a just sense of how much weight should be given to a principle that one does not see the point of. Intuitionistic decision making requires a light that heteronomy does not provide.

That is not to say that it requires an explicit rationale for every ethical decision. The art of making good intuitionistic decisions is quite different from the art of giving philosophical or theological justifications. And *seeing the point* of an ethical consideration is not so much a matter of being able to explain the point, as of having a feeling for the values involved.

Theologically, the term 'intuitionism' seems inadequate as a characterization of Christian ethics. What may be regarded from a secular viewpoint merely as "intuition" is seen by Christians as *inspiration*. And if we speak of a "discretion" that is given to us as an aspect of Christian liberty, it is not a matter of being entirely on our own. It is not only a freedom from the heteronomous control of an external law; it is also a freedom for the guidance of the Spirit of God within. It is quite explicit in Paul that the leading of the Spirit is the Christian alternative to heteronomous subjection to the letter of a law. "If you are led by the Spirit, you are not under a law" (Gal. 5:18). "For the letter kills, but the Spirit makes alive . . . And where the Spirit of the Lord is, there is freedom" (2 Cor. 3:6, 17).

The Holy Spirit is regarded, however, as working *through* the faculties of a human being, enlightening the mind and awakening, purifying, and sensitizing the heart of love. And it would be presumptuous to suppose that we can separate divine and human input so neatly as to be able to distinguish sharply in practice between inspiration and mere intuition. The Christian can still speak, therefore, of receiving "discretion," in the sense of the freedom to be guided by the faculties that are to be opened to the Spirit.

The Pauline contrast of Spirit and letter suggests another respect in which Rawls' conception of intuitionism does not correspond with the structure of Christian ethics. Rawls speaks of intuitionist decision making as based on "an irreducible family of first principles."[8] In Christian ethics one's ultimate loyalty is not supposed to be to any "principles" or theory (for that would be living by "the letter"), but to a person. To be sure, loyalty to a person will be embodied, at any given time, in an intention to pursue certain goals and act in accordance with certain principles. But what goals and principles those are can change while the loyalty to the person remains. In a lifetime of loyalty to Christ, one's ethical goals and principles may change in ways that one cannot precisely define in advance, as one's understanding of Christ develops; and all of that change may remain within the intent of the same basic Christian commitment. This openness to the modification of goals and principles is also a part of Christian liberty, and of responsiveness to the Spirit of Christ.

The friend of Christ is called to understand what is morally important, see a point in many rules, choose suitable means to morally valuable ends, weigh conflicting rules and ends according to their importance, and be open to the possibility that his principles ought to be modified. A person who fulfilled this calling would be free in a very important sense.

But he could still be governed by a morality that rigorously determined every detail of his life. It would not be to him an arbitrary collection of rules; every part of it would be charged with significance. But it would tell him that in every situation there is some one course of action that he is ethically obliged to choose. It would tell him that everything he does will be either an ethical transgression, or perhaps an error of judgment, or else something he must do. He could never say to himself, "I may do this, but I don't have to." This seems to me to be less than the fullness of Christian liberty.

A major source of this difficulty is that in what we have said about theonomy we have still been concerned with ways of forming *beliefs* or *judgments* about what one *ought* to do. But if one has such beliefs completely determining one's conduct, one will hardly be able ever to act directly and purely from any motive except conscientiousness, if one is conscientious. This does not fit very well with the conception of Christian ethics as an ethics of love. For these reasons I believe that we should look for something more in Christian liberty, besides theonomy and freedom from fear, though in going beyond this point we enter territory that is more controversial theologically.

3. SLAVERY AND FRIENDSHIP

In the social context of the New Testament, the free person, the ε'λεύθερος in the literal sense, was the person who was *not a slave*. 'Freedom' thus had a less individualistic meaning than it usually does for us. It did signify exemption from some forms of social constraint; but more fundamental it signified a social position, a status of full membership in the family or community.[9] The contrast between the slave and the free slides into a contrast between the slave and the son (John 8:31–36).

In this context, Christian liberty appears first of all as a form of personal relationship with God. Slavery, as a metaphor for our relationship with God, is treated ambivalently in the New Testament. In many passages, following a common practice in ancient religions, Christians are spoken of as slaves of God or of Christ. But there are other passages, fewer in number but striking and carefully worked out, in which it is said that Christians are no longer God's slaves, but his children (Gal. 3:23–4:11, 4:21–5:1; cf. John 8:31–36) or his friends (John 15:15). The idea of Christian liberty can be illuminated by reflecting, as we began to do in the last section, on differences between slavery and sonship or friendship. I shall concentrate on friendship here, since it is a simpler relationship which is or ought to be an element in parent-child relationships.

Slaves are treated as belonging to their masters. To want someone as a friend is also to want him or her to belong to you. But it is a different kind of belonging.

When we say a physical object "belongs to" a person, we usually mean that the person *owns* the object. To own an object is normally to have, by right if not always in fact, complete control over it. If I own a house, I have the right to go in and out whenever I like, to paint it whatever color I like, to add a room or take off a porch, or even to tear down the house entirely. And I have a right that you should not come in the house without my permission, that you should not paint it without my permission, and so forth. I also have the right to sell the house or give it away, or to rent it or lend it to someone else for a period of time. While I own it, the purpose of the house is simply that it should serve my purposes.

The master is spoken of (monstrously) as "owning" his slaves. The relationship is conceived on the analogy of ownership of a physical object.

To claim to own another person as a slave is to claim an almost unrestricted right to control that person's actions and to make your purposes the purpose of his life.

If you want another person to belong to you as a friend, you want something very different. You certainly want to have some claims on him, which will limit his freedom in some ways; but it is not primarily control that you are after. If you look on someone as "a living tool," you cannot have him as your friend, as Aristotle rightly held.[10] Neither is it compatible with true friendship to feed your ego on the experience of dominating the other person, as in the Hegelian conception of the master-slave relationship. In desiring friendship, rightly understood, you want some blurring of the line between "mine" and "thine," some taking of the other person's ends as your ends and of yours as his. But you do not want to think that he exists only to please and satisfy you; you see his happiness, his creativity, his integrity as important in themselves.

In friendship one seeks rights to intimacy, much more than control. The intimacy may be as deep and comprehensive as in marriage, or it may be something as basic and unromantic as being entitled to phone at ten o'clock at night and say, 'Hi, this is _____. How *are* you? We haven't talked in ages.' One does not want to control every detail of one's friend's life; one wants on the contrary to participate in his freely being himself. One claims the right to speak and act freely in his presence, and one claims his free response. One wants one's friends to be able to do good things for one that they did not have to do.

If you belong to another person in friendship, part of what may be involved is that your personality is to be open to the entry of your friend's emotions, so that you can be moved by his sorrows and inspired by his enthusiasms and share in his loves. One thing Christians have had in mind when they have spoken of being filled with the Holy Spirit is such an entry of God's emotions or attitudes into their own. This is a kind of influence a friend may have on you, but it is not the obedience that is demanded of a slave. Being inspired by one friend's emotions is quite different from trying consciously and voluntarily to satisfy his desires.

In a way, one should expect that an omnipotent God would rather have friends than slaves, if he were interested in having creatures like us at all. He needs no tools; why should he want "living tools"? Is he so unsure of himself that he wants to draw spiritual sustenance from the experience of dominating us? If it is astonishing that an infinite being should want us for his friends, it is not surprising that an omnipotent being should prefer not to control every detail of his creatures' lives.

To be sure, this raises certain problems. I will not discuss here the familiar metaphysical issues about how an omnipotent God could create beings not completely determined causally by him. But the idea of God leaving us morally as well as causally free raises ethical issues, which cannot be evaded here, about indifferent and supererogatory actions.

4. SUPEREROGATION

In order to have a morally free choice, we must have plurality of possibilities of action that are ethically permitted but not ethically required. Such situations must belong to one of two types. If none of the permitted alternative actions is ethically better than any of the others, we may say that all of them are (ethically) "indifferent." If one of them is ethically better than some ethically permitted alternative, we may say that the better action is "supererogatory." If no possible actions are indifferent or supererogatory, then we are never morally free to choose among alternatives.

The utilitarian doctrine that one ought always to do the action that will have the best results comes at least close to excluding morally free choice in this way. It makes indifferent actions rare, because actions will normally differ at least slightly in the value (or probable value) of their results. And it excludes supererogation entirely, because if an action will have better results than some alternative, the latter is not permitted by this utilitarian ethics. If you can do better, you are obliged to do better; so you can never do a better act than you are obliged to do. These are main reasons why such a utilitarianism is a harsh servitude, as I have already remarked. The chief loophole for liberty in this morality is the impossibility of calculating probable utilities reliably and accurately enough to get clear guidance from it in many situations.

I believe that the possibility of both indifferent and supererogatory actions should be regarded as part of Christian liberty. This possibility is important both for the sake of morally free choice and as a consequence of the idea that God, wanting to have us as his friends rather than slaves, does not wish to determine every detail of our lives by his commands. The question may be raised whether the possibility of indifferent actions would not be enough for these purposes; must we also have supererogatory actions open to us? But I think the possibility of supererogatory actions is very important for Christian or moral liberty, chiefly because an ethics that is sensitive to the finer nuances of the moral life will not leave enough possible actions indifferent. Furthermore it seems appropriate to think of God as wanting his friends to be able to do good things for him (and for each other) that they did not have to do.

The idea of supererogation has been controversial among Christians. Two main objections call for discussion here. One is that if supererogation were possible, and we could therefore do more than is commanded, we could deserve—or perhaps even more than deserve—divine salvation; whereas the objectors have insisted that we can never even come close to deserving salvation. This issue can be largely evaded here;[11] for in calling an action "supererogatory" I do not mean to imply anything about a reward that it deserves from God (whether or not that has been implied by the term in some theological contexts). I mean only that from an ethical point of view the action is not obligatory but is permitted and is better than some permitted alternative. No doubt it would in some ways be praiseworthy to do such a thing; but there are at least two reasons why we can maintain the possibility of supererogatory actions without having to admit that we can even come close to deserving divine salvation. The first reason is that as salvation consists chiefly in the enjoyment of God's love, it is not the kind of thing that a creature like us can earn or deserve at all. It is in its very nature a matter of grace rather than of merit. The second reason is that the possibility of doing a better thing than one is strictly obliged to do does not necessarily imply a possibility of living a better life than it can rightly be said that one ought to live. The occasional performance of a supererogatory action is much easier than a perfectly consistent fulfillment of all one's duties. I imagine that virtually all of us sometimes do something supererogatory but do not always do our duty. If so, we do not act as well as we ought to, in spite of our works of supererogation. Whether we are living as good a life as we ought to live depends, moreover, on our motives and attitudes as well as our actions. If we do many works of supererogation, but do them in a grudging or loveless or self-righteous spirit, we are certainly living less well than we ought.

The other main objection to supererogation is more relevant to my conception, and more disturbing to me. It is also an objection to the possibility of indifferent actions. Does only a part of our life belong to God? Shouldn't all of our actions express our devotion to God? If so, how can any action be supererogatory?

Christian ethics has always been a morality of devotion, demanding that the Christian ethical concern be at the center of the individual's whole life. It allows that there are things that we may and should do for ourselves, but it has refused to admit a sharp separation between one's own private interests, insofar as they are legitimate, and God's interests or the interests of the Kingdom. The demand for devotion may be seen as a characteristically religious feature of Christian ethics. Perhaps a secular morality could make room for supererogation by being related to individuals much as the Federal Trade Commission is related to American business corporations—not as central to the main business of life but as a constraint on it. For Christianity, however, an ethics that only sets boundaries to life-projects that may remain basically selfish would represent the loss of an essential good.

How, then, can we maintain the possibility of supererogatory action and still have an ethics of devotion? I have discussed other aspects of ideals of religious and ethical devotion more fully elsewhere than is possible here.[12] In the present context I want to explore the relation between such ideals and the possibility of supererogation. I will do this in the form of a philosophical meditation on a story from the gospel according to Mark (14:3–7):

> And while [Jesus] was at Bethany in the house of Simon the leper, as he sat at table, a woman came with an alabaster jar of ointment of pure nard, very costly, and she broke the jar and poured it over his head. But there were some who said to themselves indignantly, "Why was the ointment thus wasted? For this ointment might have been sold for more than three hundred denarii, and given to the poor." And they reproached her. But Jesus said, "Let her alone; why do you trouble her? She has done a beautiful thing to me. For you always have the poor with you, and whenever you will, you can do good to them; but you will not always have me."

"She has done a beautiful thing." The first reaction I can remember having to this story is that the people who thought it would have been better to give the money to the poor were right.[13] And I still think that might indeed have been an even better thing to do. It was a lot of money—three hundred days' wages for an unskilled laborer. Jesus could be taken, in this narrative, as arguing that the woman actually did the best possible thing. But that is not asserted, and the story need not be read that way. It is enough that she did a *beautiful* thing; we do not have to worry about whether it was the *best* thing she could have done.

The demand to maximize value—either the value of one's actions or the value of their consequences, or both—appeals greatly to the "strenuous mood" in ethics. "The good is the enemy of the best," it is said. How can our conscience be at peace with a deed that is only good, or even "beautiful"? How can it not be wrong to do less than the best that we can?

Appealing as it may be in the abstract, this demand to maximize can be repulsively unappreciative in the concrete. That is clear in this story, if in thinking about it we focus on the people rather than on the money. It is not just that the people who reproached the woman were being unkind. The more fundamental point is that it is outrageous to think of what she did as a transgression. It was a generous expression of love (which violated no one's rights), and the fact (if it is a fact) that she could have done something even better instead does not keep it from being a beautiful deed.

'But shouldn't a Christian want always to do whatever is *most* pleasing to God?' This is a subtle question, with subtle temptations. We may be tempted to assume that the action most pleasing to God will be the best—that is, the most meritorious. But this is not necessarily right. It is not by admiring us that God takes pleasure in us, and it is not by *performing* for him that we please him. "There is more joy in Heaven over one sinner that repents than over ninety-nine righteous that have no need of repentance" (Luke 15:7). What pleases God is that we accept his love, and love him and one another. A saint is not an especially meritorious person, but a person especially transparent to God's grace.

Christian liberty is freedom not only from fear of punishment but also from self-righteousness and its attendant anxieties. Christian liberty renounces the project of self-justification, of showing that one is always in the right, and accepts the fact that one never is entirely in the right. In relation to this descent from the pedestal on which we love to place ourselves, the pursuit of merit is a very questionable motive. A commitment to justice, a love of one's neighbor—those are good motives, which may lead one to highly meritorious actions. But the love of merit as such is something different; and I think it is commonly a bad motive, a desire to climb up on the pedestal.

I agree that there is a sort of perfection, or an ideal, that we ought to aspire to exemplify. But I do not think that being concerned always to do the very best thing that one can is a part of that ideal. I do not believe that God himself is concerned to do only the best. Could he not have made better creatures instead of us? I see no reason to suppose that there is a best possible life for any finite creature nor a best possible world of finite creatures (nor that a perfect God must actualize the best possible world if there is one).[14] Maximizing is not God's game. Neither is it supposed to be ours.

"She has done a *beautiful* thing." Christian liberty will sometimes be freedom for aesthetic goods and for actions of primarily symbolic value. It will also be freedom for intellectual goods and for sheer play. These are all things that can hardly flourish in an atmosphere in which it is assumed that every possible action is either obligatory or wrong—that only what has to be done may be done. They are rarely what has to be done and lose their character if they are made means to something else that has to be done. Severe moralists have often viewed some or all of these goods with suspicion. And we may wonder how there can justifiably be time or energy or other resources for such luxuries in a world in which there are such desperate needs for the bare necessities of human life.

If our calling is to belong to an omnipotent creator as his children and his friends and not as slaves, it is not a calling to a life filled to capacity with things that *have* to be done. We may find this hard to accept if we focus our attention on all the things in the world that seem to need doing. But the Christian life is not founded on need but on gift—not on our poverty but on God's wealth. It rests on the omnipotence of God. People sometimes think of belief in divine omnipotence as inimical to human freedom, but here I think it is liberating. The reason why there is room in the Christian life for things that do not need to be done is that God does not need us as his instruments. "He hath no pleasure in the strength of an horse; neither delighteth he in any man's legs" (Psalm 147:10). Any goal to which our action might be merely a means, God can accomplish without us. So if he has commanded us to pursue certain ends, it is because he cares not only about those ends but also about our pursuit of them. If he invites us to be his friends, he invites us to regard our lives as important to him for their own sakes, and to value them accordingly.

The idea of the sabbath has its place here. Sabbath is rest from work before it is specifically religious activity. Work, in the sense that is centrally relevant here, is activity that is merely or mainly instrumental and not enjoyed for its own sake. For a creator who is omnipotent and already enjoys in himself more perfection than can possibly be embodied in creatures, creation cannot be merely work. It is also play, or sabbath—doing things that do not have to be done but that he likes to do. His children and friends are bidden to share in his sabbath—to have time and take time for things that do not serve extrinsic necessities but are done or enjoyed for their own sakes. Among these things are not only (and above all) worship, but also more optional enjoyments, such as art or philosophy or play.

"Whenever you will, you can do good to them." Is it optional, then, to do good to the poor? Surely not. It is scandalous how little the world's rich do for the world's poor. A few ancient manuscripts of the New Testament accordingly correct the text to 'Whenever you will, you can do good to them *always*.'[15] But that makes nonsense of 'whenever you will.'

Jesus' saying is more profound. There is a bite to it. "Whenever you will." You have had plenty of opportunity to do good to the poor. But how often and how much have you wanted to? You who criticize this woman's action, have you really done so much for the poor that you have nothing left for any other sort of generosity? Far from telling us that caring for the economic needs of the poor is a ministry of secondary importance, Jesus' saying stands as a reproach to the weakness and intermittency of our concern for those needs. And yet it does have something to say about the relation of freedom and human need in the vocation of Christians. It recognizes that we are surrounded by a sea of needs that are urgent, that we have to care about, and that we will never finish meeting. But in spite of this it denies that the Christian life is one in which there is room only for things that *have* to be done to meet human needs. It is to be a life in which one is really free for worship, and for love, because one is free to anoint the body of Jesus for burial without worrying about whether that will accomplish something that really needed to be done.

It is important that the ideal of devotion belongs primarily to the ethics of motives, attitudes, and traits of character. As Emil Brunner has written, "God does not wish to have my obedience as something which is valuable in itself. He wants *me*, my whole personality in the totality of all my actions, both inward and outward."[16] He commands us not only to do good to other people, but to *want* to do it. He commands us to *love them*. And if (as seems clear) it is *they* who are to be the object of this love, the devotion that is demanded is more than obedience. God seeks a response from us that is inspired not only by respect for his commands, but also by love for what he loves — specifically including our neighbors. Inviting us to participate as friends in his projects, he wants us not only to see what is important to him, but also to care about it, as he does, for its own sake.

Of course motives are related to actions, and therefore the ethics of motives is not unrelated to the ethics of actions. Few if any of us care as much as we should about the good of others, and particularly of the poor. If we fully loved our neighbors as ourselves, we would, no doubt, act differently, and much more generously. It is often true that a particular individual *ought* to be *doing* more to meet the needs of others, and some (not all) of the reasons that can be given for this conclusion are based on principles about the motives that we ought to have.

It does not follow, however, that there is a level of self-sacrifice in action that is characteristic of ideal love and that we are ethically *required* to achieve (and currently fail to achieve). The ideals, and even the commandments, of an ethics of motives are not correlated so simply with imperatives in an ethics of actions. What we *would* do if we loved as we should is not necessarily something that we ought to think we *have* to do, or that a perfected saint would think she *had* to do. It might indeed be precisely something that we (and she) do not have to do.

Moreover, there is apt to be no concretely precise answer to the question, what we would do if we were perfect in love, as the directions in which the energies of saintliness may flow are indefinitely various.

This last point, about the diversity of saintly motivation, is important for avoiding a tempting error. The following question may arise. Is rigorism being removed from the ethics of actions only to be reinstated in the ethics of motives, so that while supererogatory actions are possible, supererogatory motives are not — only the best of motives being ethically acceptable? I was formerly inclined to answer this question in the affirmative, but have come to think that Christian liberty should be seen as including the possibility of supererogatory motives. A love for philosophy that might be manifested in the career of a Thomas Aquinas can be seen as a good motive from a Christian point of view. It is one way of entering into God's love for his creation and for truth. I think a passion for justice and for human well-being that might be manifested in the career of a Gandhi or a Martin Luther King, Jr., is an even better motive from a Christian point of view. And given the limitations of any human being's time and emotional energy, these two motivational patterns are probably not fully compatible. But I believe that both patterns are ethically acceptable — indeed, good — from a Christian point of view, although one is better than the other. Given the limitations of human nature, none of us can hope to be a complete expression of God's goodness, and it is good that the divine perfection should be diversely imaged in motivation (as well as in many other respects).[17]

There is much more to be said about the possibility of supererogatory motives than there is room to say in the present essay, in which my central concern is with the kind of ethics of actions that is required by the Christian motivational ideal. Let us therefore return to the issue of the possibility of supererogatory actions. I have argued that the Christian motivational ideal of devotion to God does not imply that the best action available to us is always obligatory. I want now to go further and argue that the Christian motivational ideal actually *requires* some limitation of our obligations in the ethics of actions, to leave breathing room for love. Our love for what God loves would not have free play if there were no possibility of supererogation. For conscientiousness, respect for God's commands is and ought to be a very compelling motive. If it always drove us to just one of our alternatives, then the Christian, insofar as he is conscientious, could never do anything primarily out of love for what God loves. Such love could at most be an additional motive for him to do something that he would have done anyway out of conscientiousness.

That is true, in particular, of love for one's individual neighbor. *"You always have the poor with you, . . . but you will not always have me."* That can sound arrogant, but there are contexts in which anyone could say it to his friends. If someone loves you he will want to do something sometimes because it would be nice for you or would express his love for you, and not primarily because he thinks it would do the most good on the whole. I am emphatically not endorsing the romantic idea that there is no place for duty in love relationships. Lovers will be particularly solicitous to perform their duties to each other, and will not wish to have no such duties. But they will want also to be able to do things for each other that conscience does not require them to do.

The ideal of love requires a place at least for ethically indifferent actions, and probably for supererogation. The ethics of actions, or at least its obligation department, must be limited in scope in order to leave breathing room for the ethics of motives. A concrete example may be helpful here. If whenever it occurs to me that it would be nice to take home some ice cream to my wife, it is my duty to do so unless some weightier duty is opposed to the impulse, then I must always think either that I must do it or that I must not do it. And that rather spoils it. I can never buy the ice cream simply or mainly out of a desire to please her, because conscience is such a weighty motive.

In arguing thus I do not mean to imply that actions cannot be motivated by love if the agent knows that they are ethically required (and is conscientious). Parents who are conscientious may be moved by love to provide food for their children, even though they know it is their duty to do so. In providing for their family's needs they may, indeed, be much more conscious of their love than of the thought of duty. What I have argued is only that the ideal of love demands that not all cases of loving motivation should be of this sort—that some actions should be controlled by love in a way that excludes the presence of an alternative sufficient motive of conscientiousness. It should also be noted that the case of the conscientious parents whose love makes it unnecessary for them to think about their duty in doing it is believable only insofar as there is a fairly large area in which they assume that they will not violate their duty no matter what (among likely alternatives) they do. If they were so rigoristic as to believe that every detail of their provisions for their children is a matter of obligation—for instance that on every occasion it is either obligatory or wrong to give a child a cookie—then conscientiousness would require attention to duty at every step of the way.

Perhaps it will be objected that I have been overlooking another possible ethical relation between action and motives. If love for another person prompts me to do a certain action, it may be a sin to refrain from that action, even though refraining would not be a sin if I did not have the impulse. Here the obligation in the ethics of action is an obligation *not to quench love*, and is not an obligation to do something one would not do if one did not love. I grant that this sort of obligation to act on an impulse can arise, but I do not think all permissible loving actions are to be turned into duties this way. The duty not to quench love will in general be an *imperfect* duty. If one loves someone, one *ought often* to express one's love in action. But if one does that, and therefore is not quenching love, it is not obligatory to act on *every* loving impulse, and one's loving actions are therefore not individually obligatory. To recognize an ethical obligation to act on *every* loving impulse, in order not to quench love, would be self-defeating; for the recognition of it would threaten to turn all expression of love into an exercise of conscientiousness.

The performance of duties for a loved one can be deeply satisfying to both parties, but it would surely be an impoverishment of personal relations, a loss of grace, if there were no place for free gifts not dictated by conscience. It even seems good that there should be room for extravagant actions in which calculations of prudence as well as of duty are thrown to the winds, as in breaking an alabaster jar of precious ointment and pouring it over someone you love.[18]

NOTES

1. Joseph Fletcher, *Situation Ethics* (Philadelphia: Westminster Press, 1968), especially p. 95.

2. Aristotle, *Nicomachean Ethics* 7.11.1161b4.

3. This point is central to Bernard Williams's argument in his half of *Utilitarianism, for and against*, by J. J. C. Smart and Bernard Williams (Cambridge: Cambridge University Press, 1973).

4. John Rawls, *A Theory of Justice* (Cambridge, Mass.: Harvard University Press, 1971), p. 34.

5. Ibid., p. 40.

6. Paul Tillich, *The Protestant Era*, abridged edition, trans. James Luther Adams (Chicago: University of Chicago Press, 1957), p. 56.

7. I do not mean to deny that a more theonomous interpretation of the Law than Paul's is possible in Judaism.

8. Rawls, *A Theory of Justice*, p. 34.

9. See Dieter Nestle, *Eleutheria: Studien zum Wesen der Freiheit bei den Griechen und im Neuen Testament*, Teil I: *Die Griechen* (Tubingen: J. C. B. Mohr, 1967).

10. Aristotle, *Nicomachean Ethics* 7.11.1161a35–b10.

11. This objection is characteristically Protestant, and I particularly do not want to discuss whether Protestant critics have correctly understood the Catholic position on merit. The term 'supererogation' has its original home in Catholic teaching that certain ascetical practices are "counsels of perfection," which Christians are advised but not generally commanded to follow as a way to a holy life. These ideas have been the subject of a long, and continuing, discussion in Catholic moral theology.

12. See R. M. Adams, "Saints," *The Journal of Philosophy* 81 (1984): 392–401; and "The Problem of Total Devotion," in Robert Audi and William Wainwright, eds., *Rationality, Religious Belief, and Moral Commitment* (Ithaca, N.Y.: Cornell University Press, 1986), pp. 169–194.

13. It is interesting that Fletcher's Christian utilitarianism does not get beyond this reaction, but takes sides firmly against the Jesus of the story (Fletcher, *Situation Ethics*, p. 97). For a sharply opposed view, see Karl Barth, *Church Dogmatics*, II/2, p. 462.

14. As I have argued in R. M. Adams, "Must God Create the Best?" *Philosophical Review* 81 (1972): 317–332.

15. Codex Vaticanus ("B") and a few other manuscripts.

16. Emil Brunner, *The Divine Imperative*, trans. O. Wyon (Philadelphia: Westminster Press, 1947), p. 145.

17. Here I touch on points that I have developed more fully in "Saints." Linda Zagzebski's comments helped me to see them as points about Christian liberty. Gregory Trianosky's interesting paper, "Supererogation, Wrongdoing, and Vice: On the Autonomy of the Ethics of Virtue," *The Journal of Philosophy* 83 (1986): 26–40, includes discussion of ways in which the ethics of virtue may be thought to be more rigoristic than the ethics of actions.

18. This paper has had a long gestation period, and has been presented, in various forms, to a number of groups and individuals, to whom I am indebted for comments. Special thanks are owed to Marilyn McCord Adams, Malcolm Diamond, Alan Donagan, Thomas E. Hill, Jr., Edmund Leites, Philip L. Quinn, Amelie Rorty, Jeffrey Stout, and Robert Young.

Warring Against the Law of My Mind: Aquinas on Romans 7

NORMAN KRETZMANN

ST. PAUL AMONG THE PHILOSOPHERS

Philosophers discussing *akrasia*, or incontinence, or weakness of will, have come to rely on Paul for a paradigm of that state of acting contrary to one's principles, succumbing to temptation, doing what one has decided against doing. It is hard to find a modern treatment of the subject that does not at least refer to Romans 7:14–25 as providing a classic portrayal of weakness of will.[1] Philosophers are not the only ones to read Paul in that light; Christians who are not philosophers sometimes take those verses to contain a saint's confession of backsliding, and are reassured by it.

But Gareth Matthews has recently offered a far more pejorative interpretation, discovering in Romans 7 grounds for raising doubts about Paul's moral character and the degree of his Christianity.[2] It is an interpretation Matthews himself finds distressing, and certainly not one from which any ordinary Christian could derive any reassurance. Matthews begins by agreeing with almost everyone else in viewing Romans 7:14–25 as "a classic discussion of *akrasia*."[3] That aspect of it leaves him not only untroubled but approving: "St. Paul admits that, even as a Christian, he goes on doing evil things, and failing to do good ones. 'I can will what is right, but I cannot do it', he says. 'I do not do the good I want', he adds, 'but the evil I do not want is what I do'. So far, it seems, we have the confession of an exemplary Christian, well aware of his misdeeds, but still imprisoned in 'this body of death'."[4] What distresses Matthews about Romans 7 is not what he takes to be its clear evidence of Paul's *akrasia* and resultant misdeeds, but the Apostle's disclaimers in verses 17 and 20: "What I find unsettling, even disturbing, is the way St.

Paul seems to disown these evil actions as the actions of an alien agent, of, so to speak, a 'sin brother'. 'If I do what I do not want', he says, 'it is no longer I that do it, but sin which dwells within me'. . . . The upsetting thing is that he . . . distances himself from his sinful self and, seemingly, disowns the actions of that self."[5] Matthews is favorably impressed by Paul's sophistication regarding the *role* of unconscious motivation, but verses 17 and 20 lead him to say that "Freud seems to be more Christian than St. Paul on the matter of *taking responsibility* for hidden impulses."[6] So Matthews joins certain modern biblical commentators who "are worried about what we might call 'first-order' hypocrisy in *Romans* 7 – 'shuffling out of responsibility' for one's misdeeds by ascribing them to an 'alien power'."[7] And Matthews goes further, adding a new charge of his own: "Here is where 'second-order' hypocrisy comes in – pretending that my righteous self is distinct and separate, when such distinctness as it has rests on repression."[8]

I think both these interpretations of Romans 7 are fundamentally mistaken – both the established interpretation in terms of *akrasia* alone and Matthews's in terms of *akrasia* compounded by two orders of hypocrisy. A third interpretation offers a more plausible account of Paul's moral state, explaining the inner conflict depicted in verses 14–25 in terms of a universal condition of moral life that is much less discussed than either *akrasia* or hypocrisy. I will present this alternative reading after setting the stage with some of the relevant philosophical issues. For both the moral philosophy and the biblical interpretation I will be drawing on Thomas Aquinas.

The problems raised by the *akrasia* and the hypocrisy interpretations deserve consideration in their own right, but I also had an ulterior motive for working on these issues, one that involves taking into consideration a kind of source material ordinarily ignored in philosophical scholarship. I wanted to see how a medieval philosopher's position on certain philosophical issues affects and is affected by his treatment of certain passages in his biblical commentaries.[9] I thought that Aquinas's account of *akrasia* in his best-known writings on moral philosophy would provide a particularly illuminating background for his discussion of Romans 7. It does, but not at all as I expected it would.

HUMAN NATURE AND ACTION

Aquinas's theory of human nature follows Aristotle's in analyzing the traits or functions of a human being into three sorts: those we share with all other *living things* (e.g., nutrition and growth), which he calls vegetative or natural functions; those we share with other *animals*; and those that are specifically *human*, which he calls rational. Only the higher two sorts of functions will concern us now.

Both the animal and the rational functions of the human soul are sorted out into cognitive and appetitive faculties, or powers. The rational cognitive power is *intellect*; the animal cognitive power is *sensation*. The rational appetitive power is *will*; the animal appetitive power is sensuality, more conveniently called by its other designation, the *sensory appetite*.

Human action, properly so-called, is action stemming from the distinctively human faculties of a human being. The paradigm of human action, then, is a human will's free choice from among goals proposed by its intellect, based on the intellect's deliberation regarding ends and means. The many sorts of activity a human being engages in that do not involve intellect and will at that relatively high degree are classified as *actions associated with a human being (actus hominis)* but not as *human actions (actus humani)*, and it is human actions with which moral philosophy is primarily concerned. Classifying an action as akratic may seem to call into question the degree of the action's voluntariness or the freedom of the agent's choice and so raise the possibility that it is not a human action, strictly speaking.[10]

WILL, INTELLECT, AND PASSIONS

Aquinas's account of human nature and action is marked by an emphasis on natural order. From the standpoint of moral philosophy the most significant aspects of this order are the natural ordering of the will toward goodness in general and the naturally ordered relationship between intellect and will. Even a rapid survey of his account would disclose several points at which the will's choice among actions or decision against acting can distort the natural order, introducing disorders that might count as moral shortcomings.[11] But the moral shortcoming that is *akrasia* could not, it seems, be diagnosed as a disorder introduced by the will. On the contrary, the will, far from perpetrating *akrasia*, seems somehow to be its innocent victim. As the alleged Pauline paradigm of *akrasia* puts it, "I do not do *the good that I will*; but *the evil that I will against*, that is what I do." If *akrasia* is some sort of victimization of the will, perhaps actions characterized by it ought not to count as human actions at all, much less as immoral.

But, according to Aquinas, a consideration of goodness, intellect, and will alone cannot reveal the source of this disorder. The initial disturbance that sometimes results in *akrasia* occurs among the passions of the sensory appetite, which can affect the will via the intellect by inducing illusions regarding available options, "so that insofar as a man is in a certain passion something strikes him as all right which does not seem so when he is not in that passion. For example, something that seems good to an angry man does not seem so when he is calm. And it is in that way, in connection with the [will's] object, that the sensory appetite moves the will."[12] Notice that the will retains its freedom under the influence of the passions. The passions affect the will indirectly, by distorting the intellect's proposal of an object of volition and, therefore, only via final causation, the kind of causation exercised on the will by the intellect, which the will can resist. And so even when the influence of the passions on the rational faculties has been taken into account, the will is not coerced and is still capable of initiating human action, retaining responsibility along with freedom.

But not every case of action influenced by passion is an instance of *akrasia*, and if *akrasia* really is *doing* what one *wills not* to do, or *not doing* what one *wills* to do, as the putative Pauline paradigm implies, then introducing the influence of the passions seems to have brought us no closer to finding an explanation of *akrasia* in Aquinas's terms. If behavior of that sort is even conceivable, how, if at all, could it stem from the passions? I can answer that question and advance our investigation most effectively now by presenting one of Aquinas's more important discussions of the bad moral state he calls "incontinence." Whether this incontinence is quite the same as the *akrasia* discussed by Matthews and others is one of the things that remain to be seen, but it will be apparent at once how incontinence stems from the passions.

AKRASIA, IMPETUOSITY, WEAKNESS, AND MADNESS

Passions of that sort, however, no matter how vehement they may be, are not a sufficient cause of incontinence, but only an inducement to it; because as long as a man retains the use of reason, he can always resist the passions. If, however, the passions increase to such an extent that they sweep away the use of reason altogether — as happens in those who go mad because of the vehemence of their passions — the essential character of neither continence nor incontinence will remain; for in those people reason's judgment is not preserved, [and it is that judgment] which the continent man obeys and the incontinent falls short of. And so the result is that the direct cause of incontinence lies in the soul's not resisting passion with reason. This happens in two ways, as the Philosopher says in *Ethics* VII [8, 1150b19]:

first, when a soul yields to the passions before reason has offered counsel (this is called *unbridled incontinence* or *impetuosity*); secondly, when a man does not stand firm on the things that have been counseled [by his intellect] because he is weakly grounded on reason's judgment (and so this sort of incontinence is called *weakness*).[13]

One of the most illuminating features of this passage can be seen at once by simply comparing it with a well-known modern presentation of *akrasia*, R. M. Hare's in his *Freedom and Reason*. Hare says:

Our morality is formed of principles and ideals which we do not succeed in persuading ourselves to fulfil. And this *inability* to realize our ideals is well reflected in the highly significant names given in both Greek and English to this condition: Greek calls it *akrasia* — literally 'not being strong enough (sc. to control oneself)'; and English calls it 'moral weakness' or 'weakness of will'. Nor is this the only evidence that the state of mind that most people are thinking of when they speak of weakness of will involves an inability, in some sense, to do what we think we ought.[14]

Are Aquinas and Hare describing the same state? Well, yes and no. Aquinas calls his second, more interesting variety of incontinence "weakness," and he might just as well have called it weakness of will; but neither of his varieties of incontinence is like *Hare's* weakness of will in being characterized by "an *inability* . . . to do what we think we ought." It is essential to Aquinas's conception of incontinence in either variety, impetuosity or weakness, that a person in either of those states "*can* always resist the passions." In Hare's description, on the other hand, there is nothing corresponding to Aquinas's conception of weakness (of will). I suppose the Greek word "*akrasia*" understood literally as *absence* of power does suit the case Hare describes — one that "involves an *inability* in some sense, to do what we think we ought" — but his English designations for it, "moral *weakness*" and "*weakness* of will," seem better suited to Aquinas's conception, which involves the retention of ability, albeit at a level of diminished capacity.[15] Since Aquinas's account is the one with which I want to compare his interpretation of Romans 7, I will adopt Aquinas's terminology for the remainder of this discussion.

But does anything in Aquinas's account correspond with the state at the center of Hare's account — inability to do what we think we ought? Aquinas does recognize a state in which a person is unable to do what she might *subsequently* think she ought to have done — a state of *madness*, brought on by the vehemence of a passion. But he also characterizes that state as one in which the person's use of reason has been altogether swept away, and so it cannot be a state in which she is unable to do what she *then thinks* she ought to do. On Aquinas's account of incontinence, a person free from external coercion and sincerely describing herself as (psychologically) unable to do what she thinks she ought to do would have to be recognized as suffering not from weakness of will at all, but from *self-deception* — an instance of the will's coercion of (exercising efficient causation on) the intellect.

Hare, after offering the description we have been considering, presents "two extremely well-worn passages in literature" illustrating the state he's been describing. The second of those passages is Romans 7:14–25, at which we will be looking later, and the first is Ovid's description of Medea's falling in love with Jason, which turns out to provide a particularly good illustration of the difference between Hare's and Aquinas's accounts.

> Meanwhile, Aeëtes' daughter's heart took fire;
> Her struggling Reason could not quell Desire.
> "This madness how can I resist?" she cried;
> "No use to fight; some God is on its side . . .
> Dash from your maiden breast these flames it feels!
> Ah, if I could, the less would be my ills.
> Alas I cannot quench them; an unknown
> Compulsion bears me, all reluctant, down.
> Urged this way — that — on Love's or Reason's course,
> I see and praise the better: do the worse."[16]

Hare says: "Ovid here again and again stresses the helplessness of Medea; and so does St. Paul stress his own helplessness in the famous passage from Romans vii."[17] Ovid has Medea say of herself not only that she is helpless, but that she is in the grip of madness. Aquinas would reject that diagnosis: anyone who, like Medea, sees and praises the better is rational, not mad. So unless Medea is right about being coerced by an invisible external force, "Some God," "an unknown compulsion," she is deceiving herself about being helpless to resist. What Aquinas would say of Paul's alleged declaration of helplessness we won't need to infer; we will see what he does in fact say.

THE VOLUNTARY AND THE INVOLUNTARY

In Aquinas's view, acts performed in a fit of madness are not human acts in the strict sense, and hence not part of the primary subject matter of moral philosophy, because they are not voluntary. "If [the passion of] concupiscence were to sweep reason away entirely, as happens in those who become mad with concupiscence, it would follow that the concupiscence would remove voluntariness. And yet, strictly speaking, there would not be involuntariness in that case, because in those who do not have the use of reason there is neither voluntariness nor involuntariness."[18]

All genuinely human acts, then, are voluntary; but Aquinas recognizes that some of them are involuntary *in some respect or other* even though fundamentally voluntary. Some normal passions in the agent can render his action involuntary in a certain respect. Fear, for instance, can lead a perfectly sane person to do something which "considered in itself is not voluntary" (e.g., throwing the cargo overboard when the ship is in danger of sinking). "But what is done out of fear is voluntary at that place and time—that is, insofar as in those circumstances it is a way of preventing the greater evil that was feared."[19]

TWO ACCOUNTS OF INCONTINENCE

Now if a normal agent's normal passion can sometimes bring it about that the agent's voluntary action is involuntary in a certain respect, then a simple but promising account of incontinence seems to lie ready to hand, an account that looks as if it would, incidentally, explain Paul's saying that he does what he wills against doing (if Paul is confessing incontinence): An incontinent act, done out of some passion or other, is voluntary in one respect and involuntary in another. Aquinas considers this plausible in-a-certain-respect account of incontinence in one of his discussions of concupiscence.[20] In the discussion he is claiming that the concupiscent passions do not cause involuntariness in sane people, and he takes up several objections against his position. Here is the objection most relevant to our purposes: "Just as a frightened man performs out of fear an action contrary to what he was proposing to do, so does an incontinent man because of concupiscence. But fear causes involuntariness in a certain respect"—as we have seen Aquinas acknowledging. "Therefore, so does concupiscence" in the case of an incontinent act.[21] Aquinas certainly accepts some of the presuppositions of this objection—for instance, that an incontinent person acts out of concupiscence (at least very often), and that he acts contrary to the (good) intention he has formed. And the objection gains further strength from its appeal to common sense, since it implies a sharp distinction most people would want to draw, between the glutton's eating yet another doughnut and the dieter's eating a dougnut he had intended to forgo, a distinction that might be plausibly expressed by saying that the dieter's action was invol-

untary in a certain respect while the glutton's action was purely voluntary.

But Aquinas's rejoinder to this objection is altogether unyielding.
He expressly rejects the analogy between fear and concupiscence along
with the in-a-certain-respect account of incontinence that is based on it.

> In a man who does something out of *fear*, there is *still* his will's repug-
> nance to what he is doing considered just in itself. On the other hand, in a
> man who does something out of *concupiscence*—an incontinent man, for
> instance—the earlier volition in which he repudiated [what is now] the
> object of his concupiscence does *not* remain. Instead, he has undergone a
> change: to willing that which he repudiated earlier. And so what is done
> out of fear *is* in a way involuntary, while what is done out of concupiscence
> is in *no* way involuntary. For a man who is incontinent in respect of
> concupiscence is acting contrary to what he *proposed* to do but *not* con-
> trary to what he *is willing now*, while the frightened man is acting *also*
> against what he is willing now, considered just in itself.[22]

Setting aside considerations of incontinence for a moment, it seems
clear that Aquinas has identified a significant general difference between
acting out of fear and acting out of concupiscence. The frightened merchant throwing his cargo overboard in the storm is conscious of "his
will's repugnance to what he is doing considered just in itself" even while
he is voluntarily doing it, whereas the least that must be said about acting out of concupiscence (when incontinence is not at issue) is that the
action is in no respect involuntary. In fact, as Aquinas notes in this same
context, acting out of concupiscence *enhances* the agent's willingness.[23]

But now what about the alternative account of incontinence sketched
in Aquinas's rejoinder? It considers only the agent's *will*, and in that
regard it distinguishes not at all between the glutton and the incontinent
dieter *while* they are eating their doughnuts; each of them is simply
doing what he then wills to be doing. The differences between them as
regards their wills are to be found only in the time *before* the eating,
when the dieter willed against it and the glutton did not, and, presumably, in the time *afterwards*, when the dieter will repudiate his action
and the glutton will not.

So Aquinas rejects the initially plausible in-a-certain-respect account
of the incontinent person's willing in favor of this on-again off-again
account. It deserves a much closer look than I can stop to give it now,
and I think that the closer one looks, the better it looks.[24] But I want to
raise two worries about it. In the first place, it seems to be pointing the
way to a pretty lame, disappointing analysis of the alleged classic portrayal of incontinence in Romans: according to the on-again, off-again

account, it looks as if it will turn out that what Paul really should have
said is "I do not do the good that I *used to* will; but the evil that I *used
to* will against, that is what I do." In the second place, the on-again,
off-again account seems to fail utterly to capture the inner conflict that
moral people often experience even *while* acting incontinently.

The first of those worries will be dispelled before we are finished,
and the second of them can be at least mitigated at once. Aquinas does
of course recognize inner conflict as a frequent concomitant of incontinence, and inner conflict is, I think, essential to the sort of incontinence
he calls weakness. But that conflict takes place not within the will, as in
the case of acting out of fear, but between the agent's intellect and his
will. The incontinent man who "does not stand firm on the things that
have been counseled [by his intellect] because he is weakly grounded on
reason's judgment"[25] is one who acts out of concupiscence even though
and even while he *knows* better. As Augustine puts it in Aquinas's para-
phrase of him, "The intellect flies on ahead; desire follows slowly, *or not
at all*. We *know* what is good; to *do* what is good does not please us."[26]
And in comparing the incontinent with the continent, Aquinas brings
out this inner conflict clearly:

> Reason is found in the same state in both of them, for both the continent
> man and the incontinent have right reason, and both of them make up
> their minds not to follow their illicit concupiscent passions. The primary
> difference between them shows up in their act of choice, however. The
> continent man, even though he is undergoing vehement concupiscent pas-
> sions, chooses not to follow them, because of his reason; the incontinent
> man, on the other hand, chooses to follow them *in spite of his reason's
> forbidding it*.[27]

I am aware of at least some of the gaps in this sketch of Aquinas's
account of incontinence and some other relevant bits of his moral philosophy; but what I have presented will provide a serviceable introduction to Aquinas's interpretation of Romans 7:14–25.

AQUINAS'S COMMENTARY ON ROMANS

Most of the material I have been drawing on so far comes from
Aquinas's *Summa theologiae*, written between 1266 and 1273. His commentary on Romans was probably written during some of those same
years, 1270–1272, while Aquinas was teaching for the second time at the
University of Paris.[28]

Of the Books of the New Testament, Paul's epistles were probably commented on more often than any others during the Middle Ages. Aquinas wrote commentaries on all of Paul's epistles, and one of the foremost students of medieval biblical commentary considers "St. Thomas's commentaries on St. John, and *especially* on St. Paul, to be the most fully developed product and the most perfect realization of medieval scholastic exegesis."[29] In at least two significant respects his commentary on Romans differs from most of his other biblical commentaries. With his commentary on the fourth gospel it shares the distinction of having been written down by himself rather than being transcribed by a stenographer from classroom lectures. It may, therefore, be considered an especially careful piece of work. It seems also to be an unusually philosophical biblical commentary. In his Romans commentary Aquinas refers to Aristotle far more often than in any other of his commentaries on Paul's epistles; in particular, he refers three times more often to the *Nicomachean Ethics* than in his commentary on 1 Corinthians, its nearest competitor in that respect. James Weisheipl, the author of the best intellectual biography of Aquinas, describes it this way:

> Thomas's commentary on Romans is a magnificent, superb piece of work. It is a highly polished version, replete with quotations from the Latin and Greek Fathers, an explanation of all the main heresies in the early Church, particularly Pelagianism, and numerous citations of Aristotle, particularly the *Ethics*. On the other hand, the [i.e., his] commentaries on all the other epistles seldom refer to anything but the *Glossa* and the Bible itself.[30]

ROMANS 7:14–25

In writing his commentaries Aquinas of course used the Latin Bible, the Vulgate. Since no published English translation I know is close enough to the text as he had it, I have translated Romans 7:14–25 from the Vulgate for purposes of this discussion. Here are the verses to be considered:

14: For we know that the law is spiritual; but I am carnal, sold under sin.

15: For that which I do, I do not understand. For I do not do the good that I will; but the evil that I hate, that is what I do.

16: Now if I do what I will against, I am agreeing with the law, that it is good.

17: Now, then, it is no more I who do it, but sin, which dwells in me.

18: For I know that good does not dwell in me, that is, in my flesh.

19: For I do not do the good that I will; but the evil that I will against, that is what I do.

20: Now if I do what I will against, it is no more I who do it, but sin, which dwells in me.

21: I find, therefore, a law, that when I will to do what is good, evil is here with me.

22: For I am delighted with the law of God, as far as the inner man is concerned;

23: But I see another law in my members, warring against the law of my mind and capturing me in the law of sin, which is in my members.

24: Unhappy man that I am, who will deliver me from the body of this death?

25: The grace of God, through Jesus Christ our Lord. Therefore, I myself with the mind serve the law of God, but with the flesh, the law of sin.

AQUINAS'S ANALYSIS OF ROMANS 7:14-25

The first thing Aquinas does with this material is to extract the pattern of thought expressed in it. I have mentioned a couple of respects in which his commentary on Romans differs from his other biblical commentaries, but it is like all the others I have seen—-indeed, like Aquinas's academic writings of every sort—in its superhuman orderliness. Paul's epistles are, of course, not treatises but letters, and they often read like letters, passionate letters. Nevertheless, in his commentaries on them Aquinas untiringly, unfailingly, finds in Paul's words a more or less elaborate pattern of exposition and argumentation. I can imagine the scorn with which most modern biblical scholars would dismiss such an approach to the text. Even Thomists have sometimes written in embarrassed, apologetic tones of the "dialectical cast of St. Thomas' interpretation of the literal sense" with its "omnipresent divisions and subdivisions," in which "Syllogisms are disclosed in St. Paul and the correct sequence of thoughts is commended in St. John."[31] But I think it is splendid. In my use of his biblical commentary I have found this technique of his always helpful, never insupportable by the text, and sometimes illuminating in a way no less dialectical approach could be. I realize that there must be textual archeology, but surely there is room, and need, for textual architectonics, too.

Still, I will not take time now to set out all of Aquinas's twenty-nine divisions and subdivisions of those twelve verses. It will be enough for my purposes to point out his main division, which falls between verses 14–23 and verses 24–25. In the first of those two parts, according to Aquinas, Paul "proves the goodness of the [divine] law on the basis of the very opposition to good that is found in man, an opposition which the law cannot remove";[32] and then in verses 24 and 25 Paul shows "how the opposition associated with that sort of law *can* be removed," ending, in the second sentence of verse 25, with a summary conclusion.[33] Except for the summary conclusion, it is only the first and much bigger of these two parts that figures in the alternative interpretation I want to provide, and I neither can nor want to take account now of all he has to say even about the first part. My present purpose is only to find out and assess what Aquinas does with what nearly everyone considers to be the Pauline paradigm of weakness of will and with what has recently been presented as a particularly repulsive instance of hypocrisy.

THE REFERENT OF PAUL'S "I"

The first problem of interpretation Aquinas has to face arises over identifying the referent of "I" in these verses. Here is how Aquinas introduces it: "And this passage ['I am carnal', the second clause in verse 14] can be interpreted in two different ways. In the first way, the Apostle is speaking in the person of a man in a state of sin [*in peccato existentis*]; Augustine interprets it this way in his *Book of Eighty-Three Questions*.[34] Later, however, in his *Treatise Against Julian*,[35] he interprets it in such a way that the Apostle is understood to be speaking in *his own* person—i.e., in the person of a man firmly established under grace [*sub gratia constituti*]."[36] Aquinas then undertakes to develop both of these interpretations side by side in his commentary, "even though," as he says, "the second interpretation is the better one."[37]

Four elements of interpretation in two contrary pairs appear in this introductory analysis:

(A1) Paul himself is firmly established under grace
(A2) Paul himself is in a state of sin
(B1) Paul is playing a role
(B2) Paul is speaking in his own person.

They can be combined to form four, not just two, different interpretations (although the (A2)–(B1) combination is bizarre and can be ignored). The first interpretation Aquinas recognizes combines (A1) and B1): Paul himself is firmly established under grace, but in speaking these verses he is donning the mask of a man in a state of sin. A point in favor of the (A1)–(B1) interpretation is that it adopts the natural reading of the *content* of the verses, as a confession of evil deeds, but its account of the first-person *construction* is not the natural one. The (A1)–(B2) interpretation is the one Aquinas himself adopts: Paul himself is firmly established under grace, and in these verses he is speaking in his own person. Aquinas calls this the better interpretation, but offhand it looks as if its inclusion of the natural reading of the first-person construction is outweighed by the perplexing combination of (A1) and (B2), a combination that seems to fly in the face of the verses' content.

The (A2)–(B2) combination—Paul himself is in a state of sin, and in these verses he is speaking in his own person—underlies most modern interpretations, whether they take Paul to be confessing or hypocritically wriggling out of his incontinence.[38] Although the (A2)–(B2) interpretation has the unique advantage of providing a natural reading of both the construction and the content of Romans 7:14–25, Aquinas does not even acknowledge it as a possibility because, I think, he was convinced by the rest of what he read in the epistles that Paul was indeed firmly established under grace. Moreover, Aquinas's theology and moral philosophy provide a way of filling out his combination of (A1) and (B2) that must have struck him as the only plausible interpretation of the passage. It deserves consideration as at least a serious rival of the formidable (A2)–(B2) interpretation. We will uncover it most naturally by following Aquinas's development of the (A1)–(B1) (man-of-sin) and (A1)–(B2) interpretations through some of these verses. I will refer to this development as the dual interpretation.

MORAL TROUBLE FOR THE IDEALLY MORAL MAN

The very first first-person statement—"I am carnal"—has no obvious direct bearing on our interest in incontinence, but in commenting on it Aquinas makes some general claims that constitute part of the basis for his treatment of the more clearly relevant passages. In "I am carnal," Aquinas claims, no matter which branch of the dual interpretation is being considered—man-of-sin or man-of-grace—"the 'I' is interpreted as the man's *reason*, that which is first and foremost in a man. That is why every individual man seems to *be* his reason or intellect, just as a political state seems to *be* the head of the state, in the sense that the state seems to do what the head of state does."[39]

On the basis of that first general claim Aquinas begins the promised dual interpretation. If Paul is taken to be playing the role of a man
of sin, his reason "is called carnal . . . because it is *subjugated* to his
flesh, *consenting* to things urged by the flesh"—that is, by the sensory
appetite.[40] But "reason is called carnal in the other [man-of-grace] respect
because it is *under attack* by the flesh . . . And in this respect even the
reason of a man firmly established under grace," such as Paul himself,
"is understood to be carnal."[41] For our present purposes only the moral
aspect of a man firmly established under grace is relevant, and so I offer
"ideally moral man" as an ad-hoc counterpart of "man firmly established under grace." Seen in that light, this man-of-grace interpretation
already contains a hint of something we have not seen till now: even the
ideally moral man is in some sort of moral trouble.[42]

Aquinas identifies the nature and source of the trouble as he takes
the dual interpretation one step further.

> Carnality of these two kinds stems from sin, which is why he [the Apostle]
> adds "sold under sin." But it is important to understand that this [second
> kind of] carnality, which has to do with the *rebellion* of the flesh against
> the spirit, stems from the sin of our first parent. For this [state of affairs]
> pertains to the *fomes*, [that spark] whose ravages derive from that [first]
> sin. On the other hand, the kind of carnality that has to do with *subjec-
> tion* to the flesh stems not only from original sin but also from actual sin,
> through which a man makes himself a slave of the flesh by obeying the
> concupiscent passions of the flesh.[43]

Beginning with the less difficult and less pertinent man-of-sin interpretation, we can, I think, conveniently adopt a secularized understanding of *actual* sin here as immoral action (which, for Aquinas, is irrational action). But *original* sin, which figures in the man-of-grace
interpretation, is not interpretable in purely secular terms at all. Fortu-
nately, it can be set aside for our present purposes because it is introduced here only as the deeper explanation for the immediate source of
the trouble experienced even by the ideal moral man. That source is
identified as "the *fomes*," the inextinguishable spark of unreason in human
nature. Aquinas sometimes identifies it as "the inclination of sensuality,"
or the natural bent of the sensory appetite, which is neither removed by
baptism nor absent from the state of grace.[44] The fact that he takes this
insidious incendiary ingredient in human nature to be a consequence of
original sin is interesting and important to his theology, but we need not
stop now to consider that explanation of our having it. We know we
have it, however we get it, whatever we call it, and that not even the best
of us can relax his guard against it. Take the *fomes* as the beast within,

the unpredictable source of impulses selfish, loutish, lascivious, and perverse, a theologized *id*. That is the source of the moral trouble in which even, or especially, the ideally moral person knows himself to be.

Those impulses Aquinas sometimes aptly calls "first movements" of concupiscence or of sensuality.[45] His recognition of their ubiquity, ineradicability, unpredictability, and irrationality is an essential part of his preferred, man-of-grace interpretation of Paul's first-person statements. In commenting on the second of them — "For that which I do, I do not understand" — he says regarding the man of grace that he

> does indeed do evil — not, of course, by committing evil in fact or with a consenting mind, but only by concupiscently desiring in accord with some passion of the sensory appetite. And that sort of concupiscence is out of range of reason or intellect, because it precedes reason's judgment, which, as soon as it comes, blocks activity of that sort. And so he [the Apostle] says . . . "I do not understand" because that sort of activity of concupiscence arises when the intellect has not yet deliberated, or is not yet aware.[46]

Is this attenuated evil-doing in the man of grace to be identified as "impetuosity" or "unbridled incontinence," the sort that occurs "when a soul yields to the passions before reason has offered counsel"?[47] Obviously not, since although these first movements do precede reason's counsel, the soul of the man of grace does *not* yield to but rather *"blocks* activity of that sort" with reason's judgment as soon as the impulse is noticed. *Neither* sort of incontinence has yet made its appearance in these verses on *either* side of Aquinas's dual interpretation.

AQUINAS'S MAN-OF-SIN INTERPRETATION
OF THE PAULINE PARADIGM

Aquinas's characterization of what has been taken to be the Pauline paradigm of incontinence in verses 15 and 19 begins with his application of the man-of-sin interpretation to "I do not do the good that I will" in verse 15:

> Interpreted in that way, his [the Apostle's] saying "I do *not do*" has to be taken in connection with a completed action that is carried out in fact, overtly, with reason's consent. His saying "I *will* to do," on the other hand, is of course not to be interpreted as having to do with a *completed* volition, the sort that commands action, but rather with the sort of *uncompleted* volition with which people will what is good in general, just

as they also have in general a correct judgment of what is good. Nevertheless, through a habit or a perverse passion that judgment is perverted and that sort of [uncompleted, general] volition is spoiled regarding a particular case, so that [the man] does not do that which he understood[48] in general was to be done, and which he willed in general to do.[49]

(Elsewhere Aquinas calls an "uncompleted volition" a favorable predisposition [*velleitas*].[50]) So the statement "I do not do the good that I will" when attributed to the man of sin means something like this: "I know what is good in general, and I am favorably disposed to do whatever will contribute toward it, but I fail to apply my understanding to certain particular cases, and so my uncompleted volition for the good in general is overridden by a completed, commanding volition for what only seems good on such occasions." Culpable ignorance, bad practical reasoning, and probably other shortcomings can be discerned in this situation, but not, I think, incontinence.[51]

AQUINAS'S MAN-OF-GRACE INTERPRETATION
OF THE PAULINE PARADIGM

On the other hand, when this [first-person statement in verse 15] is interpreted regarding the man restored through grace, it must be interpreted the other way around. *His* saying "I *will* to do" must be interpreted as having to do with a *completed* volition that lasts until a particular action has been selected, so that *his* saying "I do *not do*" is interpreted as having to do with an uncompleted *action* [or first movement], one that takes place only in the sensory appetite, not attaining to reason's consent. For of course the man firmly established under grace wills to preserve his mind from improper concupiscent desires, but that good he does *not do* because of the disordered movements of concupiscence arising in the sensory appetite.[52]

So when the statement "I do not do the good that I will" is attributed to the man of grace, it is simply a statement of his recognition of the inescapable moral trouble that is part of the human condition, a trouble more readily noticed and more keenly felt by a person firmly established under grace.[53] It is certainly not a confession of incontinence.[54]

But how can Aquinas say of the Apostle, of the man of grace, in these unhappy but unavoidable circumstances that *he* does evil, or that it is *he* who does not do that good? We have already seen Aquinas identifying the agent with the agent's reason, and these are circumstances in which everything that can be attributed to the agent's reason is just as it should be.

The first thing to notice is that the agent is not being *blamed* for anything. Even verse 24 is a cry of misery, not of self-condemnation. Furthermore, "*malum*," the Latin word for evil (with all its connotations of blameworthiness), is also the word for just plain bad. Moral people often recognize that they have done something bad even when they are not to blame for it, and the ideally moral man would not will against his inadvertent perverse impulses if he did not recognize them as a bad thing to have, as a flaw though not a fault.

All the same, further exoneration is available for the man of grace in these circumstances, and Aquinas finds Paul offering it in verses 17 and 20, the passages that are particularly repugnant under Matthews's hypocrisy interpretation: "it is no more I who do it, but sin, which dwells in me." Aquinas comments:

> This, too, can be correctly and readily interpreted regarding the man firmly established under grace. For the fact that what is evil is concupiscently desired by him in accord with the sensory appetite, pertaining to the flesh, stems not from the activity of the reason but from the bent of the *fomes*. But the man is said to do what his reason does, because a man is what he is in accord with his reason. And so [in the case of] movements of concupiscence, which stem not from reason but from the *fomes* (which is here named "sin"), it is not the man but the *fomes* of sin that is operative.[55]

And with verse 17, the first of these two—17 and 20—that fit the man-of-grace interpretation so well, Aquinas's project of a dual interpretation hits its first real snag: "But this cannot be interpreted properly regarding the man firmly established under sin, because his reason consents to sin, and so he himself is acting."[56] (Notice that on this point Aquinas would agree with Matthews.) But, despite this difficulty of interpretation, for this passage and others later that present the same sort of problem Aquinas does dutifully contrive a man-of-sin interpretation, "albeit tortuously," as he admits.[57]

CONCLUSION

There is much more to see and appreciate in Aquinas's commentary on these verses, but we have seen enough, I think, to answer this question confidently: Where does incontinence, or *akrasia*, fit into this account of Romans 7:14–25? The answer is, of course, that it does not.

It is not just that Aquinas is sure that Paul was not an incontinent man. More generally and more importantly, Aquinas's conception of incontinence simply does not fit "I do not do what I will to do" (or "I do what I will against"), no matter *who* is supposed to be saying it. Even in the mouth of a man of sin such a statement has to be interpreted in terms of an uncompleted, general volition, a mere favorable predisposition, in order to make sense at all. If incontinence is taken to be instantiated in a person's performing a human action while willing—i.e., engaged in a complete volition—against performing that action, then incontinence cannot be instantiated. Socrates was right about the impossibility of *akrasia* in that sense, at least. Aristotle devoted much of Book VII of the *Nicomachean Ethics* to incontinence or *akrasia*, and Aquinas knew that book well, commented on it, and often cited it elsewhere. But not a single one of his many citations of Aristotle in his Romans commentary occurs in his discussion of chapter 7, verses 14–25, because (I think) he believes Aristotle has nothing relevant to say, not even in Book VII, about the moral circumstances Paul is portraying here.

Romans 7:14–25 is no more a confession of incontinence than it is a portrayal of hypocrisy or of Matthews's "second-order hypocrisy." Matthews's reluctant espousal of the third interpretation may have presented itself to him as a forced option not only because it is the interpretation that incorporates natural readings of both the construction and the content of those verses, but also because he saw no obvious reasonable alternative to it. I hope to have shown that there is an alternative philosophical interpretation that is both reasonable and better, one that is less apparent than it should be because the facts of moral life on which we have seen Aquinas's man-of-grace interpretation to be based have been neglected in moral philosophy.

As I see it, then, Aquinas has read Paul with ingenuity and insight, embedding in this model of rational biblical commentary some rare philosophical observations on certain universal features of the human condition that are brought into high relief in the inescapable plight of even the ideally moral person or the Christian saint, who must, like the rest of us, contend throughout his life against the disorderly promptings of his animal nature, which is implacably warring against the law of his mind.[58]

NOTES

1. References to the parallel in Galatians 5:17 are rare, however.

2. Gareth B. Matthews, "It Is No Longer I That Do It . . . ", *Faith and Philosophy* 1 (1984): pp. 44–49.

3. Ibid., p. 44.

4. Ibid., p. 45.

5. Ibid.

6. Ibid., p. 46; emphasis added.

7. Ibid., p. 48.

8. Ibid., p. 49.

9. Commentaries on the opening verses of Genesis have long been recognized as valuable sources for medieval natural philosophy, but medieval biblical commentaries have otherwise remained closed books to students of medieval philosophy. The number of those closed books is huge, even if we count only those that still survive and were written by medievals who also wrote philosophy. From the middle of the twelfth century almost all medieval philosophers taught at universities where they were required to offer courses of biblical exegesis at a certain stage in their careers, and very many of the resultant commentaries can still be found in manuscript. Students of medieval philosophy have recognized for some time that philosophers' commentaries on the *Sentences* of Peter Lombard constitute a vast, rich source of philosophy along with the theology that is their principal subject matter. I think it is likely that biblical commentaries by medieval philosophers warrant the same sort of recognition.

10. Aquinas's theory of the will is an essential part of the background against which his diagnosis of *akrasia* should be viewed. For a brief, relevant account of it, see pp. 359–362 of Eleonore Stump and Norman Kretzmann, "Absolute Simplicity," *Faith and Philosophy* 2 (1985): 353–382.

11. See, e.g., the survey mentioned in n. 10 above.

12. *Summa theologiae* (*ST*) I-II, q. 9, a. 2.

13. *ST* II-II, q. 156, a. 1.

14. R. M. Hare, *Freedom and Reason* (Oxford: Clarendon Press, 1963), p. 77.

15. Hare's account of *akrasia* is almost as controversial as it is well known. For a good introduction to the controversy, see G. W. Mortimore, ed., *Weakness of Will* (London: Macmillan & Co., 1971), esp. the six articles in Part II, "Hare's Paradox."

16. *Metamorphoses*, vii, 20.

17. Hare, *Freedom and Reason*, p. 78.

18. *ST* I-II, q. 6, a. 7, ad 3.

19. *ST* I-II, q. 6, a. 6.

20. In this context "concupiscence" (*concupiscentia*) is a general name for the passions prompting pursuit or avoidance, as distinct from the passions prompting aggression or resistance, which are designated generally by "irascibility." But sometimes, as in the passage I quoted on pp. 177–178, above about people who are "mad with concupiscence," it means sexual desire in particular, and sometimes it means covetousness. Cf. *ST* I-II, q. 82, a. 3, and 2.

21. *ST* I-II, q. 6, a. 7, obj. 2.

22. *ST* I–II, q. 6, a. 7, ad 2.

23. *ST* I–II, q. 6, a. 7. Cf. Donald Davidson's appreciation of Aquinas on this point, in his "How is Weakness of the Will Possible?" in Joel Feinberg, ed., *Moral Concepts* (Oxford: Oxford University Press, 1970), p. 99, n. 1.

24. In commenting on my treatment of Aquinas's account of weakness, Edward Wierenga said that "it seems that what's really crucial in weakness of the will is that there be a conflict between what the person wills and what the person thinks is best. So why is the on-again, off-again feature included?" One answer is provided in n. 51 below, which discusses a case in which the conflict between what the person thinks best and what he wills on a particular occasion goes unnoticed by him, a case which is not to be characterized as weakness of will just because it does not include the on-again, off-again feature. But there is also a bolder answer, one that seems to require recognizing a stage of immorality *between* Aristotle's and Aquinas's recognized stages of incontinence and intemperance. For there seems to be a kind of despair in which the agent consciously wills against his reason *without* having earlier willed in keeping with it, as in the case of a self-loathing, unrepentant alcoholic. Since such a person loathes his sin, he is not intemperate; and since the on-again, off-again feature is excluded, it is not a case of weakness of will.

25. *ST* II–II, q. 156, a. 1; see pp. 175–176 above.

26. *Ennarationes in Psalmos*, Ps. 118 (119), serm. 8, n. 4; PL 37, 1522; *Corpus Christianorum (Series Latina)* XL, p. 1689.59–63; paraphrased in *ST* I–II q. 9, a. 1, obj. 1.

27. *ST* II–II, q. 155, a. 3.

28. For bibliographical information on Aquinas' writings, see the appendix to James A. Weisheipl's *Friar Thomas d'Aquino* (New York: Doubleday, 1974). See also P. Glorieux, *"Essai sur les commentaires scripturaires de s. Thomas et leur chronologie,"* *Recherches de théologie ancienne et médiévale* 17 (1950): 237–266.

29. C. Spicq, "Saint Thomas Exégéte," *Dictionnaire de théologie catholique*, vol. 15-A, col. 695. See also C. E. B. Cranfield, *A Critical and Exegetical Commentary on the Epistle to the Romans*, vol. 32 *The International Critical Commentary*, (Edinburgh: T. & T. Clark, 1975), pt. I, p. 36: "But altogether outstanding among medieval commentaries is that of Thomas Aquinas . . . One does not have to read very far in it to realize that one is observing an immensely powerful intellect at work. His commentary is admirably succinct and beautifully clear (with a very liberal use of 'primo', 'secundo' and 'tertio'). It is notable for its close attentiveness to, and extraordinarily precise logical analysis of, the Pauline text." (I am grateful to Terry Irwin for having called my attention to Cranfield's appreciation.)

30. Weisheipl, *Friar Thomas d'Aquino*, p. 248.

31. Matthew L. Lamb in the introduction to his translation of Aquinas's commentary on Ephesians (Albany, N. Y.: Magi Books, 1966), p. 26.

32. *Super epistolam ad Romanos lectura (SR)*, n. 556.

33. Ibid.

34. *Liber de diversis quaestionibus LXXXIII*, q. 66, 5; ed. Maur., vol. VI, col. 46e; *Corpus Christianorum (Series Latina)* XLIV A, p. 158.169–178.

35. *Contra Iulianum* II, 3; ed. Maur., vol. X, col. 529c.

36. *SR* n. 558.

37. Ibid. On the dual interpretation, see also *De veritate* q. 24, a. 12, ad 1, where the man-of-sin interpretation is characterized as concerned with mortal sin, the man-of-grace interpretation with venial sin, the first movements of concupiscence. See also Cranfield, *Commentary* (n. 29 above), p. 37:

> The humility characteristic of the true scholar shows itself . . . in the fairness and fulness with which he expounds alternative interpretations which he himself does not accept. A good example . . . is to be seen in the discussion of 7.14ff . . . [where he offers two interpretations while] at the same time indicating clearly his own judgment (which is surely right!) that the explanation which understands Paul to be speaking of the man who is under grace is to be preferred . . .

38. I do not know of a medieval version of the view that Paul is confessing *incontinence* here, but around the time Aquinas was commenting on Romans he argued against a thirteenth-century interpretation that had Paul confessing in Romans 7 at least that he *lacked temperance*. See n. 54 below.

39. *SR* n. 559.

40. *SR* n. 560.

41. Ibid.

42. The extent to which the man of grace is the ideally moral man and the nature of the moral trouble even he is in can be seen in, for instance, *ST* I–II, q. 109, a. 8:

> In the [present, earthly] state of corrupted nature, however, a man needs habitual grace for healing his nature so that he may altogether abstain from sin. In the present life this healing is brought about first in respect of the mind, while the carnal appetite is not yet altogether rectified. That is why the Apostle says in Romans 7:[25], in the person of a man who has been restored [through grace], "I myself with the mind serve the law of God, but with the flesh, the law of sin." And in that state [of grace] a man can indeed abstain from mortal sin, which occurs in the reason, as was claimed above [q. 74, a. 5]. But because of the corruption of the lower appetite, sensuality, a man cannot abstain from every venial sin. Reason can, indeed, prevent *any* of its individual movements—it is on that basis that they have the character of sin and are voluntary—but not *all* of them. For while it is trying to resist one, another may arise, and, furthermore, reason cannot always be alert to these movements that are to be avoided, as was said above [q. 74, a. 3, ad 2].

Cf. *ST* I–II, q. 81, a. 3, ad 2; II–II, q. 104, a. 6, ad 1; *De virtutibus in communi* q. un., a. 10, ad 14; *Super epistolam ad Galatas lectura* n. 314.

43. *SR* nn. 560, 561.

44. See, e.g., *ST* I–II, q. 74, a. 3, ad 2; q. 81, a. 3, ad 2; q. 89, a. 5, ad 1; q. 91, a. 6, *passim*.

45. See, e.g., *De malo* (*DM*) q. 7, a. 6, ad 8; q. 7, a. 8, *passim*; *ST* I–II, q. 89, a. 5.

46. *SR* n. 563.

47. *ST* II–II, q. 156, a. 1; pp. 175–176 above.

48. Reading "*intelligeret*" for "*intelligi*."

49. *SR* n. 565.

50. Here is a particularly helpful passage:

> A man's will considered unconditionally [*simpliciter*] is his reason's will, since we will absolutely [*absolute*] what we will in accord with our reason's deliberation. On the other hand, what we will in accord with a movement of sensuality, or even in accord with a movement of our simple [*simplicis*] volition [for the good in general], which is considered as our nature, we will not unconditionally but on condition [*secundum quid*] – that is, *if* nothing else uncovered by reason's deliberation should get in the way. That is why a volition of that sort is called a favorable predisposition rather than an absolute volition – i.e., because a man *would* will this thing if nothing else got in the way (*ST* III q. 21, a. 4).

Cf., e.g., *ST* I–II q. 13, a. 5, ad 1; *DM* q. 16, a. 3, ad 9. On uncompleted volitions and mixed voluntary-involuntary acts more generally, see, e.g., *Summa contra Gentiles* II 32, n. 1091; *ST* I–II q. 20, a. 4; II–II q. 142, a. 4.

51. In commenting on my paper Edward Wierenga said, quite rightly, that one reason I think "there is no incontinence in this case is that there is no conflict between what the person believes is good . . . and what the person wills." The difference between incontinence and this situation might also be brought out by observing that the incontinent person *does* know better while the man of sin in this case *should* know better but does not. But Wierenga also wondered whether this person's will does not change over time as Aquinas says an incontinent person's will changes. It seems to me that this man of sin's volition gets more complex without being altered in a way that would ordinarily be described as a change in his will. At 8:00 he forms this uncompleted volition for the good: "I should give up eating between meals." The rational outcome of that uncompleted volition would be his completed, commanding volition against having a doughnut at 10:30, but instead he then wills to have one, and has it. The contrariety between his uncompleted volition and his commanding volition goes unrecognized by him (there's the culpable ignorance or bad practical reasoning), and so there is no willing on his part to repudiate the uncompleted volition (as there would be if this situation were one of incontinence), just a commanding volition that is in fact, unrecognizedly, in conflict with it. So there is not a full-fledged change in the will – in the conscious direction of the will – as there would be if this man of sin's reason were doing its job. He does not have to say to himself "I'll have a doughnut *anyway*," as the incontinent person would.

52. *SR* n. 565.

53. Everyone knows that "improper concupiscent desires" are likely to lead to moral evil, that they are therefore morally dangerous. That is one reason, the obvious reason, why every moral person must be on guard against "the disordered movements of concupiscence" and contend against them when they arise. But the fact of moral life I think has been neglected is that those promptings are not only morally dangerous but are also themselves morally deplorable, considered just as such. They are ineradicable moral flaws, beyond the agent's power to prevent, and so not flaws for which the agent considered as an individual is responsible. That means that they are not to be counted as moral evils of his, just moral flaws. What is special about the saint or the ideally moral person in this connection is that it is he rather than the rest of us who has a low enough level of moral background noise in his soul to be able to focus on and deplore what is sin in him without being his sin in the full sense of those words. (Since what is at issue here is the *fomes*, a residue of original sin, an unusual and perhaps unorthodox account of the moral status of original sin seems to be just around the corner.)

54. Aquinas considers Paul to be not merely continent but, rather, temperate, as is shown in his reply to an objection in *De virtutibus cardinalibus* q. un., a. 1, obj. 6:

> Temperance seems not to be a virtue; for it is not possessed by people who have the other virtues, as is clear in the case of Paul, who had all the other virtues and yet did not have temperance. For in his members there was still concupiscence, according to Romans 7:[23]: "But I see another law in my members, warring against the law of my mind." Now the temperate man differs from the continent man in this, that the *temperate* man does not *have* perverse concupiscent desires, while the *continent* man has them but does not *follow* them, as is clear from what the Philosopher says in *Ethics* VII [9].

Ad 6:

> It must be said that it is not of the essence of temperance [in a man] that he exclude all perverse concupiscent desires, but rather that he not allow vehement and powerful concupiscent desires of that sort, as those who have not applied themselves to restraining concupiscent desires do allow. Paul, therefore, was undergoing *disorderly* concupiscent desires because of the corruption associated with the *fomes*, but not *powerful or vehement* concupiscent desires, because he was applying himself to repel them by chastising the body and reducing it to servitude. Thus he was genuinely temperate.

Cf. *Super epistolam ad Galatas* n. 315, where Aquinas is commenting on Galatians 5:17:

> But it should be noted that as regards concupiscent desires there are four types of human beings, *none* of whom does the things he wills. [1] For the *intemperate* ones — those who follow their carnal passions on purpose (in

keeping with Proverbs 2:14, "Who rejoice when they have done evil")—do indeed do what they will insofar as they do follow those very passions; but insofar as their reason murmurs against it and is displeased with it, they do not do the things they will. [2] On the other hand, the *incontinent* ones, who have the aim of abstaining and are nevertheless overcome by their passions, of course do what they do not will insofar as they follow those passions contrary to their aim. (And so the intemperate ones do more of what they will.) [3] Those who are *continent*, however—i.e., those who would will not to be concupiscent at all—do what they will as long as they are not concupiscent; but because they cannot remain entirely without concupiscence, they do what they do not will. [4] Finally, the *temperate* ones do indeed what they will, insofar as in their tamed flesh they are not concupiscent. But because it cannot be *entirely* tamed, so that it does not struggle against the spirit in any respect at all—just as malice cannot grow to such an extent that reason will not murmur against it—so, when on occasion they are concupiscent, they do what they will not to do. Nevertheless, they do more [than any of the others] of what they will.

55. *SR* n. 570.

56. Ibid.

57. *SR* nn. 571, 576.

58. I am grateful to all those who raised thoughtful questions about this paper on various occasions, particularly to Robert Adams, Joel Feinberg, Paul Helm, Alvin Plantinga, and Holly Smith. I was generously supplied with written comments by John Boler, Terry Irwin, Ron Milo, David Widerker, and Edward Wierenga, and I am grateful to all of them for having helped me to improve the paper. And I am grateful to Eleonore Stump, whose criticisms and suggestions at every stage of writing this paper made it better than it could otherwise have been.

Suffering Love

NICHOLAS WOLTERSTORFF

My heart grew sombre with grief, and wherever I looked I saw only death. My own country became a torment and my own home a grotesque abode of misery. All that we had done together was now a grim ordeal without him. My eyes searched everywhere for him, but he was not there to be seen. I hated all the places we had known together, because he was not in them and they could no longer whisper to me, 'Here he comes!' as they would have done had he been alive but absent for a while. . . . My soul was a burden, bruised and bleeding. It was tired of the man who carried it, but I found no place to set it down to rest. (Augustine, *Confessions* IV, 4; IV, 7)[1]

It is in passages such as this, where he exposes to full view the grief which overwhelmed him upon the death of his dear friend from Tagaste, that Augustine is at his most appealing to us in the twentieth century. We are attracted both by the intensity of his love and grief, and by his willingness to expose that grief to his friends and the readers of his *Confessions*. To any who may have experienced torments similar to those Augustine here describes, the passage also has the mysteriously balming quality of expressing with delicate precision the grief they themselves have felt. All the places and all the objects that once whispered "Here he comes" or "Here she comes" have lost their voice and fallen achingly mute.

It is a rough jolt, to discover that at those very points in his life where we find Augustine most appealing, he, from the time of his conversion onward, found himself thoroughly disgusting. His reason for exposing his grief was to share with his readers his confession to God of the senselessness and sinfulness of a love so intense for a being so fragile that its destruction could cause such grief. "Why do I talk of these things?" he asks. And he answers, "It is time to confess, not to question" (*Confessions* IV, 6).

In the years between the death of his friend and the death of his mother Augustine embraced the Christian faith. That embrace made his response to his mother's death very different from that to his friend's. "I closed her eyes," he says,

> and a great wave of sorrow surged into my heart. It would have overflowed in tears if I had not made a strong effort of will and stemmed the flow, so that the tears dried in my eyes. What a terrible struggle it was to hold them back! As she breathed her last, the boy Adeodatus began to wail aloud and only ceased his cries when we all checked him. I, too, felt that I wanted to cry like a child, but a more mature voice within me, the voice of my heart, bade me keep my sobs in check, and I remained silent. (*Confessions* IX, 12)

On that earlier occasion, tears and "tears alone were sweet to him, for in his heart's desire they had taken the place of his friend" (*Confessions* IV, 4). In his reminiscences he asked why that was so, "why tears are sweet to the sorrowful." "How . . . can it be that there is sweetness in the fruit we pluck from the bitter crop of life, in the mourning and the tears, the wailing and the sighs?" (*Confessions* IV, 5) But now, on the occasion of his mother's death, he "fought against the wave of sorrow" (*Confessions* IX, 12).

His struggle for self-control was not successful. He reports that after the burial, as he lay in bed thinking of his devoted mother, "the tears which I had been holding back streamed down, and I let them flow as freely as they would, making of them a pillow for my heart. On them it rested . . ." (*Confessions* IX, 12). So now, he says to God, "I make you my confession. . . . Let any man read it who will. . . . And if he finds that I sinned by weeping for my mother, even if only for a fraction of an hour, let him not mock at me . . . but weep himself, if his charity is great. Let him weep for my sins to you . . . " (*Confessions* IX, 12). The sin for which Augustine wants the person of charity to weep, however, is not so much the sin of weeping over the death of his mother as the sin of which that weeping was a sign. I was, says Augustine, "guilty of too much worldly affection."

Obviously there is a mentality coming to expression here which is profoundly foreign to us. In our own day there are still those who hold back tears — usually because they think it unbecoming to cry, seldom because they think it sinful. But rare is the person who believes that even to *feel* grief upon the death of a friend or one's mother is to have been guilty of too much worldly affection. The mentality expressed not only shapes Augustine's view of the proper place of sorrow and suffering in human life; it also contributes to his conviction that in God there is no sorrow or suffering. God's life is a life free of sorrow — indeed, a life free of upsetting emotions in general, a life free of passions, a life of apathy, untouched by suffering, characterized only by steady bliss. In thus thinking of God, Augustine was by no means alone. Indeed, the view that God's life is that of blissful non-suffering apathy enjoyed near total consensus until the twentieth century. Among the church fathers, only Origen and Lactantius thought differently — and Origen, only inconsistently so.

But why would anyone who placed himself in the Christian tradition think of God's life as that of non-suffering apathy? The identity of that tradition is determined (in part) by the adherence of its members, in one way or another, to the scriptures of the Old and New Testaments. And even those who read while running cannot fail to notice that God is there pictured as one who sufferingly experiences his world and therefore grieves. What was it, then, that led the tradition to 'bracket' this dimension of the biblical picture of God? Many of our modern theologians reject the proposition that God acts miraculously in history; if they remain within the Christian tradition, they 'bracket' that part of the biblical narrative and picture. But 'bracketing' did not begin with the Enlightenment. It was practiced already by the church fathers, on all the passages which spoke of the passions and the suffering of God. In this paper I wish to dig down to the roots of this practice; and having done that, to go on to ask: Were they right in this claim of theirs, that God does not sufferingly experience the world?

We cannot do better than begin with Augustine. But we would be ill-advised to move at once to what Augustine said about emotions and suffering in the life of God. For it was true of Augustine, as it was of most others in the tradition, that his reflections on the place of emotions and suffering in God's life were merely a component within his more comprehensive reflections on the place of emotions and suffering in the ideal life of persons generally — divine and human together. We must try, then, to grasp that totality. Let us begin with what Augustine says about the proper place of emotions and suffering in human experience.

Augustine frames his thought within the eudaemonistic tradition of antiquity. We are all in search of happiness — by which Augustine and the other ancients did not mean a life in which happiness outweighs grief and ennui but a life from which grief and ennui have been cast out — a life of uninterrupted bliss. Furthermore, Augustine aligns himself with the Platonic tradition in his conviction that one's love, one's *eros*, is the fundamental determinant of one's happiness. Augustine never imagined that a human being could root out *eros* from his existence.[2] Incomplete beings that we are, we inescapably long for fulfillment. The challenge, accordingly, is to choose objects for one's love such that happiness ensues.

Now it was as obvious to Augustine as it is to all of us that grief ensues when that which we love is destroyed or dies, or is altered in such a way that we no longer find it lovable. Says he, in reflecting on his grief upon the death of his friend, "I lived in misery like every man whose soul is tethered by the love of things that cannot last and then is agonized to lose them. . . . The grief I felt for the loss of my friend had struck so easily into my inmost heart simply because I had poured out my soul upon him, like water upon sand, loving a man who was mortal as though he were never to die" (*Confessions* IV, 6; IV, 8). The cure is to detach one's love from such objects and to attach it to something immutable and indestructible. For Augustine, the only candidate was God. "Blessed are those who love you, O God. . . . No one can lose you . . . unless he forsakes you" (*Confessions* IV, 9).

What might be called Augustine's "evangelistic strategy" follows straightforwardly. If it is happiness and rest for your soul that you desire—and who does not?—then fix your love on the eternal immutable God. Addressing his own soul and thereby all others as well Augustine says: "[In God] is the place of peace that cannot be disturbed, and he will not withhold himself from your love unless you withhold your love from him. . . . Make your dwelling in him, my soul. Entrust to him whatever you have. . . . All that is withered in you will be made to thrive again. All your sickness will be healed" (*Confessions* IV, 11).

Part of what obstructs our detachment from the world and attachment to God is illusion as to where happiness can be found. Much of Augustine's endeavor in his early writings was devoted to penetrating his readers' veil of illusions. But a striking feature of Augustine's thought—here he departs decisively from the Platonic tradition—is his conviction that illumination is not sufficient to redirect love. Though we may *know* that only in loving God is abiding happiness to be found, yet the beauties of the world sink their talons so deep into our souls that only by the grace of God and the most agonizing of struggles can we break loose. Nowhere is this anti-Platonic point made more vividly in Augustine's writings than in the brilliant description of his experience in the garden just before his conversion:

> I now found myself driven by the tumult in my breast to take refuge in this garden, where no one could interrupt that fierce struggle, in which I was my own contestant, until it came to its conclusion. . . . I was frantic, overcome by violent anger with myself for not accepting your will and entering into your covenant. Yet in my bones I knew that this was what I ought to do. In my heart of hearts I praised it to the skies. And to reach this goal I needed no chariot or ship. I need not even walk as far as I had

come from the house to the place where I sat, for to make the journey, and to arrive safely, no more was required than an act of will. But it must be a resolute and wholehearted act of the will. . . . I tore my hair and hammered my forehead with my fists; I locked my fingers and hugged my knees; and I did all this because I made an act of will to do it. . . . Yet I did not do that one thing which I should have been far, far better pleased to do than all the rest and could have done at once. . . . My lower instincts, which had taken firm hold of me, were stronger than the higher, which were untried. And the closer I came to the moment which was to mark the great change in me, the more I shrank from my purpose; it merely left me hanging in suspense. (*Confessions VIII, 8; VIII, 11*)

I see no reason to interpret Augustine as opposed to all enjoyment of earthly things: of food, of drink, of conversation, of art. Wary, Yes; opposed, No. What he says is only that we should root out the *love* of such things — root out all attachment to them such that their destruction would cause us grief. "Let my soul praise you for these things," he says, "O God, creator of them all; but the love of them, which we feel, through the senses of the body, must not be like glue to bind my soul to them" (*Confessions* IV, 10). To enjoy the taste of kiwi fruit is acceptable provided that one's enjoyment is not such that if it proves unattainable, one grieves. Though we must not love the world, we may enjoy the world. Admittedly Augustine says little by way of grounding the legitimacy of such enjoyment. For example, the theme of the things of the world constituting God's blessing extended to us is subdued in him. In the famous passage in Book X of the *Confessions* where the things of creation 'speak', what they say is not "Receive us with enjoyment as God's blessing" but "Turn away from us to our maker." Nonetheless I think we must allow that for Augustine, the detached life need not be a joyless life.[3]

But suppose that one has torn oneself loose from love of the things of this world and turned oneself to loving God — detached oneself from world and attached oneself to God. Has Augustine not overlooked the fact that this is to open oneself to a new mode of grief? When Augustine recommends to us the love of God as the only source of abiding happiness, he is not recommending that we find delight in our own acts of devotion. He is not an arch-Calvinist urging that we delight in our acts of social obedience nor an arch-Orthodox urging that we delight in our celebration of the liturgy. He is urging that we delight in the experience of the presence of God. It was the presence of his friend, he says, that "was sweeter to me than all the joys of life as I loved it then" (*Confessions* IV, 4). This sweetness was to be replaced by the sweetness of God's presence. Augustine knew of that sweetness. Looking out from a window into the courtyard of a house in Ostia, he was discoursing with his mother, shortly before her death, about God. "And while we spoke of the eternal Wisdom," he says, "longing for it and straining for it with all the strength of our hearts, for one fleeting instant we reached out and touched it" (*Confessions* IX, 10). He imagines that blissful experience prolonged.

But it never is prolonged, not in our world. The experience of the saints through the ages is the experience of the sweet presence of God interrupted with long aching stretches of his absence. They experience the dark night of the soul, and in that night, they grieve. God "will not withhold himself from your love unless you withhold your love from him," says Augustine (*Confessions* IV, 11). Many of the great mystics would disagree. But in any case, if humanity's greatest lovers of God find their love plunging them into grief, then one cannot recommend turning one's love to God as the way to eliminate grief from one's experience.

In fact Augustine, by the time of writing his *Confessions*, agreed that to reorient oneself toward loving God is to open oneself to a new mode of grief. But the grief he had in mind is not that of which I have just spoken, that of the lover of God grieving because God hides himself. It was that of the lover of God grieving because her own love proves weak and inconstant. The response Augustine urged to the grief which ensues upon change and decay in the objects we love is that we detach ourselves from such objects and attach ourselves to God in whom there is no shadow of turning. But this newly oriented self never wholly wins out over the old. And over that repetitious reappearance of the old self, the new now grieves. The *passive* grief of negated affection is replaced by the *active* grief of lamenting over the faults of one's religious character—over those persistent habits of the hearts that one now recognizes as sin.

Prominent in the ethical philosophy of middle and late antiquity were discussions over the proper place of emotions in life. In those discussions, the Stoic view was famous. Augustine, in *The City of God*, participates in those discussions by staking out his own position on the proper place of emotions in the life of the godly person in opposition to the Stoic position.

Now the Stoics did not say that in the ideal life there would be no emotional coloring to one's experience. They insisted, on the contrary, that in such a life there would be various non-perturbing emotions which they called *eupatheiai*. They regularly cited three of these: Joy, wishfulness, and caution. Their thought was that the ideal life, the happy life, is the life of the wise person—of the person who, by virtue of directing his life by reason, is a person whose character and intentions are morally virtuous. To make it clear that, in their judgment, the only thing good in itself is moral good, they typically refused even to *call* anything else "good." Certain other things are, at best, *preferable*. The wise person, then, will rejoice over the moral status he has attained, will wish for the continuation of that status, and will be watchful for what threatens it.

The Stoics went on to say, though, that the sage would be without *pathos*, without passion. He would be *apathés*, apathetic. His condition would be that of *apatheia*—apathy, impassibility, passionlessness. What did they mean?

In the interpretation which he offers of their position, Augustine takes a *pathos* to be simply a perturbing, upsetting emotion such as fear, grief, and ecstasy. He does not incorporate into his concept of *pathos* any theory as to the rightness or wrongness of such emotions. And he was of the opinion that, in spite of all the verbal differences between the way in which the Peripatetics expressed their view as to the place of the passions, thus understood, in the life of the moral person, and the way in which the Stoics expressed theirs, there was no substantive difference between them.[4]

The Peripatetics said that though passions may befall the moral person as well as the non-moral, they will not overthrow the rule of reason in his life; while the Stoics said that "the wise man is not subject to these perturbations" (*City of God* IX, 4).[5] To illustrate why, in his judgment, there was no substantive difference between these two positions, Augustine cited an anecdote from Aulus Gellius. Gellius was once at sea with a famous Stoic when a storm came up and the Stoic became pale with fear of shipwreck. After the storm had passed, Gellius courteously asked the Stoic why he had become fearful. Thereupon the Stoic pulled out a book of Epictetus and pointed to a passage in which the point was made that

> When these impressions are made by alarming and formidable objects, it must needs be that they move the soul even of the wise man, so that for a little he trembles with fear, or is depressed by sadness, these impressions anticipating the work of reason and self-control; but this does not imply that the mind accepts these evil impressions, or approves or consents to them. For this consent is, they think, in a man's power; there being this difference between the mind of the wise man and that of the fool, that the fool's mind yields to these passions and consents to them, while that of the wise man, though it cannot help being invaded by them, yet retains with unshaken firmness a true and steady persuasion of those things which it ought rationally to desire or avoid. (*City of God* IX, 4)

In short, whatever emotions befall the wise person, his *will* and judgment remains morally intact.

Augustine goes on to speculate that perhaps the Stoics meant to assert that "the wisdom which characterizes the wise man is clouded by no error and sullied by no taint, but, with this reservation that his wisdom remains undisturbed, he is exposed to the impressions which the goods and ills of this life (or, as they prefer to call them, the advantages or disadvantages) make upon them." And he goes on to remark, somewhat wryly, that even though the Stoic refused to call his bodily safety a "good," preferring some other such word as "thing preferred" or "advantage," his turning pale with fear indicated that he esteemed his bodily safety rather highly — as highly, indeed, as the Peripatetic who was quite willing to call bodily safety a "good" and in the same situation would probably also have turned pale from fear over the threat to it.

But if this is what the Stoics mean, then, says Augustine, all parties agree that though the wise person may well experience such passions as fear and grief, he will not allow them to overthrow the rule of reason in his life — will not allow them to damage his virtue. Though the wise person may not be free *of* passions, he will be free *from* them. Though they may *befall* him, he will not be *subject* to them; they will not influence his intentions and judgments. It is in that sense that the sage is characterized by *apatheia* — by apathy, passionlessness, impassibility.[6]

Since our concern here is with Augustine's formulation of his own view in contrast to that of the Stoics, what is directly relevant is not what the Stoics actually said on the proper place of emotions in life but what Augustine interpreted them as saying. Nonetheless it is worth observing that probably Augustine has described a late, nonstandard version of Stoicism.[7] For it is clear that the founding fathers of Stoicism, Zeno and Chrysippus, said that a *pathos* is "an excessive impulse," "a 'disease' which affects our basic impulses," "an irrational movement of the soul," "an unnatural movement of the soul which is contrary to reason," etc. And by such sayings they meant to imply, among other things, that a *pathos* is based on, or is even to be identified with, a judgment which is false and contrary to reason. Passions are based on (or identical with) erroneous judgments of evaluated fact that lead to (or are) irrational feelings and excessive impulses. But if this is one's understanding of a *pathos*, then obviously one will hold that passions will in no form whatsoever appear in the life of the fully wise person. And that in fact is what the mainline Stoics claimed when they said that the wise person will be characterized by *apatheia*.

In principle the question remains open, however, whether all emotional disturbances — with fear, grief, and ecstasy as prime examples —

are *passions* on this concept of passion. It is clear that the classic Stoics thought they were. One grieves, they would have said, only over what one evaluates as evil; but the sage, finding no trace of moral evil in himself, has nothing over which to grieve. So too, one fears what one evaluates as an evil threatening; but for the sage, who is steady in virtue, there are no threatening evils. And one goes into ecstasy over something that happens to come one's way which one evaluates as good. But for the sage, there are no goods which just happen to come his way; that which is the only thing good for him, namely, his own moral character, is entirely of his own making. It was, thus, the contention of the classic Stoics that as a matter of fact the upsetting emotions are all passions, and will, on that account, have no place in the life of the wise person. The true sage experiences no emotional disturbances.[8]

The dispute between the classic Stoics and the late Gellius-type Stoics was thus a subtle one: Does one become emotionally upset only over what one judges as evil or also over what one judges as nonpreferable? Can there be emotional disturbances not based on false evaluations? That dispute we need not enter. However, a decision on terminology is necessary. It will be far and away most convenient for our purposes here to use the word *"pathos"* in its neutral sense. A *pathos*, in the remainder of my discussion, will simply be an emotional upset, an emotional disturbance. (And probably most of us would not even speak of those phenomena which the Stoics called *eupatheiai*, and which were thought to lack any element of disturbance, as *emotions*.)

His own position, says Augustine, is that the Stoics and Peripatetics were correct in their central contention: A life free "from those emotions which are contrary to reason and disturb the mind, . . . is obviously a good and most desirable quality . . . " (*City of God* XIV, 9). The context makes clear that Augustine means to say something much stronger: A life *entirely* free of passions (emotional upset) is to be desired. For ideal existence is incompatible with being 'overcome' in the way in which one is overcome by emotions. And beyond that, it is incompatible with the suffering, the 'vexation', which is a component in such 'negative' emotions as fear and grief.

However, Augustine's main emphasis does not fall on this point of agreement between himself and the Stoics. It falls instead on his insistence that *in this present life* a person who desires to live in truly godly fashion will *not* try to live a life devoid of *pathos*, of passion, of emotional upset. She will not be apathetic. If "some, with a vanity monstrous in proportion to its rarity, have become enamoured of themselves because they can be stimulated and excited by no emotion, moved or bent by no affection, such persons rather lose all humanity than obtain true tranquillity," says Augustine (*City of God* XIV, 9).

The reason is that none of us avoids sin. And the godly person will grieve over the sins into which she has fallen as well as fear falling into new ones. She will grieve over the state of her soul. If *apatheia* be understood as "a condition . . . in which no fear terrifies nor any pain annoys, we must in this life renounce such a state if we would live according to God's will . . . " (*City of God* XIV, 9). An ethic for the perfect sage is not an ethic for the imperfect lover of God. Such a person will not just let the emotions of fear and grief take their natural course in her life, merely seeing to it that they do not lead to bad intentions and false judgments. Nor will she try to root them out entirely. She will *cultivate* fear and sorrow—fear and sorrow over the right things, however; namely, over sin. The decisive point in Augustine's departure from the classic Stoics lies in his conviction that some fear and some sorrow is based on *correct* evaluation. The issue, he says, is "not so much . . . whether a pious soul is angry, as why he is angry; not whether he is sad, but what is the course of his sadness; not whether he fears, but what he fears" (*City of God* IX, 5; cf. XIV, 8). The eudaemonistic ideal of antiquity begins to creak and crack before our eyes. Though we are to *long* for eudaemonia, says Augustine, it would be wrong in *this* life to pursue it.

Now most certainly the Stoics did not recommend the cultivation of passion in the life of the non-sage, not even in the life of the person *committed* to becoming a sage who falls prey every now and then to weakness or temptation. Yet it is hard to see how they could object in principle to adopting in their own way what Augustine here holds. Augustine has argued that *eros* must be turned away from the things of this world to God, on the ground that we must abolish that grief which follows upon the change or destruction of objects of *eros*. Yet this does not mean for him the elimination of grief and fear from life. We struggle now to reorient our love to God. But the self does not turn freely on its axis. And so we grieve—grieve over not being able to turn right round. We grieve over our persistent failure to achieve the project of reorientating our love.[9] Now the Stoics said that the sage would both rejoice over his moral perfection and be wary of the temptations that lie in wait. But, having said that, it is hard to see what grounds they could have for resisting admitting the propriety of *grief over moral failure* by the person struggling to become a sage. For such an emotional upset would be based on a true, not a false, evaluation. In the classic Stoic sense of "*pathos*," it would not be a *pathos*. It is true that Augustine stood in the Platonic tradition of seeing happiness as lying in the satisfaction of *eros* while the Stoics saw happiness as lying in the elimination of *eros* and the achievement of the project of being a fully moral self. Yet grief over one's moral failure seems as appropriate in the Stoic universe as does grief over one's religious failure in the Augustinian.

It is in what Augustine went on to say next that he burst outside not only what any Stoic *said* but what any Stoic *could possibly* have said—indeed, what any ancient pagan ethicist could have said. Augustine says that we are not only to grieve over *our own* sins and be fearful of falling into new ones. We are also to grieve over the sins of others and to rejoice in their repentance (*City of God* XIV, 9). And, motivated by pity, we are to work for their deliverance. We are to be merciful.

We must understand Augustine aright here. He is not suddenly bringing *eros* back in. He is not saying that our lives are incomplete unless they are attached by *eros* to our fellows. *Eros* is to remain fixed on God. Yet we are to grieve over the religious condition of the souls of all humanity—or, more concretely, of all those whom we know.

What is Augustine's thought here? He never quite spells it out. I see no alternative, however, but to interpret it along the following lines: Each of us is to be joined in a solidarity of joy and grief with all human-ity—joy and grief over the right things, be it added; namely, over the state of our souls. I am to rejoice and grieve over the religious condition of my soul and, in the very same way, to rejoice and grieve over the condition of yours. In the most strict of senses, I am to love my neigh-bor as myself—as if he *were* myself. The idea is not that I am to recog-nize some value in *you* which fulfills *me*; that would be the snake of earthly *eros* slinking back in. Rather, I am to live in emotional solidarity with you. Instead of my project being simply to achieve my own true happiness, my project must be to achieve *our* true happiness. My happi-ness is not to be achieved without yours being achieved. Often this soli-darity will consist in bearing your grief and sharing your joy. But the identification Augustine has in mind goes beyond even such sympathy. For it may be that you are not grieving over your soul when you should be. Then I will grieve on your behalf, grieving even over your not griev-ing.

Implicit in this vision is a recognition of the worth of each human self. If one aims exclusively at happiness for one's own self, the tacit attribution of a certain kind of worth to one's self which this project presupposes scarcely comes to light. But if one exists in a solidarity of grieving and rejoicing with all humanity, then it is clear that one is thereby ascribing a certain worthiness to each and every human being which one is not ascribing, say, to any animal.[10] Human beings are worthy of being caught up in one's solidarity of grieving and rejoicing. One is to honor every human soul by grieving and rejoicing over its religious successes and failures just as one honors one's own soul by grieving and rejoicing over its successes and failures. The worthiness thereby tacitly ascribed to each and every human soul is not that worthiness which consists in a person's degree of godliness; after all, one grieves most intensely over those who are least godly. Rather, if it be asked why it is appropriate to exist in this mysterious honoring solidarity with all human beings, the answer Augustine gave, all too cryptically, is this: Because we are all icons of God.[11]

Thus in the Augustinian universe there is a quadripartite distinction among modes of worth and valuing. God has one mode of worth; we express our recognition of that worth by loving him and him alone. Human beings as icons of God have another kind of worth; we exhibit our recognition of that mode of worth by rejoicing and grieving over the religious health of their souls. The morally admirable person has another mode of worth, one which the morally despicable person lacks. And the things of the world have yet a different kind of worth; we value them as useful and, perhaps, as enjoyable.

The Stoic universe was profoundly different — at least as interpreted by that fine scholar of late antiquity, J. M. Rist. The Stoic, says Rist, regarded only human beings as of value, and regarded the value of human beings as determined entirely by their moral status. The Augustinian split between *their worth as persons, and their moral status*, has no counterpart in the Stoics. Marcus Aurelius, observes Rist, "tells us that each man is worth as much as what he is concerned with. . . . The implication is clear: those whose character is preoccupied with right reason and virtue are of value, those whose tastes are lower can be graded accordingly. Some people are presumably worth nothing at all; and these should be treated accordingly."[12] And Epictetus remarked that "neither the nose nor the eyes are sufficient to make a man, but he is a man who makes properly human judgments. Here is someone who does not listen to reason — he is an ass. Here is one whose sense of self-respect has become numbed: he is useless, a sheep, anything rather than a man."[13]

It is true that such Stoics as Epictetus and Marcus praised *philostorgia*, benevolence.

> Yet along with their emphasis on *philostorgia* these writers are inclined to point out that the wise man is not concerned over the death of a child. . . . Marcus expressly points out both that the wise man is benevolent (*philostorgos*) and that he is the most devoid of passions contrary to reason. . . . Hence we have to conclude that *philostorgia* neither confers nor recognizes value in its objects, nor does it think of its objects as unique

and irreplaceable, nor does it demand any overwhelming emotional commitment in those who exhibit it.[14]

"It is clearly incumbent on each man to be emotionally committed to one human being, or rather one human phenomenon alone, namely, one's own moral character and moral dignity."[15] For the only good is moral character. And the only moral character any of us can be responsible for is our own. Hence if I come across another moral character I can respect it; but it cannot be for me a good. The sole good for me is my own moral character. "Each man has one and only one object of value to be cherished, namely, his own higher self. By a law of nature he is not able to love others as he loves himself. Only another individual can love *himself*, just as only I can love myself. There is only one canon by which the wise man is able to judge his own behavior: Is it conducive to my own virtue, or does it risk compromising the moral self which it is my unique prerogative to preserve?"[16]

A Stoic, then, would put to Augustine this fundamental challenge:[17] Your recommended solidarity of grief and joy is incoherent. You cannot bear to the religious character of others the relation you bear to your own. It makes no sense to grieve and rejoice over theirs as you do over yours. To this deep challenge Augustine might well have made two responses: Even if it is true that I cannot constitute any one else's religious character in the same way that I can constitute my own, it does not follow that the only thing good in my universe is my own character. For it is not true that only what is in a person's control is of value for that person. And second, the assumption of self-reliance must be replaced by a doctrine of co-responsibility. We are social creatures capable of influencing each other; it is on that account that we are responsible for the religious condition of others as well as for that of ourselves. Religious character is not formed by isolated self-determining individuals.

I would be doing a disservice to Augustine if I did not mention, before concluding this section of our discussion, that now and then he indicates that it is also appropriate to grieve over the innocent misfortunes that come our way — over things like hunger and physical pain. "What is compassion," he asks in one passage, "but a fellow-feeling for another's misery, which prompts us to help him if we can? And this emotion is obedient to reason, when compassion is shown without violating right, as when the poor are relieved, or the penitent forgiven" (*City of God* IX, 5). But just as it would have been a disservice not to have mentioned this point, so also it would be a disservice to give it any more emphasis than Augustine himself gave it — which is, very little.

We have been speaking of the place of the passions in the life of the imperfectly godly person in this imperfect world of ours. But, we must be reminded that Augustine also points us away from life in this world to a perfected life in a perfected world—a life not earned or achieved but granted. In that life there will be no such emotional disturbances as grief and fear. For that will be a life of uninterrupted bliss; and "who that is affected by fear or grief can be called absolutely blessed?" Even "when these affections are well regulated, and according to God's will, they are peculiar to this life, not to that future life we look for" (*City of God* XIV, 9). Augustine's argument, as we have seen, is not the Stoic argument that the passions are always based on false evaluations; they are not. His argument is that having emotions always involves *being overcome*, and that the pain embedded within such emotions as grief and fear is incompatible with full happiness. Grief and fear are not as such incompatible with *reason*. They are as such incompatible with *eudaemonia*. Hence the abolition of those passions from our lives will not occur by way of illumination as to the true nature of things. It will occur by way of removal from our existence of that which it is appropriate to fear or grieve over.

So our perfected existence will exhibit not only *eros* attached entirely to God, but apathy. For attachment to God and detachment from world, we struggle here and now. For *apathy*, we merely long, in the meanwhile fearing and grieving over the evil worth fearing and grieving over. Struggle and longing, aiming and hoping, pull apart in the Augustinian universe. It is not, though—let it be repeated—a feelingless apathy for which we long. We long for a life of joy and bliss. If *apatheia* be understood as the condition "where the mind is the subject of no emotion," says Augustine, "then who would not consider this insensibility to be worse than all vices? It may, indeed, reasonably be maintained that the perfect blessedness we hope for shall be free from all sting of fear or sadness; but who that is not quite lost to truth would say that neither love nor joy shall be experienced there?" (*City of God* XIV, 9)[18]

And now the eternal life of God, as understood by Augustine, can be very simply described: God's life satisfies the eudaemonistic ideal implicit in all that has preceded. God's life is through and through blissful. Thus God too is free of negative *pathe*. Of *Mitleiden* with those who are suffering, God feels nothing, as also he feels no pain over the short-fall of godliness in his errant creatures. His state is *apatheia*—an *apatheia* characterized positively by the steady non-perturbing state of joy. God dwells eternally in blissful non-suffering *apatheia*. Nothing that happens in the world alters his blissful unperturbed serenity. Certainly God is not oblivious to the world. There is in him a steady disposition of

benevolence toward his human creatures. But this disposition to act benev-
olently proceeds on its uninterrupted successful course whatever transpires in the world.

In sum, the Augustinian God turns out to be remarkably like the
Stoic sage: devoid of passions, unfamiliar with longing, foreign to suffering, dwelling in steady bliss, exhibiting to others only benevolence.
Augustine fought free of the Stoic (and neo-Platonic) vision when it
came to humanity; when it came to God, he succumbed.

The result, as one would expect, was unresolved tension in his
thought. What difference is there between God and us which brings it
about that, for us, authentic existence in the presence of evil is a suffering awareness whereas, for God, it is a nonsuffering, perpetually blissful, awareness? Augustine never says. Sometimes he suggests that when
reality is seen whole as God sees it, then nothing appears evil but everything is seen to make its contribution to the goodness of the whole. Thus
God has no suffering awareness of evil because there is no evil of which
to be aware. But if this were Augustine's steady conviction, then he
would seek to illuminate us as to the illusoriness of evil rather than urging us to cultivate suffering over evil.

Augustine does indeed make clear that in one important respect
God's life is not to be identified with our eudaemonistic ideal. In
humanity's perfected existence *eros* is fixed steadily on God. God, in
contrast, has no *eros*. Since there is in him no lack, he does not reach
out to what would fulfill him. God reaches out exclusively in the mode
of benevolence, not in the mode of *eros*. But this difference, though real,
does nothing to relieve the tension.

Are we to say, then, that in his picture of God as dwelling in blissful non-suffering apathy Augustine shows that, whatever be the qualifi-
cations he wishes to make for human beings, he still embraces the late
antique, Stoic notion of what constitutes perfect existence? Is that the
bottom line? Yes, I think we must indeed say this—not only for Augustine
but for the tradition in general. Shaped as they were by the philosophical traditions of late antiquity, it was inconceivable to the church fathers
that God's existence should be anything other than perfect and that ideal
existence should be anything other than blissful. But though this must
be said, perhaps one or two more things must be said as well.

I have suggested that in his reflections on how we human beings
should live in this present fallen condition of ours, Augustine not only
departed from the Stoics but even drove a splintering wedge into the
eudaemonistic framework of antiquity. Though we long for eudaemonia,
we are not, while surrounded by evil, to pursue it. So long as evil is

present among us we are to cultivate suffering over evil. I suggest that, in addition to the grip on him of the late antique picture of ideal existence, two additional considerations prevented Augustine from saying a similar thing about God. For one thing, Augustine and the church fathers in general believed that the longing of our hearts for eudaemonia will be satisfied by sharing in the life of God—a conviction which lies at the heart of that long-enduring tradition of contemplative Christianity to which Augustine helped give birth. But if the goal of our existence is happiness, and if our ultimate happiness consists in sharing in the life of God, then that life must itself be a life of peace and joy. If, upon entering into the life of God, we there find vexation and disturbance and suffering, then our own eudaemonia remains unattained. And second, it was agreed by almost everyone in the tradition that God is immutable. Thus it was impossible for them to say that the divine joy, in the sharing of which lies our own eudaemonia, is a joy which God himself does not fully enjoy until the coming of his perfected Kingdom. I suggest, in short, that what leaped to Augustine's eye when he surveyed the picture he had drawn was this feature of it: In God's eternal life is to be found the joy and peace in the sharing of which lies our own true end. To that feature of the picture, he was deeply attached.

It is possible, however, to be struck by quite a different aspect of the picture; namely, God remains blissfully unperturbed while humanity drowns in misery. When looked at in this way the picture's look is startlingly reversed, from the compelling to the grotesque. It is this grotesque look of the picture which has forcefully been called to our attention by various contemporary thinkers as they have launched an attack on the traditional picture of the apathetic God—with the foremost theologian, of recent years, being Jürgen Moltmann.[19]

One of the arguments, more purely theological than the others and developed most elaborately by Moltmann, is that if one grants both that Jesus suffered and that Jesus is the second person of the Trinity, then one cannot avoid concluding that in Jesus' suffering, God was suffering—or to speak more amply, that the second person of the Godhead was suffering. Moltmann reviews the struggles of the church fathers and the early church councils to avoid this conclusion and judges them all to be failures.[20] In my discussion I shall have to neglect entirely this theological argument for the suffering of God.

Far and away the most commonly used argument in the contemporary discussion is that if God truly loves his suffering children, then he himself will feel their misery with them. God's love must include that mode of love which is sympathy, *Mitleiden*. Perhaps the most vivid statement of this argument was composed by an English writer, Maldwyn Hughes, early in the century in his book, *What is Atonement? A Study in the Passion of Christ.* Hughes says:

> We must choose whether or not we will accept the Christian revelation that 'God is love.' If we do, then we must accept the implications of the revelation. . . . It is an entire misuse of words to call God our loving Father, if He is able to view the waywardness and revelation of His children without being moved by grief and pity. . . . It is of the very nature of love to suffer when its object suffers loss, whether inflicted by itself or others. If the suffering of God be denied, then Christianity must discover a new terminology and must obliterate the statement 'God is love' from its Scriptures.[21]

It is clear that between this view of the life of God and the Augustinian view there is a deep clash of ideals: The ideal divine life for Augustine was that of uninterrupted suffering-free bliss; the ideal divine life for the moderns is a life of sympathetic love. In effect the moderns insist that the solidarity of grieving and rejoicing which Augustine recommends for humanity on this earth is to embrace God as well. How can we adjudicate between these profoundly different visions?

Little will be gained by the moderns' simply citing biblical passages about God as loving. For Augustine and the other church fathers who defended the non-suffering apathy of God had not overlooked the fact that the Bible speaks of God loving. And they too were committed to the teachings of the prophets and apostles. It was their conviction, however, that all the statements about God's love could be, and should be, interpreted in a manner consistent with God's apathy and his freedom from suffering.

Augustine's proposal became classic.[22] Scripture everywhere witnesses that God is pitiful, he says. But the pity of God differs from human pity. Human pity brings "misery of heart"; whereas "who can sanely say that God is touched by any misery?" "With regard to pity, if you take away the compassion which involves a sharing of misery with whom you pity, so that there remains the peaceful goodness of helping and freeing from misery, some kind of knowledge of the divine pity is suggested."[23] In short: The love that we are to attribute to God is not the love of sympathy, of *Mitleiden*, in which one shares the feelings of the other; it is the love of well-doing, of benevolence, of agape.

And in general, as to the predication of the language of the emotions to God: this must all be interpreted as attributing to God those *effects* of his agency which are similar to the effects of the perturbing emotions in us:

> God's repentance does not follow upon error, the anger of God carries
> with it no trace of a disturbed mind, nor his pity the wretched heart of a
> fellow-sufferer, . . . nor His jealousy any envy of mind. But by the repen-
> tance of God is meant the change of things which lie within His power,
> unexpected by man; the anger of God is His vengeance upon sin; the pity
> of God is the goodness of His help; the jealousy of God is that providence
> whereby He does not allow those whom He has in subjection to Himself
> to love with impunity what He forbids.[24]

The conclusion is that "when God repents He is not changed but He
brings about change; when He is angry He is not moved but He avenges;
when He pities He does not grieve but He liberates; when He is jealous
He is not pained but He causes pain."[25]

So it is clear that the classical tradition of the apathetic God will
not come crashing down simply by observing that the Scriptures speak
of God as loving and then adding that if God loves his suffering human
creatures, he must himself suffer. The tradition interpreted the biblical
passages in question as speaking of God's non-suffering benevolence. We
seem to be at an impasse.

Perhaps some advance can be made if we pause to reflect a bit on
the nature of the emotions; for these, after all, are central in the discussion. Let me here make use of the results of some probing discussions
on the nature of emotion to be found in the philosophical literature of
the past fifteen years or so, results skillfully pulled together and ampli-
fied by William Lyons in his recent book, *Emotion*.[26] The upshot of the
philosophical discussions is decisively in favor of the so-called *cognitive*
theory of emotion—a theory already prominent, in its essentials, among
the ancients and the medievals.

The cognitive theory holds, in the first place, that every episode of
emotion incorporates a *belief* that such and such a state of affairs has
occurred or is occurring or may well occur, along with an *evaluation* of
that state of affairs (proposition). Every emotion has, in that way, a
doxastic/evaluative component, and thereby a propositional content. Of
course the belief which the emotion incorporates may well be mistaken:
Emotions may be either veridical or non-veridical. Suppose, for example
(to take one of Lyons' illustrations) that I am afraid that the large dog
approaching will attack me. The proposition (state of affairs) that the
large dog will attack me is then the propositional content of the emotion; and a central component of the emotion will be my believing and
evaluating, be it negatively or positively, that state of affairs.

The reference to evaluation is important and must not be lost from
view. The propositional content of an emotion is not only believed but

evaluated. If I were indifferent to being attacked by the large dog, rather than evaluating such an attack with distinct negativity, I would feel no emotion in that regard. Or if I evaluated this state of affairs positively, out of exhibitionism or a desire for martyrdom, I would feel not fear but exhiliration.

The propositional content of an emotion, along with one's negative or positive evaluation of that content, plays a central role in the identification of an emotion. But it is not the whole of the emotion. There is no emotion unless the belief and evaluation cause a physiological disturbance in the person (the sympathetic nervous system being central here), along with certain characteristic feelings which are, in part, awareness of one's physiological disturbance. What proves to be the case is that the physiological disturbance and the accompanying feelings differ remarkably little from one kind of emotion to another. One cannot, for example, differentiate anger from fear on this basis.

Lastly, many if not all emotions incorporate a characteristic appetitive component — a desire to do something or other so as, for example, to eliminate the state of affairs in question or to continue it, etc. The person afraid that the large approaching dog will attack him is strongly desirous of doing something to avert the attack — though it may happen that his physiological disturbance becomes so severe that, instead of running like a gazelle so as to implement his desire to avoid attack, he sinks down helpless as a jellyfish. It is the appetitive component in emotions that accounts for the fact that emotions can function as motives for intentionally undertaken actions: a person may run away *out* of fear, may send a blistering letter *out of* anger, etc.

Now if this schematic analysis of the nature of emotions is correct in its main outlines, it follows directly that God has no emotions: No grief, no anger, no fear, and so forth. For a person can have an emotion only if that person is capable of being physiologically upset. And God, having no physiology, is not so capable. I am not aware that Augustine ever used this argument for God's *apatheia*: he had other arguments. But Aquinas, for example, makes explicit use of it in *Summa Theologiae*, Book I, 20, art. 1; and in *Summa contra Gentiles* I, 89, 3. In the sense of *pathos* which we have been using in our discussion, we can conclude that God is lacking in *pathos*. The tradition was right: God is apathetic. He does not grieve, neither in sympathy nor, as it were, on his own.

But we must not conclude from this that the contest is over and that the ancients are victorious in their combat with the moderns. For though the issue of whether God suffers is regularly blurred with the issue of whether God has passions, I suggest that suffering is in fact a distinct phenomenon from grief and the other 'negative' emotions, and that the conclusion that God has no passions still leaves open the question whether God suffers. It remains an open question whether God's apathy is a *suffering* apathy.

A person grieving over some loss is suffering. It will be recalled that the recognition that grief has a component of suffering is what led Augustine to conclude that God does not experience the passion of grief. But human suffering is by no means confined to emotional states. There is also the suffering caused by physical pain, the suffering caused by mental depression, the suffering caused by the desperate wish that one's sexual orientation were different from what it is, and so forth. Furthermore, it is often the case that even when the emotional state of grief subsides, the suffering continues.

What then are the connections among the belief that some loss has occurred, the emotional state of grieving over that loss, and the suffering comprised in that grieving? Well, clearly the cause of the suffering that one experiences in grieving is not the physiological disturbance or the accompanying feelings. These are not to be thought of as one of the sources of suffering in our existence, on a par with physical pain and mental depression. For as we have seen, the actual feelings involved in grief are little different from those in great joy. There are tears of joy as well as tears of grief. And it is worth recalling Augustine's observation that the grieving person may even find sweetness in the tears of his grief.

One is tempted to conclude, then, that the cause of the suffering that one experiences when grieving is the event over which one is grieving: the death, the maiming, the defeat, whatever. But this too cannot be correct. For there may be no such event! One may *believe* that the death, the maiming, the defeat, occurred when it did not. There may in fact be no event such that one grieves over it and it caused one's grief. And conversely, if some event occurred but one does not believe it did, the event causes no grief.

The conclusion must be, I think, that the cause of one's suffering, when grieving over loss, is simply *one's believing* that a loss occurred. For whether or not a loss of the sort in question occurred, the *believing* definitely exists. When someone suffers from physical pain, eliminating the pain eliminates the suffering. When someone suffers over mental depression, getting rid of the depression gets rid of the suffering. So too, the suffering one experiences when grieving over loss is eliminated by elimination of the belief that the loss occurred. When the prodigal son, thought to be dead, returns home alive, the father's tears of grief are transmuted into tears of joy. Physical pain and mental depression and unsatisfied desire cause suffering. But so also do certain of our ways of representing reality. And it makes no difference whether those ways be faithful to reality or unfaithful — veridical or non-veridical.

We speak naturally of the suffering *caused* by pain, of the suffering *caused* by mental depression, etc. But we must not think of the connection between some facet of our experience, on the one hand, and joy or suffering, on the other, as the connection of efficient causality. The suffering *caused* by pain is not some distinct sensation caused by the pain sensation. Suffering and joy are, as it were, adverbial modifiers of the states and events of consciousness. Pain and depression and the belief that someone we love has died are episodes of consciousness that occur sufferingly. The experience of art and the taste of good food and the belief that one of our projects has succeeded are episodes of consciousness that occur joyfully. A fundamental fact of consciousness is that the events of consciousness do not all occur indifferently. Some occur unpleasantly, on a continuum all the way to suffering; some occur pleasantly, on a continuum all the way to joy; and some, indeed, occur in neither mode.

Suffering, when veridical, is an existential No-saying to something in reality. With one's very existence one says "No" to the pain, "No" to the mental depression. But when that state of consciousness which causes the grief is one which has a propositional content, then that to which one existentially says "No" pulls apart from the cause of the suffering. One existentially says "No" to the loss, not to the believing; "No" to the desire's being unfulfilled, not to the desiring. (The suffering may of course lead one to say "No" to the desire itself.)

Earlier we spoke of emotions as including an evaluative component. But quite clearly there is no emotion if we just coolly evaluate something as meeting or not meeting some criterion that we happen to embrace. The evaluation must be an existential *valuing* of which we have just now been speaking. At the core of an emotion will be our *valuing* of the facts and supposed facts of the world. And that valuing may continue even though the emotion subsides.

One more observation is relevant: The fact that suffering consists of the (intensely) aversive occurrence of some state or event of consciousness is compatible with the fact that often we choose to do what we anticipate will cause us suffering. We choose the surgery knowing that pain will follow. In this there is nothing complex or mysterious. To understand it, we need only remind ourselves that, as means to achieving what one desires, one may do that which (as such) one does not desire. Truly mysterious, however, is the fact that one may get *joy out of suffering* — as, for example, the person of intense religiosity who shares in the sufferings of Christ and 'counts it all joy'. In such a case, the person joyfully experiences his sufferingly experiencing pain.

And now back to the issue: Let us suppose that God knows what transpires in this world. The question before us then is whether some of that knowledge is sufferingly experienced and some of it joyfully. And notice that the issue of whether God sufferingly experiences some of what transpires in this world does indeed join hands with whether he also experiences some of it joyfully. Unless it be the case that everything in this world is good to the eye of God or everything bad, whatever be the answer we give to one of these questions must also be the answer we give to the other.

Our answer must be postponed for a few pages, however, so as to introduce into the discussion a new and distinct line of thought, also embraced with near unanimity by the patristics and medievals, leading to the same conclusion as the perfection argument which we have thus far considered. This additional argument for the conclusion that God experiences neither passions nor suffering may be called the *ontological* argument. The fact that the perfection argument and the ontological argument join to yield the same result is what made the tradition of God's non-suffering apathy so enormously powerful. There is more that divides the moderns from the ancients than a clash of moral ideals— though to this 'more', the moderns rarely give any attention.

Suppose that God suffered on account of the pain experienced by the people in Stalin's Gulag camps and of the evil in the heart of Stalin who put them there. Then it would be the case that what one human being did, and what happened to other human beings, would determine the quality of God's life. Stalin's acting as he did would bring about God's suffering awareness of the evil in Stalin's heart. The victims' experience of pain would bring about God's suffering knowledge of their pain. Or to take another example: If God suffered on account of humanity's destructive impact upon his earth, then again what transpires in the world would determine the quality of his life.

But to imagine that what transpires in the world could in this way determine the quality of God's life is to bump up against an assumption which, ever since Plotinus, has been deeper than any other in classical Christian theology; namely, the assumption that God is unconditioned. "The Supreme," says Plotinus, "can neither derive its being nor the quality of its being. God Himself, therefore, is what He is, self-related, self-tending; otherwise He becomes outward-tending, other-seeking—He who cannot but be wholly self-poised."[27]

On most Christian theologians this deliverance of Plotinus has had the grip of obvious and fundamental truth. From it has been extracted a truly astonishing list of conclusions: that God is simple, thus having no nature as we would nowadays understand 'having a nature'; that he is immutable; that he is eternal; that he is entirely lacking in potentialities, thus being pure act; that he exists necessarily, since his essence and his existence are identical; that no predicate correctly predicated of something other than God can with the same sense be correctly predicated of God; and — to break off the listing — that God has no passions.[28] Of course, these conclusions were not all derived *directly* from God's status as unconditioned. Chains of argument were used. John of Damascus, for example, takes it that God is "without flux because He is passionless and incorporeal," and that he is by nature passionless "since he is simple and uncompound."[29] But the classic argument for God's simplicity, in turn, came from Plotinus, whose key premise was that reality must comprise a being which is entirely unconditioned.

Beyond a doubt it was Aquinas who, after Plotinus, worked out most profoundly the implications of the assumption that God is the unconditioned condition of everything not identical with himself. No doubt he saw it as rendering the biblical teaching of God's sovereignty. At the same time it was he who struggled most intensely to construe the teachings of the scriptures as a whole in the light of this assumption and its implications. Let us, then, follow him in his thought.

In *Summa contra Gentiles* I, 89, 9, Aquinas says that the passion of *sorrow* or *pain* has for its "subject the already present evil, just as the object of *joy* is the good present and possessed. Sorrow and pain, therefore, of their very nature cannot be found in God."[30] No doubt in this particular formulation Aquinas is alluding to the perfection argument.[31] But what has already brought him to this conclusion is an elaborate development of the ontological argument and its ramifications.

Aquinas has just argued that God has no passions at all. And in addition to offering as ground for this conclusion that God lacks the "sensitive appetites" and the bodily physiology necessary for experiencing passions (I, 89, 2-3), he argued, more relevantly to our purposes here, that "in every passion of the appetite the patient is somehow drawn out of his usual, calm, or connatural disposition. . . . But it is not possible for God to be somehow drawn outside His natural condition, since He is absolutely immutable, as has been shown" (I, 89, 4). This argument, of course, militates as much against God's suffering as against his passion.

But if God cannot be "drawn outside his natural condition" of unalloyed abiding bliss, does it not follow that God is either ignorant of the suffering and evil that transpire in the life of his human creatures, or is indifferent to their plight? Yet the former is incompatible with God's omniscience. And as to the latter, how would indifference to the plight of humanity be compatible with the love of God?

Though he does not sorrow over evil, yet God *knows* evil, says Aquinas. To understand in what way Aquinas thinks this to be true, we must first understand in what way, as he sees it, God knows anything at all other than himself.

It must be granted, says Aquinas, "that primarily and essentially God knows only Himself." For this conclusion, Aquinas gives several arguments, most of which consist in spinning out the implications of the doctrine of divine simplicity. He says, for example, that "the operations of the intellect are distinguished according to their objects. If, then, God understands Himself and something other than Himself as the principal object, He will have several intellectual operations. Therefore either His essence will be divided into several parts, or He will have an intellectual operation that is not his substance. Both of these positions have been proved to be impossible" (I, 48, 4).

From this argument it would seem to follow not merely that God "primarily and essentially" knows only himself but that, *without qualification*, he knows only himself. Yet Aquinas immediately goes on to argue that "God understands things other than Himself." His reason is that "an effect is adequately known when its cause is known. So 'we are said to know each thing when we know the cause' [Aristotle]. But God Himself is through His essence the cause of being for other things. Since He has a most full knowledge of His essence, we must posit that God also knows other things" (I, 49, 2). Thus it is simply *in* knowing his own simple undifferentiated self that God knows all other things — on the two principles that God is the cause of all things other than himself, and that in knowing a thing's cause one knows the thing.[32]

And how is God the *cause* of other things? He is the cause by virtue of his will, says Aquinas. Yet it must be granted that "the principal object of the divine will is the divine essence." For if we allowed that God directly willed things other than himself, the principle of divine simplicity would again be violated.[33] "If . . . God should principally will something other than Himself, it will follow that something other is the cause of His willing. But His willing is His being, as has been shown. Hence, something other will be the cause of His being — which is contrary to the nature of the first being" (I, 74, 4).[34]

But if the divine self is the principal object of the divine will, how does God cause other things? In *Summa contra Gentiles* I, 74, 4, Aquinas says that in every case of willing something "the principle object" is just the *ultimate end* for which the thing is willed. But that is misleading for the case before us. We are not to think of God as willing other things as means to the end of himself. Rather, Aquinas' thought is this: "God wills and loves His essence for its own sake." Now "the things that we love for their own sake we want to be most perfect, and always to become better and be multiplied as much as possible." But "the divine essence cannot be increased or multiplied in itself." There is only one way in which the divine self can be enriched or enhanced, namely, by way of there being other entities which resemble it. The divine essence "can be multiplied solely according to its likeness, which is participated by many," says Aquinas. It is in that way, then, that *in* "willing and loving His own essence and perfection" God "wills the multitude of things." If we look at the multitude of beings other than God and ask, what is the ultimate ground of their existence, our answer is this pair of phenomena: That this whole array of beings, each in its own way and degree resembling God (including their being "ordered to God as their end") is a sort of enhancement of the divine perfection; and that God wills the enhancement of his own self.

We have been looking at Aquinas' construal of God's knowing and willing of things other than himself. Before we move on we should also consider his construal of the love of God for things other than himself, since all the relevant phenomena are already before us. God wills himself. Now to will something is perforce to regard it as good; "the understood good is the proper object of the will, the understood good is, as such, willed" (I, 72, 2). And in turn, it "belongs properly to the nature of love, that the lover wills the good of the one he loves" (I, 91, 2). But we have also found it appropriate, says Aquinas, to speak of God as willing other things. Now we have just seen that it is a necessary truth about willing that one wills what one judges good. So God wills the good of those other things. And since, as we have also seen, to love something is to will the good of the thing — Aquinas, be it noted, construes love simply as benevolence — it follows straightforwardly that God loves things other than himself.[35]

But now, is it not stretching the sense of the words beyond their breaking point to call "knowledge of other things" those phenomena in the Plotinian God to which Aquinas applies that phrase; and so, similarly, for "willing of other things" and "loving of other things"? Consider: God knows himself, and God is the cause of all things other than himself: This pair of phenomena is what Aquinas calls *God's knowing of things other than himself*, on the principle that to know the cause of a thing is to know the thing. And consider: God wills his perfection, and the ensemble of things other than God enhances his perfection by resembling him: this pair of phenomena Aquinas calls *God's willing of things other than himself*. He furthermore proposes calling this last pair of phenomena, *God's loving of things other than himself*, on the grounds that one only wills what one regards as good, and that to love something is to will its good. But is not the former of these so distant from the knowledge of things as not to deserve the title? And is not the latter so distant from the intentional making and the loving of things as also not to deserve those titles? What is missing throughout is any awareness of, any acquaintance with, things other than himself by God. God has no concept nor anything like a concept of anything other than himself. "Our intellect knows singular things through singular species that are proper and diverse," says Aquinas. By acquiring such "singular species," we actualize our potentials for knowledge. Not so for the divine intellect. "If it knew something through a species that is not itself, it would necessarily follow that its proportion to that species would be as the proportion of potency to act. God must therefore understand solely through the species that is his own essence" (I, 71, 11-12). (Aquinas might, of course, have reached the same conclusion from the premise of God's simplicity.)

It appears that Aquinas himself regarded the point to which I have objected as one of the weak points in his theory; for when he returned to the topic of God's knowledge in his later work, *Summa Theologiae*, he reworked his thought on the topic of "whether God knows things other than himself by proper knowledge?" (*ST* I, 14, a. 6) He still holds, of course, that God has a proper and not merely a general knowledge of things other than himself, his reason being that "to know a thing in general and not in particular, is to have an imperfect knowledge of it" (resp.). But now he attempts in a somewhat different way than before to meet the challenge of explaining how it can be that the Plotinian God has a proper knowledge of things other than himself.

Other than God himself, everything whatsoever bears to God a unique relation or resemblance with respect to its perfections. Not only do human beings, for example, resemble God with respect to their perfections in a way different from horses; but also Socrates resembles God with respect to his perfections in a way distinct from Plato. Furthermore, a thing's unique resemblance to God can be thought of as the nature of the thing. "The nature proper to each thing consists in some degree of participation in the divine perfection" (ibid.). But the multiplicity of ways in which God can be resembled is, in turn, a necessary and not an accidental feature of him. "His essence contains the similitude of things other than Himself" (a. 5, resp.). But if so, then "God could not be said to know Himself perfectly unless He knew all the ways in which His own perfection can be shared by others" (a. 6, resp.). Hence, says Aquinas, "it is manifest that God knows all things with proper knowledge, in their distinction from each other" (ibid.).

I think it is clear, however, that this argument will not do. Aquinas assumes that to know the 'proper nature' of a thing is to know the thing. Perhaps we can grant that assumption—though, of course, its truth depends on how we construe 'proper nature'. He also assumes that a thing's particular way of resembling God constitutes the nature of the thing. That seems more controversial; but let us not contest the matter. He further assumes, in classic Chain of Being fashion, that for every possible mode of resemblance to God, there is (or was, or will be) something which actually bears that mode of resemblance to God. That assumption is even more controversial; but let us still not boggle. It is because of these three assumptions that Aquinas can say that in God's knowing of all the particular ways in which his perfection *can* be shared, he knows all the particular ways in which it *is in fact* shared; and in his knowing of all the particular ways in which it is in fact shared, he knows all the particular things of the world. Let us, on this occasion, content ourselves with questioning Aquinas on the move that he makes before these three: the move from God's knowledge of his essence to his knowledge of the distinct and multiple ways in which things can resemble his essence.

Now it is indeed true that the ways in which a thing can be resembled belong to its essence. But it is not sufficient for Aquinas' purposes to hold that a perfect knowledge of God's essence implies a knowledge of all the ways in which he can be resembled. The demands of the simplicity doctrine are such that he must say that God's knowing of his essence just *is* his knowing of the various ways in which he can be resembled. Perhaps, indeed, the demands of the simplicity doctrine are even more stringent than that. For someone might contend that one's knowledge of *x* may be identical with one's knowledge of *y* even though *x* is not identical with *y*. But if that is indeed true, then what must be said is that the doctrine of Divine Simplicity requires not only that God's *knowing* is single but that *what he knows* is single.

But now consider some one of the ways in which God can be resembled. Is that way of resemblance identical with God's essence? Surely not. For Aquinas identifies a way of resembling God with the nature of some thing other than God; and if such a way of resembling was identical with God's essence, the nature of some thing other than God would be identical with God's essence—from which it would follow that that thing which was other than God was identical with God. The conclusion must be that Aquinas' adherence to the simplicity doctrine makes untenable this attempt at explaining how God knows things other than Himself.

Aquinas' struggle to find in the Plotinian God something that might appropriately be called "knowledge of other things" becomes even more transparently a struggle when it comes to God's knowledge of evil. I will not here rehearse all his arguments; he gives some seven of them. But the basic line of thought running through all of them is evident from the first: "When a good is known, the opposite evil is known. But God knows all particular goods, to which evils are opposed. Therefore God knows evils" (I, 71, 2). God, Aquinas would say, knows that particular human evil which is blindness because he knows that 'particular good' which is human sight to which this evil of blindness is 'opposed'. Now it is obscure in Aquinas' argument whether he means to say that God knows, of some particular human being, that she enjoys that good which is sight, or whether he means to say that God just knows abstractly what is that good which is human sight. But suppose he means the former. At most what can be said is that anyone who has such knowledge will also know what blindness is. That leaves such a person well short of knowing, say, that some particular elderly woman has gone blind — which is what all of us would regard as knowing one of the actual evils of our world.

The conclusion is unavoidable: Aquinas does not find, in the Plotinian God, anything which could appropriately be called, *knowing the suffering and evil which transpire in our world*. But if God does not know the suffering and evil which transpire in our world, then he does not *sufferingly* know it. Now suppose we assume, as seems reasonable, that Aquinas has done as well as can be done by way of finding in the Plotinian God something which could be called "knowledge of things other than himself" and "knowledge of the suffering and evil of our world." Then we must conclude that on the Plotinian concept of God, God does indeed not have a suffering awareness of the world. He does not have such an awareness because he does not have an awareness of the world at all.

So we are faced with a choice. If one adopts the Plotinian concept of God, the conclusion falls out that God does not suffer, and, of course, does not have passions. But one gets the conclusion by paying the price of removing from God all knowledge of, and love for, the particular things of this world. The question, then, is whether this price is too high. Virtually the entire Christian tradition would say it is. The Christian cannot surrender the conviction that God knows and loves his creation. Or to put it differently: to pay the price charged by the Plotinian concept of God is to move away from Christianity toward some other form of religion.

So we are back to where we were: Does God sufferingly experience what transpires in the world? The tradition said that he does not. The moderns say that he does — specifically, that he sufferingly experiences our suffering. Both parties agree that God loves the world. But the tradition held that God loves only in the mode of benevolence; it proposed construing all the biblical passages in the light of that conviction.[36] The moderns insist that God's love includes love in the mode of sympathy. The moderns paint in attractive colors a moral ideal which is an alternative to that of the tradition, and point to various biblical passages speaking of God's suffering love — passages which the tradition, for centuries, has construed in its own way. The tradition, for its part, offered essentially two lines of defense. It argued that the attribution of emotions and suffering to God was incompatible with God's unconditionedness, an argument which, so we have concluded, should be rejected. And second, it offered a pair of what it took to be obvious truths: that suffering is incompatible with ideal existence, and that God's existence is immutably ideal. We saw that the supposition that those truths are obvious was endangered in Augustine's case by his insistence that we human beings are to cultivate a solidarity of grieving over evil and rejoicing over repentance. But we did not ourselves offer any argument directly against those supposed truths.

How can we advance from here? Perhaps by looking more intently than we have thus far at that claim of the tradition that God's love consists exclusively of benevolence. Benevolence in God was understood as his steady disposition to do good to his creatures. And since as long as there are creatures — no matter what their condition — there is scope for God's exercise of that disposition, and since his exercise of that disposition is never frustrated, God endlessly takes joy in this dimension of himself. He does not take joy — let us carefully note — in his awareness of the condition of his creatures. He does not delight in beholding the creaturely good that he has brought about. If that were the case, his joy would be conditional on the state of things other than himself. What God joyfully experiences is simply his own exercise of benevolence. God's awareness of our plunge into sin and suffering causes him no disturbance; his awareness of the arrival of his perfected kingdom will likewise give him no joy. For no matter what the state of the world, there is room for God's successful exercise of his steady disposition to do good; and it is in *that* exercise that he finds delight.

An analogue which comes to mind is that of a professional health-care specialist. Perhaps when first she entered her profession she was disturbed by the pain and limping and death she saw. But that is now over. Now she is neither perturbed nor delighted by the condition of the people that she sees. What gives her delight is just her inner awareness of her own well-doing. And always she finds scope for well-doing—so long, of course, as she has clients. To those who are healthy she gives reassuring advice on health maintenance. To those who are ill she dispenses medicine and surgery. But it makes no difference to her whether or not her advice maintains the health of the healthy and whether or not her proferred concoctions and cuttings cure the illness of the ill. What makes a difference is just her steadiness in well-doing; in this and in this alone she finds her delight. If it falls within her competence she will, of course, cooperate in pursuing the elimination of smallpox; that is doing good. But should the news arrive of its elimination, she will not join the party; she has all along been celebrating the only thing she finds worth celebrating—namely, her own well-doing. She is a Stoic sage in the modern world.

I dare say that most of us find such a person thoroughly repugnant; that shows how far we are from the mentality of many of the intellectuals in the world of late antiquity. But beyond giving vent to our feelings of repugnance, let us consider whether the picture I have drawn is even coherent. Though this person neither rejoices nor suffers over anything in the condition of her patients, nonetheless she rejoices in her own doing of good. But what then does she take as *good*? What does she *value*? The health of her patients, one would suppose. Why otherwise would she give advice to the one on how to maintain his health, and chemicals to the other to recover his, and all the while rejoice, on account of thus acting, in her own doing of good? But if she does indeed value the health of her patients, then perforce she will also be glad over its presence and disturbed by its absence (when she knows about these). Yet we have pictured her as neither happy nor disturbed by anything other than her own well-doing. Have we not described what cannot be?

Perhaps in his description of moral action that great Stoic philosopher of the modern world, Immanuel Kant, can be of help to us here. In the moral dimension of our existence, the only thing good in itself is a good will, said Kant. Yet, of course, the moral person will do such things as act to advance the health of others. Insofar as she acts morally, however, she does not do so because her awareness of health in people gives her delight and her awareness of illness proves disturbing. She may indeed be so constituted that she does thus value health and sickness in others and act thereon. But that is no moral credit to her. To be moral she must act not out of delight over health nor out of disturbance over illness but out of duty. She must act on some rule specifying what one ought to do in her sort of situation—a rule to which, by following, she accords 'respect'. That is what it is to value good will: to act out of respect for the moral law rather than out of one's natural likings and dislikings, rejoicings and grievings. And the moral person is the person who, wherever relevant, thus values the goodness of her will. Her valuing of that will mean, when her will is in fact good, that she will delight therein. But if she acts out of a desire to delight in having a good will, that too is not moral action; she must act out of respect for the moral law.

Suppose then that our health-care specialist values the goodness of her will and acts thereon by dutifully seeking to advance the health of her patients — delighting in thus acting. She may or may not also value the health of her patients, being disturbed by its absence and delighted by its presence. But if she does not in that way value her patients' health, that does not in any way militate against her delighting in her own well-doing.

We have here, then, a way of understanding how it can be that God delights in his doing good to human beings without either delighting in, or being disturbed by, the human condition. God acts out of duty. Thus acting, he values his own good will without valuing anything in his creation. If we interpret God's benevolence as his acting out of duty, then the traditional picture becomes coherent.

But of course it buys this coherence at great price. For to think thus of God is to produce conflict at a very deep level indeed with the Christian scriptures. These tell us that it is not out of duty but out of love that God blesses us, not out of obligation but out of grace that he delivers us. To construe God's love as purely benevolence and to construe his benevolence along Kantian-Stoic lines as his acting out of duty, is to be left without God's love.

So we are back with the model in which God values things other than his own good will — values positively some of the events and conditions in his creation, and values negatively others. To act out of love toward something other than oneself is to value that thing and certain states of that thing. And on this point it matters not whether the love be erotic or agapic. If one rejects the duty-model of God's action, then the biblical speech about God's prizing of justice and shalom in his creation will have to be taken at face value and not construed as meaning that God has a duty to work for justice and shalom.

These reflections place us in a position to see better than we could before the cause of tension in Augustine's thought. Augustine urged us to value the religious condition of our fellow human beings. But, as we saw, he does not hold that our *eros* is to be attached to our fellows. Rather it was his assumption that the religious condition of our fellow human beings has its own mode of value, distinct from that mode of value which those things have for us that satisfy our need, our *eros*. We are to love our fellow human beings without being attached to them. But if we are indeed to value in this noneerotic way the religious condition of our fellows, why would God not do so as well? Or conversely, if God does not do so, why is it nonetheless appropriate for us to do so? The tension in Augustine's thought is due to the fact that our (non-erotic) valuing and God's valuing arbitrarily part ways.

In my argument I have assumed that if, believing some state of affairs to be occurring, one *values* that occurrence, whether negatively or positively, then one is correspondingly delighted or disturbed. I have assumed that one's believing is then either a delightedly believing or a disturbedly believing, an avertive believing or an 'advertive' believing. Some might question this assumption. Can valuing not be existentially colorless? Can God not value justice and shalom in his creation while yet his awareness of its presence gives him not a flicker of delight nor his awareness of its absence a twinge of unhappiness? My answer is that I do not know how to envisage such a possibility. The Kantian duty-model gives us a way of understanding how one might act intentionally to bring about some state of affairs without valuing that state of affairs. But even Kant, along with the ancient Stoics, assumed that valuing displays itself in the aversive and adversive qualities of our experience. It is true, of course, that one can *evaluate* things coolly and impartially. One can work in a farmer's shed evaluating potatoes without valuing positively those to which one gives top grade or negatively those that one tosses out. But that is a different matter. Evaluating is not valuing.

I come then to this conclusion: The fact that the biblical writers speak of God as rejoicing and suffering over the state of the creation is not a superficial eliminable feature of their speech. It expresses themes deeply embedded in the biblical vision. God's love for his world is a rejoicing and suffering love. The picture of God as a Stoic sage, ever blissful and nonsuffering, is in deep conflict with the biblical picture.[37]

But are we entitled to say that it is a *suffering* love, someone may ask — a love prompted by a *suffering* awareness of what goes on in the world. An unhappy awareness, Yes; but does it reach all the way to suffering?

What the Christian story says is that God the Father, out of love for humanity, delivered his only begotten Son to the suffering and abandonment and death of the cross. In the light of that, I think it grotesque to suggest that God's valuing of our human predicament was so mildly negative as to cause him no suffering. But in any case, nothing of importance hangs on degrees. The claim of the tradition was that God's knowledge of the world gives him no vexation *at all*, no disturbance, no unhappiness. We have seen reason to think that that claim is false.

In closing let me observe that if we agree that God both sufferingly and joyfully experiences this world of ours and of his, then at once there comes to mind a question which the tradition never asked; namely, What in our world causes God suffering and what in it causes him joy? And then at once there also comes to mind a vision of the relation between *our* suffering and joy and *God's* suffering and joy which is profoundly different from that to be found in the tradition. In the tradition the relation was simply that here in this life we long to share in that uninterrupted bliss which God from eternity enjoys. What now comes to mind instead is the vision of *aligning ourselves* with God's suffering and with his joy: of delighting over that which is such that his awareness of our delight gives him delight and of suffering over that which is such that his awareness of our suffering causes him suffering.

The embrace of this new vision will then lead us to look once again at the *content* of the Augustinian vision, according to which the only thing in our earthly lives of sufficient worth to merit suffering is the religious condition of our souls. The company of friends and relatives is to become to us as kiwi fruit which we enjoy while we have it but whose disappearance causes us no suffering. And so too for whatever else one wants to mention — justice, for example. We are to grieve over the souls of those who perpetrate injustice with evil heart; but over the violation of our rights as such we are not to grieve. Our rights we are to enjoy if we have them, but not grieve over if we do not.

In short, what one finds in Augustine and in that long tradition of Christian piety which he helped to shape is a radical and comprehensive lowering of the worth of the things of this world. In the presence of all those griefs which ensue from the destruction of that which we love, Augustine pronounces a "No" to the attachments rather than a "No" to the destruction — not a "No" to death but a "No" to love of what is subject to death. Thereby he also pronounces a "Not much" concerning the worth of the things loved. Nothing in this world has worth enough to merit an attachment which carries the potential of grief — nothing except the religious state of souls. The state of my child's soul is worth suffering love; the child's company is not.[38]

But there is another way to go. To some of the things in this world one can pay the tribute of recognizing in them worth sufficient to merit a love which plunges one into suffering upon their destruction. In one's love one can say a "Yes" to the worth of persons or things and in one's suffering a "No" to their destruction. To friends and relatives one can pay the tribute of loving them enough to suffer upon their death. To justice among one's people one can pay the tribute of loving it enough to suffer upon its tyrannical denial. To the delights of music and voice and birdsong one can pay the tribute of loving them enough to suffer upon going deaf. One can pay to persons and things the existential tribute of suffering love. "The world is better," says Richard Swinburne in a fine passage,

> if agents pay proper tribute to losses and failures, if they are sad at the failure of their endeavours, mourn for the death of a child, are angry at the seduction of a wife, and so on. Such emotions involve suffering and anguish, but in having such proper feelings a man shows his respect to himself and others. A man who feels no grief at the death of his child or the seduction of his wife is rightly branded by us as insensitive, for he has failed to pay the proper tribute of feeling to others, to show in his feeling how much he values them, and thereby failed to value them properly — for valuing them properly involves having proper reactions of feeling to their loss.[39]

Suffering is an essential element in that mode of life which says not only "No" to the misery of our world but "Yes" to its glories.

And if one does pay to friends and relatives the tribute of a love that may suffer, then also one will struggle to prolong their lives rather than to reorient a self cast into suffering by the snuffing out of their lives. If one does pay to justice among one's people the tribute of a love that may suffer, than also one will struggle to overthrow the tyrant rather than to reconstruct one's self so as to be content under tyranny. Suffering contributes to changing the world. Suffering must sometimes be cultivated. We are indeed to live in a solidarity of grieving and rejoicing — but of grieving and rejoicing over the absence and presence of that mode of human flourishing which the biblical writers call *shalom*; not just over the religious condition of our souls.

This, I said, was a different way to go — the way of "No" to death rather than to love of that which dies, the way of "No" to injustice rather than to love of justice, the way of "No" to poverty rather than to the struggle to alleviate poverty — and Yes, the way of "No" to our distance from God rather than to love of God. It is also, in my judgment, a better way. For it is in line with God's suffering and with God's joy. Instead of loving only God we will love what God loves, including God. For it is in the presence of justice and shalom among his human creatures that God delights, as it is for the full realization of justice and shalom in his perfected Kingdom that he works. To love what is of worth in this world and to suffer over its destruction is to pay to that Kingdom the tribute of anguish over its delay. "Our hearts are restless until they find their rest in thee, O Lord," said Augustine. What must be added is that our hearts will not find their full rest and *should not* find their full rest until the heart of our Lord is itself fully at rest in his perfected Kingdom.

NOTES

1. Translated by R. S. Pine-Coffin (Harmondsworth, Middlesex: Penguin Books, 1961). All my citations from the *Confessions* will be from this translation.

2. No doubt for the reason which is vividly stated in this passage from Plotinus:

> And so this being, [Love Eros] has from everlasting come into existence from the soul's aspiration towards the higher and the good, and he was there always, as long as Soul, too, existed. And he is a mixed thing, having a part of need, in that he wishes to be filled, but not without a share of plenitude, in that he seeks what is wanting to that which he already has; for certainly that which is altogether without a share in the good would not ever seek the good. So he is born of Plenty and Poverty, . . . But his mother is Poverty, because aspiration belongs to that which is in need. (*Enneads* III, 5, 9; Armstrong tr. in Loeb Classical Library [Cambridge, Mass.: Harvard University Press, 1967])

For arguments that the *full* notion of *eros* in Plato and Plotinus included some component of self-giving, see A. H. Armstrong, "Platonic Eros and Christian Agape" in Armstrong, *Plotinian and Christian Studies* (London: Variorum Reprints, 1979); and John M. Rist, *Eros and Psyche: Studies in Plato, Plotinus, and Origen* (Toronto: University of Toronto Press, 1964).

3. I see no other way to make the point in the text than with the word "enjoy" or some near synonym such as "delight." But to do so is to risk introducing serious confusion into the interpretation of Augustine. For he was fond of drawing a distinction between *use* (*uti*) and *enjoyment* (*frui*), to equate enjoying with loving, and then to say that God alone must be enjoyed — earthly things are only for use. (See the chapter "Marius Victorinus and Augustine" by R. A. Markus in *The Cambridge History of Later Greek and Early Medieval Philosophy* [Cambridge: Cambridge University Press, 1970], pp. 389-391.) My point, however, is that the "use" to which earthly things may be put is probably not to be conceived in grimly utilitarian fashion; we may "enjoy" them. On the other hand, Augustine was ever conscious of the fact that *delight* in earthly things may become *love*. See his reflections on the enjoyment of food, music, etc. in *Confessions* X, 31-34.

Here is perhaps also the best place to discuss a terminological point about love — *amor*. I think there can be no doubt that most of the time Augustine says that we should love God alone. And to explicate his thought on this, I have taken *love* to be that mode of attachment to a thing which is such that the destruction or change of that thing would cause one grief. But there are also passages in which Augustine, with the great "chain of being" in mind, says that we should love things in proportion to their worth. One finds a few such passages in *Of True Religion*. But Markus (*Cambridge History*, pp. 386–387) cites one of the most elaborate of them, taken from *de doctrina christiana* I, 27.28: the righteous man is "the man who values things at their true worth; he has ordered love, which prevents him from loving what is not to be loved, or not loving what is to be loved, from preferring what ought to be loved less, from loving equally what ought to be loved either less or more, or from loving either less or more what ought to be loved equally." Probably all of us, in our first approach to Augustine, are inclined to give such passages as this prominence, rather than those in which he says that God alone is to be loved. They sound so much more humane! But I think there can be absolutely no doubt that Augustine generally meant by 'love', that degree of attachment to something such that the destruction or change of that object will cast one into grief; and that he meant to say that, in that sense, God alone is to be loved. Other things are only to be used, this use including what I have called "enjoyment." Now naturally use and enjoyment *is* a form of "attachment" to things. Hence it is not inappropriate for Augustine sometimes to speak of a properly tempered love for these things. But the crux of the issue is this: Our "love" for such things is not to be such that it can cause us grief. As we shall see shortly, Augustine also says, as one would expect, that each of us is to "love" our neighbor as ourselves. *But* — how are we to "love" ourselves?

4. Augustine was not alone in antiquity in holding this view. Carneades held it as well — or at least went around asserting it. Cf. J. M. Rist, *Stoic Philosophy* (Cambridge: Cambridge University Press, 1969), p. 1. My understanding of the Stoics is very much indebted to this book by Rist. Also helpful is F. H. Sanbach, *The Stoics* (New York: W. W. Norton Co., 1975).

5. Augustine, *The City of God*, trans. Marcus Dods (New York: Random House, 1950). My citations will be from this edition.

6. It is interesting that J. M. Rist gives essentially the same formula in one passage: "The Stoic wise man is a man of feeling, but his feelings do not control, or even influence, his decisions and his actions. In this terminology he is passionless (*apathés*), but not without rational feelings." From Rist's full discussion it becomes clear, however, that the classic Stoics thought that, in fact, the perturbing emotions never were fully in accord with reason.

7. See Chapter 3, "Problems of Pleasure and Pain," in Rist, *Stoic Philosophy*.

8. In the above I follow A. C. Lloyd, "Emotion and Decision in Stoic Psychology" in John M. Rist (ed.) *The Stoics* (Berkeley, Calif.: University of California Press, 1978). Compare the summary by A. A. Long, *Hellenistic Phi-*

losophy (New York: Charles Scribner's Sons, 1974), pp. 206–207:

> The Stoic sage is free from all passions. Anger, anxiety, cupidity, dread, elation, these and similar extreme emotions are all absent from his disposition. He does not regard pleasure as something good, nor pain as something evil. . . . The Stoic sage is not insensitive to painful or pleasureable sensations, but they do not 'move his soul excessively'. He is impassive towards them. But he is not entirely impassive. . . . His disposition is characterized by 'good emotional states'. Well-wishing, wishing another man good things for his sake; joy: rejoicing in virtuous actions, a tranquil life, a good conscience . . . ; and 'wariness', reasonable disinclination.

Augustine himself, in various scattered passages, uses the classic Stoic concept of *pathos*. He speaks, for example, of "that state which the Greeks call pathos, whence our word passion is derived; *pathos*, and passion, being a motion of the mind against reason" (*City of God* VIII, 16). Using this definition, one would have to express Augustine's interpretation of the Stoic position as that such a perturbing 'phenomenon' as fear or grief might or might not, in a given case, be a pathos. It would be so if it overthrew the rule of reason in the person experiencing it; otherwise it would not be. And then to say that the wise person is characterized by apathy would be to say that such perturbing 'phenomena' as fear and grief would not function in him as passions; it would not be to say that he never experiences these.

9. This is the theme of Chapter 15, "The Lost Future" in Peter Brown's superb biography, *Augustine of Hippo* (London: Faber & Faber, 1967). Consider especially this passage on p. 156:

> Augustine is a man who has realized that he was doomed to remain incomplete in his present existence, that what he wished for most ardently would never be more than a hope, postponed to a final resolution of all tensions, far beyond this life. Anyone who thought otherwise, he felt, was either morally obtuse or a doctrinaire. All a man could do was to 'yearn' for the absent perfection, to feel its loss intensely, to pine for it. . . . This marks the end of a long-established classical ideal of perfection: Augustine would never achieve the concentrated tranquility of the supermen that still gaze out at us from some mosaics in Christian churches and from the statues of pagan sages.

10. Thus we see in Augustine, and in all those who accept with 'Augustinian seriousness' the biblical injunction to love one's neighbor as one's self, the seed of that plant which eventually blossomed into the recognition of natural human rights, a blossom which, as it has gone to seed, has tended to destroy that sense of human solidarity from which it sprang.

11. This whole line of interpretation is confirmed, I judge, by a fascinating and, to most of us, astonishing and even offensive, passage in Augustine's *Of True Religion*, written at virtually the same time as the *Confessions*:

> Only he is overcome who has what he loves snatched from him by his

adversary. He who loves only what cannot be snatched from him is indubitably unconquerable. . . . He cannot lose his neighbour whom he loves as himself, for he does not love even in himself the things that appear to the eyes or to any other bodily sense. So he has inward fellowship with him whom he loves as himself.

The rule of love is that one should wish his friend to have all the good things he wants to have himself, and should not wish the evils to befall his friend which he wishes to avoid himself. He shows this benevolence towards all men. . . . If a man were to love another not as himself but as a beast of burden, or as the baths, or as a gaudy or garrulous bird, that is for some temporal pleasure or advantage he hoped to derive, he must serve not a man but, what is much worse, a foul and detestable vice, in that he does not love the man as a man ought to be loved. . . .

Man is not to be loved by man even as brothers after the flesh are loved, or sons, or wives, or kinsfolk, or relatives, or fellow citizens. For such love is temporal. We should have no such connections as are contingent upon birth and death, if our nature had remained in obedience to the commandments of God and in the likeness of his image. . . . Accordingly, the Truth himself calls us back to our original and perfect state, bids us resist carnal custom and teaches that no one is fit for the kingdom of God unless he hates these carnal relationships. Let no one think that is inhuman. It is more inhuman to love a man because he is your son and not because he is a man, that is, not to love that in him which belongs to God, but to love that which belongs to yourself. . . .

If we are ablaze with love for eternity we shall hate temporal relationships. Let a man love his neighbour as himself. No one is his own father or son or kinsman or anything of the kind, but is simply a man. Whoever loves another as himself ought to love that in him which is his real self. Our real selves are not bodies. . . . Whoever, then, loves in his neighbour anything but his real self does not love him as himself. . . .

Why should not he be unconquered who in loving man loves nothing but the man, the creature of God, made according to his image?. . . . It is never improper to live aright. Whoever does this and loves it, not only does not envy those who imitate him, but also treats them with the greatest possible kindness and good will. But he does not stand in any need of them. What he loves in them he himself completely and perfectly possesses. So when a man loves his neighbour as himself, he is not envious of him any more than he is envious of himself. He gives him such help as he can as if he were helping himself. But he does not need him any more than he needs himself. He needs God alone, by cleaving to whom he is happy. No one can take God from him. He, then, is most truly and certainly an unconquerable man who cleaves to God. . . . " (xlvi, 86–xlvii, 90; trans. by J. H. S. Burleigh [Chicago: Henry Regnery Co., 1959])

In his *Retractions* Augustine discusses this passage and says that he should not have said, "hate temporal relationships"; if our forebears had done this, we their descendants would never have been born and God's company of the elect would not have been filled up. So hating is inappropriate. And of course in the text I have not interpreted Augustine as proposing 'hatred'. The thing remarkable about the *Retractions* passage, for my purposes, is that Augustine does not retract the doctrine of *love* expounded in this passage from *Of True Religion*.

12. John M. Rist, "The Stoic Concept of Detachment" in John M. Rist (ed.) *The Stoics* (Berkeley, Calif.: University of California Press, 1978), pp. 261–262.

13. Rist, ibid., p. 264.

14. Rist, ibid., p. 263.

15. Rist, ibid., p. 264.

16. Rist, ibid., p. 265.

17. A Plotinian would do the same. See Chapter 12: "The Self and Others" in J. M. Rist, *Plotinus: The Road to Reality* (Cambridge: Cambridge University Press, 1967).

18. Augustine saw that if the bliss of our perfected existence is to be entirely unalloyed, regret will have to be eliminated by forgetfulness. In its perfected existence, the soul will enjoy "an everlasting pleasure of eternal joys, forgetful of faults, forgetful of punishments, but not therefore so forgetful of her deliverance, that she be ungrateful to her deliverer" (*City of God* XXII, 30). There is another issue in the region which, so far as I know, Augustine does not consider. Presumably the solidarity in which we are to exist with our fellows continues into our perfected existence. But if some souls are lost from God's abiding Kingdom, then the absence of grief and the presence only of joy, which is to characterize our perfected existence, can be achieved only by lack of awareness by those who are rejoicing of those who are lost.

19. An important and highly influential book in biblical studies has been Abraham J. Heschel, *The Prophets* (New York: Harper & Row, 1962). Heschel argues that the theology underlying the Old Testament prophets was that of the *pathos* of God. For biblical studies, see also Terence E. Fretheim, *The Suffering of God: An Old Testament Perspective* (Philadelphia: Fortress Press, 1984). In between biblical studies and systematic theology is Kazoh Kitamori, *Theology of the Pain of God* (Richmond, Va.: John Knox Press, 1958). Also see Dorothee Sölle, *Suffering* (Philadelphia: Fortress Press, 1975). An important overview of the discussion is to be found in J. K. Mozley, *The Impassible God* (Cambridge: Cambridge University Press, 1926). In addition to surveying the discussions affirming God's passibility by a number of English theologians in the first quarter of this century, Mozley surveys the long tradition in Christian theology of divine impassibility from its beginnings. Also very useful is the recent book by Richard E. Creel, *Divine Impassibility* (Cambridge: Cambridge University Press, 1986).

20. Jürgen Moltmann, *The Crucified God* (New York: Harper & Row, 1981); and *The Trinity and the Kingdom* (New York: Harper & Row, 1981).

21. Quoted in Mozley, pp. 165–166. Compare these passages from Hartshorne: "The lover is not merely the one who unwaveringly understands and tries to help; the lover is just as emphatically the one who takes unto himself the

varying joys and sorrows of others, and whose own happiness is capable of alteration thereby. . . . Love *is* joy in the joy (actual or expected) of another, and sorrow in the sorrow of another" (*Man's Vision of God* [New York: Harper & Bros., 1941], pp. 111, 116). "Sympathetic dependence is a sign of excellence and waxes with every ascent in the scale of being. Joy calls for sympathetic joy, sorrow for sympathetic sorrow, as the most excellent possible forms of response to these states. The eminent form of sympathetic dependence can only apply to deity, for this form cannot be less than an omniscient sympathy, which depends upon and is exactly colored by every nuance of joy or sorrow anywhere in the world" (*The Divine Relativity: A Social Conception of God* [New Haven, Yale University Press, 1964], p. 48).

22. See, for example, Anselm in *Proslogion* 8: "How art Thou at once pitiful and impassible? For if Thou art impassible, Thou dost not suffer with man; if Thou dost not suffer with man, Thy heart is not wretched by compassion with the wretched, which is the meaning of being pitiful. But if Thou are not pitiful, whence can the wretched gain so great comfort? How then art Thou, and art Thou not pitiful, Lord, except that Thou art pitiful in respect of us, and not in respect of Thyself? Truly Thou art so in respect of our feeling, and art not in respect of Thine. For when Thou lookest upon us in our wretchedness we feel the effect of Thy pity, Thou feelest not the effect. And therefore Thou art pitiful, because Thou savest the wretched, and sparest the sinners who belong to Thee; and Thou art not pitiful, because Thou art touched by no fellow-suffering in that wretchedness." And Aquinas in *Summa theologiae* I, 19, a. 11, resp.: "When certain human passions are predicated of the Godhead metaphorically, this is done because of a likeness in the effect. Hence a thing that is in us a sign of some passion is signified metaphorically in God under the name of that passion. Thus with us it is usual for an angry man to punish, so that punishment becomes an expression of anger. Therefore punishment itself is signified with anger, when anger is attributed to God."

23. Quoted in Mozley, p. 105.

24. Ibid., p. 106.

25. Ibid., p. 106–107.

26. William Lyons, *Emotion* (Cambridge: Cambridge University Press, 1980).

27. *Enneads* VI, viii, 17.

28. In "God Everlasting" in Orlebeke & Smedes, *God and the Good* (Grand Rapids, Mich.: Eerdmans Publ. Co., 1975), I discussed the issue of whether God is eternal and immutable. Alvin Plantinga, in *Does God Have a Nature?* (Milwaukee, Wisc.: Marquette University Press, 1980) has discussed another dimension of the Plotinian concept of God—namely, the contention that God has no properties, in particular, no nature.

29. John of Damascus, *Exposition of the Orthodox Faith* I, 8; translation in Vol. 9 of *Nicene and Post-Nicene Fathers*, Second Series, ed. Schaff and Wace (Grand Rapids, Mich.: Eerdmans Publ. Co., 1983).

As to what he means by "passion," John says this in *Exposition* II, 22:

"Passion is a sensible activity of the appetitive faculty, depending on the presentation to the mind of something good or bad. Or in other words, passion is an irrational activity of the soul, resulting from the notion of something good or bad. For the notion of something good results in desire, and the notion of something bad results in anger. But passion considered as a class, that is, passion in general, is defined as a movement in one thing caused by another."

30. My citations from the *Summa contra Gentiles* are from the Pegis translation (Notre Dame, Ind.: University of Notre Dame Press, 1975).

31. Aquinas uses the perfection argument more explicitly in *Summa Theologiae* I, 20, a. 1, ad 2. It is interesting to note that one of Augustine's reasons for regarding our human emotions as part of "our present infirmity" is that the *being acted upon* which they involve is something from which we should look toward to being delivered in our perfected existence: "We are often overpressed by our emotions. A laudable desire of charity may move us: yet shall we weep whether we will or no. For we have them by our human infirmity, but so had not Christ; for He had His infirmity itself from His own power" (*City of God* XIV, 9).

32. Cf. *ScG* I, 68, 3: "In knowing His essence, God knows other things in the same way as an effect is known through a knowledge of the cause. By knowing his essence, therefore, God knows all things to which his causality extends." And *ScG* I, 70, 2: "God knows things not by receiving anything from them, but, rather, by exercising His causality on them."

33. Also the principle of perfection would be violated: "If . . . the principal object of the divine will be other than the divine essence, it will follow that there is something higher than the divine will moving it. The contrary of this is apparent from what has been said" *ScG* I, 74, 3.

34. And always, in addition, there was *this* Plotinian thought haunting medieval reflections on God's creation: "That . . . which does not want to generate suffices more to itself in beauty, but that which desires to create wants to create beauty because of a lack and is not self-sufficient" Plotinus, *Enneads* III, 5, 1).

35. In *ST* I, 20, a. 2, resp., Aquinas' argument would seem to run just a bit differently: God wills the existence of all things; and since a thing's existence is good, God wills the existence of all things. But to love something is to will good to that thing. Hence God loves all things. This is the text: "God loves all existing things. For all existing things, in so far as they exist, are good, since the existence of a thing is itself a good; and likewise, whatever perfection it possesses. Now it has been shown above . . . that God's will is the cause of all things. It must needs be, therefore, as it is willed by God. To every existing thing, then, God wills some good. Hence, since to love anything is nothing else than to will good to that thing, it is manifest that God loves everything that exists."

36. So when Aquinas speaks of God's *mercy* (*misericordia*), he has no choice but to turn it into mere benevolence: "Mercy is especially to be attributed to God, provided it be considered in its effect, but not as an affection to passion.

In proof of which it must be observed that a person is said to be merciful [*misericors*] as being, so to speak, sorrowful at heart [*miserum cor*]; in other words, as being affected with sorrow at the misery of another as though it were his own. Hence it follows that he endeavors to dispel the misery of this other, as if it were his; and this is the effect of mercy. To sorrow therefore, over the misery of others does not belong to God; but it does most properly belong to Him to dispel that misery, whatever be the effect we call misery" (*ST* I, 21, a. 3, resp.).

37. For a full consideration of our topic, there is an argument of Charles Hartshorne which would have to be considered. He argues that God's *benevolence* must itself be understood as a suffering love—or strictly speaking, as a love that yields suffering. For God in his benevolence wants his human creatures to be happy. Yet so often they are not. God suffers, then from the frustration of his benevolent intention. This, of course, is something that the tradition would never have granted: that God's benevolent intention could be frustrated. Theologians, says Hartshorne,

> sought to maintain a distinction between love as desire, with an element of possible gain or loss to the self, and love as purely altruistic benevolence; or again between sensuous and spiritual love, *eros* and *agape*. . . . Benevolence *is* desire for the welfare of others. . . . Of course it must be a superrationally enlightened, an all-comprehending, never wearying desire for others' good, that is attributed to God. But still desire, so far as that means partial dependence for extent of happiness upon the happiness of others. . . . Lincoln's desire that the slaves might be free was not less desire because it was spiritual, or less spiritual because it was desire—that is, a wish, *capable of being painfully disappointed or happily fulfilled.* . . .

> To hold that God "wills" or purposes human welfare, but is absolutely untouched by the realization or non-realization of this or that portion of the purposed goal (due, for instance, to human sins or unfortunate use of free will), seems just non-sense. . . .

> Does this not introduce the tragedy of unfulfilled desire into God? Yes, it does just that.

(Charles Hartshorne, *Man's Vision of God* [New York: Harper & Brothers, 1941], pp. 116, 135, 294). Compare Fretheim, in *Suffering of God*, p. 134: "In terms of Jeremiah 45, we need to speak in some sense of a temporary failure in what God has attempted to do in the world. Because of this, the mourners should take up a lamentation for God as well."

38. "Love [Eros] is an activity of soul reaching out after good," says Plotinus in *Enneads* III, 5, 4. Augustine would agree. His argument is that the things of this world do not have sufficient good to be worth reaching out after— or strictly, the good they have does not outweigh the grief they cause sufficiently to make it worth reaching out after them.

39. Richard Swinburne, *The Existence of God* (Oxford: Oxford University Press, 1979), p. 192.

PART III

Christian Doctrine and the Possibilities for Truth

And Yet They Are Not Three Gods But One God

PETER VAN INWAGEN

1

Christians believe that the love of one person for another is an essential part of the internal life of God. This is consonant with the Christian belief that all good things in creation are, in some way or other, copies or images of the uncreated. God himself, Christian theology teaches, could not invent the idea of a good that was not prefigured in his own nature, for in the radiant plenitude of that nature, all possible goods are comprehended. And this holds for the supreme good, love. All forms of human love are (we believe) copies of the love that is internal to God. The natural affections of the family, friendship, sexual love (insofar as it is uncorrupted), the charity that will endure when faith has been swallowed up in sight and hope in fulfillment — all of these are creaturely images of the love that already existed, full and perfect and complete, when Adam still slept in his causes.

Like Christians, Jews and Muslims believe that power and goodness and wisdom and glory are from everlasting to everlasting. But only Christians believe this of love, for the eternality of love is a fruit of the uniquely Christian doctrine of the Holy Trinity. The doctrine of the Trinity is no arid theological speculation. It is not a thing that Christians can ignore when they are not thinking about philosophy or systematic theology. The doctrine of the Trinity ought to have as central a place in Christian worship and religious feeling as the doctrines of the Crucifixion and Resurrection.

Let me give one example of how the doctrine of the Trinity touches the deepest concerns of Christians. When we think of our hope of salvation, we tend to think of something individual. If you had asked me a year ago what I thought salvation consisted in, I think I should have said something like this: Each of us bears within him an image of God that has been distorted by sin, and his salvation will be accomplished when—if—that image has been restored in Christ. I do not mean to imply that I now think that this answer is wrong; but I do now think that it is incomplete. The Christian hope is not merely a hope about what will happen to us as individuals. The Beatific Vision is not something that each of the saints will enjoy separately and individually, alone with God. *Vita venturi saeculi* is a corporate life, the life of the Church Triumphant. And the establishment of this corporate life will consist in the whole Body of Christ coming to be an undistorted image of God. If you and I are one day members of the Risen Church, then you will indeed be a restored image of God and I, shall indeed be a restored image of God. But there is more: The love we have for each other will be a restored image of the love that the Persons of the Trinity have for one another.

But can this really be? If the "eternal life we are by grace called to share, here below in the obscurity of faith and after death in eternal light"[1] is the life of the Trinity, had we not better worry about the very logical possibility of the Christian hope? For how can the love of one person for another be internal to the life of God, who is, after all, one being? ("Hear, O Israel, the Lord our God is one Lord.") Must not Jew and Muslim and unbeliever join in demanding of us that we disclose the ill-concealed secret of all the Christian ages: that we are mere polytheists? Or if we are not mere polytheists, then are we not something worse: Polytheists who are also monotheists, polytheists engaged in a pathetic attempt to remain loyal to the God of Israel through sheer force of reiterated logical contradiction? For do we not say all of the following things? There is one divine Being, but there are three distinct Persons, each of whom is a divine Being; and the one divine Being is a Person, though not a fourth Person in addition to those three; nor is he any one of the three.[2]

My primary purpose in this paper is to explore one way of replying to the charge that Christians are either simple polytheists or else polytheists and monotheists at the same time. I shall not be terribly unhappy if the reply I propose to explore turns out to be unsatisfactory. The Trinity has always been described as a mystery, as something that surpasses human understanding. If one is unable to answer satisfactorily questions posed by a mystery—well, what should one expect?

Now if the Christian faith were a human invention, a theory devised by human beings to explain certain features of the world, then we should be wrong to be complacent about our inability to answer pointed questions about it. In such a case, if, after lengthy, determined, and serious effort to answer these questions, we should find ourselves still unable to answer them, then we ought to consider replacing our theory with one that does not pose these apparently unanswerable questions. But, as the pope recently had occasion to remind the Roman Church in Holland, the faith is no human invention. It is, quite simply, news.

Have we ever been promised by God that we shall understand everything he tells us well enough to resolve all the intellectual difficulties it raises? God's concern with us — just at present, at any rate — is not the concern of a tutor who fears that we shall fail to grasp some nice point: God fears that we shall lose the end for which we were made. His concern with us is entirely practical. It may well be that if I had the opportunity to ask God to explain his triune nature to me, he would say, "What is that to thee? Follow thou Me." It is, as Thomas à Kempis observed, better to be pleasing to the Holy Trinity than to be able to reason about the mysteries of the Holy Trinity.[3] It may be that it is important for us to know that God is (somehow) three Persons in one Being and not at all important for us to have any inkling of how this could be — or even to be able to answer alleged demonstrations that it is self-contradictory. It may be that we *cannot* understand how God can be three Persons in one Being. It may be that an intellectual grasp of the Trinity is forever beyond us. And why not, really? It is not terribly daring to suppose that reality may contain things whose natures we cannot understand. And if there were such natures, it would not be so very surprising if the highest nature of all were among them. As to alleged demonstrations of contradiction — well, our faith is: There is some way to answer these demonstrations, whether or not *we* can understand it.

The world, of course, has a handy word for this sort of thing: "obscurantism." I would remind the world of certain cases that have arisen in twentieth-century physics. An electron, we are told, is both a wave and a particle. One can ask pointed questions about *this* thesis. A wave is a spreading, periodic disturbance; a particle is lump of stuff; How can something be both? I think that there are two equally respectable answers to this question: (1) No one knows; (2) Quantum field theory explains how something can be both a wave and a particle.[4] Let us suppose that the second of these answers is correct, and that some people, those who are at home in quantum field theory, know how something can be both a wave and a particle. Still, there was an interval during which physicists went about saying that electrons were both waves and particles, and had no satisfactory reply to the childishly simple question, "How can something be both a disturbance and a lump of stuff?" (I do not think anyone would say that there was a good answer to this question before Dirac formulated quantum field theory. I am willing to be corrected on this point, however.) And I do not think that anyone should blame the physicists for this. I do not think that anyone should have blamed them even if quantum field theory had somehow never been discovered. There were certain undeniable but absolutely astounding experimental data (a "revelation" from nature, as it were); there was a theory that explained those data (a human invention, to be sure, and an extraordinarily brilliant one at that, but not a human invention in the way a motet or an abstract painting is — the theory purported to represent physical reality); and that theory implied that an electron had both a mass and a wavelength.

Might it not be that the Christian who accepts the doctrine of the Trinity, even though he is unable to answer certain pointed questions about it, is in a position analogous to that of quantum physicists before the advent of quantum field theory? The world, of course, will reply that the Christian "revelation" is a fantasy, while the revelation disclosed by nature in the double-slit experiment or in the phenomenon of electron diffraction comprises hard facts of observation. But may we not ask the world to consider the question hypothetically? Suppose the Christian revelation were *not* a fantasy. If the Holy Spirit really existed and had led the mind of the Church to the doctrine of the Trinity,[5] *then* might not the Trinitarian be in a position analogous to that of the physicist to whom nature had revealed the doctrine of the Duality? The world may abuse us for believing in God and revelation if it will, but I think the world should admit that once we have accepted something as a revelation, it is reasonable for us to retain it even if we cannot answer all the intellectual difficulties it raises; or at least the world should admit this if the subject matter of the putative revelation is one that it is plausible *a priori* to suppose we should find it very difficult to understand.

While I accept all this as a Christian, I could not help being disappointed as a philosopher if there were no good, humanly accessible replies to the pointed questions raised by the doctrine of the Trinity. These questions are, after all, questions about number, identity, discernibility, personhood, and being. That is to say, they are logical and metaphysical questions, and therefore questions that I am professionally interested in. In this paper, my main purpose is to explore one way of responding to these questions. I should say, first, that I do not endorse the way of looking at the Trinity I shall ask you to consider, but I do think it is worth considering. It is worth asking whether the theses I shall put forward for your consideration are coherent and whether such light as they cast on the doctrine of the Trinity is orthodox and catholic (in the nondenominational senses of those words). I should say, secondly, that I do not propose to *penetrate* the mystery of the Trinity. I propose to state the doctrine of the Trinity (or part of it: the part that raises all those pointed logical and metaphysical questions) in such a way that it is demonstrable that no formal contradiction can be derived from the thesis that God is three persons and, at the same time, one being.

I do not propose to *explain* how God can be three persons and one being. Here is an analogy. I believe (and I hope that you do, too) that God exists necessarily—that, like a number or a proposition, he exists in all possible worlds; and I also believe (as I am sure you do, too) that, unlike numbers or propositions, he is a concrete being possessing causal powers. I have no idea how something could both exist necessarily and possess causal powers. And I think that no other human being does. How there could be something with both these features is a mystery. But I do not see any reason to suppose that a contradiction might be derivable from the thesis that God is both necessary and concrete, or from this thesis taken together with any plausible logical or metaphysical assumptions. It is in more or less this condition that I should like to leave the doctrine of the Trinity. But, as I have said, I shall not achieve even this modest goal in the present paper. I wish only to propose a way of stating that doctrine that can be shown to be free from formal inconsistency. Whether the doctrine, so stated, actually is the catholic faith (which I mean to keep whole and undefiled) will be a matter for further discussion.

The device I shall exploit for this purpose is the notion of relative identity, familiar to us from the work of Professor Geach. Professor Geach has discussed the abstract notion of relative identity in some detail, and has made some helpful and suggestive remarks about relative identity and the Trinity.[6] What I shall try to do is to expand these suggestive remarks in such a way as to enable us to see what a systematic and thoroughgoing attempt to express the propositions of Trinitarian theology in terms of relative identity would look like.[7] While the entire impetus of the thoughts of this paper is thus due to Professor Geach, we should not suppose that the idea of applying the notion of relative identity to the problems about identity and counting posed by the doctrine of the Trinity is an idiosyncratic whim of one twentieth-century Roman Catholic logician. Professor Geach, when alluding to the historical antecedents of his views—and rarely if ever does he do more than allude—usually manages to mention Thomas Aquinas. But the following (rather scattered) quotation from the *Quicunque Vult*—a document that was certainly in more or less its present form by about 500 A.D.—speaks for itself:

> The Catholic Faith is this: That we worship one God in Trinity, and Trinity in Unity, neither confounding the Persons, nor dividing the Substance.
>
> For there is one Person of the Father, another of the Son, and another of the Holy Ghost . . .
>
> The Father eternal, the Son eternal, and the Holy Ghost eternal.
>
> And yet they are not three eternals, but one eternal . . .
>
> So likewise the Father is Almighty, the Son Almighty, and the Holy Ghost Almighty.
>
> And yet they are not three Almighties, but one Almighty.
>
> So the Father is God, the Son is God, and the Holy Ghost is God.
>
> And yet they are not three Gods, but one God.
>
> So likewise the Father is Lord, the Son Lord, and the Holy Ghost Lord.
>
> And yet not three Lords, but one Lord.
>
> For like as we are compelled by the Christian verity to acknowledge every Person by himself to be both God and Lord,
>
> So we are forbidden by the Catholic Religion, to say, There be three Gods, or three Lords.[8]

Before turning to a detailed treatment of relative identity and the Trinity, I shall make some remarks on the meaning of the word *person* in Trinitarian theology.

2

Anyone who undertakes to give an account of the Trinity will find it hard to avoid falling into some heresy that is summarized in a helpful little article in the *Oxford Dictionary of the Christian Church*. Roughly speaking, these heresies are bounded on the one side by Modalism and on the other by Tritheism. Modalism, in its crudest form, holds that the Father, the Son, and the Holy Spirit are the same person and the same being, this one being or person being conceived, on various occasions, under each of these names in relation to an office, function, or "mode" appropriate to that name. (I say "in its crudest form" because Modalism may be variously disguised.) Thus, 'the Father' is simply a name of God, one we use when we are thinking of him as our creator and judge, rather than as (say) our redeemer or our comforter. Modalism is associated historically with Sabellius (it is sometimes called Sabellianism), and with Peter Damien. Tritheism is, of course, the thesis that there are three Gods. Of these two heresies, Tritheism would seem to be the more serious. If Modalism subverts the doctrine of the Incarnation of the Word by flatly contradicting either our lord's divinity or else his consistent representation of himself and his Father as distinct persons, Tritheism strikes, by definition, at the very root of monotheism.

Nevertheless, it is Tritheism that I shall risk. I have two reasons. First, the language of the Creeds is as safe from a modalistic interpretation as any language could be. If a philosopher or theologian is guided by the Creeds, he will be directed resolutely away from Modalism, and I propose to be guided by the Creeds. Secondly, I think that Modalism is a far easier heresy than Tritheism to fall into in our time, and is, therefore, a doctrine that a Christian thinker ought to stay as far away from as possible. I have recently heard a priest of my own communion, guided, I suppose, by a desire to avoid saying anything that implied that God had a sex, bless the people at the end of Mass not with the prescribed words, ' . . . the blessing of God Almighty, the Father, the Son, and the Holy Ghost . . .' but rather with the words ' . . . God our Creator, God our Redeemer, and God our Sanctifier.' Note that what are enumerated in this formula are not persons but functions, offices, or modes, and that this formula has been used in place of a customary and familiar formula in which the divine Persons are enumerated. The "new" formula is no more a Trinitarian formula than is 'the God of Abraham, the God of Isaac, and the God of Jacob'. You may tell me that the three offices enumerated have been, in liturgy and tradition, associated respectively with the Father, the Son, and the Holy Spirit. I will reply that that is true, but does not affect my point. (Moreover the nature of that "association" or "appropriation" is a nice theological problem. Whatever it means, it does not mean that, e.g., only the Father was involved in the creation. The Nicene Creed says of the Son: 'by whom (*per quem*) all things were made', and in this it echoes Colossians 1:15–17 and the opening words of John's gospel.) My priest, of course, was not a Modalist and did not intend to preach Modalism. But note how easy it is for one whose purposes are remote from questions of Trinitarian theology inadvertently to use words that are, in context, Modalistic in tendency.

It is my intention in this paper to avoid Modalism by adhering rigorously to the doctrine that there are three distinct divine Persons. Two comments are in order.

(1) I shall ignore all problems related to the predication of wisdom, goodness, knowledge — and personality itself — and other attributes predictable of created persons to the divine Persons. Such predication is, I think, as much a difficulty for the Unitarian (i.e., the Jew or Muslim) as for the Trinitarian, and I think it is the *same* difficulty for the Unitarian and the Trinitarian. In any case, I cannot attend to all the problems of philosophical theology at once.

(2) It is sometimes contended that 'person' in Trinitarian theology does not mean what it means in everyday life or in the philosophy of mind or even in non-Trinitarian applications of this word to God. Professor Geach has answered this contention with his usual vigor, and I am of his party:

> [S]ome will protest that I am equivocating between the normal use of the term 'person' and its technical theological use. I reject the protest. The concept of a person, which we find so familiar in its application to human beings, cannot be clearly and sharply expressed by any word in the vocabulary of Plato and Aristotle; it was wrought with the hammer and anvil of theological disputes about the Trinity and the Person of Christ.[9]

He goes on to say, "The familiar concept of a person finds linguistic expression not only in the use of a noun for 'person' but also in the use of the personal pronouns. . . . " In addition to the uses of personal pronouns in connection with the divine Persons that Geach proceeds to cite, we may call attention to the English translation of the *Quicunque Vult* quoted above (" . . . to acknowledge every Person by himself to be both God and Lord"), and the closing words of Proper 27 of the Episcopal Church: " . . . where with thee, O Father, and thee, O Holy Ghost, he liveth and reigneth ever, one God, world without end."[10]

3

In this section, I shall outline a system of formal logic I shall call Relative-Identity Logic, or RI-logic for short.[11] I shall also attempt to answer the question: On what assumptions is a logic of relative identity of philosophical interest?

A formal logic comprises a vocabulary and a set of formation rules, a set of rules of inference, and, sometimes, a set of axioms. We shall require no axioms.

The vocabulary of RI-logic will consist of certain predicates of English (including 0-place predicates: closed sentences), the usual sentential connectives, variables, the universal and existential quantifiers, and suitable punctuation marks.[12] It will *not* include the identity sign, the description operator, or any terms other than variables.

We shall assume that our vocabulary contains all English predicates that conform to the following three constraints.

(1) Our stock of English predicates will not include any that contain the informal analogues of the things we have pointedly excluded

from our formal apparatus: identity, descriptions, demonstratives, and names. Thus we exclude 'α is identical with some Albanian', 'The tallest man is rich', 'That is a dog', and 'α is Jack's father'. It would cause no *formal* difficulties to include such predicates in the language of RI-logic, since a formal logic does not "interact" with the semantic content (if there is any) of the items it manipulates formally, but to do so would be confusing and contrary to the motivating spirit of RI-logic.

(2) With the exception of a special class of predicates noted in (3) below, our stock of English predicates will include no predicates containing count-nouns. (A count-noun is a noun that has a plural form and which can be modified by the indefinite article.) Thus we exclude: 'α is an apple', 'α owns three horses', and 'α has more children than β'. Some acceptable predicates are: 'α is heavy', 'α is made of gold', 'α is spherical' and 'α is taller than β'. We shall not, however, be really fanatical about excluding count-nouns. We shall be liberal enough to admit count-nouns that are mere grammatical conveniences. For example, we shall admit 'α has six sides' because one might just as well express what is expressed by this predicate by writing 'α is six-sided'. The rough rule is: A count-noun is "all right" if its use does not commit its user to there being things it counts. If one says, "The box weighs four pounds," one does not lay oneself open to the following sort of ontological interrogation: "Just what is a 'pound'? What properties do these 'pounds' have? You say the box weighs four of them; but how many of them are there (in all, I mean)?"

(3) Consider phrases of the form 'α is the same N as β', where 'N' represents the place of a count-noun. Sometimes predicates of this form are used in such a way as to imply that α and β are Ns and sometimes they are not. If I say, "Tully is the same man as Cicero," I imply that Tully and Cicero are men. If I say, "The Taj Mahal is the same color as the Washington Monument," I do not imply that these two edifices are colors. Let us call a predicate of the form 'is the same *N* as' a *relative-identity predicate* (or "RI-predicate") if it is satisfied only by Ns. A predicate that is not an RI-predicate we call an *ordinary* predicate. Thus, 'is the same man as' is an RI-predicate, and 'is the same color as' is an ordinary predicate—as are 'is green', 'is round', and 'is taller than'. (Actually, we should not say that predicates of the form 'is the same *N* as' are or are not RI-predicates *in themselves*, for a predicate of this form may be used sometimes as an RI-predicate and sometimes as an ordinary predicate. Consider, for example, 'Magenta is the same color as bluish-red'. In this sentence, 'is the same color as' functions as an RI-predicate.

In the sequel, I shall ignore this complication.) Count-nouns — seriously meant count-nouns like 'apple', 'horse', and 'child' — may turn up in our stock of English predicates in just one way: as components of RI-predicates. Thus we admit 'α is the same apple as β', 'α is the same horse as β', and so on.

Having introduced RI-predicates, we may introduce ordinary predicates of the form 'α is a(n) N' (e.g., 'α is an apple'; 'α is a child') by abbreviation: 'α is an apple' abbreviates '$\exists\beta$ α is the same apple as β,' and so on. To be an apple, in other words, is to be the same apple as something.

The formation rules of RI-logic are the obvious ones.

The rules of inference of RI-logic are simply the rules of ordinary quantifier logic — developed as a system of natural deduction — supplemented by two rules for manipulating RI-predicates. Since RI-predicates are closely connected with the idea of identity, we should expect these rules to be in at least some ways analogous to the inference-rules governing classical identity. This is indeed the case. The two rules are:

> *Symmetry* From $I\alpha\beta$, infer $I\beta\alpha$
> *Transitivity* From $I\alpha\beta$ and $I\beta\gamma$, infer $I\alpha\gamma$.

Here, of course, 'I' represents any RI-predicate and the Greek letters represent any variables. Using these two rules, we may prove something that will be a minor convenience to us, the general fact of which the following statement is an instance: '$\exists y$ x is the same apple as y' is equivalent to 'x is the same apple as x'.[13] "Right-to-left" is simply an instance of Existential Generalization. We proceed from left to right as follows: We have 'x is the same apple as z' by Existential Instantiation; from this we infer 'z is the same apple as x' by Symmetry; from these two sentences, 'x is the same apple as x' follows by Transitivity.

This result is a convenience because it allows us to regard, e.g., 'x is an apple' as an abbreviation for 'x is the same apple as x' instead of for '$\exists y$ x is the same apple as y', which will simplify the typography of the sequel. This result also makes it clear why we have no rule corresponding to the reflexivity rule of classical identity logic. A reflexivity rule for RI-predicates would look like this: From any premises, infer $I\alpha\alpha$. But if we had this rule, we could prove, e.g., that everything is the same apple as itself — that is to say, we could prove that everything is an apple.

Do we need further rules for manipulating RI-predicates? It might be argued that we must have such rules if RI-logic is to be at all interesting. Developments of the classical logic of identity always include some rule or axiom motivated by the intuitive idea that if x is identical with y, then x and y satisfy all the same predicates. In fact, all the classical principles of identity can be derived from a reflexivity rule ('From any premises, infer $\alpha = \alpha$') and an "indiscernibility" rule: 'From any premises, infer

$$\alpha = \beta \rightarrow (F \ldots \alpha \ldots \leftrightarrow F \ldots \beta \ldots).\text{'}$$

Here $F \ldots \alpha \ldots$ represents a sentence in which β does not occur, and $F \ldots \beta \ldots$ represents the result of replacing any (or all) free occurrences of α in $F \ldots \alpha \ldots$ with β. For example:

$$x = y \rightarrow (\exists w \ z \text{ is between } x \text{ and } w. \leftrightarrow \exists w \ z \text{ is between } y \text{ and } w).$$

If RI-logic is to be interesting (it might be argued), it must be supplied with some analogue of this rule. What would this analogue be? It will certainly *not* do to have the following rule (call it 'The Proposed Rule'): 'Where I is any RI-predicate, from any premises infer

$$I\alpha\beta \rightarrow (F \ldots \alpha \ldots \leftrightarrow F \ldots \beta \ldots)\text{'}.$$

For example:

$$x \text{ is the same man as } y \rightarrow (z \text{ is west of } x \leftrightarrow z \text{ is west of } y).$$

If we added the Proposed Rule to RI-logic, we should get a logic that treated RI-predicates as if they were all of the form 'x is an N & $x = y$', where N is a count-noun and '$=$' represents classical, absolute identity.[14] For example, the resulting logic would treat 'x is the same apple as y' as if it had the logical properties ascribed to 'x is an apple & $x = y$' by the classical logic of identity.

We may put this point more precisely as follows. Call a sentence like 'x is the same apple as y' that is formed from an RI-predicate and two occurrences of variables, an *RI-expression*. Call the sentence 'x is an apple & $x = y$' the *classical image* of the RI-expression 'x is the same apple as y'. Similarly 'z is a horse & $z = w$' is the classical image of 'z is the same horse as w'; the definition is obvious. More generally, the classical image of a *sentence* of the language of RI-logic is got by replacing each occurrence of an RI-expression in that sentence with its classical image.

Adding the Proposed Rule to RI-logic has this consequence:

A sentence is a theorem of RI-logic if and only if its classical image is an instance of a theorem of the classical logic of identity.

By an instance of a theorem of the classical logic of identity, I mean a sentence that results from such a theorem by substituting English predicates (consistently) for all of its predicate-letters. (Of course most instances of theorems of the classical logic of identity are not classical images of any sentence of RI-logic; '$x = y$ & x is green. $\rightarrow y$ is green', for example, is not.) The following three sentences are instances of theorems of the classical logic of identity:

x is an apple & $x = y$. $\rightarrow.y$ is an apple & $y = x$

x is an apple & $x = y$ & y is an apple & $y = z$. $\rightarrow.x$ is an apple & $x = z$

w is an apple & $w = y$. $\rightarrow$ (w is green $\leftrightarrow$ y is green).

Therefore (if the above thesis about adding the Proposed Rule to RI-logic is correct), the sentences of which these are the classical images are theorems of RI-logic supplemented by the Proposed Rule. (Hereinafter, 'RI-logic + '.) For example, the sentence

w is the same apple as $y \rightarrow$ (w is green $\leftrightarrow$ y is green).

is a theorem of RI-logic + . And it is, I think, intuitively obvious that a sentence is a theorem of RI-logic + if and only if its classical image is an instance of a theorem of the classical logic of identity. It does not seem to be overstating the case to say that RI-logic + treats 'α is the same N as β' as a stylistic variant on 'α is an N & $\alpha = \beta$'. If RI-logic + is the correct logic for reasoning about relative identities, then there is no point in having a special logic for reasoning about relative identities. The correct principles for reasoning about relative identities follow from the correct principles for reasoning about absolute identities. One need do no more than put a check mark beside each instance of a theorem of the logic of classical identity that is a classical image of some sentence in the language of RI-logic and say, "These are the formal truths about so-called relative identities. You may pronounce, e.g., 'z is an apple & $z = y$' as 'z is the same apple as y' if you care to."

A logic of relative identity will be interesting only if there are instances of theorems of the classical logic of identity that are the classical images of *non-theorems* of that logic of relative identity. A philosophically interesting logic of relative identity must be (in that sense) "weaker" than the classical logic of identity. (As with para-consistent logic, "intuitionist" logic, quantum logic, and David Lewis's counterfactual logic, a good deal of the philosophical interest of the topic arises from the fact that certain sentences that one might expect to be theorems are not theorems.) I propose to achieve this end as follows: to resist the temptation to supply RI-logic with any special rules of inference beyond Symmetry and Transitivity. This, of course, will not insure that RI-logic is of any philosophical interest. It is certainly of no formal interest. Considered formally, it is simply the quantifier calculus with its two-place predicates partitioned into two classes, within one of which Symmetry and Transitivity apply. What interest it has must come from two sources: first, from the thesis that this rather weak logic does indeed embody all the formal principles of inference that one should have when one reasons about relative identities, and, secondly, from such applications as it may have. The main philosophical interest of "intuitionist" logic lies in the claim that it embodies all the principles of formal reasoning the mathematician can legitimately employ. Quantum logic has no philosophical interest apart from its intended application.

The effect of having no special rules of RI-logic beyond Symmetry and Transitivity (and that comes down to having neither the Proposed Rule nor any restricted version of it) is exemplified by the following case:

x is the same apple as $y \rightarrow$ (x is green $\leftrightarrow$ y is green)

will not be a theorem of RI-logic, despite the fact that its classical image

x is an apple & $x = y$. $\rightarrow$ (x is green $\leftrightarrow$ y is green)

is an instance of a theorem of the classical logic of identity. More generally, RI-logic differs from RI-logic + in the following way. Call sentences of the following form *dominance sentences*:

$$I\alpha\beta \rightarrow (F \ldots \alpha \ldots \leftrightarrow F \ldots \beta \ldots),$$

where $F \ldots \alpha \ldots$ is a sentence in which β does not occur, and $F \ldots \beta \ldots$ is like $F \ldots \alpha \ldots$ except for having free occurrences of β at some or all places at which $F \ldots \alpha \ldots$ has free occurrences of α. All dominance sentences are theorems of RI-logic + . In general, dominance sentences are not theorems of RI-logic — unless they are instances of theorems of the sentential calculus, or are of the type 'x is the same apple as $y \rightarrow$ (x is the same apple as $z \leftrightarrow$ y is the same apple as z)'.

In refusing to add the Proposed Rule (or any restricted version of it) to RI-logic, we are in effect saying that each dominance sentence embodies a substantive metaphysical thesis — or perhaps in some cases a trivial metaphysical thesis, but at any rate a *metaphysical* thesis, one that ought not to be underwritten by the formal logic of relative identity. If there were a formal criterion by which we could separate the trivial metaphysical theses from the substantive ones, then we might consider adopting a restricted version of the Proposed Rule, one that yielded only the trivial theses. But there could not be such a formal criterion: If some dominance sentences are substantive and some trivial, the distinction lies in the English meanings of the predicates they contain.

In refusing to adopt the Proposed Rule we are (in effect) saying to whoever proposes to construct a derivation containing RI-predicates: "If you think that a dominance sentence like 'x is the same apple as $y \rightarrow$ (x is green $\leftrightarrow y$ is green)' is *true*, you are perfectly free to introduce it into your derivation *as a premise*. But then defending it is your responsibility. Formal logic alone does not endorse it." If someone does regard the dominance sentence 'x is the same apple as $y \rightarrow$ (x is green $\leftrightarrow y$ is green)' as true, let us say that he regards the RI-predicate 'is the same apple as' as *dominating* the predicate 'is green'. (If he believed that x and y might be the same apple and nevertheless be of different colors, then he would deny that sameness among apples "dominated" color.) Informally, for I to dominate F is for I to "force indiscernibility" in respect of F. Formally, an RI-predicate I dominates a predicate F (F may be of any polyadicity and be either ordinary or RI) if all sentences of the form '$I\alpha\beta \rightarrow (F \ldots \alpha \ldots \leftrightarrow F \ldots \beta \ldots)$' are true. We say that an RI-predicate that dominates every predicate is *dominant*. It seems a reasonable conjecture that most of us would regard, e.g., 'is the same apple as' and 'is the same horse as' as dominant.

The question now arises, *are* there any RI-predicates that are not dominant? Are there any false dominance sentences? If all dominance sentences are true (if all RI-predicates are dominant), then the Proposed Rule can never lead from truth to falsity. And if the Proposed Rule can never lead from truth to falsity, then the project of constructing a logic of relative identity is of no interest. It can be accomplished by stipulating that a sentence is a "theorem of the logic of relative identity" if and only if its classical image is an instance of a theorem of the classical logic of identity. There is, after all, no point in refusing to include the Proposed Rule among the rules of inference of a logic of relative identity if that rule can never lead from truth to falsity. And the Proposed Rule can lead from truth to falsity only if some RI-predicates are not dominant.

A trick of Professor Geach's shows that some RI-predicates are not dominant.[15] Let us introduce an RI-predicate 'is the same surman as' by the following definition:

α is the same surman as $\beta = df \alpha$ is a man and β is a man and
$$\alpha \text{ and } \beta \text{ have the same surname.}$$

Thus, John Locke is the same surman as Don Locke. It is evident that 'same surman' fails to dominate a great variety of predicates: 'is alive in the twentieth century', 'has never heard of Kant', 'is the same man as', and so on. Or, at least, 'same surman' fails to dominate these predicates if it really is an RI-predicate. But it would seem to be: 'surman' is a count-noun ("John Locke is a surman"; "Geach and Locke are two surmen") and if x is the same surman as y, then x and y are both surmen (i.e., each is the same surman as himself).

But this trick, it seems to me, does not show that the project of constructing a logic of relative identity is of interest. It is true that 'is the same surman as' is non-dominant. But it is also easily eliminable from our discourse. Anything we can say using 'is the same surman as' we can say without it; we need only use the (presumably dominant) RI-predicate 'is the same man as' and the ordinary predicate 'has the same surname as'. Let us say that if a non-dominant RI-predicate has these features, it is *redundant*. More explicitly: a non-dominant RI-predicate is redundant if everything we can say by making use of it we can say using only dominant RI-predicates and ordinary predicates. If the *only* non-dominant RI-predicates are in this sense redundant, then there is no real point in having a special logic of relative identity. If the only non-dominant RI-predicates are redundant, then—at least when we are engaged in constructing formal derivations—why not just translate all of our premises into sentences containing only dominant RI-predicates and ordinary predicates? Having done that, we may replace each premise that contains RI-predicates with its classical image and employ the classical logic of identity. If it pleases us, we may replace all occurrences in our conclusion of, e.g., 'x is a man & y is a man & x and y have the same surname' with 'x is the same surman as y'. In short, the "surman" trick provides us with no motivation for constructing a logic of relative identity. A logic of relative identity will be of interest only if there are *non-redundant* RI-predicates that are not dominant.

Are there non-redundant RI-predicates that are not dominant? Is there a non-redundant RI-predicate that fails to dominate some predicate? It is tempting to think that if there is such a relation as classical, absolute identity, the answer must be No. (If that is right, the project of constructing a logic of relative identity is interesting only on the assumption that classical, absolute identity does not exist.) Consider, say, 'is the same apple as'—which we shall suppose for the sake of the example not to be redundant—and 'is green'. Suppose that there is such a relation as classical identity. Obviously (one is tempted to say), if x is the same apple as y, then $x = y$. We have as an instance of a theorem of the logic of classical identity: $x = y \rightarrow (x$ is green $\leftrightarrow y$ is green). Hence, if x is the same apple as y, then x is green if and only if y is green. That is, 'is the same apple as' dominates 'is green'. Essentially the same argument could be constructed for the general case: to show that for any non-redundant RI-predicate I and any predicate F, I dominates F.

The tricky step in the argument for the general case will be the premise that, for just any non-redundant RI-predicate *I*, if *Ixy* then *x* = *y*. (A redundant RI-predicate *R* may, of course, be such that *Rxy* & ~*x* = *y*. The two Lockes are the same surman but not absolutely identical.) Is this true? Does every non-redundant RI-predicate dominate classical identity, assuming there to be such a relation as classical identity? Put the question this way. Call a predicate *subdominant* if it is dominated by every RI-predicate other than those that, like 'same surman', are redundant; Is it a part of the *concept* of classical identity (whether or not any relation in fact falls under that concept) that it be subdominant?

If the answer to this question is Yes, then RI-logic is an interesting topic only if classical identity does not exist. (And it seems to be the consensus among the friends of relative identity that classical identity does not exist.)

I am unsure what to say about the subdominance of classical identity. I know of only three relevant arguments, and they are inconclusive.

First, one might argue that if there is such a relation as classical identity, then, for any non-redundant RI-predicate 'is the same *N* as', the following equivalence should hold:

x is the same *N* as *y* ↔ .*x* is an *N* & *x* = *y*.

And it obviously follows from this that every non-redundant RI-predicate dominates classical identity. I think that those friends of relative identity who assume that their position is incompatible with the existence of classical identity have something like this in mind. (But why exactly should one accept this equivalence? Call a count-noun *proper* if, unlike 'surman', it does not form a redundant RI-predicate. Why is it incoherent to suppose that, where *N* is a proper count-noun, *x* is an *N*, *y* is an *N*, *x* and *y* are the same *N*, and *x* and *y* are not absolutely identical?)

Secondly, one might argue *ad hominem* that the philosopher who believes that RI-logic is an interesting topic should not mind denying that classical identity is subdominant. After all, he must hold that *some* predicate is not subdominant. Now the really puzzling thing—one might argue—is that *any* predicate should fail to be subdominant. Once someone has admitted *that*, he should have no scruples about saying of any *given* predicate—classical identity, for example—that *it* is not subdominant.

Thirdly, one might point out that all the theorems of the logic of classical identity follow from '$x = x$' and '$x = y \rightarrow (F \ldots x \ldots \leftrightarrow F \ldots y \ldots)$' by quantifier logic. This fact suggests that only two properties are constitutive of the *idea* of classical identity: identity is *universally reflexive* and it *forces absolute indiscernibility*. And it is hard to see how these two properties might entail subdominance.

As I have said, I regard these arguments as inconclusive. In the sequel, therefore, I shall neither assume that classical identity exists nor that it does not exist.

We may note in this connection that it is possible for one to employ in certain contexts a symbol that behaves like the classical identity-sign without thereby committing oneself to the existence of classical identity. The contexts in which one may do this can be described as follows. Let G be a one-place predicate. Let us say that an RI-predicate I *G-dominates* a predicate F if all sentences of the form

$$G\alpha \ \& \ G\beta. \ \rightarrow [I\alpha\beta \rightarrow (F \ldots \alpha \ldots \leftrightarrow F \ldots \beta \ldots)]$$

are true. Suppose that, for the duration of a certain project, one is willing to restrict the scope of one's generalizations to objects that satisfy G. And suppose that one believes (1) that all of the RI-predicates one is employing in this project G-dominate all of the predicates one is employing, and (2) that, for any x, if Gx, then for some RI-predicate I that one is employing, Ixx. Then one may introduce a predicate '$=$' as the disjunction of all the RI-predicates that one is employing and one may regard this predicate as governed by the two rules that define the logical behavior of the classical identity-sign. (That is, Reflexivity and the Indiscernibility of Identicals; see above.)

A philosopher who denies the existence of classical, absolute identity may find materials in the procedure I have outlined for an explanation of the fact that most philosophers and logicians have assumed that there is such a relation as classical identity. Might it not be that all commonly used RI-predicates G-dominate all commonly used predicates, where G is some predicate that comprehends all the objects that philosophers typically think of as central or paradigm cases of "objects"? If this were so, it would go a long way toward explaining how a belief in absolute identity could be pervasive but incorrect. (One might compare an explanation of this sort with the usual explanations of how a belief in absolute, Euclidean space could be pervasive but incorrect. Each sort of explanation postulates a natural but unwarranted inference from "local" features of the world to the features of the world as a whole.)

Now whether or not there is such a relation as classical identity, RI-logic is of interest only if there is an RI-predicate I (from now on, when making generalizations about RI-predicates, I shall regard the qualification 'non-redundant' as "understood") and a predicate F such that I does not dominate F. We should have such an I and F if there were some count-noun of English N (from now on, when making generalizations about count-nouns, I shall regard the qualification 'proper' as "understood") such that, for some x and y, x is green and y is not green and x is the same N as y. (In this case 'is the same N as' fails to dominate 'green'.) Or we should have such an I and F if there were two count-nouns of English, M and N, such that, for some x and y, x is an M and x is an N and y is an M and y is an N and x is the same N as y and x is not the same M as y. (In this second case, 'is the same N as' fails to dominate 'is the same M as'. This second case has been said to be a necessary and sufficient condition for RI-logic being of interest; but it is not necessary, as the first case shows.)

How plausible is it to suppose that there is some RI-predicate that fails to dominate some predicate? (In the present section I shall examine the question whether there are such predicates insofar as this question touches on objects belonging to the natural world. Theological speculations are reserved for section 4.) The literature on relative identity suggests several candidates for this position, several of which are worthy of careful examination. I pick one as representative. It is sometimes said that there are such things as "quantities of clay" (and of other stuffs, of course). A clay vase is a quantity of clay, a clay statue is a quantity of clay, and an unformed lump of clay that no potter or sculptor has touched is a quantity of clay. ('Quantity' does not here mean *amount*; 'quantity' is like 'lump', only even less demanding: a lump has to be in one piece— one would suppose—while a quantity may be scattered to the four corners of the earth.) It is sometimes suggested that the RI-predicate 'is the same quantity of clay as' does not dominate, e.g., 'is less than one hour old'. It is suggested that it may be that there is a vase and there is a lump of clay (currently vase-shaped and coincident with the vase) such that the former is the same quantity of clay as the latter, despite the fact that the vase is less than one hour old and the lump more than one hour old. (For no vase could ever have been of a radically different shape—spherical, say—while a lump of clay might be vase-shaped now and have been spherical yesterday.) A philosopher who doubts the philosophical utility of the concept of relative identity will not be moved by these suggestions, however. He will contend that there is no need to suppose that 'is the same quantity of clay as' fails to dominate 'is less than one hour old'. He will suggest that it is simpler to suppose (a) that there is such a relation as absolute identity, (b) that 'x is the same quantity of clay as y' is equivalent to 'x is a quantity of clay & $x = y$', and (c) that it *can* be true of a vase that *it* was once spherical; he will suggest that a clay vase *is* (absolutely) just a quantity of clay; one that was once (say) spherical and is now vase-shaped. In other words, this philosopher will suggest that "being a vase" is a *status* that a quantity of clay may temporarily acquire, much as "being a president" is a status that Ronald Reagan has temporarily acquired: Just as the President existed before he was a president, so the vase existed before it was a vase. I have not the space to consider all the cases that have been devised by philosophers in the attempt to show that there are non-dominant RI-predicates (ones having only natural objects in their extensions), but I think that the enemies of relative identity will be able to produce replies to them as effective as the reply I have suggested for the case of the clay vase. I can find nothing in the natural world to suggest that there are any non-dominant RI-predicates. As far as I am able to tell, RI-logic has no utility outside Christian theology. (This need not raise doubts about the coherency of Christian doctrine. Like quantum mechanics and the more rarefied parts of pure mathematics, the doctrine of the Trinity treats of objects extraordinarily different from the objects of ordinary experience, ones that are perhaps *sui generis*. If it could be shown that a certain exotic non-classical logic had an application—if anywhere—in quantum physics or in the study of the non-constructive infinite, this result would not necessarily raise doubts about the coherency of quantum physics or the non-constructive infinite. Of course, someone who already believed that one of these things was incoherent might regard this result as providing indirect confirmation for his belief: if, e.g., quantum mechanics is hospitable to a logic in which conjunction fails to distribute over disjunction— he might say—that's one more strike against quantum mechanics.)

Let us close our discussion of RI-logic with a brief look at the topic of singular reference. The language of RI-logic contains no singular terms. Given our decision to be non-committal about the existence of classical, absolute identity, this is no accident. The philosopher who eschews classical, absolute identity must also eschew singular terms, for the idea of a singular term is—at least in currently orthodox semantical theory—inseparably bound to the classical semantical notion of reference or denotation; and this notion, in its turn, is inseparably bound to the idea of classical identity. It is a part of the orthodox semantical concept of reference that reference is a many-one relation. And it is a part of the idea of a many-one relation—or of a one-one relation, for that matter—that if x bears such a relation to y and bears it to z, then y and z are absolutely identical. (That's what it says on the label.) For example, if 'the tallest man' denotes y and denotes z, then y and z are absolutely identical. (This point "works" better in respect of descriptions than in respect of proper names. The friends of singular terms must concede that, e.g., 'John Frederick Harris' might, and in fact does, name numerically distinct objects. Let us ignore this awkward fact, which can be dealt with in various ways, and remarkably messy and *ad hoc* ways they are, too.)

If the RI-logician has no singular terms at his disposal, how shall he accomplish singular reference? Must he be content with general statements? In a sense, the answers are: He shan't accomplish it, and he must be content with them. In *what* sense does he face these unpleasant consequences? In any sense of "singular reference" in which the idea of singularity is infected with the idea of classical, absolute identity. This is pretty evident when you think about it. Nevertheless, the RI-logician is not without resources. He has the resources to accomplish *relative* singular reference, a sort of singularity of reference that stands to classical, absolute singularity of reference—the sort that is supposedly accomplished by singular terms—as relative identity stands to classical, absolute identity. Relative singular reference can be accomplished by a device suggested by Russell's theory of descriptions. It is illustrated by the following examples of translations of English sentences containing (what are traditionally called) definite descriptions into the language of RI-logic.

The king is bald

$\exists x$ (x is a king & $\forall y$ (y is a king $\rightarrow$ y is the same king as x) & x is bald).

The queen is the monarch

$\exists x$ (x is a queen & x is a monarch &
$\forall y$ (y is a queen $\rightarrow$ y is the same queen as x) &
$\forall y$ (y is a monarch $\rightarrow$ y the same monarch as x)).

Or, at any rate, this is one way to translate these two English sentences into the language of RI-logic; this is the way to do it without making any suppositions about dominance. But if we assume, e.g., that 'is the same man as' dominates 'is the same king as', it might be more natural and useful to translate 'The king is bald' as

$\exists x$ (x is a king & $\forall y$ (y is a king $\rightarrow$ y is the same man as x) & x is bald).

4

In the present section, I shall show how to translate certain central theses of Trinitarian theology into the language of RI-logic. The vocabulary we shall employ would hardly do for devotional purposes, but (I hope) we can use it to express certain of the *propositions* that are expressed in devotional discourse about the Trinity. It will not be difficult to show that what we want to say about the Trinity in this vocabulary is free from formal contradiction.

We have, to start with, two undefined RI-predicates:

is the same being as[16]

is the same person as.

We shall not assume that either of these predicates dominates the other. And, of course, we shall not assume that either of them is eliminable in favor of dominant RI-predicates and ordinary predicates. It is of particular importance that we not assume that 'same being' dominates 'same person', for that would entail that if x is the same being as y and x is a person, then x is the same person as y. (In at least one other context — the theology of the Incarnation — it would be important not to assume that 'same person' dominates 'same being'.)

I do not refrain from defining these predicates because I think that there is any particular difficulty about what it is to be a being or a person. Something is a being (is the same being as something) if it has causal powers. A being is a person (something that is the same being as something is also the same person as something) if it is self-aware and has beliefs and plans and acts on the basis of those beliefs to execute those plans. (As Boethius says, a person is an individual substance of a rational nature.) But to say this much is not to give a general account of '*same* being' or '*same* person'. If we regard a definition of a sentence in the austere fashion of logicians as a recipe for eliminating that sentence *salva extensione* in favor of another sentence containing the same variables free, then the account I have given of 'person' and 'being' provides us with definitions of 'x is the same being as x' (or, equivalently, of 'x is the same being as something') and 'x is the same person as x', but not of 'x is the same being as y' or 'x is the same person as y'.[17] (It allows us, for example, to define 'x is the same being as x' as 'x has causal powers'.)

If we believed that there were such a relation as classical, absolute identity, and if we believed that this relation was subdominant, then we *could* extract from our account of 'person' and 'being' definitions of 'same person' and 'same being'. For example:

x is the same being as $y = df\ x$ has causal powers & $x = y$.

The reason that the existence and subdominance of classical identity would enable us so to turn a definition of 'x is the same being as x' into a definition of 'x is the same being as y' is that the subdominance of classical identity (its domination by all RI-predicates) entails the conditional

x is the same being as $y \rightarrow x = y$;

and from this conditional one may infer (by the rules of the classical logic of identity) the biconditional

x is the same being as $y \leftrightarrow .x$ is the same being as x & $x = y$.

But if the above definition of 'is the same being as' were correct, it would follow that if a person x and a person y are the same being, then x and y are the *same* person.[18] The Trinitarian must, therefore, assume either that classical, absolute identity does not exist, or that, if it does exist, it is not dominated by 'is the same being as'. (Or, at least, he must make one or the other of these assumptions if his thinking about the Trinity is to be based on a logic of relative identity. This result is essentially an application to the case of a relative-identity treatment of the Trinity of a point made in section 3 about relative-identity treatments of anything: If there is such a relation as classical, absolute identity, and if it is subdominant, then all RI-predicates are dominant.) Nothing, of course, prevents him from introducing by the device outlined in section 3 a predicate that behaves within a certain restricted area of his discourse—say, the part that does not have to do with the Trinity—in the way the classical identity-predicate is supposed to behave throughout all discourse.

We shall have several ordinary predicates, which will be introduced as we need them. The first is 'is divine'. A *definiens* for 'x is divine' might look something like this:

x is necessarily existent; essentially almighty, all-knowing, and perfect in love and wisdom; essentially such that nothing contingent would exist unless x willed it.

But you may have your own ideas about how to define this predicate. Since any reasonable list of the attributes constitutive of divinity must include attributes implying power and knowledge, the following would seem to be a conceptual truth, and I shall assume it to be such:

CT1 $\forall x$ (x is divine $\rightarrow .x$ is a being & x is a person).

Indeed, the first conjunct of the consequent is, strictly speaking, redundant, since any person is, necessarily, a being:

CT2 $\forall x$ (x is a person $\rightarrow$ x is a being).

It follows from CT1 that something is a divine Person if and only if it is a divine Being:

CT3 $\forall x$ (x is a person & x is divine. $\leftrightarrow$ .x is a being & x is divine).[19]

We shall assume that 'is the same being as' dominates 'is divine'; that is we shall assume

CT4 $\forall x \forall y$ (x is the same being as y $\rightarrow$ (x is divine $\leftrightarrow$ y is divine)).

The most important consequence of CT4 is that if a being is divine, then any being who is the same being as that being is divine. (We shall not assume that 'same person' dominates 'divine'. We shall not need this assumption, and it might cause difficulties for the theology of the Incarnation, since, on the obvious interpretation of the doctrine of the Incarnation, there is an x such that x is divine and there is a y such that y is not divine and x is the same person as y. Owing to similar considerations, we should not want to assume that 'same person' dominated such predicates as 'is a man' and 'was born in the world'.) It follows from CT1 and CT4 that if x is a divine Person and y is the same being as x, then y is *a* person. It does not, of course, follow that y is the *same* person as x.

Let us now introduce abbreviations for 'same being', 'same person', and 'divine':

$\underline{B}\alpha\beta$ α is the same being as β

$\underline{P}\alpha\beta$ α is the same person as β

$D\alpha$ α is divine.

(In virtue of CT1, 'Dx' may be read, 'x is a divine Person' or 'x is a divine Being'. If 'a God' is equivalent to 'a divine Being'—as I suppose it to be—, 'Dx' may also be read 'x is a God'.) We underline '$\underline{B}$' and '$\underline{P}$' to remind us that they abbreviate RI-predicates. We shall further abbreviate, e.g., '$\underline{B}xx$' as '$\underline{B}x$'.

We may express using only these three predicates three central propositions of Trinitarian theology:

(1) There is (exactly) one God
   $\exists x$ (Dx & $\forall y(Dy \rightarrow \underline{B}yx)$)

(2) There are (exactly) three divine Persons

$\exists x \exists y \exists z$ *(Dx & Dy & Dz &~Pxy & ~ Pxz & ~ Pyz &*
$\forall w(Dw \rightarrow. \underline{P}wx \vee \underline{P}wy \vee \underline{P}wz))$

(3) There are three divine Persons in one divine Being

[There are three divine Persons] & $\forall x \forall y(Dx \& Dy. \rightarrow \underline{B}xy)$.

It is easy to see that (1) through (3) and CT1 through CT4 together compose a set of sentences from which no contradiction can be derived in RI-logic.

To show this, let us consider the following reinterpretation of our three predicates. (Admittedly, it is rather unedifying; it has been chosen for its mnemonic virtues.)

$\underline{B}\alpha\beta$ α is the same breed as β

$\underline{P}\alpha\beta$ α is the same price as β

$D\alpha$ α is a dog

Now assume that there are exactly three dogs and that nothing besides these dogs has either a breed or a price. Assume that these dogs are for sale at different prices and that each is a purebred dachshund. Given these assumptions, it is easy to verify by inspection that the sentences (1) through (3) and CT1 through CT4 are true on the proposed reinterpretation of '$\underline{B}$', '$\underline{P}$', and 'D'.

This reinterpretation of our predicates shows that no formal contradiction can be deduced from (1) through (3) and CT1 through CT4 by standard quantifier logic, since (by a well-known property of quantifier logic), no formal contradiction can be deduced in that logic from a set of sentences that are true on some interpretation. The only rules of RI-logic other than those of quantifier logic are Symmetry and Transitivity. Since 'x is the same breed as y' and 'x is the same price as y' express symmetrical and transitive relations, it follows that no formal contradiction can be deduced from (1) through (3) and CT1 through CT4 by the rules of RI-logic. (Nothing I have said should be taken to imply that 'is the same breed as' and 'is the same price as' are relative-identity predicates. In fact these predicates are *not* RI-predicates, at least as we are using them. On this point, see our discussion of 'is the same color as' on p. 249.)

Our consistency result shows that 'Something is a divine Person if and only if it is a divine Being' [CT3] is formally consistent with 'There are three divine Persons' [(2)] and 'There is one divine Being' [(1)]. This formal result can be understood philosophically as follows. Without classical identity, there is no absolute counting: there is only counting by

*N*s. For example, if propositions (1) and (2) are true: Counting divine Beings by beings, there is one; counting divine Persons by beings, there is one; counting divine Beings by persons, there are three; counting divine Persons by persons, there are three. But if someone asks us how many divine Beings there are, it is presumably a "conversational implicature" of his question that he wishes us to count divine Beings by beings—that is, by the count-noun *he* used. And the same goes for, "How many divine Persons are there?" That is why 'There is one divine Being' is a natural English translation of the symbolic sentence (1) and 'There are three divine Persons' is a natural English translation of the symbolic sentence (2). If, on the other hand, there is such a thing as absolute identity, there is such a thing as absolute counting. For example, if absolute identity exists, it follows from (2) and CT3 that there are three divine Beings and three divine Persons, counting absolutely. If absolute identity not only exists but is subdominant, an absolute count of *N*s will force the same count on all relative counts of *N*s. (In that case, of course, CT3, (1), and (2) could not all be true.) If absolute identity exists but is not subdominant—if, in particular, it is not dominated by 'same being'— then it may be true that there is one divine Being counting by beings and, at the same time, true that there are three divine Beings counting absolutely.

Let us now turn to the problem of singular reference.

We must find some way, using only the resources of RI-logic, to do the work of the English singular terms 'God', 'the Father', 'the Son', and 'the Holy Spirit'.[20] We have seen how to supply a relative-identity surrogate for classical definite descriptions. The singular term 'God' should obviously be thought of as an abbreviation for 'the divine Being' or (like the Arabic 'Allah') 'the God'. Thus, using our relative-identity surrogate for classical definite descriptions, we may translate the English sentence 'God made us' into the language of our RI-logic as

$$\exists x \, (Dx \, \& \, \forall y(Dy \rightarrow \underline{B}yx) \, \& \, x \text{ made us}).$$

It will be convenient to abbreviate '$Dx \, \& \, \forall y \, (Dy \rightarrow \underline{B}yx)$' as '$Gx$' (and similarly for other variables). 'Gx' may be read 'x is one God' (*cf.* Deut. 6:4) or 'x is the only God' or 'x is the divine Being'. The word 'God' in English is sometimes a common noun ('There is one God') and sometimes a proper noun ('In the beginning, God created the heavens and the earth'). When 'God' is a common noun in English, it is a count-noun. In the special vocabulary of the present section of this paper, the work done by the English count-noun 'God' is done by the predicate 'is divine': 'There is a God' is read 'Something is divine'. The work done by the English proper noun 'God' is also done by 'is divine': to say what is said by an English sentence of the form 'God is ø', we say 'The only God (the one God, the divine Being) is ø'. Or, making use of the above abbreviation, '∃x(Gx & øx)'.

But how shall we translate English sentences containing the terms 'the Father', 'the Son', and 'the Holy Spirit'?[21] It is a commonplace of Trinitarian theology that the Persons of the Trinity are individuated by the relations they bear to one another. Two relations, the Creeds tell us, individuate the Persons; we may express them by these predicates:

α begets β

α proceeds from β through γ.

(I hope that the wording of the second of these is acceptable to both the Eastern and the Western Churches.)[22] These two relations hold only within the Godhead:

CT5 ∀x∀y(x begets y →.Dx & Dy)

CT6 ∀x∀y∀z(x proceeds from y through z →.Dx & Dy &Dz).

Every divine Person enters into the "procession" relation:

CT7 ∀x(Dx → .(∃y∃z x proceeds from y through z)v
            (∃y∃z y proceeds from x through z)v
            (∃y∃z y proceeds from z through x)).

If x, y, and z enter into the "procession" relation with one another, then x, y, and z are distinct Persons:

CT8 ∀x∀y∀z(x proceeds from y through z →.~Pxy & ~Pxz & ~Pyz).[23]

If x, y, and z enter into the "procession" relation with one another, then no other Persons do (nor do x, y, and z enter into it in more than one way):

CT9 ∀x∀y∀z∀t∀u∀v (x proceeds from y through z & t proceeds from u through v. →. Pxt & Pyu & Pzv).

The two relations, procession and begetting, are not independent:

CT10 ∀x∀y∀z(x proceeds from y through z → y begets z)

CT11 ∀x∀y ∃z(x begets y → z proceeds from x through y).[24]

Begetting has features analogous to the features ascribed to procession in CT8 and CT9:

CT12 ∀x∀y(x begets y → ~Pxy)

CT13 $\forall x \forall y \forall z \forall w(x$ begets y & z begets $w. \rightarrow. \underline{P}xz$ & $\underline{P}yw).$[25]

It will be convenient to introduce three one-place predicates by definition:

α begets $= df \, \exists \beta \, \alpha$ begets β

α is begotten $= df \, \exists \beta \, \beta$ begets α

α proceeds $= df \, \exists \beta \exists \gamma \, \alpha$ proceeds from β through γ.

Propositions CT5–13 entail that each of these predicates is satisfied (if at all) by a divine Person; that if x and y satisfy any given one of them, then $\underline{P}xy$; and that if x satisfies one of them and y another, then $\sim \underline{P}xy$. We may therefore treat 'the Father', 'the Son', and 'the Holy Spirit' as equivalent to, respectively, 'the Person who begets', 'the Person who is begotten' and 'the Person who proceeds'. More exactly, we shall read, e.g., 'The Father made us' as

$\exists x(x$ begets & $\forall y(y$ begets $\rightarrow \underline{P}yx)$ & x made us).

Let us abbreviate 'x begets & $\forall y(y$ begets $\rightarrow \underline{P}yx)$' as '$Fx$'("$x$ is the Father"). Let us abbreviate 'x is begotten & $\forall y(y$ is begotten $\rightarrow \underline{P}yx)$' as '$Sx$' ("$x$ is the Son"). Let us abbreviate 'x proceeds & $\forall y(y$ proceeds $\rightarrow \underline{P}yx)$' as '$Hx$' ("$x$ is the Holy Spirit"). (And similarly for other variables.)

I now present a list of Trinitarian sentences of English and some proposed translations into our formal vocabulary. All of the translations are provable from (1) through (3), and CT1 through CT13. Note, by the way, that (2) and (3) are provable from (1) and the CTs.

(4) God is the same being as the Father
   $\exists x \, \exists y(Gx$ & Fy & $\underline{B}xy).$

(5) God is a person[26]
   $\exists x(Gx$ & $\underline{P}x).$

(6) God is the same person as the Father
   $\exists x \, \exists y(Gx$ & Fy & $\underline{P}xy).$

(7) God is the same person as the Son
   $\exists x \, \exists y(Gx$ & Sy & $\underline{P}xy).$

(8) The Son is the not the same person as the Father
   $\sim \exists x \, \exists y(Fx$ & Sy & $\sim \underline{P}xy).$[27]

Or we might write (giving 'not' "narrow scope"),

$\exists x \, \exists y(Fx$ & Sy & $\sim \underline{P}xy).$[28]

We should note that (6), (7), and both versions of (8) are — formally, at least — consistent. More generally: let S be the set of sentences containing (1) through (8) and CT1 through CT13; we can show that no formal contradiction is deducible from S in RI-logic.[29] We can show this by an extension of the "three dogs" reinterpretation of '$\underline{B}$', '$\underline{P}$', and '$\underline{D}$' that we employed earlier. Reinterpret our "Trinitarian" predicates as follows:

α begets β	α barks at β
α proceeds from β through γ	α prances from β to γ

Now let our three dogs be A, B, and C. Suppose that C prances from A to B and does no other prancing and that nothing besides C prances. Suppose that A is barking at B and at nothing else and that nothing besides A barks. Given these assumptions, and our earlier assumptions about prices and breeds, it is easy (if somewhat tedious) to verify by inspection that all the members of S are true on the proposed reinterpretation. Note that the reinterpretation for 'Px' in (5) should be 'x is the same price as x'. It follows that no formal contradiction is deducible from S in RI-logic.

In order to verify by inspection that all members of S are true, it is necessary to remove the abbreviations in (4)-(8). For example, here is sentence (4) in unabbreviated form:

$$\exists x \exists y (Dx \ \& \ \forall z (Dz \rightarrow \underline{B}zx) \ \& \ \exists w(y \text{ begets } w) \ \& $$
$$\forall z (\exists w \ z \text{ begets } w. \rightarrow \underline{P}zy) \ \& \ \underline{B}xy).$$

The tedium of verifying (4) - (8) on the "three dogs" reinterpretation can be somewhat reduced if we supply appropriate "derived" reinterpretations for the defined predicates 'G', 'F', and 'S':

$G\alpha$	α is a member of the only breed of dog
$F\alpha$	α barks and any barking dog is the same price as α
$S\alpha$	α is barked at and any dog that is barked at is the same price as α.

It is important to realize that the "three dogs" reinterpretation of our predicates is not intended to provide a model (in any sense) for the Trinity. For one thing, as we have noted, 'is the same price as' and 'is the same breed as' are not even RI-predicates. The only purpose of the reinterpretation is to show that for no sentence is it possible to derive both that sentence and its negation from S by Transitivity, Symmetry, and the rules of quantifier logic. The argument is essentially this: If a contradiction can be formally deduced from S, then the story of our three dogs is inconsistent; but that story is obviously consistent.

Does it seem paradoxical that (6), (7), and (8) are consistent? We must remember that it is an essential part of the position we are exploring that the English sentences (6), (7), and (8) do not wear their real, underlying logical structures on their sleeves: They are not really of the forms '$\underline{P}gf$', '$\underline{P}gs$', and '$\sim\underline{P}fs$'. According to this position, the underlying logical structures of these sentences are given by their RI-translations; and no sentence in the language of RI-logic could be of these forms, for that language contains no terms but variables. We should note that '$\sim(\underline{P}xy \,\&\, \underline{P}xz \,\&\, \sim\underline{P}yz)$' is an easily proved theorem of RI-logic, and is, therefore, by our consistency result, formally consistent with (6), (7), and (8). The tendency to think that the consistency of (6), (7), and (8) is paradoxical is rooted, I think, in our tendency to suppose that 'God', 'the Father', and 'the Son' are singular terms (in the orthodox semantical sense).

Other "paradoxical" groups of sentences can be found. For example:

(9) God is begotten
  $\exists x \,(Gx \,\&\, x$ is begotten)

(10) God is unbegotten
  $\exists x \,(Gx \,\&\, \sim x$ is begotten).

These two sentences are formally consistent with, and, in fact, provable from, the members of **S**. Are they theologically acceptable? Well, one sometimes sees references in Christian theological writing (usually in rhetorical opposition) to begotten and unbegotten Deity, so I suppose that they are.

A perhaps more serious problem of the same sort is raised by the Incarnation. It seems plausible to define 'x is incarnate' as '$\exists y(y$ is a human being $\& \,\underline{P}xy)$'. On this reading, however, 'God is unincarnate'—'$\exists x(Gx \,\&\, \sim\exists y(y$ is a human being $\& \,\underline{P}xy))$'—will "come out true."[30] I think that the best course for the philosopher who proposes to express the doctrines of the Trinity and the Incarnation in the language of RI-logic is to insist that this sentence is literally true but misleading. He will be able to adduce in his support the demonstrable facts that (if Jesus of Nazareth is the same person as one of the divine Persons), then 'God is incarnate' is true and 'it is not the case that God is incarnate' is false. But I can do no more than allude to the problems raised by the Incarnation.

I have shown how to represent certain Trinitarian sentences of English in our formal vocabulary, and I have shown that no contradiction can be deduced in RI-logic from the formal translations of these sentences. I note in passing that there are interesting sentences expressible in terms of the predicates we have at our disposal that allow us to make distinctions that cannot be made easily in English. Consider this sentence

(11) $\exists x(Gx \, \& \, Fx)$.

This sentence expresses a truth; or at least it is provable in RI-logic from the members of **S**. How shall we express its content in English? Not, certainly, as 'God is the same being as the Father' or 'God is the same person as the Father', for these are the equivalents, respectively, of the RI-sentences (4) and (6). I would suggest: 'God and the Father are one absolutely'. It might be said that the ideas conjured up by the predicate 'are one absolutely' are contrary to the spirit of RI-logic. Perhaps so; but sentence (11) is a perfectly respectable sentence, and I am at a loss for a better informal expression of its content. We may note that if my suggestion for translating (11) into English is followed out consistently, the English sentence 'God and the Son are one absolutely' will express a truth, and the English sentence 'The Father and the Son are one absolutely' will express a falsehood.[31]

I have said that in this paper I should risk Tritheism. Have I fallen into Tritheism? What can be said with certainty is this. The sentence (1)

$\exists x(Dx \, \& \, \forall y(Dy \rightarrow \underline{B}yx))$,

which — it may be argued, at any rate — expresses the thesis of monotheism, does not yield a formal contradiction in RI-logic; nor does the whole set of sentences **S** that we have "endorsed," and to which (1) belongs, yield a contradiction. Consider, moreover, the sentence

$\exists x \exists y(Dx \, \& \, Dy \, \& \, \sim\underline{B}xy)$,

which — it may be argued, at any rate — expresses the thesis that there are two or more Gods. The negation of this sentence can be formally deduced from (1). But these results do not protect us from all the dangers of Tritheism. Perhaps the most objectionable — I do not say the only objectionable — feature of polytheism is that if one believes that Zeus and Poseidon are real and are two divine beings and two divine persons, one must admit that one has no guarantee that Zeus and Poseidon will not demand contrary things of one. And there is nothing in the notion of "same being," taken by itself, that entails that two divine Persons who are the same Being will not, despite their being the same Being, demand contrary things of one. It must certainly be a feature of any adequate Trinitarian theology that whatever is demanded of one by any divine Person is demanded by all, and, more generally, that the idea of a clash of divine wills is as impossible as the idea of a round square. I am pointing out only that the impossibility of a clash of wills among the divine Persons is not a simple consequence of their being one Being. (It may be that, owing to their perfect knowledge and wisdom, no two divine Persons could will differently. If so, this has nothing in particular to do with the unity of being of the divine Persons: the same consequence would follow if there were two divine Persons who were also two beings.)

I believe that the (conceptual) danger of a clash of divine wills can be eliminated in a conceptually satisfying (i.e., non-arbitrary) way if we accept what I shall call the Principle of the Uniformity of the Divine Nature. This principle turns on the notion of a non-Trinitarian—or, as I shall say, "normal"—predicate applicable to God. Roughly speaking, a normal predicate is one that someone who believed that there was exactly one divine Person might coherently apply to that Person.[32] For example: 'made the world'; 'is compassionate'; 'spake by the Prophets'. The Principle of the Uniformity of the Divine Nature is simply this: 'is the same being as' dominates all normal predicates. Formally (where 'N' represents any normal predicate), all sentences of the following form are true:

$$\underline{B}\alpha\beta \rightarrow (N \ldots \alpha \ldots \leftrightarrow N \ldots \beta \ldots).$$

(We may note that CT4 is of this form.) Since such predicates as 'commands Moses to return to Egypt' and 'tells Saul to enter Damascus' are normal, the Principle of the Uniformity of the Divine Nature rules out the possibility of a Homeric clash of divine wills. And it rules out a good many other things; it entails, for example, that it is false that the Father made the world and the Son did not. It is a way of saying formally what the *Quicunque Vult* says in the words, "*Qualis Pater, talis Filius, talis et Spiritus Sanctus*"[33]—although the writer of those words was not thinking primarily of the relations God bears to his creation, but rather of his *intrinsic* normal attributes.[34]

I will close by mentioning some important philosophical questions about the Trinity that I have not touched on. Consider, for example, the relations that individuate the Persons. Are the Persons individuated *only* by these relations, as most of the classical Trinitarian theologians seem to have supposed? Or might it be that each of the Persons has certain intrinsic (non-relational) attributes that are not shared by the others? Put the question this way. The Father begets the Son, and the Holy Spirit proceeds from the Father through the Son. Why do these two relations hold among the three divine Persons in just *this* way? Is it a brute fact, the three Persons being absolutely descriptively identical except for the manner in which they are related? Or does each of the three Persons have a proper nature of his own, in addition to the nature (Divinity) that is common to all three, in which these relations are "grounded"? To say so might threaten the traditional doctrine of the Divine Simplicity. But the doctrine of purely relational individuation seems to imply the (surely repugnant) thesis that it is intrinsically possible that the Person who is in fact the Holy Spirit beget the Person who is in fact the Father.

A second problem we have not considered, but which has bulked large in the speculations of the great Trinitarian theologians, can be stated very succinctly: Why *three* Persons? I could go on at some length about the problems I have not considered, but I will not. I have been concerned in this paper to touch only on those features of Trinitarian theology most closely connected with problems of counting, identity, and predication.

Even in this limited area of investigation, I have left the mystery of the Holy Trinity untouched. It is one thing to suggest that 'is the same being as' does not dominate 'is the same person as'. It is another thing to explain how this could be. I have no explanation of this fact (if it is a fact); nor do I think that we could hope to discover one in this life, in which we see only disordered reflections in a mirror. One day, perhaps, we shall see face to face and know as we are known.[35]

NOTES

1. Paul VI, "Credo of the People of God" (pronounced 30 June 1968), *Acta Apostolicae Sedis* 60 (1968), 9.

2. Keith Yandell has called my attention to the following passage from St. Augustine's *On Christian Doctrine* (I, 5, 5):

> Thus there are the Father, the Son, and the Holy Spirit, and each is God and at the same time all are one God; and each of them is a full substance, and at the same time all are one substance. The Father is neither the Son nor the Holy Spirit; the Son is neither the Father nor the Holy Spirit; the Holy Spirit is neither the Father nor the Son. But the Father is the Father uniquely; the Son is the Son uniquely; and the Holy Spirit is the Holy Spirit uniquely.

Yandell has also called my attention to the marvelously splenetic Socinian attacks on the doctrine of the Trinity that are cited in Leonard Hodgson's *The Doctrine of the Trinity* (New York: Charles Scribner's Sons, 1940), pp. 219 ff. I wish I had the space to reproduce them all. Here is my favorite, from a work that was (understandably) published anonymously in 1687. It has been ascribed to the notorious Socinian John Biddle.

> You may add yet more absurdly, that there are three persons who are *severally and each of them true God*, and yet there is but one true God:

this is *an Error* in counting or numbering; which, when stood in, is of all others the most brute and inexcusable, and not to discern it is not to be a Man.

3. Thomas à Kempis, *The Imitation of Christ*, I, 1.

4. The idea of drawing an analogy between a Christian mystery and the wave-particle duality is due to John Polkinghorne (formerly Professor of Mathematical Physics in Cambridge University, and now an Anglican parish priest). See his book of Christian apologetic *The Way the World Is* (Grand Rapids, Mich.: Eerdman's, 1983). Fr. Polkinghorne's position on the wave-particle duality is that quantum field theory *shows* how an electron can be both a wave and a particle (i.e., can be both diffracted on its way to a detector and give up its energy to the detector in a particle-like manner). My impression from reading popular works on quantum mechanics is that not all physicists and philosophers of physics are willing to say this. If there is indeed real disagreement on this point, I expect it is philosophical disagreement: disagreement about what counts as *really* having "shown how something can be." One man's "showing how something can be both *X* and *Y*" is another man's "constructing a formalism that allows you to treat something as both *X* and *Y* without getting into trouble." Fr. Polkinghorne, by the way, has written an excellent popular book on quantum mechanics, *The Quantum World* (New York: Longman, 1984).

5. Some might prefer to say: to an explicit and systematic statement of that which is present implicitly and in an unsystematic form in scripture.

6. I have paid special attention to "Identity" and "Identity — A Reply" in *Logic Matters* (Oxford: Basil Blackwell, 1972), pp. 238–249, and to "Ontological Relativity and Relative Identity" in Milton K. Munitz, ed., *Logic and Ontology* (New York: New York University Press, 1973). On the matter of relative identity and the Trinity, my main sources are *The Virtues* (Cambridge: Cambridge University Press, 1977), pp. 72–81 and Peter Geach and G. E. M. Anscombe, *Three Philosophers* (Oxford: Basil Blackwell, 1963), pp. 118–120. I do not claim that Geach would agree with everything I say about relative identity in this paper, either in the abstract or in relation to the Trinity.

7. This has been attempted at least once before, by A. P. Martinich. See his papers, "Identity and Trinity," *The Journal of Religion* 58 (April 1978), pp. 169–181, and "God, Emperor, and Relative Identity," *Franciscan Studies* 39 (1979): pp. 180–191. The relative-identity treatment of Trinitarian doctrine of the present paper was devised when I was unaware of these papers; the two treatments are thus independent developments of Geach's work. My treatment differs from Martinich's principally in devoting a good deal of attention to the problem of translating English sentences containing the singular terms — at least they have the syntax of singular terms — 'God', 'the Father', 'the Son', and 'the Holy Spirit' into the language of relative identity. I do not accept any of Martinich's supposed examples of non-theological "cases of relative identity."

8. The translation is that of *The Book of Common Prayer* (According to the Use of the Episcopal Church, New York: Seabury Press, 1979), p. 864f. In the Prayer Book of 1662, the *Quicunque Vult* is printed following the Order for

Evening Prayer. The Latin text I have used (on the advice of Eleonore Stump) is that of J. N. D. Kelly, *The Athanasian Creed* (London: Adam & Charles Black, 1964), pp. 17–20. The Prayer Book translation is accurate enough (allowing for changes in English since 1549), although it sometimes departs from the literal sense of the Latin in aid of liturgical euphony. (For example, the title of the present paper, literally translated, would be 'And yet [they are] not three Gods, but there is one God'.) I do not know what Latin text Cranmer — or whoever — used, but it does not seem to have been significantly different from the text in Kelly's book. We may note that in several places the Creed makes use of a grammatical device that English idiom resists: the use of adjective as substantive: 'And yet not three eternals [*aeterni*] but one eternal [*aeternus*]'. "Three eternal *whats*?" the English speaker wants to ask. (After all, they *are* three eternal *personae*.) I take '*tres aeterni*' to be equivalent to '*tres substantiae aeternae*'; I would defend this reading on the basis of the earlier warning about "dividing the substance." It is possible that the earliest users of the Creed — and the Scholastics as well — would dispute my contention that there are, after all, three eternal *personae*, on the ground that this implies that the *aeternitas* of the three *personae* is "divided." I am not sure what that means, however. *I* mean only that there are three *personae* and that it is true of each that *he* is eternal. The eternity ascribed to each person can be "the same," though I am not sure what that is supposed to imply. I certainly want to say that the word 'eternal' is applied to each Person in the same *sense*, if that helps.

9. *The Virtues*, p. 75.

10. Geach cites Ps. 89:26, Ps. 2:7 (it is, of course, rather a controversial reading of these verses to regard them as describing exchanges between two Persons of the Trinity!), and John 17:5. My two citations represent not "intra-Trinitarian" discourse, but unreflective and incidental creedal and liturgical recognition of the personhood (in the ordinary sense) of the Father, the Son, and the Holy Spirit. The sources I cite are not supposed to be authoritative (the personal aspect of 'by himself' has no basis in the Latin Creed, which says only 'acknowledge each Person *singillatim* to be') but merely typical.

11. I have learned something from all of the following papers and books: John Perry, "The Same F," *The Philosophical Review* 79 (1970); Eddy M. Zemach, "In Defense of Relative Identity," *Philosophical Studies* 26 (1974); Nicholas Griffin, *Relative Identity* (Oxford: the Clarendon Press, 1977); John Perry, "Relative Identity and Number," the *Canadian Journal of Philosophy* 8 (1978); Harold W. Noonan, *Objects and Identity* (The Hague: Martinus Nijhoff, 1980); David Wiggins, *Sameness and Substance* (Cambridge: Harvard University Press, 1980); William P. Alston and Jonathan Bennett, "Identity and Cardinality: Geach and Frege," *The Philosophical Review* 93 (1984). But the first drafts of section 3 and 4 of the present paper were written before I had read any of these papers and books, and I have found no reason to revise anything I have said in the light of their content. I do not, of course, mean to imply that what is said in this paper supersedes all previous work on the subject; I mean only that what I say here

about the concept of relative identity and its logic does not seem to me to require any revisions in the light of what I have read in the authors cited above.

12. "To avoid accusations of provincialism, we should mention that the preferred status of English is a matter only of the authors' convenience; the subsequent treatment would apply as well to French, German, or Coptic" (Donald Kalish and Richard Montague, *Logic: Techniques of Formal Reasoning* [New York: Harcourt, Brace & World, 1964], p. 5).

The somewhat unusual employment of English predicates as items in the vocabulary of a formal logic will make our exposition more compact. Thereby we generate "directly" as theorems what Kalish and Montague (p. 9) call 'literal English translations of theorems', and it is these that we shall be primarily interested in. The description of the content of our stock of English predicates that follows in the text is of no formal significance. As long as we restrict our attention to purely formal matters—the statement of formation-rules and rules of inference—we need assume nothing more definite than that we have gone through the class of English predicates and have picked out (somehow) a certain set of them to be our vocabulary items. We must also assume, of course, that each of the chosen predicates has a clear and definite number of "places." And we must assume that our two-place predicates have (somehow) been partitioned into two classes, the "ordinary two-place predicates" and the "relative-identity" predicates (*vide infra*). Exactly how these things are to be done is irrelevant to our statement of the formation- and inference-rules of RI-logic, which presupposes only that we have a stock of predicates and a partition of the two-place predicates.

In the text that follows, there are examples and illustrations that presuppose that particular English predicates (e.g., 'is green') belong to the vocabulary of RI-logic. The specially scrupulous may wish to replace illustrative statements of the type "'x is green $\rightarrow$ x is green" is a theorem of RI-logic' with the corresponding statements of the type 'On the assumption that "is green" belongs to the vocabulary of RI-logic, "x is green $\rightarrow$ x is green" is a theorem of RI-logic'.

13. Two sentences are equivalent in RI-logic if their biconditional is a theorem of RI-logic. In the present section, I shall assume that the reader is familiar with the usual conventions for omitting universal quantifiers.

14. I shall not pretend to be careful about use and mention in the remainder of this paper. The content of general statements about words and symbols will be conveyed impressionistically.

15. See the article "Identity" cited in n. 6.

16. Or 'is the same substance as' or 'is the same *ousia* as'. Geach employs the predicate 'is the same God as' to do essentially the task that I assign to 'is the same being as', as does Martinich in the articles cited in n. 7.

17. I can imagine here someone making the following remarks: "Say that a being that is self-aware, etc., is *rational*. You have said, in essence, that 'person' means 'rational being'. But, then, by what we may call 'the principle of intensional substitution',

x is the same person as $y \leftrightarrow x$ is the same rational being as y.

But, evidently,

> x is the same rational being as y ↔ .x is the same being as y &
> x is rational & y is rational.

It is obvious that 'same being' dominates 'rational':

> x is the same being as y → (x is rational ↔ y is rational).

But from these three sentences there follows by RI-logic:

> x is the same being as y → (x is the same person as z ↔ y is the same person as z).

That is, 'same being' dominates 'same person'."

But I have not said that 'person' means 'rational being'; not if that entails that 'person' and 'rational being' can replace each other in any context *salva extensione*. I have said only that 'x is the same person as x' and 'x is the same being as x & x is rational' can replace each other in any context *salva extensione*.

18. The subdominance of classical identity entails 'x is the same being as y → ($x = x$ ↔ $x = y$)', since '$x = x$' does not contain 'y' and '$x = y$' is like '$x = x$' except for containing a free occurrence of 'y' where '$x = x$' contains a free occurrence of 'x'. '$x = x$' is a theorem of the logic of classical identity. From these two sentences the conditional in the text follows. The biconditional is proved as follows. *Left-to-right*: assume the antecedent; '$x = y$' follows from the antecedent and the just-proved conditional; the other conjunct of the consequent, 'x is the same being as x', follows from '$x = y$' and the antecedent by Substitution of Identicals. *Right-to-left*: assume the antecedent; the consequent follows by Substitution of Identicals.

Suppose 'x is the same being as y' means 'x has causal powers & $x = y$'. If x is the same person as x (i.e., if x is a person), and if x is the same being as y, then it follows by Substitution of Identicals (since '$x = y$' follows from the definition of 'x is the same being as y'), that x is the same person as y.

19. "But doesn't CT3 entail that the number of divine Persons is the same as the number of divine Beings?" No. This apparent paradox will be cleared up in a moment.

20. I call these phrases 'singular terms' because they have the syntax of singular terms: they are noun-phrases that require a singular verb. But I do not mean to imply that they have the *semantic* features that orthodox philosophical semantics ascribes to what it calls "singular terms" (and which orthodox semantics, for all I know, takes to be part of the meaning of 'singular term'). In particular, I do not mean to imply that there is a relation — call it 'reference' or what you will — such that if, e.g., 'God' bears this relation to x and to y, then x is absolutely identical with y. I do not know of a phrase that has the syntactical but not the semantical implications of 'singular term'.

21. And what of the phrase 'the Holy Trinity" itself? I take these words to be short for 'the Father, the Son, and the Holy Spirit', much as 'the Holy Family' is short for 'Jesus, Mary, and Joseph'. One might say, "In this painting, the

Holy Trinity *is* represented as present in the Eucharist." But then one might say, "In this painting, the Holy Family *is* shown entering Jerusalem."

22. I allude, of course, to the *filioque* controversy. As I understand the present state of this controversy, the concern of the Eastern Church is to say nothing that could be taken as a denial of the doctrine that the Father alone is the *fons et origo* of Deity, while the concern of the Western Church (i.e., Rome) is to do justice to Jesus' statements about his relation to the Paraclete, especially John 16:14-15. It is my understanding that many theologians, both Roman Catholic and Orthodox, believe that the formula 'the Holy Spirit proceeds from the Father through the Son' does justice to both of these concerns. But I speak under correction.

23. It is perhaps tendentious to call CT7 and CT8 "conceptual truths," since they together entail that if there are any divine Persons, there are at least three (a thesis shared by Catholic Christians and atheists, but rejected by Arians, Jews, Muslims, and, probably, most agnostics). What I mean by calling CT5-13 "conceptual truths" is this. Trinitarians *allege* that certain relations hold within the Godhead — that is, among the various divine Persons. CT5-13 display certain properties that Trinitarians *say* are essential to these relations. Arians, Jews, and Muslims can agree that CT5-13 display properties that are essential to the Trinitarian concepts of "procession" and "begetting" (just as they can agree that *being square* is an essential component of the concept of a round square), and go on to comment that these concepts are like the concept of a round square in that nothing could possibly fall under them.

24. Since 'x begets $y \leftrightarrow \exists z$ (z proceeds from x through y)' is a logical consequence of CT10 and CT11, it is formally possible to define 'begets' in terms of 'proceeds'. But I doubt whether such a definition would be seen as a fruitful "move" by Christologists or by Trinitarian theologians whose concerns are wider than the logical issues addressed in the present paper.

25. CT12 and 13 are redundant; they can be deduced from CT8-11.

26. That is, God is an "individual substance of a rational nature"; (5) is not meant to imply that God is a *prosopon* or an *hypostasis*.

27. The formal translations of the following English sentences are also deducible from (1) through (3) and CT1-13: 'The Father is the same being as the Son'; 'The Father is the same being as the Holy Spirit'; 'The Son is the same being as the Holy Spirit'; 'God is the same person as the Holy Spirit'; 'God is the same being as the Son'; 'God is the same being as the Holy Spirit'; 'The Father is not the same person as the Holy Spirit'; 'The Son is not the same person as the Holy Spirit'.

28. The "wide-scope" version of (8) would be accepted by Catholic Christians, Arians, Jews, Muslims, and atheists. The "narrow-scope" version would be accepted by Catholic Christians alone.

29. S is logically somewhat redundant. Given (1), CT1, CT2, CT4, and CT6-11, one can prove (2), (3), CT3, CT5, CT12, and CT13.

30. This sentence will "come out true" in the sense that its symbolic translation is deducible from S and the proposition that some divine Person is unincarnate: ' $\exists x$ (Dx & ~$\exists y$ (y is a human being & $\underline{P}xy$))'.

31. I.e., ' $\exists x(Gx$ & $Sx)$' and '~$\exists x(Fx$ & $Sx)$' are deducible from S.

32. 'Normal' should not be confused with 'ordinary'.

33. As the Father is, so also are the Son and the Holy Spirit.

34. I say "primarily" because the sharing of the predicate 'is Lord' equally by the Persons is asserted in the section of the Creed that is introduced by these words; and this predicate expresses a relational attribute of God.

35. A part of this paper was read at the December, 1985 meeting of the Society of Christian Philosophers. The commentator was Eleonore Stump. An overlapping part was read at the University of Notre Dame, at the conference on which this book is based. The commentator was Keith Yandell. The two commentators have had considerable influence on the final form of this paper. Michael Detlefsen made extremely valuable comments on section 3. He is, of course, not responsible for the confusions that remain — all the more so because I have imprudently resisted some of his criticisms.

Eschatological Pragmatism

JAMES ROSS

1. INTRODUCTION

What is the truth maker for Christian faith in the Second Coming, the final resurrection, judgment, heaven and hell? Is it the reality to come? Not in the way many suppose. For one thing, a belief's 'being so' does not often consist in some part-by-part match with reality. For another, there are special features of the historical elements of the faith (both backward and forward looking) that suggest that truth, in these matters, consists in cognitive consonance between belief *in via* and cognition in the end.[1]

Truth is rightness of understanding, measurable by the mind alone. In these cases, the right way of understanding (the faith) is the way that is cognitively consonant with how the last things will be experienced. In other cases, there are other measures of "right understanding."

There are two special features of Christian faith in "the last things" that suggest that " 'being so' consists in *cognitive consonance*, the fulfillment of our expectations." The two factors are the *analogia fidei* and "the development of doctrine," as theologians call them.[2] First, what the formulated faith means is determined at a *remove* from the believer. It is determined by the faith of the church, and that by the scripture, which in turn, interprets God's saving acts, some of which continue through to the end of the world, and are thus not completed yet, and others of which are yet to come, like the last things. Second, how the faith is understood by the church and individuals varies with time. Contrast a fourth-century Byzantine understanding of universal kingship and fatherhood with what we would think now; they would never have imagined universal kingship in a world without kings.[3] And it has to work out that every believer, united in faith with the church, no matter at what time he lives, has the truth. That means, too, that every later community of faith has no *less* authority in proclaiming and interpreting the faith than the earliest communities after the deaths of the apostles.

Both features can be accounted for. First, the faith is made true (as from an efficient cause) by being God's word. And second, its 'being true' *is* its being-found-fulfilled by each who holds it, regardless of their differences of historical position (in the development of faith). Analogously to "for some things 'being so' is 'seeming so'," for the eschatological faith, "being so" (now) is "being found to be fulfilled" (later). That, of course, is not what the truth of future contingents, generally, consists in. And considered as a formal cause, the truthmaker of faith *in via* is the consonant cognition of the believer at the Second Coming.

I call this "eschatological pragmatism" because it is truth by fulfillment of human thoughts, without a match-up part-by-part between a thought, ideally decomposed into its ultimate meaning units, and a compliant reality, ideally decomposed into its ultimate ontological parts, with some "final fit" (picturing?) by which the compliant reality makes the conforming belief true.

Even if you could carry that decomposition out in general to provide a correspondence account of truth (which I doubt), it would not do for the faith, because of the these two factors. Truth of faith is the *rightness of thinking that achieves fulfillment of expectation in the life to come.* Fulfillment of faith consists in each believer's finding that things are "as he expected," though he could never have imagined that! More simply, "being so" is "being as expected." It is cognitive consonance.

That is oversimplified, of course, but it indicates the elements of the problem and the shape of the solution I am considering.

Where truth does require a compliant reality, as the faith does, the reality may not be what makes the belief true.[4] That is a far more general feature of truth than has yet been explained. The fact that one and the same reality is compliant with developing faith may be puzzling and require explanation, but so does the fact that any contingent truth conforms to an infinity of incompossible situations.

My wondering what is the truth maker for what we believe and await in the "last things" and what their "being so" consists in, is thus, (1) *partly* because of the transcendent determinacy of the contingent that allows ontologically incompatible realities to be compliant realities for the same truth; (2) partly because of the peculiarity of future contingents in general, where present truth is supposed to be explained by a not-yet, a future, reality to which it "corresponds," when I cannot find any basis for thinking a correspondence analysis of truth will succeed; partly (3) because of the completability of historical events where "what happened" is "spread out" over time until its "identifying" effects occur (so again, reality seems not to have caught up with the truth);[5] and (4) partly because the reality to come (often thought to be the truth conditions) is *unimaginable*.[6]

I have already mentioned (5) the illusions in standard correspondence theories as a contributor to this puzzlement. The distinctive flavor of the eschatological faith is that a person's faith is at "the third interpretive remove" from God's saving acts and that the content of the faith develops culturally and historically. Those factors are (6) *analogia fidei*, and (7) the development of doctrine.

2. ANALOGIA FIDEI

The *analogia fidei* is the dependence of the content of the individual's faith on the faith of the church, and that, in turn, on the scripture, and that, in turn on the saving acts of God. The four-element proportionality (my faith: faith of the church; Scripture: God's saving acts) is like Plato's divided line. The left half (A:B) depends in being and content on the right half (C:D); and the same holds within each segment-pair. Cognition goes from left to right; authentication, content, and being goes from right to left. And the (C:D) relation is, analogously, the same as that between the two halves, A:B and C:D. Everything to the left of "God's saving acts" is an interpretation. It seems clear why it is called "*analogia fidei*" by some theologians including, prominently, Karl Barth. The proportionality expresses the interlocked dependence of interpretation in the one direction and of reality contained as meaning in the other. Individual faith is at "a third interpretive remove" from the divine acts, a hermeneutical "distance."

Yet *shared* individual faith is the basis for the authority to *proclaim* this faith, as God's word, in every generation. There is a linguistic analogy in the proportionality for another reason, too: The words for the relations between segments, when they have the same name, "depends on" or "interprets," and others, differ in meaning, because they are dominated by their contexts.[7]

3. DEVELOPMENT OF DOCTRINE

Besides, what the church believes, while not increased by further revelation, develops through the Holy Spirit. The faith in the things to come, like other elements, develops toward the faith of the Communion of Saints at the Second Coming, "the fullness of truth" that the Second

Vatican Council says the Holy Spirit is "leading the Church to believe." Since development cannot come by addition, it must come by realization and appreciation, by changed cultural perspectives, changed imagery and associations, sometimes even by more nourishing secular philosophy, literature, science, and art. In any case, the faith develops by understanding. It is unpacked, reformulated, and reflected. I hope I need not argue that point. It is a problem-making premise of this paper.

The faith develops from the initial realities in history, as recorded in scripture, as understood in the church, and believed by the faithful. What significance the scripture *actually* attributes to certain events is itself something *settled by the religious experience of the church*. So the faith of the church, the proclaimed faith, is no less authoritative as to the word of God than was the teaching of the Apostles themselves.[8] It is secondary, of course, because interpretive; but it is certain, and so, both authoritative and final.

There is a last stage, the belief of the Communion of Saints at the Second Coming, the fullness of truth, when we are no longer describing realities that are only partially completed and describing what God has done from a partial record (that requires interpretation) that we are reading "in the midst" of what it describes (interprets). That cognition of the faithful is the truth maker, the compliant "reality" for all that went before.

When we in imagination peer into a future so long that millenia are like seconds, we can guess that immense changes in our understanding of the faith, like those brought by the advent of Platonism, and then the advent of Aristotelianism, of modern science, will flip by like pages in a telephone book. Those notions come and go (and sometimes, remain far after their "scientific" status has waned) as part of our understanding of the scriptural faith. The faith will develop with page after page of human secular learning and religious understanding. (With advances of holography, who knows what understanding of "bodily presence" will be achieved.) Yet all the faith of all who hold the word of God, no matter at what time, must be true, yet develop to a fullness of truth.

We cannot claim that beliefs that differ so much will "correspond" by one and the same "double decomposition" and "final fit" to the one reality to come. That seems a mere hope, kept alive by our failure to deliver a true decomposition for any significant truths whatever,[9] and thus, by our not having to apply a worked-out correspondence account to *these* peculiar circumstances. We need another look at what is true, what makes it true, and what being true consists in, with lively attention to the prospect that there may be varieties of each.

For the eschatological faith, I adapt pragmatic truth making, (which, I think, also applies well for parts of physical science). This is truth making by (a) an authenticating belief-producing and refining process (revelation, scripture, tradition, and proclamation), (b) aimed at a final output, the knowledge of the Communion of Saints at the Second Coming (like the beliefs of the ideal ultimate community of scientists, the "net" all of observable reality, roughly as conceived by C. S. Peirce), with 'being true' *in via* consisting in the fulfillment, then, of all expectations, in accord with scripture and the faith of the church, from the earliest times to the last.[10]

So, a person's understanding the linguistic meaning of the proclaimed faith, as it is situated scripturally and used religiously in his time, is enough for knowledge of the world to come, even for the least literate. (Such a threshold grasp is available even for the mysteries.) Other people have more elaborate understandings of the faith that need differing fulfillments from the same reality. The same reality can produce a variety of cognitive states in differently thinking observers, e.g., a forest fire to a primitive human, to a forest ranger, to a physicist. Where truth is fulfillment of prior cognitive states by later ones, enormously different expectations can be satisfied by the same event.

Still, why call this pragmatism? A reality is to come, a reality that does not acquire its character from what we believe about it, but is instead caused by the same cause that produces our belief, and causes the cognitions that satisfy our beliefs. But that reality is not the *cause*, either efficient or formal, of the truth of *our* belief; and "being true" does not consist in some single match-up with parts or components of that reality, but with multiple cognitive *effects* of that reality, multiple fulfillments of belief.[11]

A true belief can be time and culture bound in imagery (like a Greek Orthodox conception of fathership and kingship), or marked with emphases caused by a dispute that is later non-functioning (versions of atonement), or marked by Platonism, Aristotelianism, or other conceptual schemes that wither, yet generate successor beliefs expressed, sometimes in the same words ("For his soul and all the souls of the faithful departed . . . ") but understood without those angularities and in a culturally less restricted context, like the understandings of the universal kingship of Christ, or the changing conceptions of the soul. In other words, though a third-century Roman Christian's belief about the kingdom of Christ on earth might appear to a fortieth-century Christian to differ from a twentieth-century Christian, especially in its imagery of kingship and power, each, at the parousia, will "find his faith fulfilled," each finding that "This is just what I expected," and, as I said, also beyond all expectation. (We all have had experiences of "Oh wow! I was right!" that are a fulfillment of expectancy, yet not remotely to be analyzed as a simple match of earlier words to features of facts.)

This is pragmatism because truth is fulfillment of expectation, a kind of harmony among ordered cognitive states, not some other kind of "match-up" with reality. The same reality can "match-up" with the same words, differently understood, or even differing words, by fulfilling the whole conviction of the believer, while even disclosing something infinitely more. Having the truth for this purpose is a successful expectation of later experience.

This is a different sense of 'true', from, say, "It is true that we are humans," because crucial elements of what we *mean* by "being so" are different.[12] It is also clear that nothing can be true, as fulfillment of cognitive expectations, unless there are things true in other ways: the fulfilling cognitive states have to root, eventually, in compliant realities, where conformity of cognition and compliance of reality have a different analysis. Pragmatic truth of this kind cannot be a basic kind of truth.

4. WHY NOT CORRESPONDENCE?

My objection to a correspondence account of the prophetic faith begins with my noting the historical indeterminacy of truth-making realities that are supposed to have "happened" but are not "completed" (redemption and sanctification of the earth) — and so, we lack a determinate reality as truth maker, when we already have the truth. Next, I doubt that truths about the future are made true by "backward" causation from the realities that have not happened yet, or that the realities to come somehow timelessly are (so as to do that truth making without "backward" causation).[13]

Far more serious is that whatever "final fit" might explain truth by correspondence would have to be too "tight" to allow the faith from *all* times to "fit" the final reality. If it were loose enough to allow semantically *opposed* experiences ("*extra ecclesia nulla salus*") to express the truth, it would be too *weak* to be the universal truth-making relation. And if it did *now* allow that, it would conflict with doctrinal history.[14] Still, that is a warning on the label. The poison inside correspondence "theory" is the sensible sounding but actually incoherent project, as understood in our time, of a double decomposition (of truth-bearer and compliant reality) and a "final fit," the correspondence, by which the one becomes the scale-model or replica of the other. The relation of "final fit" cannot be explained without invoking the notion of truth.

Briefly, the double decomposition of truth-bearer and compliant reality into their genuine ultimate parts is impossible; because there are none. False images of language suppose there is some ultimate semantic decomposition and also treat units of *language* as the primary truth-bearers. From logical atomism onward, the myth hangs about that there is an ultimate *ontological* decomposition of realities (facts), and that truth and reality, ultimately decomposed, "fit" or are, somehow, the same; that the semantic assembly is, somehow, "the same" as the real assembly. Even if there were parallel ultimate decompositions, there is no describable "final fit" (say picturing, for example) to make a "match-up," a correspondence, that we would see to be truth making. You need the notion of "truth" to get a strong enough characterization of "matching" for there to be any particular reason to regard *that* as what truth consists in.

The whole idea that truth is mental, or semantic, *replication* is misleading. Not all truth can be by replication because that notion, itself, involves the idea of truth. Besides, a contingent truth can have incompos-sible compliant realities, an infinity of them; it replicates one as well as another (if it replicates any at all), and so, to replicate what is, it must replicate an infinity of what is not. That cannot be the basic idea involved in truth. Moreover, the reality that really does constitute the *p*-out-of-quotes for any contingent '*p*' is only schematically picked out by '*p*' (where I let '*p*' be any truth-bearer, statement, judgment, thought, belief, etc.) We need to look at that point more closely. For now, notice that right understanding, say of what you are doing, is *not* right *replication* (representation); it is much more a matter of "right focus" (where what *counts* as right focus depends on the form of understanding and its uses).

5. TRANSCENDANT DETERMINACY

It takes a lakeful of reality for a drop of contingent truth. So, also, for natural necessities. A contingent situation needs "accidental" qualities, an infinity of them, not contained in a true belief that it will occur, overflowing the meaning of what is said, no matter what is said. That is so for all contingencies: the reality required to make what we say true is infinitely more determinate than anything we can say, no matter how definite we try to be, or whether we talk forever.

That is the transcendent determinacy of reality[15] that more that has to be so than we can ever say, in order for anything we say to be so. "John is here" can be satisfied by his being in one chair, or another, right there, an inch away, etc. No amount of refinement will reduce the indeterminacy below infinity. Yet no reality that is not infinitely determinate (but not necessarily determinate in every respect) can ever comply with a contingent truth.

That also means that *incompossible* realities would comply with any contingent truth.[16] If the realities are the truth makers, then any one of an infinity of incompossible ones would do for any contingent truth. There seems to be no special attachment of what is true by content to what is so. It could have been true when something else was so because the truth-bearer would "fit" with any of them, so it does not by semantic *content* "pick out" the actual reality, from all the others, with which it conforms. (There are more situations that do not obtain to which the truth conforms than the single actual one.) Something quite different from "fit" has to be added to semantics or other scale modeling to get truth; namely, *reference*. The way truth picks out the actual reality is by the chain of indexicality (of experience); without the chain of reference it would "fit" as well with an infinity of incompatibles. That tells us that "fit" does not explain truth.

What kind of "fit" would both allow an infinity of incompatible realities to satisfy it, and yet allow the truth bearer to pick out the one and only reality that obtains? None. If a shoe fits a lot of different feet, it cannot by fit alone pick out the very foot that will wear it. So "final fit" fails as to what *constitutes* truth. It is the same thing with a single photograph. It looks as much like an infinity of other people as you. It gets to be *your* picture by a chain of causation and reference, *not* by the excellence of the resemblance.[17]

The development of faith needs a reality that satisfies a vast number of differing expectations. Two things provide for that. First there is no unique "perfect fit," between true thought and compliant reality. A lot of feet can wear the same shoe. Second, the compliant reality is, in this case, a reality *perceived*; experience is moulded by expectation and reshaped as it continues.

6. TRUTH IS ANALOGOUS

Influenced by the Tarski formula, " '*p*' iff *p*," philosophers think a statement is true just in case things are as it says, or are not, as it says they are not, (to adapt Aristotle), and that is all there is to it. So (1) they do not remark that there is a *family* of uses of "is true" that satisfy " '*p*' iff *p*," but differ in the explanatory condition, perhaps even in meaning-relevant conditions, that express the *truth-making* relation. Nor (2) do they notice there are differing conditions of "being so," for different kinds of thinking, e.g., logical, mathematical, future contingent counterfactual, and others, too; *p*-out-of-quotes may be as diverse as rules of chess, mathematical truths, logical abstraction, conventions, natural necessities, simple "facts," and more. (3) It also eludes them that the truth-making relation may *not* hold between '*p*' in quotes, the truth-bearer (nowadays often mistaken by Davidson, Dummett, and Wiggins, for example, for a sentence or other linguistic entity) and *p*-out-of-quotes, the compliant reality.

There are truth-making relations *other* than some kind of *match* between the truth-bearer (judgment, thought, belief, statement) and its *compliant reality* (the designated reality, see definition below). There are *alien* truth makers. In fact, many philosopher-theologians, who are systematically committed to saying that, are contributors to this volume.

Turn from the notion of truth Tarski needed for logical purposes to Anselm: "truth is rightness of understanding perceptible to the mind alone" (*De Veritate*). What *is* right understanding depends on what sort of thinking is going on, e.g., perception, mathematics, topology, card playing, empirical science. *Sometimes* thinking that achieves a certain "fit" between our expression of thought sententially, or in another medium, and a designated reality (some reality picked by reference as well as sense) is right thinking. *Sometimes*, thinking in such a way that the thinking itself provides the complete certification of what is to be said is right thinking. Sometimes there are still other conditions for right thinking. Right thinking, in the way of understanding (as against willing), *is* truth. Truth is a feature of judgmental thought, and only derivatively of anything else. Without thought, there is no truth as was recognized by, among others, Aquinas and Frege.

What *is* rightness of understanding depends on what we are thinking about and the uses of thought. A certain disposition of chess pieces is to be regarded as "check"; a certain hand of cards as a "straight"; a certain baseball situation as an "out"; those are distinct conditions for right understanding of situations. Far more subtle are the conditions for understanding human situations of love, deception, support, abandonment, faith, and comprehension. Distinct, again, are the conditions of right understanding (right conception and judgment) for doing arithmetic, proving number-theoretic theorems, reading a musical score, weighing the force of circumstantial evidence, discovering analogies, making deep metaphors.

It is hard to say whether life is one thing for all living things. I think it certainly is not, others disagree. Far less hard, it seems to me, is it to see and say that rightness of understanding (in the judgmental, assetoric modes) is *not* one thing but a family of things, bearing marked resemblances in the predicate appropriate (true, false, erroneous, mistaken, correct, right, wrong, etc.). The different senses of "rightness of understanding" are not like "painted," applied to a painting and to the trim of a house; they are more like "collected," applied to debts and donations, shading off to be like "enjoyed," applied to classical music and a long life. "Is true" is not univocal; there are distinct families in which " '*p*' iff *p*" holds, for example, earned and inherited truth,[18] and an "extreme" and most important case, inflationary truth (to be discussed below).

If there are different kinds of truth-makers, there may be different *meanings* of "truth," or "right understanding"—depending on whether the distinct truth-making conditions form part of what we *mean*, analogously to whether the "fourth condition" for "knowing" is "meaning-relevant." There certainly are different kinds of truth depending on what "*p*-out-of-quotes," the compliant "reality" is. If "*p*-out-of-quotes" is a *product* of right understanding, as well as a content, that is quite a different reality from the contents of our contingent judgments. Purely formal truth, for example, is only analogous to contingent truth, as I will show. In any case, we have to take another look at truth makers and truth-bearers and what "being so" consists in.

The condition that explains a statement's (or other truth-bearer's) having a compliant reality varies with the area of discourse. The condition that is the 'being so' also varies with our thinking, and, of course, with the analogy of being (*analogia entis*).[19] No single analysis of "is true" will do for science, law, mathematics, logic, or, *a fortiori*, for theology, and certainly not one for all parts of all; not, that is, if an *explanatory* objective is in view. All the same, analogous definitions, "truth is rightness of understanding perceptible to the understanding alone" (Anselm) or "*veritas est adequatio mentis et rei*" (Aquinas), whose meanings adjust to the context, can be very useful, as was Aristotle's definition of life as self-movement which he applied to souls and to God. For instance, "agreement of mind and reality" can be applied to mathematical truths by someone who does not think there is a truth-making world of mathematical objects, or even an independent mathematical reality; "reality" adjusts in meaning to the belief-context. Such definitions are, as I said, linguistically analogous; their value is measured, in part, by their adaptability to what we can see to be similar (and what some, unfortunately, find to be the same). Further, they focus what might otherwise appear to be *unrelated* things. There really is a range of right understanding, measurable by the mind alone, that is truth.

There are a variety of truth *makers*. For example:

(a) Truth by *efficacious utterance* (within a behavior network)
"I promise."
"I bid two dollars."
"I find for the defendant,"

(b) Truth by *rule-bound judgment*
"That's a winning hand."
"Whether a heifer is a cow is not a matter of fact." (but of law in law!)
$$x^2y^2 = z^2$$

(c) Truth by *provenance* (by guarantee from the method of production) e.g., *legislation* "the standard meter is the length that equals 1650763.73 wavelengths in a vacuum of the radiation corresponding to the transition between the levels 2p10 and 5d5 of the krypton-86 atom."

(d) Truth by *authentication*: some feature of the *method* (or form) of production *excludes* disconformity or failure of conformity (e.g., formal truths and revelation) between the "objects" and "situations" it countenances and the judgments (or statements) it authorizes: geometry, logic. This does *not* have to include only *pure* formal truths.

(e) Truth by linguistic (or conceptual) *meaning relations*, what were traditionally called analytic truths, "Bachelors are unmarried," "whales are mammals." But what of "warm blooded animals have hearts," "creatures with hearts have kidneys"? Inclusions, conceptual and linguistic, are often mistaken for *originating* devices, when they are only *storage* devices for truth.

(f) Truth by *logical* and *pragmatic* relations, "Some of my beliefs are false," "Not everything I think is false," "If I err, I am."

Granting that those are distinct truth makers, they are only distinct truth producers. That does not show that *truth* does not consist in one and the same thing. The way to do that, I think, is to show that rightness of understanding is quite different for two *very* important ranges of truth: the natural necessities and formal truths.

6a. ALIEN TRUTH MAKERS

Can anything really be made true by something other than what it states to be so (the designated reality)? You would naturally think not. How could "there are philosophers in Ann Arbor" be *made true* by anything other than there being philosophers in Ann Arbor?

Yet nearly everyone, from Plato through medieval divine exemplarists, Kantian apriorists, positivist conventionalists, and modern modal actualists, explicitly holds the opposite: that a proposition, expressed sententially, can and often is made true (or false) by something quite other than what it says is so. Sometimes relations of linguistic meaning, conceptual inclusion, or logical construction are said to be truth makers. And sometimes the truth maker is said to be *exemplification* or instantiation of *abstract objects* (for some modal actualists) or divine ideas. I do not like that proposal, though it clearly illustrates the prevalance of appeal to alien truth makers.

The oddity of some of the truth makers alleged is no more apparent, at first, than the oddity of thinking truth is a feature of sentences, (linguistic entities), or even of languages, or talking as if there might be truths even if there were no minds. It takes a while before the incoherence is obvious.

Designated Reality. Taking linguistic, contextual, speaker-meaning, and other meaning-determinates into account, when you say "It is cold today," "Numbers are of many kinds," "Some things are really necessary," "Humans are necessarily living," and so forth, what has to be so for what you say to be true, as far as it is determined by what you mean, is the designated reality for your statement. It is the *p*-out-of-quotes that has to be for '*p*' in-quotes to be true.

In general true statements (or whatever truth-bearers you privilege) are not made true by their *designated* realities, not straightforwardly at least. The most typical and influential philosophical theories commit themselves to that. And it is an important feature of truth, especially for formal truths.[20]

Dismissing Revisionism. I reject "revisionist" accounts of what we mean, accounts that tell us we really mean something quite different from what we *think* we mean, or that we are talking *about* something quite different from what we thought we were talking about. They are just attempts to force the identity of truth maker and compliant reality. For example, suppose a dedicated counterpart theorist says the *real* designated reality for "I might have gone to Canada yesterday" is "A counterpart of mine goes to the Canada-counterpart, at the yesterday-counterpart, at the (relatively) nearest possible world" (e.g., David Lewis).

Whatever one thinks of counterpart theory, to tell me that is what I meant is just pushy. Yet even Frege seems to have sinned that way when he said "Whales are mammals" is not about whales but about the concepts.

Plenty say that "humans are animals" is made true by the linguistic meaning-inclusion of the terms, but fewer, that what one means when saying 'humans are animals' is that the ideas are inclusive, though some positivists, like A. J. Ayer, went that far.

"Inclusion" explanations of necessary truth, whether linguistic or conceptual inclusions (whether Kantian, Humean, or Leibnizian), all appeal to alien truth makers (that is, a truth maker that is not the designated reality). Platonist and neoplatonic participation accounts of truth and predication also postulate outside truth makers, though they usually go on to explain that the truth maker is *really* the ontological constituent of what we have said. That is a kind of ontological realism, where we are being told what are the real constituents of common sense things. That is not revisionism. We still have to be careful, though. If I am talking about tables and tables are really only arrangements of atoms, what I am talking about may be only arrangements of atoms, but I am not "really" talking about arrangements of atoms only. So, too, for all the "real constitution of things" ontologies; the designated reality may be only intentionally distinct from the ontological constitution, if the ontology is right, but it is what I refer to and mean, not the constituents, even if they are the truth maker (which, of course, I doubt).

6b. ALIEN TRUTH MAKERS FOR ETERNAL TRUTHS

What about the truth maker for eternal and necessary truths about created natures, like "humans are mortals" when there are no humans? That was debated vigorously from about 1250 to 1375, with a later flareup from about 1450 to 1600, just before Descartes' "king's laws" account (1630). The standard earlier answers appealed to outside truth makers, *really* alien ones, usually relations among the divine exemplar ideas. I say they were *really, extremely*, alien because they are not *constituents* of the natural necessities.[21] Descartes' "kings laws" account is also an alien truth maker, of course: the divine will.

A similar device is virtually universal among present-day modal semanticists. "Lincoln lived in the middle nineteenth century" has as truth maker that, *inter alia*, the individual essence, Lincolneity, (or the abstract 'human', contracted by haecceity, for others) was exemplified in the nineteenth century. If that is what makes the statement true, it is certainly not what the speaker states. It is not the designated reality.

Maybe they intend to tell us this is the real constitution of the designated reality. Even so, we have, again, a very broad commitment that what makes a truth-bearer (proposition, statement, thought, judgment, even sentence) true is not its designated reality, even if they were right about the metaphysical constitution of the designated reality, (and even if they think these are cases of real and necessary identities).

In general, I think philosophers have correctly noticed that earned truth is typically explained by something different (at the very least intentionally, and typically, as with exemplarists and analyticity defenders, different in real being) from what is stated. Earned truth is typically explained with alien truth makers! (Obviously, inherited truth is always acquired from something other than what is stated.)

6c. THE CASE OF FORMAL TRUTH

The basic idea of alien truth makers is irresistible for formal truths, like pure logic, and discloses that there is inflationary truth: a certain kind of understanding, done the right way, achieves truth, even though there is no independent reality for it to be true-of; and the "being so" of such understanding consists in its complete verification (satisfaction) by the designata of such thinking, and by the exclusion (by the method of understanding) of disconfirmation in any real situation whatever. The understanding that achieves the truth supplies the designata for the naming expressions.

The conforming objects have objective intensionality (intentional being that is not belief dependent) because of what is understood of them, and they completely confirm everything the activity "authorizes" to be thought, and nothing else (like a material thing, say, or an object from a different activity) can ever disconfirm or disconform with something authorized by the activity (a kind of understanding). Formal truth is produced the way money is, by an activity (like owing, having, transferring, and, crucially, borrowing and lending). The activities in this case are kinds of understanding. I say that the formal objects (the designata of general expressions, for example, of mathematics or geometry) are *entia rationis*.

The crucial metaphysical option facing us is to decide *whether* such objects are a product of the mirror-reflective understanding *we* have of such pure formalities, and, thus, conceptual figments, or to allow that divine formal understanding, which is formal truth, has such projected objects, too. At first, because of the beauty of the objects I thought it appropriate to say they are objective and universal *entia rationis*, necessary consequences of God's understanding. Now, I think they are products of our secondhand understanding. For God's mathematical and formal understanding there need be no such object which, after all, are at most a *consequence* of truth.

I am not, of course, denying the objectivity of the pure formal objects, or suggesting mere conventionalism or mere conceptualism. I am talking about *another kind of real truth, the kind where being is a consequence of truth,* which is why we call the objects "*entia rationis.*" We are definitely able to create systems of such objects.[22]

For now, drawing on Descartes, Husserl, Frege, and others, let me say that a *formal object* (a) cannot be realized in space-time, (b) has the features it has independently of any belief we have about it, (c) has all its features essentially, (d) yet cannot be except as an object of understanding (thus, Godel's argument for the existence of God), (e) and has being in consequence of truth (and not vice versa, as is the case with non-intentional things), (f) is not transcendentally determinate (i.e., has no reality that overflows, by being logically independent, whatever can be said of it), and (g) may be explanatory (in part) of causal and structural situations involving real things.[23]

Formal objects, *entia rationis*, as far as their attributes and existence go, are as independent of what we believe about them as are *entia realia*, as Descartes observed when denying numbers really exist. "Independence of what we believe about it" is not the mark of reality, only objectivity. You may wonder how it can be true that such objects are logically the product of understanding and, nevertheless, independent of our beliefs. That is the clue to objective intentionality.

In brief, we have formal truth, truth by *inflation*, when we understand by a systematic abstraction that specifies *all* the features of its formal objects, so that whatever so authorized (e.g., statements, propositions, etc.) is positively and wholly satisfied by the objects designated (under any conditions whatever), and when no real thing whatever can disconfirm anything authorized by the form of understanding. Thus the authorized statements, the truths, are fully verified by their designata and irrefutable by anything else. The result is inflationary truth. You only have to know how to think that way to have all the truth you want. Moreover, there is no limit to the number of forms of understanding that have that structure.

We can *invent* abstractions (e.g., the propositional calculus) that have objects (e.g., atomic propositions, and molecular ones), all of whose features are determined by the system of understanding, and we can, as in that case, determine the abstraction *itself* to have certain formal features (e.g.) consistency, completeness, provable consistency and completeness, etc.). That should make it obvious that, while there are such "objects," for example, propositions, as *entis rationis*, as objects of the abstraction interpreted designatively and extensionally (as we usually do), there are no such eternal and necessary objects, anymore than there are real Euclidean scalene triangles. Furthermore, though the truths of such systems are necessary truths (i.e., positively satisfied by the objects under any conditions of real being whatever, and never disconfirmed by real things or by statements authorized by the system), we *made* them. We can *make* necessary truths, even ones with designating terms and, so, objects!

That tells us that to say such objects exist, or that there *are* such objects, is, theoretically, to say something about the success of such an abstractive understanding. And to speak existentially *within* a system, to settle which, for instance, is the first prime larger than a million, is theoretically, to say something about the extent of the definite commitments of the form of understanding.

The same, for all we know at the moment, may not be true of God's mathematical understanding; *we* may have to understand arithmetic and set theory *designatively*, as having objects of which the truths are true. God's understanding may, however, be a single comprehension of the forms for multiplicity of being, without any objects at all. So we do not need divine ideas to *be* the numbers to account for the eternal and necessary truth of pure mathematics. We need only divine understanding of the forms for multiplicity of being, to account for the *eternal* necessary truth of mathematics.

If I am even nearly right, and I think the case is far stronger than mere approximation, about inflationary truths whose objects are *entia rationis*, there is more than one kind of 'being so'. Not just more than one way of producing truths, but more than one kind of thing that being true consists in, still within the general family where "being true is being so." Rightness of understanding is proportionate to what is to be understood. Truth is not all of a piece, any more than being is. So it is not surprising that I should consider 'being true' for the eschatological faith (indeed, the faith in large part) to consist in a fulfillment of earlier cognitive states by later ones, produced by God.

7. UNIMAGINABILITY

Lastly, let us look at the unimaginability of the eschaton. Does that make any difference? I do not think the unimaginability of what will actually happen, as it happens, has anything to do with whether our belief is true, or, more importantly, with whether we understand what we believe, or know what we believe.

We do not have to have cinematic previews to expect the last judgment. We do not even have to imagine things compatibly with other believers. We can substitute the image of a vulture (as did Brother Antoninus in a poem) for that of a shepherd in our imagining.

The theologians, like Brian Hebblethwaite, who want to make up new truth-conditions, usually far outside what we normally understand by our beliefs, in order for them "to come out true" (because they cannot think of any that could possibly make them true in their natural meanings), and others, like Don Cupitt, who declare that on no analysis of truth-conditions for what we mean can such beliefs come out true (and so they must be regarded as false but anthropologically vindicated by their social and historical utility and fertility), are all acting beside the point. They think our imaginings, and even our conceptual analyses, have to line up photographically with the future and our beliefs have to come apart into truth-conditions that are like blueprints for the things to come. They have an unanalysed notion of "realism" for our expectations that has all the defects Goodman[24] pointed out in common talk about art. What is it for our present imaginings and believing to *resemble* the things to come? Our beliefs, our expectations subsist in the media of words, images, and feelings, (basically presented by scriptures, traditional and current religious awareness in the believing community) which, taken as representations are 'realistic' just to the extent that they are easily found fulfilled by the last things. Realism in the medium of thought is not a structural relation to the world, but a relation to the successor understanding. Realism, as Goodman said about art, is a matter of ease of access.

Our imaginings, guided by scripture, liturgy, prayer (*lex orandi, lex credendi*), etc., are the medium for our expectations. We can, of course, make up movie sequences for the end of the world; but we can have no confidence in their depictive qualities when they go beyond the scripture; and we can be sure they leave less room for nourishment of the understanding than the fragmentary images to be found in scripture, the fathers, the liturgy, and music.

To know what we mean and to know that it is true, we do not, except trivially, need to know truth-conditions or conditions of empirically justified assertion for such claims. We do not even have to have a generalized skill for assessing such claims. We can have expectations that are to be fulfilled, perhaps quite detailed ones, formed by religious interactions in a praying community,that we cannot express.

"That's not what I imagined at all" is compatible with one's beliefs' coming true. One may know, even, what will happen when one cannot say more about what one means than the plain meaning, adjusted to scriptural and religious contexts, and even when one pictures it "all wrong." What two believers hold in common may be imagined by each incompatibly with the other and both differently from the way things happen, yet each may find that what he thought was so.

We cannot go "outside" the faith to fix either the reference of the words or the conditions for the reality.[25] There is no access to the revealed realities outside their scriptural traces and the church's understanding through scripture. What believers, in unity of faith, thought would happen does, and they recognize it, without there having to be any match, beyond the *cognitive condition of fulfillment.*

The point of my discussing alien truth makers, and mentioning the diversity of what being true consists in, is to motivate our seeing that thoughts can be true without there having to be some match-up of semantic assembly, or of other thought-assembly, with the ontological constitution of the designated reality. For a very important class of thoughts truth consists in our having experience as one would expect. That seems to me to be an easy and obvious understanding of what the truth of the faith about the last things consists in.

Terrence Penelhum has asked why the same analysis would not apply to the developing faith about the *originating* revelatory and salvific events. On reflection, I think that may be so too: The faith of each believer that God spoke to Moses is true exactly in that his understanding of what *did* happen (to be acquired in the Beatific Vision) will fulfill his "expectations" (in unity with the church) as to what did happen. The same holds for "The son of God became man," but not for "Jesus existed and died." Expectations are cognitive anticipations of later cognitive states; they do not have to stand in the *same order* as the events. Maybe this will serve as a general account of the claim that the faith of believers in unity with the church is true, regardless of their epoch and culture.[26]

NOTES

1. Terrence Penelhum, February, 1986, at the Notre Dame Conference, suggested that there should be a symmetry between the historical reality of the past, accessible to us only through privileged reports, like scripture, and the realities of the future. On reflection, I think he is right, though the cognitive

consonance about the past still lies in *our* future. I have also benefitted from some interesting written comments kindly sent to me by George Mavrodes.

2. I say something about each of the points I mentioned, as well as some others. Yet I have a larger background in mind to explain truth makers and truth-bearers in general so as to account for the eternal truths, and God's relationship to logic, a project in which the truth makers for the faith are just a part.

3. In addition to what I am considering, there has to be some kind of truth-by-ancestorship in the development of faith to the final belief of the Communion of Saints at the Second Coming of Christ, because there are real changes of understanding, e.g., of *"nulla salus extra ecclesiam"* and of the "transparency of scripture."

4. Not all truth requires a distinct compliant reality, see, below, on formal truths.

5. *What* an event fully is depends on its future effects; thus whether teaching theology in the "street of straw" in Paris was founding the Western University system depended on what happened later on. It looks as if some belief can be true, a right thinking, *before* its compliant reality came to be. What is the efficient and formal cause of truth *then*?

6. It is, however, remarkable how little we expect what we think *of*, for example, Jesus on a cloud, and other painter's images, to *resemble* what we believe and await, and how often we realize "I cannot imagine it," without disbelieving it.

7. See James F. Ross, *Portraying Analogy* (Cambridge: Cambridge University Press, 1982).

8. This is another theological premise that would have to be argued separately. The successors of the Apostles had the authority Jesus conferred on them, to transmit and understand. Each age's understanding of the faith is guided by the Spirit and authoritative; the faith of the church is the faith *they* proclaim. Otherwise, access to the true faith would become mediated by historical investigations that had to be sciences applied to uncover and "preserve" the "original" faith.

9. I mean "correspondence" has not appeared as a special problem for theology because it has had no conspicuous success elsewhere to contrast with theology. But that tends to mislead theologians.

10. Were the cognitive harmony of belief and final understanding not *caused* by a veracious deity, the unison might be error rather than truth.

11. From that we can generate the indeterminacy of translation, inscrutibility of reference, grue problem, world-versions problem, and similar issues, but resolve them as epistemic barriers, not ontic gaps.

Instead of adopting the skepticism Kripke attributes to Wittgenstein, or the world-weary pluralism of Goodman, we should get the *order* right: There is a fact of the matter as to which, up to a point, counterfactuals are true, *because* the natures of things are determinate. Goodman reasoned from the epistemic indeterminacy, because of inaccessibility of discriminating observations, to an ontic gap. That is a non-sequitur. Kripke's adaptation reasons from the constitutive indeterminacy of material things, plus vs quus machines, (because of the actual finitude of operations, after which the differentiating outputs would appear) still in the finite, to an outcome where "there is no fact of matter." Instead, he should have concluded that the machine only *simulates* the function that *we* carry out, and, thus that genuine understanding is beyond the capacity of any purely material thing.

The explanatory order between what a thing is and how it does, or would, appear is reversed. Pure functions, like "adding," "mean," and "chose," *do* determine, not appearances, but what happens in all counterfactual cases (even when you add incorrectly). Real kinds are not that definite, at least not the ones we know. Its diverse manifestations are the "riddle of induction" and the generalized world-making consequences for Goodman, and the plus-quus skepticism, with the resulting 'no-fact-of-the-matter', that Kripke ascribes to Wittgenstein. The origin of both is in the Quinean errors about our knowledge of real necessity and the status of logic.

Realization is relative to capacity. So if a thing is not a definite realization, it is no thing of a kind at all.

12. See Ross, *Portraying Analogy.*

13. These difficulties might be surmounted by calling the beliefs true in the sense that they are *going* to be true when the compliant reality is completed. To say future reality is contained in present *causes*, which are actually the truth makers of present beliefs about the future and exactly determine the reality to come, not only will not "work" in general because it is too deterministic, it is particularly defective for eschatological beliefs because the causes of the last things and the world to come are not included in the *natural* order of things.

14. I know that it is contested by theologians, but I cannot see how Augustine, Aquinas, and Descartes could, with their full understandings of "soul," be saying the *same* thing when they say "Jesus is present, body and blood, soul and divinity in the eucharist."

15. See James F. Ross, "God, Creator of Kinds and Possibilities," in *Rationality, Religious Belief, and Moral Commitment: New Essays in the Philosophy of Religion*, edited by Robert Audi and William J. Wainwright (Ithaca, N. Y.: Cornell University Press, 1986).

16. Ibid.

17. On this, see Nelson Goodman, *Languages of Art* (Indianapolis, Ind.: Bobbs-Merrill, 1968). In part, by conventions of reference, what is *causally* a statue or a picture of a fifteenth-century model *becomes* a statue or painting of Christ. So there are many crucifixion paintings, with different Christ figures, all depictions of one reality, only the reality is picked out by reference, not resemblance.

Goodman was not so far from Anselm, when in *Ways of Worldmaking* (Indianapolis, Ind.: Hackett, 1978) he emphasized that truth is a matter of rightness of rendering far more than any kind of look-alike, and that what *is* right rendering depends on *what* one is doing and, perhaps, on the developmental stage of the activity (for abstract understanding matures, or can, just as human capacity in gymnastics or violin playing, take startling leaps of proficiency, dexterity, depth, and passion as the highest achievements of the past become the starting routines of new masters.

18. The difference is easily appreciated. We construct logical systems and analyses that are truth preserving and have various truth-value *transmissions* from one proposition to another. Getting a truth-value by *transmission* is getting it by inheritance. A consequence of interpreting strict implication as material implication that holds under all conditions is that a conditional with an impossible antecedent is true. That is a truth-value inherited syntactically. One can ignore that, and apply a different mode of transmission: a conditional with a semantically (*not* syntatically) impossible antecedent is always false: "If I were a monad, I'd see gravitons." We can use either kind, as long as we keep our accounts straight, just as French inheritance law could be matrilineal when England's was patrilineal. See Ross, *God, Creator of Kinds and Possibilities*.

19. I am still amazed that something so central to the Platonic and Aristotilian sources of western science is ignored in the hot flush of initial scientific success—despite the evident bafflement the model science, physics, now confronts.

20. In the two most important cases, necessities of nature and simple contingent truths, where the designated realities do make the expressed judgments true, we have no satisfactory explanation of how it is done.

21. We encounter a contemporary alien truth maker in Plantinga's neo-Augustinean explanation. See his book, *Does God Have A Nature?* (Milwaukee, Wisc.: Marquette University Press, 1981).

22. Thomas Satre gave me an example from computer theory that I've forgotten, that clearly shows *we* make formal objects by constructing systems of necessary truths.

23. Some people wonder whether formal truths can have any explanatory function when formal objects have no causal power. I take it that "the gravitational constant at the earth's surface is 32 ft. per sec., per sec.," and that "F = MA," and the like, explain why a rocket engine of certain power is both required to and is able to escape the earth's gravitational field. If formal truths are entirely without explanatory power there would be no point to the elegant mathematizations we invent. *How* such abstractions can be genuinely explanatory is another matter.

24. Goodman, *Languages of Art*.

25. Nothing outside the faith provides the *full* sense of "Christ will come again to judge the living and the dead." Of course, the key expression for the human condition for which the faith provides the real story, anchored "outside" the faith. See chapter 7 of Ross, *Portraying Analogy*.

26. Truth by authentication, in general, is conditions of production of thought that assure (by actually producing) a final product that "nets" all of what is to be experienced. That means that the believer's expectation about all of reality (as far as it is encompassed as designated by his beliefs) will be fulfilled.

Revelation as truth maker makes each stage of the faith such that its holders will find all (the relevant) reality completely "netted," that is, all their expectations fulfilled by what happens.

The second coming is, I take it, a supernatural intervention. I am not certain how to regard the general resurrection, since it appears that Christians think immortality is a natural human property, like being sentient.

There is an analogue here to the "grue" problem. For me, doing one definite thing rather than another that is incompatible with the first, certain things have to be counterfactually determinate; yet there is nothing about the actual to determine all those things. If what is actually so does not uniquely determine the situation, what I am doing is indefinite. But only what is necessary uniquely determines all relevant counterfactuals with content. Does that mean every contingent situation is indeterminate between incompatible counterfactual situations, and thus, indefinite?

That is a rather interesting difference between formal objects and real ones. In both cases, an infinity of things I have not said have to be so for what I say (whatever it is) to be so; but in the one case, none of them are logically independent of what I do say, and in the other, an infinity are, despite however many are logically included in what I say. The reality of the real overflows anything we can say about it.

Truth is a matter of focus, not fit. It is *adequatio mentis et rei*, not like a ruler and a stone, more like performance and the music. Anselm was right, truth is a kind of rightness perceivable to the mind alone.

This is not a "wait to be" account that says "to be true is to be believed by the Communion of Saints at the Second Coming," like Pierce's ultimate scientific community. Nor is it a "wait to see" theory, that says "to *have* the truth now is to believe, or approximate by suitable ancestry, the belief of the Communion of Saints at the Second Coming." Nor is this a "Wait and See" story that definite truth-conditions for what is to come do obtain, but are cognitively unavailble to us until the last day.

This is an account of an alien truth maker, the word of God, and one that says 'being so' for the relevant beliefs is being fulfilled in experience, having what one expected, happen. "That things are really the way they appear to be" is not part of the analysis of fulfilled expectation.

The church is always trying to find its faith in one respect or another, just as individuals typically are, thus developing to the belief of the Communion of Saints.